FOUNDATIONS OF SUPPLY-SIDE ECONOMICS

Theory and Evidence

FOUNDATIONS OF SUPPLY-SIDE ECONOMICS
Theory and Evidence

VICTOR A. CANTO
DOUGLAS H. JOINES
ARTHUR B. LAFFER
Department of Finance and Business Economics
School of Business Administration
University of Southern California
Los Angeles, California

With Contributions by

PAUL EVANS
MARC A. MILES
ROBERT I. WEBB

 1983

ACADEMIC PRESS
A Subsidiary of Harcourt Brace Jovanovich, Publishers
New York   London
Paris   San Diego   San Francisco   São Paulo   Sydney   Tokyo   Toronto

ACADEMIC PRESS, INC.
111 Fifth Avenue, New York, New York 10003

United Kingdom Edition published by
ACADEMIC PRESS, INC. (LONDON) LTD.
24/28 Oval Road, London NW1 7DX

Library of Congress Cataloging in Publication Data
 Main entry under title:

Foundations of supply-side economics.

    Includes index.
    1. Supply-side economics--Addresses, essays, lectures.
I.   Canto, Victor A. II. Joines, Douglas H. III. Laffer,
Arthur B.
HB241.F64   1983   338.973   82-8809
ISBN 0–12–158820–3   AACR2

Contents

Chapter 3 A NEOCLASSICAL MODEL OF FISCAL POLICY, EMPLOYMENT, AND CAPITAL ACCUMULATION

Douglas H. Joines

Chapter 4 THE REVENUE EFFECTS OF THE KENNEDY TAX CUTS

Victor A. Canto, Douglas H. Joines, and Robert I. Webb

Chapter 5 FISCAL POLICY AND THE LABOR MARKET

Paul Evans

Chapter 6 ESTIMATES OF EFFECTIVE MARGINAL TAX RATES ON FACTOR INCOMES

Douglas H. Joines

Chapter 7 GOVERNMENT FISCAL POLICY AND PRIVATE CAPITAL FORMATION—SOME AGGREGATE TIME-SERIES ESTIMATES

Douglas H. Joines

Chapter 8 WHAT DOES A TAX CUT DO?

Paul Evans

Chapter 9   **PERSISTENT GROWTH RATE DIFFERENTIALS AMONG STATES IN A NATIONAL ECONOMY WITH FACTOR MOBILITY**

Victor A. Canto and Robert I. Webb

Chapter 10 **THE MISSING EQUATION: THE WEDGE MODEL ALTERNATIVE**

Victor A. Canto and Marc A. Miles

Preface

When an adjective is applied to the word economics, the resulting expression can identify either a specific type of economic analysis or a set of policy prescriptions. The term supply-side economics has in recent years become closely associated with such a set of policy prescriptions, the most prominent of which has been a recommendation that tax rates be lowered both in the United States and in many other countries.

This volume contains no policy prescriptions. (Indeed, it is likely that the authors would have disagreed on many such prescriptions had they decided to include them.) Instead, it is composed of a series of papers containing both theoretical and empirical analyses of a set of issues in government fiscal policy. The type of analysis employed is standard neoclassical economics, and this analysis is used to study the macroeconomic incentive effects of taxation. One might use the term supply-side economics to describe the application of neoclassical analysis to these issues in order to distinguish the resulting models from others (notably the Keynesian ones) in which the macroeconomic effects of fiscal policy operate largely through income rather than substitution effects.

Collaboration on this book began several years ago. A common interest in the macroeconomics of taxation arose in the course of discussions among the contributors dating back to the period when they were all at the

University of Chicago. Arthur Laffer was then on the faculty at Chicago, and all the other contributors were graduate students. They specialized in different fields, including international economics, monetary theory, public and private finance, and labor economics. They were all influenced by a set of ideas common at Chicago—that people respond to incentives, that the resulting substitution effects can frequently be larger than is generally believed, and that the government's behavior can have an important effect on private incentives. Starting from those premises, the various authors proceeded to analyze different aspects of the macroeconomics of taxation.

The first chapter, by Canto, Joines, and Laffer, deals with some basic issues in the macroeconomics of taxation. It contains a simple, static, one-sector, two-factor model which analyzes the effects of taxes imposed purely for generating revenues. The paper develops the four following propositions:

1. There exists a trade-off between taxes on labor and capital necessary to maintain a given level of output;

2. there exists a tax structure that maximizes government revenue;

3. there exists a tax structure that maximizes output at a given level of government revenue; and

4. there exists a tax structure that maximizes welfare at a given level of government revenue.

It is shown that the output-maximizing and welfare-maximizing tax structures are not necessarily the same. However, if the tax structure is such that either tax rate is in the prohibitive range, then there exists another tax structure that yields the same revenues but higher output *and* welfare. Finally, the chapter contains some illustrative calculations of the revenue-maximizing tax structures resulting from alternative combinations of factor-supply elasticities.

The next two chapters, by Victor Canto and by Douglas Joines, extend the model of Chapter 1 to a dynamic setting with explicit consideration of the process of capital formation. The Canto paper presents a continuous-time model with infinitely lived individuals. The Joines paper presents a discrete-time, overlapping-generations model with finite-lived individuals who have a bequest motive. Despite the different structures, the two papers reach many of the same conclusions, and the results are generally consistent with those of the static model.

The following six chapters report empirical evidence on taxation and economic activity. Chapter 4, by Victor Canto, Douglas Joines, and Robert Webb, begins with a very simple one-sector, one-factor model which derives some propositions concerning the conditions under which changes in tax rates and changes in government revenues will be negatively related. It briefly traces the historical antecedents of these propositions back as far as David Hume and Adam Smith. It then examines a specific instance of broad-based tax cuts, the Kennedy tax cuts of the early 1960s, in order to determine whether the changes in revenue, output, the government deficit, and inflation were significantly different after the tax cuts than they otherwise would have been. The evidence is consistent with a significant increase in output and no significant changes in the other variables.

Chapter 5, by Paul Evans, develops a model to explore the relation between fiscal policy and labor market activity, taking explicit account of the ways in which fiscal authorities dispose of their tax revenues. It is shown that the fraction of potential workers who are employed and the average number of hours worked by each employed person depend on the real before-tax wage rate, the shares of each type of government spending, and the distribution of government benefits between workers and nonworkers. The model is estimated using annual U.S. data for the period 1931–1977. The estimated functions satisfy the restrictions implied by the theoretical model. Increases in most types of government spending reduce employment and hours of work both in the short run and in the long run. The effects are large enough to be economically important.

Chapter 6, by Douglas Joines, describes a method of calculating effective marginal tax rates on factor incomes using available U.S. data. The method is employed to calculate a time series of tax rates on incomes of labor and capital in the United States for the period 1929–1975. These results provide some support for the idea that the United States has been moving in the direction of a pure consumption tax since World War II. They also support the contention that the effective corporate tax rate on the income of corporate capital has declined since the 1950s and that this decrease has been only partially offset by an increase in the taxation of such capital at the personal level.

Chapter 7, also by Joines, employs the above-described tax rates to estimate the effect of fiscal policy on private investment in plant and equipment. It is found that increases in the tax rate on income from capital reduce capital formation. No reliable effect of labor income taxation can be estimated, however. In addition, it is found that a one-dollar increase in government purchases of goods and services crowds out only approximately 3 to 5 cents' worth of private investment.

Chapter 8, by Paul Evans, reports the estimation of a small macroeconomic model of the United States for the postwar period. It uses some of the methodology recently suggested by Sims and others. The basic results indicate the following:

1. A permanent increase in real federal purchases of goods and services causes a transitory (one-year) increase in nominal income and a permanent increase in real income;

2. a permanent increase in the monetary base causes a permanent equiproportional increase in nominal income but no permanent change in real income;

3. a permanent increase in real federal debt causes (with a one-year lag) a permanent increase in nominal income but no permanent change in real income; and

4. a permanent increase in marginal tax rates on income from labor or capital has no effect on nominal income, but causes a permanent reduction in real income. For the tax on income from capital, this effect is so strong that the increase in tax rates may well reduce government revenue.

Chapter 9, by Victor Canto and Robert Webb, contains a theoretical section which extends the previously described models to a multicountry, integrated economy. Within the model, there are two types of adjustment processes. Relative price changes serve to equilibrate worldwide demand and supply. Quantity adjustments serve to relieve excess demand or supply within each country. Worldwide equilibrium is determined in part by the sum of fiscal policies of all countries. Country-specific equilibrium is determined in part by that country's fiscal policies relative to those of the rest of the world. The model is applied to the U.S. economy with each state treated as a small, open economy. It is found that states which increase their tax rates faster than the national average tend to experience slower output growth than the national average. The evidence also suggests that there is a substantial mobility of factors of production among states.

The final chapter, by Victor Canto and Marc Miles, is an attempt to integrate supply-side analysis into a traditional macroeconomic framework. The traditional IS–LM framework is underdetermined. The goods market clearing condition (IS) and money market clearing condition (LM) are not sufficient to determine the price level, output, and the interest rate. This indeterminacy problem is frequently solved by introducing an output/inflation trade-off, or Phillips curve, an approach which has been under strong attack in recent years. This paper develops an alternative specification by explicitly considering factor markets. In addition to aggregate demand policies (income effects), the position and slope of the IS curve also depends upon tax *rates* (substitution effects). As a consequence, output, employment, and the price level depend upon tax rates.

Books, of course, are not written in a vacuum. The process of writing a book such as this involves constant interaction with the thoughts of other people, especially since most of us were still in our formative, graduate student years when these ideas started to take shape. It is very difficult to delineate where the thoughts of one's colleagues end and one's own ideas begin. In lieu of such an impossible task, we should like to thank those who have been particularly helpful in instilling in us the basic ideas that led to the writing of this book.

In addition to our fellow collaborators, our greatest debt is to those faculty members at the University of Chicago who have had the strongest influence on our thinking. These include Arnold Harberger, Robert Barro, Gary Becker, John Gould, Merton Miller, and Arnold Zellner.

Others who have contributed in one way or another in developing these ideas include Robert Mundell, Jude Wanniski, Onwochei Odogwu, and R. David Ranson.

We are grateful to The University of Chicago Press for permission to reprint the quotes in Chapters 3 and 4 from *The Journal of Political Economy* (copyright © 1942, 1974, and 1976, The University of Chicago Press).

Introduction

This volume represents the first compilation of papers specifically designed to illustrate formally the theory underlying supply-side economics. With me as the sole exception, each of the authors received his doctorate at the University of Chicago at a time when existing demand theories were experiencing difficulties explaining what was happening. My good fortune was to be a faculty member at the University of Chicago when so many gifted people were attending that institution. For me, the real pride is to be associated with a group of my students who have proven themselves so adept at the tools of our trade.

Supply-side economics is little more than a new label for standard neoclassical economics. In layman's terms supply-side economics provides a framework of analysis which relies on personal and private incentives. When incentives change, people's behavior changes in response. People are attracted toward positive incentives and repelled by the negative. The role of government in such a framework is carried out by the ability of government to alter incentives and thereby affect society's behavior.

Whether it be through fiscal, monetary or regulatory policy, government actions affect the incentives of individuals. The response of those individuals and others around them represents the impact of government policy for horizons both near and far. In its most basic form, if an action is taken that makes an activity more attractive, people will do more of that activity. If, on the other hand government actions make an activity less attractive people will shun or otherwise avoid that activity. Subsidies and taxes are the *lingua franca* of governmentally altered positive and negative incentives.

The debate or controversy between demand- and supply-side economics is truly as old as economics itself. In fact, the very issues discussed in this volume can be traced back in the annals of both economic and political tracts. The current political debate is no exception.

Tax, spending, and monetary policies stand on the forefront of current controversy. While seemingly unique, the events of the past decade fit easily into the mosaic of the more distant past. The politics of the presidential contest between the Harding/Coolidge ticket and their unsuccessful counterparts Cox and Roosevelt is strikingly similar to Reagan's defeat of Carter. But then again the rhetoric of presidential contender Jack Kennedy, lauding bigger defense and lower taxes, doesn't sound so unfamiliar either. Harry Truman in 1944 and 1945 carried out a supply-side program that others only discussed. And so the litany proceeds.

Perhaps most fearsome was Hoover's rejection of supply-side economics in permitting the Smoot–Hawley tariff to become law and then, as the economy collapsed, his search for solace by raising other taxes as well. Roosevelt's tax increases in 1936 stand as a grim reminder that even powerful natural forces can be thwarted by perverse policy. During the Great Depression the highest marginal income tax rate was raised from 24 to 79%. Other taxes were boosted sharply as well. Is it any wonder that the depression lasted as long and went as deep as it did? The deficits—for a markedly smaller government—were proportionately as great if not greater than those today.

The United States is not alone in reenacting time and again the melodrama surrounding economic policy. Prime Minister Sir Robert Peel in the 1840s era of British politics said it all as others had done even before him. Somewhat later the Gladstone–Disraeli debates became vintage reminders that we relive this past.

This volume is an attempt to consolidate the paramount political and economic issues into a formal analysis for the technical economist. As such it struggles to uncover the theoretical and empirical underpinnings of what the popular press calls supply-side economics. This volume is for those who truly care.

ARTHUR B. LAFFER

Chapter 1

Tax Rates, Factor Employment, Market Production, and Welfare

Victor A. Canto, Douglas H. Joines, and Arthur B. Laffer

An increasing amount of attention has recently been devoted to the effects of alternative tax structures on the pattern of economic activity, on the level of taxable economic activity, and on the aggregate amount of revenue generated by the tax system. In this chapter, a static, one-sector, two-factor model is developed in order to analyze the effects of taxes imposed purely for the purpose of generating revenues.[1] For simplicity, these taxes are assumed to be proportional taxes on the incomes of factors of production. We derive some properties of the tax structure needed to maximize output while raising a given level of government revenue.

The model we present is a highly simplified one. We call our two factors of production capital and labor, but we do not distinguish one as fixed and

---

[1] More accurately, our model only has one market output. It is in fact a two-sector model in the sense that it has a household production sector which also employs capital and labor in proportions which depend upon their relative cost.

the other as variable. Since the model is static, we do not attempt to analyze the process of capital formation.[2] Instead, we assume that at any point there exist fixed stocks of capital and labor and that these stocks must be allocated either to household production or to market-sector production.[3]

1. THE MODEL

Two factors are combined in the market sector according to a Cobb–Douglas production function to produce the market good Q:

$$Q = K^{\alpha}L^{1-\alpha} \tag{1}$$

where α and $1 - \alpha$ are the partial output elasticities of capital K and labor L, respectively, and $0 < \alpha < 1$. The market good, capital, and labor are inputs into the household production process. Capital and labor thus have identical analytical properties except that they are not perfect substitutes in either household or market production.

We assume that factors employed in the market sector are paid their marginal products and that the rental rate received by capital R^* and the wage rate received by labor W^* differ from the rates paid because of the taxation of factor income:

$$W^* = W(1 - t_l) \tag{2}$$

$$R^* = R(1 - t_k) \tag{3}$$

where W and R are the gross-of-tax wage and rental rates on labor and capital services, and t_l and t_k are the tax rates on incomes of labor and capital, respectively. These tax rates are assumed to be both marginal and average rates and are expressed as percentages of the rental and wage rates paid. The gross-of-tax factor payments are denominated in terms of the market good Q.

A change in the ratio of W to R will cause a change in the ratio of capital to labor demanded by firms for production of any level of market goods. One of the characteristics of the Cobb–Douglas production function is the constancy of the shares of the factors of production. Accordingly, the demands for labor and capital and the optimal factor proportions are

$$K^{d} = \frac{\alpha Q}{R} \tag{4}$$

$$L^{d} = \frac{(1 - \alpha)Q}{W} \tag{5}$$

$$\frac{K^{d}}{L^{d}} = \frac{\alpha}{1 - \alpha}\frac{W}{R} = \frac{\alpha}{1 - \alpha}\frac{1 - t_k}{1 - t_l}\frac{W^*}{R^*} \tag{6}$$

---

[2] For dynamic models which treat capital formation as the outcome of an intertemporal utility maximization process see Canto (1977) and Joines (1979).

[3] For a discussion of household production see, for example, Becker and Ghez (1975).

A change in the ratio of W^* to R^* will cause a change in the ratio of capital to labor demanded by households for production of any level of the household commodity. In addition, an increase in the absolute levels of W^* and R^*, given the same ratio of W^* to R^*, will cause households to substitute market goods for capital and labor in the production of a given level of the nonmarket commodity. We assume that an equiproportional increase in W^* and R^* causes households to supply more of both capital and labor to the market sector and that the supply functions for capital and labor take the following form[4]:

$$K^s = \left(\frac{R^*}{W^*}\right)^{\sigma_k} R^{*\varepsilon}, \qquad \varepsilon + \sigma_k > 0, \quad \sigma_k \leq 0 \tag{7}$$

$$L^s = \left(\frac{W^*}{R^*}\right)^{\sigma_l} W^{*\varepsilon}, \qquad \varepsilon + \sigma_l > 0, \quad \sigma_l \leq 0 \tag{8}$$

It is assumed that the government derives its revenue entirely from proportional taxes on factor income, that its budget is always balanced, and that revenue collections are returned to the economy in a neutral fashion so that no income effects are generated.[5]

---

[4] The assumption that the cross-price elasticities σ_l and σ_k are nonpositive deserves some attention. The imposition of a 100 percent tax rate on a factor of production, say, labor, will set the net-of-tax wage rate and the amount of labor services supplied to the market sector equal to zero. Given this net-of-tax wage rate, the quantity of capital services supplied to the market sector depends critically on the value of σ_k. If $\sigma_k > 0$, the quantity of capital services supplied to the market sector is undefined, in which case taxation of a factor of production in excess of 100 percent may result. This possibility is ruled out in this model by assuming nonpositive values for σ_l and σ_k. Notice also that when σ_l and σ_k are strictly negative, a 100 percent tax on one factor of production implies that neither factor is supplied to the market sector. When σ_l and σ_k are both equal to zero, the supply of a factor of production is independent of the other factor's reward, a common assumption in two-factor models. (See, for example, Feldstein 1974a,b.) Finally, notice that our assumptions imply that the own-price factor supply elasticities $\sigma_l + \varepsilon$ and $\sigma_k + \varepsilon$ are positive.

[5] For simplicity it is assumed that

a. government expenditure takes the form of transfer payments to individuals, receipt of which is unrelated to factor supply,

b. there is no waste or inefficiency on the part of the government, and

c. taxes and transfers are costless to collect and distribute, respectively.

Under these conditions, government spending will have no net income effect, only a substitution effect due to the relative price changes resulting from the taxes. Joines (1979) and Canto (1977) develop a similar analysis of government fiscal policy in which deficit financing is possible. Canto and Miles (1981) consider the possibility of income effects resulting from different types of government expenditure, collection costs, and the government efficiency level.

Combining Eqs. (7) and (8), the ratio of factors supplied to the market sector is

$$\frac{K^s}{L^s} = \left(\frac{R^*}{W^*}\right)^{\sigma_s} \tag{9}$$

where σ_s, the elasticity of substitution in factor supply, is assumed to be positive and is defined as $\sigma_k + \sigma_l + \varepsilon$. Equation (9) says that the ratio of capital to labor supplied to the market sector depends only upon the after-tax wage–rental ratio. On the other hand, Eq. (6) says that the proportion of capital to labor demanded by the market sector depends only upon the gross-of-tax wage–rental ratio. Combining the two equations, one can solve for the equilibrium level of the gross- and net-of-tax wage–rental ratio as a function of the tax rates:

$$\frac{W^*}{R^*} = \left[\left(\frac{1-\alpha}{\alpha}\right)\left(\frac{1-t_l}{1-t_k}\right)\right]^{1/(1+\sigma_s)} \tag{10}$$

$$\frac{W}{R} = \left(\frac{1-\alpha}{\alpha}\right)\left[\left(\frac{1-\alpha}{\alpha}\right)\left(\frac{1-t_l}{1-t_k}\right)\right]^{-\sigma_s/(1+\sigma_s)} \tag{11}$$

Equations (10) and (11) show that both the net-of-tax wage–rental ratio and the gross-of-tax wage–rental ratio depend upon tax rates, factor supply elasticities, and output elasticities of the two factors.

It can be shown that if producers maximize profits, the cost function of the market good will also be of the Cobb–Douglas form:

$$1 = \left(\frac{W}{1-\alpha}\right)^{(1-\alpha)}\left(\frac{R}{\alpha}\right)^{\alpha} \tag{12}$$

where the market good has been defined as the numeraire.

Rearranging Eq. (12) and substituting for the gross-of-tax wage–rental ratio [Eq. (11)], one can solve for the gross-of-tax wage rate:

$$W = (1-\alpha)\left[\left(\frac{1-\alpha}{\alpha}\right)\left(\frac{1-t_l}{1-t_k}\right)\right]^{-\alpha\sigma_s/(1+\sigma_s)} \tag{13}$$

Similarly, the gross-of-tax rental rate can be expressed as

$$R = \alpha\left[\left(\frac{1-\alpha}{\alpha}\right)\left(\frac{1-t_l}{1-t_k}\right)\right]^{(1-\alpha)\sigma_s/(1+\sigma_s)} \tag{14}$$

Substituting Eqs. (13), (14), (2), and (3) into the factor supply equations, one can determine the equilibrium quantities of each factor and the proportions of capital to labor employed in the market sector:

$$K = [\alpha(1 - t_k)]^\varepsilon \left[\left(\frac{1 - \alpha}{\alpha} \right) \left(\frac{1 - t_l}{1 - t_k} \right) \right]^{[\varepsilon(1 - \alpha)\sigma_s - \sigma_k]/(1 + \sigma_s)} \tag{15}$$

$$L = [(1 - \alpha)(1 - t_l)]^\varepsilon \left[\left(\frac{1 - \alpha}{\alpha} \right) \left(\frac{1 - t_l}{1 - t_k} \right) \right]^{(\sigma_l - \alpha\sigma_s\varepsilon)/(1 + \sigma_s)} \tag{16}$$

$$\frac{K}{L} = \left[\left(\frac{1 - \alpha}{\alpha} \right) \left(\frac{1 - t_l}{1 - t_k} \right) \right]^{-\sigma_s/(1 + \sigma_s)} \tag{17}$$

The equilibrium level of market output as a function of the tax rates is obtained by substituting Eqs. (15) and (16) into the production function:

$$Q = [(1 - \alpha)(1 - t_l)]^\varepsilon \left[\left(\frac{1 - \alpha}{\alpha} \right) \left(\frac{1 - t_l}{1 - t_k} \right) \right]^{[\sigma_l - \sigma_s(1 + \varepsilon)\alpha]/(1 + \sigma_s)} \tag{18}$$

2. TAXATION AND MARKET ACTIVITY

Upon inspection of Eqs. (13), (14), and (11), it is apparent that an increase in the labor tax rate will unambiguously increase the equilibrium levels of the gross-of-tax wage rate W and wage–rental ratio W/R and decrease the equilibrium level of the gross-of-tax rental rate.[6] The increase in the gross-of-tax wage–rental ratio will generate a substitution effect away from labor into capital in market production. The capital–labor ratio will unambiguously increase.[7]

---

[6] Defining E as the d log operator, $T_l = (1 - t_l)$ and $T_k = (1 - t_k)$, and differentiating logarithmically Eqs. (13), (14), and (11), one obtains

$$EW = \frac{\alpha\sigma_s}{1 + \sigma_s} E\left(\frac{T_k}{T_l} \right) > 0$$

$$ER = -\frac{(1 - \alpha)\sigma_s}{1 + \sigma_s} E\left(\frac{T_k}{T_l} \right) < 0$$

$$E\left(\frac{W}{R} \right) = \frac{\sigma_s}{1 + \sigma_s} E\left(\frac{T_k}{T_l} \right) > 0$$

Notice that $ET_k = -dt_k/T_k$ and $ET_l = -dt_l/T_l$.

[7] For a Cobb–Douglas production function, $E(K/L) = E(W/R)$. Thus, from footnote 6,

$$E\left(\frac{K}{L} \right) = \frac{\sigma_s}{1 + \sigma_s} E\left(\frac{T_k}{T_l} \right) > 0$$

The increase in the labor tax rate will unambiguously reduce the equilibrium level of labor and capital employed in the market sector, resulting in a net reduction of the level of production of market goods.[8] The effects of an increase in the tax rate on income from capital can be analyzed in a similar manner.

Using the simplified model developed in the previous section, we derive certain propositions concerning the effects on output and government revenue of changes in the two tax rates. The specific forms taken by the proofs of these propositions depend upon the structure we have assumed for our model. This structure allows us to obtain a closed form solution for the variables of interest. Despite its simplifications, we feel the present model is useful as a pedagogic device for demonstrating the propositions. Most of these propositions can be proved using less restrictive models which derive the factor supply decisions as explicit results of utility maximization, treat capital accumulation in a dynamic framework of intertemporal choice, and allow for the possibility of government debt.

Proposition 1.   There exists a trade-off between the tax rates on labor and capital necessary to maintain output at a given level.

---

[8] Differentiating Eqs. (15) and (16) logarithmically, one obtains

$$EL = \varepsilon ET_l - \left[\frac{\sigma_l - \alpha\sigma_s\varepsilon}{1 + \sigma_s}\right] E\left(\frac{T_k}{T_l}\right)$$

$$= \left[\frac{\alpha\sigma_s\varepsilon - \sigma_l}{1 + \sigma_s}\right] ET_k + \left[\frac{\varepsilon + \sigma_l + (1 - \alpha)\sigma_s\varepsilon}{(1 + \sigma_s)}\right] ET_l$$

$$EK = \varepsilon ET_k - \left[\frac{\varepsilon(1 - \alpha)\sigma_s - \sigma_k}{1 + \sigma_s}\right] E\left(\frac{T_k}{T_l}\right)$$

$$= \left[\frac{\varepsilon(1 - \alpha)\sigma_s - \sigma_k}{1 + \sigma_s}\right] ET_l + \left[\frac{\varepsilon + \sigma_k + \alpha\varepsilon\sigma_s}{1 + \sigma_s}\right] ET_k$$

Since $\sigma_l < 0$, $\sigma_s\varepsilon > 0$, $\eta_l = \varepsilon + \sigma_l > 0$, and $\eta_k = \varepsilon + \sigma_k > 0$, the coefficients for ET_l and ET_k are positive in both of the two equations above, implying that an increase in either of the tax rates unambiguously reduces the employment of both factors of production. Differentiating Eq. (18) logarithmically gives

$$EQ = \varepsilon ET_l - \left[\frac{\sigma_l - \sigma_s(1 + \varepsilon)\alpha}{1 + \sigma_s}\right] E\left(\frac{T_k}{T_l}\right)$$

$$EQ = \left[\frac{(1 - \alpha)(1 + \varepsilon)\sigma_s - \sigma_k}{1 + \sigma_s}\right] ET_l + \left[\frac{\alpha(1 + \varepsilon)\sigma_s - \sigma_l}{(1 + \sigma_s)}\right] ET_k$$

The signs of the coefficients for T_l and T_k are both positive.

The percentage change in output is

$$EQ = \varepsilon ET_l - \left[\frac{\sigma_l - \sigma_s(1 + \varepsilon)\alpha}{1 + \sigma_s} \right] E\left(\frac{T_k}{T_l}\right) \tag{19}$$

At a given level of output (i.e., on an isoquant), $EQ = 0$. Thus, the previous equation implies that

$$\frac{ET_k}{ET_l} = -\frac{(1 - \alpha)(1 + \varepsilon)\sigma_s - \sigma_k}{\alpha(1 + \varepsilon)\sigma_s - \sigma_l} < 0 \tag{20}$$

from which one can derive the marginal rate of factor tax substitution.[9] This is merely the rate at which the economy can substitute the tax on a given factor of production for a tax on another factor (i.e., dt_l/dt_k), while keeping output constant. The marginal rate of factor tax substitution is the slope of an isoquant in the (t_l, t_k) space.

The above assumptions ensure that only one isoquant will pass through any point in the retention rate (T_l, T_k) space and that the family of isoquants is homothetic in the retention rates. However, the curvature of the isoquants remains to be determined. This can easily be done by considering the zero-output isoquant. The assumed factor supply functions are such that at a 100 percent tax rate on a factor of production, none of that factor will be supplied to the marketplace. Since both inputs are indispensable in the production process, zero market output will be forthcoming. At tax rates below 100 percent, positive amounts of both factors will be supplied to the market sector, and market production will be positive. It thus follows that the zero-output "isoquant" consists of all points in the tax space where at least one of the factor tax rates is 100 percent or greater. Consider the locus of points where one tax rate is exactly equal to 100 percent and the other tax rate is less than or equal to 100 percent. This locus, which for simplicity we call the zero-output isoquant, is shown in Fig. 1 as the curve BAC. Notice that the zero-output isoquant is concave from below. This and the facts that the iso-output curves are homothetic in the retention rate space (the origin of which is point A) and that only one isoquant goes through a point are sufficient to ensure that the set of iso-output curves will be concave from below. In addition, the closer an isoquant is to the origin of the tax space, the higher is the level of output to which it corresponds. Finally, since it is possible to produce some output without one of the factors being taxed, or for that matter with one of the factors being subsidized, the isoquants intersect each axis with a nonzero, finite slope and are defined even if one of the tax rates is negative.

---

[9] The negative sign is unambiguous. See footnote 8.

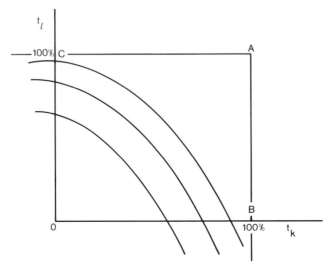

Figure 1. Iso-output curves.

3. TAXATION AND REVENUE

Here we seek to demonstrate that increases in tax rates are not always accompanied by increases in tax revenue, and the reverse may in fact be the case.

Proposition 2.   There exists a tax structure that maximizes government revenue.

Total government receipts can be expressed

$$G = Q[(1 - \alpha)t_l + \alpha t_k] = Q[(1 - \alpha)(1 - T_l) + \alpha(1 - T_k)] \qquad (21)$$

Differentiating logarithmically, we have

$$EG = \frac{(1 + \varepsilon)(1 - \alpha)\sigma_s - \sigma_k}{1 + \sigma_s} ET_l - \frac{(1 - \alpha)T_l}{1 - [(1 - \alpha)T_l + \alpha T_k]} ET_l$$

$$+ \frac{(1 + \varepsilon)\alpha\sigma_s - \sigma_l}{1 + \sigma_s} ET_k - \frac{\alpha T_k}{1 - [(1 - \alpha)T_l + \alpha T_k]} ET_k \qquad (22)$$

Equation (22) shows that the percentage change in tax revenue induced by changes in tax rates depends on the elasticity of output with respect to tax rates (the first and third terms) and the levels of the tax rates on capital and labor. The coefficients of ET_l and ET_k in the first and third terms are positive constants, implying that increases in positive tax rates (reductions in T_l and T_k) tend to reduce revenue indirectly by reducing output. The coefficients on ET_l and on ET_k in the second and fourth terms are negative, implying that increases in tax rates exert a direct effect tending to increase revenue. These coefficients are not constant, however, but depend upon the levels of the tax rates. At high tax rates (low values of T_l and T_k), these coefficients are close to zero and the indirect revenue-reducing effect of the first and third terms dominates the revenue-increasing effect of the second and fourth terms. Equation (22) thus implies that tax revenue will increase initially with increases in the tax rates, but at a decreasing rate. The marginal tax revenue raised decreases with increases in tax rates, finally reaching some point where the marginal tax revenue raised is zero. Beyond this point, any tax rate increases will reduce revenue collection. Tax revenue is maximized at the point at which the marginal tax revenue is zero. Figures 2 and 3 illustrate government tax revenues as functions of the tax rates on labor and capital, respectively, assuming that the tax rate on the other factor remains constant.

In Figs. 2 and 3, two distinct ranges of tax rates can be identified. In the normal range,

$$\frac{\partial G}{\partial t_l} > 0 \quad \text{and} \quad \frac{\partial G}{\partial t_k} > 0$$

and increasing tax rates increases government receipts, and vice versa. In the prohibitive range,

$$\frac{\partial G}{\partial t_l} < 0 \quad \text{and} \quad \frac{\partial G}{\partial t_k} < 0$$

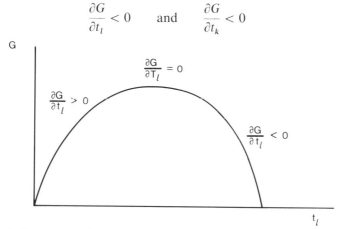

Figure 2. Revenue as a function of the tax rate on labor income, given the tax rate on income from capital.

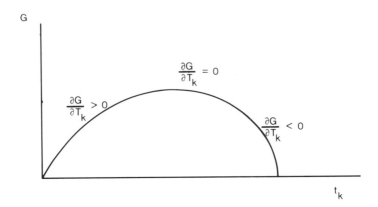

Figure 3. Revenue as a function of the tax rate on income from capital, given the tax rate on labor income.

and increases in tax rates on labor and capital decrease government receipts, and vice versa. In both ranges, the change in government revenue arising from changes in the tax rates depends on the elasticities of the factor supply curves, the output elasticities of the factors, and the level of the tax rates. The foregoing analysis shows that there exists a tax structure at which government tax receipts are maximized.

The first-order conditions imply that G is maximized when

$$-A + (1 - \alpha)(A + 1)T_l + \alpha A T_k = 0 \tag{23}$$

$$-B + (1 - \alpha)BT_l + (B + 1)\alpha T_k = 0 \tag{24}$$

where

$$A = \frac{(1 + \varepsilon)(1 - \alpha)\sigma_s - \sigma_l}{1 + \sigma_s} \tag{25}$$

$$B = \frac{(1 + \varepsilon)\alpha\sigma_s - \sigma_l}{1 + \sigma_s} \tag{26}$$

From Eqs. (23) and (24), one can solve for the factor income retention rates:

$$T_l = \frac{A}{(1 - \alpha)(A + B + 1)} = \frac{(1 + \varepsilon)(1 - \alpha)\sigma_s - \sigma_k}{(1 + \varepsilon)(1 - \alpha)(1 + \sigma_s)} \tag{27}$$

$$T_k = \frac{B}{\alpha(A + B + 1)} = \frac{(1 + \varepsilon)\alpha\sigma_s - \sigma_l}{(1 + \varepsilon)\alpha(1 + \sigma_s)} \tag{28}$$

These are the marginal retention rates which maximize government tax revenues. Using these results, one can then solve explicitly for the tax rates, the maximum amount of revenue that the government can produce, and the corresponding level of output. It is apparent also that these results depend on the supply and output elasticities of the factors of production. Furthermore, these retention rates may take on values greater than unity, implying that the revenue-maximizing tax structure may involve subsidizing one of the factors of production. Even though the maximum revenue point M depicted in Fig. 4 corresponds to positive tax rates on both factors, this need not be the case.

Corollary. There exists a trade-off between the tax rates on labor and capital necessary to maintain a given level of government tax receipts.

On a given iso-revenue curve, $EG = 0$. Therefore, from Eq. (22) we have

$$\frac{ET_l}{ET_k} = -\frac{(EG/ET_k)}{(EG/ET_l)} = -\frac{[1 - (1 - \alpha)T_l - \alpha T_k]B - \alpha}{[1 - (1 - \alpha)T_l - \alpha T_k]A - (1 - \alpha)} \quad (29)$$

which one can define as the government's marginal rate of factor tax substitution. This is simply the rate at which the government can trade off the tax on labor for the tax on capital while maintaining total revenue (spending) constant.

There is an iso-revenue curve which deserves some attention—the zero-revenue curve. There are two alternative ways of raising zero revenue. One method involves a tax system in which each tax rate yields zero revenue. This in turn can be accomplished in one of two ways: setting both factor tax rates equal to zero or setting tax rates so high (in this model, 100 percent on one of the factors of production) that no market output is produced. These arguments imply that the zero-revenue curve overlaps the zero-output isoquant and that it also goes through the origin. Another way to collect zero revenue involves a system in which one tax collects positive revenue and the other collects an equal but negative amount, that is, a tax on one factor of production matched by a subsidy to the other factor. This implies that the zero-revenue curve need not be constrained to the positive quadrant of the tax space. Finally, given that zero revenue is collected at both 0 and 100 percent tax rates, it follows that each of the tax-cum-subsidy segments of the zero-revenue curve must intersect each tax rate axis twice, once at the zero tax rate and again at a rate equal to 100 percent. The locus OBAC describes the zero-revenue curve.

Several properties of the family of iso-revenue curves are easily deduced. First, it is apparent that the area outside the locus OBAC corresponds to zero revenue whenever one of the tax rates is equal to or larger than 100 percent and the other tax rate is positive. Elsewhere, this area corresponds to negative tax revenue. The area inside the locus OBAC corresponds to positive revenue. Second, in contrast to the set of iso-output curves, the iso-revenue

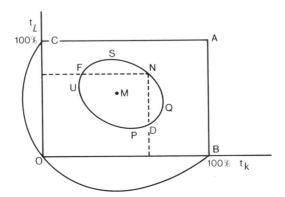

Figure 4. Iso-revenue curves.

curves are not homothetic in the retention rate space. Third, the assumptions made guarantee that, as was the case with the iso-output curves, there is only one iso-revenue curve passing through each point. In addition to the maximum and zero iso-revenue curves (M and OBAC, respectively), Fig. 4 shows a representative iso-revenue curve UPQS.

An increase in a factor tax rate tends to reduce the equilibrium level of that factor's employment and thus the taxable income base. It also increases the revenue collected per unit of income earned by the factor. The net effect on total revenue depends on whether this latter effect dominates the first. Revenue increases if the tax rate is in what we have called the normal range and decreases if the tax rate is in the prohibitive range. With two tax rates, each possible combination of tax rates falls into one of three distinct cases:

1. Both tax rates are in the normal range;
2. Both tax rates are in the prohibitive range; or
3. One tax rate is in the prohibitive range while the other is in the normal range.

If both tax rates are in the normal range, an increase in one of the rates with the other rate unchanged yields an increase in revenue collected. If the amount collected is to remain unchanged, the other tax rate must decrease and the iso-revenue curve must therefore slope downward. A diminishing marginal rate of factor substitution implies that the iso-revenue curve must be the convex from below. Case 1 corresponds to segment UP of the iso-revenue curve in Fig. 4.

If both factor income tax rates are in the prohibitive range, an increase in either tax rate (the other rate constant) leads to a reduction in total revenue collected. Since both tax rates are in the prohibitive range, the other factor tax rate must be reduced if revenue is to remain unchanged. Hence, the iso-revenue curve is also downward sloping in this region, which corresponds to segment QNS in Fig. 4.

In case 3, one of the factor tax rates is in the prohibitive range while the other is in the normal range. An increase in the prohibitive tax rate leads to a reduction in revenue. If revenue is to remain unchanged, the tax rate in the normal range must increase, and the iso-revenue curve is therefore upward sloping. Case 3 corresponds to segments UFS and PDQ in Fig. 4.

Higher-valued iso-revenue curves lie inside lower-valued curves. In the limit, the iso-revenue curve shrinks to a point, the maximum revenue point (Proposition 2).

4. THE TAX STRUCTURE, MARKET OUTPUT, AND WELFARE

Here we show how changes in the tax structure, holding total revenue (expenditure) constant, affect the levels of market output and economic welfare.

Proposition 3. There exists a tax structure that maximizes output at a given level of government expenditures.

The graphical solution to this problem is quite simple.[10] The level of revenue collection determines the iso-revenue curve. Once this is known, the objective becomes to find the lowest possible isoquant that satisfies the revenue constraint. At this point the two curves are tangent. The graphical solution is presented in Fig. 5.

The locus of points describing the tangency of the different iso-revenue and iso-output curves, shown as OM in Fig. 5, describes the tax structure that maximizes market output for a given amount of revenue. Notice that the ratio of the factor tax rates varies with the level of tax revenue. This is due to the fact that the iso-output curves are homothetic in the retention rates, while the iso-revenue curves are not. Therefore, the locus of tangency points does not lie along a ray through the origin of the retention rates (point A).

Proposition 4. There exists a tax structure that maximizes welfare at a given level of government expenditures.

The design of an optimal tax system has long been a matter of concern to economists.[11] In order to design an optimal tax system (since value judgments must be made as to the objective function to be maximized),

---

[10] For a formal derivation of this proposition, see Canto *et al.* (1978).

[11] See, for example, Harberger (1974), Mirrlees (1971), Atkinson and Stiglitz (1972), Cooter (1978).

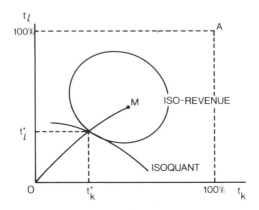

Figure 5. Output maximization subject to revenue constraint.

some sort of social welfare function has to be specified. The issue of inter-personal comparisons is not considered in this paper since the economy is modeled in terms of a representative individual. Therefore, changes in welfare can be measured in terms of compensating and equivalent variations. Willig (1976) has shown that observed consumer surplus can be rigorously utilized to estimate unobservable compensating and equivalent variations and that these are correct theoretical measures of the welfare impact of changes in prices and income for the individual. Harberger (1964) has derived the follow-ing welfare indicator to analyze distortions in the factor markets:

$$WC = -\frac{1}{2}\sum_i \sum_j N_{ij} T_i T_j \tag{30}$$

where N_{ij} denotes the reduced-form coefficients showing how the equilibrium level of factor employment depends on the degree of distortion to which each activity is subject and where T_i and T_j are positive.[12]

[12] In the development of the welfare cost expression, we have chosen the origin in such a way that the welfare cost can be expressed in terms of the retention rates. This choice of origin does not yield the traditional result that at zero tax rate the welfare cost is zero. Since the welfare cost measured from the origin implicit in Eq. (30) is monotonically related to the welfare cost measured from the more traditional origin, they both yield the same welfare cost ranking. The expression for the N_{ij} coefficients is easily derived from Eqs. (15) and (16) as follows:

$$N_{kl} = \frac{\partial K}{\partial T_l} = \frac{\partial L}{\partial T_k} = N_{lk}$$

$$N_{kk} = \frac{\partial K}{\partial T_k}$$

$$N_{lk} = \frac{\partial L}{\partial T_l}$$

In the context of our model, Harberger's welfare indicator can be expressed as

$$WC = -\left[\frac{1}{2}LT_l\left(\frac{\varepsilon + \sigma_l + (1-\alpha)\sigma_s}{1+\sigma_s}\right) + \frac{1}{2}KT_k\left(\frac{\varepsilon + \sigma_k + \alpha\sigma_s}{1+\sigma_s}\right)\right]$$

(31)

Differentiating Eq. (31) logarithmically and equating to zero, one can define the combinations of tax rates that yield a given welfare cost, that is an iso-welfare-cost curve. The marginal rate of factor tax substitution (i.e., the slope of the iso-welfare-cost curve in the tax space) can be expressed

$$\frac{ET_k}{ET_l} = -\left\{1 + \left[\frac{(\varepsilon + \sigma_l) + (1-\alpha)\sigma_s\varepsilon}{1+\sigma_s}\right]\left(\frac{KT_k}{LT_l}\right)\left(\frac{\varepsilon + \sigma_k + \alpha\sigma_s}{\varepsilon + \sigma_l + (1-\alpha)\sigma_s}\right)\right.$$

$$\times \left[\frac{\varepsilon(1-\alpha)\sigma_s - \sigma_k}{1+\sigma_s}\right]\right\}\bigg/\left\{\left[\frac{\alpha\sigma_s\varepsilon - \sigma_l}{1+\sigma_s}\right] + \left(\frac{KT_k}{LT_l}\right)\right.$$

(32)

$$\left.\times \left(\frac{\varepsilon + \sigma_k + \alpha\sigma_s}{\varepsilon + \sigma_l + (1-\alpha)\sigma_s}\right)\left[1 + \frac{(\varepsilon + \sigma_k) + \alpha\varepsilon\sigma_s}{1+\sigma_s}\right]\right\}$$

Several features of Eq. (32) deserve attention, the first one being the negative slope of the iso-welfare-cost curve. This is easily shown by noting that although σ_l and σ_k are negative, $\eta_l = \varepsilon + \sigma_l$ and $\eta_k = \varepsilon + \sigma_k$ are nonnegative. The second is that upon inspection of Eq. (17), it is apparent that the capital–labor ratio depends only on the ratio of the two retention rates. Therefore, Eq. (32) is invariant to equiproportionate changes in T_l and T_k. Alternatively stated, the iso-welfare-cost curves are homothetic in the retention rate space.

Since taxation of nonmarket activities and forced labor are ruled out of our model by assumption, it follows that the lowest iso-welfare curve (i.e., highest welfare-cost curve) will result when there is zero market production, in which case the highest iso-welfare-cost curve coincides with the zero-output curve. Furthermore, given the concavity of the zero iso-welfare-cost curve (combined with the fact that enough assumptions have been made to ensure that only one iso-welfare-cost curve passes through a given point) and the homotheticity of the iso-welfare-cost curves, it then follows that the family of welfare cost curves will be concave from below.

In addition, since each factor welfare cost "triangle" increases more than proportionately with respect to that factor's tax rate, the iso-welfare-cost curve is of greater curvature than the iso-output curves; i.e., at a tangency point the iso-welfare-cost curve lies inside the iso-output curve. Finally, since both the iso-output and iso-welfare-cost curves are homothetic in the retention rates, the locus of tangency points between the two sets of curves must lie along a ray from the origin of the retention rates, such as AV in

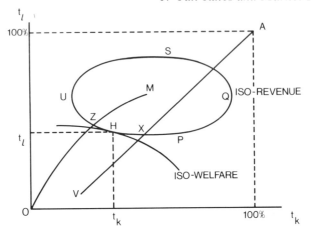

Figure 6. Welfare maximization subject to revenue constraint.

Fig. 6. The actual slope of AV is obtained by equating Eqs. (20) and (32).

To summarize, we have shown that one can define a set of iso-welfare-cost curves in the tax rate space, the values of which increase the further away the curves are from the origin and reach a maximum of zero when one of the two tax rates reaches 100 %. The graphical illustration of Proposition 4 is shown in Fig. 6. As for Proposition 3, the level of revenue collection determines the iso-revenue curve. Once this is known, the objective becomes to find the lowest possible isoquant that satisfies the iso-revenue constraint.

Proposition 5.   For a given level of tax revenue, the tax structure that maximizes market output is not in general the same as the tax rate structure that minimizes the welfare cost of taxation.

It has been shown that both the iso-output and iso-welfare-cost curves are homothetic in the retention rates. The locus of tangency points between the two sets of curves lies on a ray such as AV through the origin of the retention rates. On the other hand, the tax structures that maximize output for a given level of revenue collection (locus OM) do not lie on a ray through the origin. Since the loci AV and OM do not coincide, it follows that the tax structure that maximizes output does not necessarily minimize the welfare cost of taxation. Furthermore, since the iso-welfare-cost curve has a greater curvature than the iso-output curve at any point to the left of the AV locus, the absolute magnitude of the slope of the iso-output curve going through that point will be less than that of the iso-welfare-cost curve. Thus, it is apparent that at a point like Z, which maximizes output for a given amount of revenue, the iso-welfare-cost curve will be flatter than that of the iso-revenue curve. The tangency between the iso-revenue and iso-welfare-cost curves will occur somewhere on the ZHX segment. One must keep in mind that since the constrained maximization rules out the possibility of the economy's being in the prohibitive range, the feasible tax rates are on the segment UZHXP. Notice that as one moves in the southeast direction along this locus, the slope declines. Therefore, the tangency between the iso-revenue and iso-welfare-cost curves necessarily occurs in the ZHX segment.

Notice that in the range ZUSQPXH, movements along the iso-revenue curve change market output and welfare in the same direction, and in the range HZ, such changes in the tax structure move output and welfare in opposite directions. This raises the possibility that the government might institute a marginal change in tax rates which, holding revenue constant, might appear desirable, since it would increase empirically observable output, but which would, in fact, be undesirable because it would reduce the more important but unobservable quantity, welfare. However, there exists a situation in which the government might be able to enact an output-increasing (and possibly nonmarginal) reduction in tax rates and be assured that welfare would also increase (again holding revenue constant). This situation holds if one or more of the tax rates is so high as to be in the prohibitive range.

For example, if the economy is at point N in Fig. 4, with both tax rates in the prohibitive range, then there exists a nonmarginal reduction in t_k (moving the economy to point F) or in t_l (movement to point D) or in both t_k and t_l (movement to a point on the segment FUPD) which will increase both output and welfare while holding revenue constant. It is not clear which of these tax rate changes would result in the optimal tax structure (subject to the government's revenue constraint), but it is clear that any of them would constitute a welfare-improving or second-best movement from the initial point N. If the economy is initially operating on either of the segments UFS or PDQ, where only one of the tax rates is in the prohibitive range, then there also exists a *marginal* change in the tax structure which would simultaneously increase output and welfare, while satisfying the revenue constraint. This change involves a reduction in the prohibitive tax rate and a corresponding increase in the other tax rate. Given the strong welfare implications of prohibitive taxation, it is worth examining more closely the conditions under which such a situation could arise within our model.

5. THE EMPIRICAL RELEVANCE OF THE PROHIBITIVE RANGE

In Section 3, we demonstrated that there is a tax structure which maximizes government revenue (Proposition 2) and that it is possible for tax rates to be so high as to generate less revenue than would be raised from lower tax rates. Whether any real-world governments have ever operated in the prohibitive range, however, is an empirical issue. There are several ways of analyzing this question, the most common of which is what might be called the "elasticities" approach. This approach consists of examining existing estimates of, for example, factor supply elasticities and tax rates. These estimates are applied to some theoretical model in order to simulate the revenue effects of tax rate changes. In general, the higher the elasticities and the tax rates, the more likely it is that the tax rates are in the prohibitive range.

While this approach can undoubtedly provide valuable information on the revenue effects of tax cuts, it has several shortcomings. The first of these is that the effective tax base may be smaller than total economic activity. Some economic activity may escape taxation because it is legally exempt from taxation or because of outright tax evasion. The factor supply elasticities relevant for an analysis of revenue effects are the elasticities of supply of factors to *taxable* activities. If there is a reasonable degree of substitutability between taxable and nontaxable activities, then these elasticities may well be higher than the conventionally measured overall factor supply elasticities. This problem can be quite severe as concerns saving, since there are many uses to which saving can be put which involve a partial or complete tax exemption of the resulting income. Notable among these are residential capital and municipal bonds. Recent discussions of the "underground economy" suggest that underreporting of income may well make the distinction between taxable and nontaxable activity important for labor supply as well.[13]

Another difficulty with employing this elasticities approach in a highly aggregated model is that there are in fact many tax rates which apply to different types of economic activity and also many categories of productive factors, each of which potentially has a different elasticity of supply to taxable economic activity. Given this multiplicity of tax rates and of types of factors, it seems quite likely that some tax rates somewhere in the system are in the prohibitive range. This, in fact, is the very essence of certain tariffs on international transactions which are imposed for protectionist purposes rather than for revenue generation. Certain features of the domestic U.S. tax system may also result in a high tax rate being imposed on an elastically supplied factor. For example, the federal personal income tax imposes a "marriage penalty" which taxes the income of a secondary worker at the marginal rate of the primary worker in the family. This fact, combined with evidence that married women have substantially higher labor supply elasticities than do prime-age males, makes it at least reasonable to conjecture

---

[13] The factor supply functions [Eqs. (7) and (8)] attempt to take these effects into account. As tax rates alter the relative price of factors of production, they also alter the relative price of the nonmarket (i.e., nontaxed) activities. The change in the factor supply to the market sector thus depends on two effects, a substitution effect in household production and a scale effect. The substitution effect is captured by the ε term in both factor supply equations.

that some features of the current tax system result in prohibitive taxation. Also, recent evidence indicates that proprietors of small businesses, who have more control over hours worked than do most employees, may have a considerably higher supply elasticity than do males in general.[14] Finally, effective marginal tax rates can be quite high for those in upper-income brackets and can be even higher for the poorest workers and those receiving social security, who stand to lose benefit payments as their earnings increase.

The relevant question to ask is thus not whether the United States or some other real-world economy is operating in the prohibitive range. It is quite likely that somewhere in the system there exists a tax rate on some type of activity which results in less revenue than would a lower tax rate. The relevant issue concerns the revenue effects of a specific set of tax rate changes. Of particular interest are recent proposals for broad-based cuts in federal income tax rates. Such broad-based changes might be viewed as approximating changes in the two-factor income tax rates in a highly aggregated model such as that presented in Section 1. Therefore, in spite of the shortcomings of such simulations using the elasticities approach, we present in the next section some illustrative calculations in an attempt to show the levels at which tax rates become prohibitive in our model, given alternative assumptions concerning the size of the factor supply elasticities.

6. SOME NUMERICAL EXAMPLES

Table 1 reports the tax rates on income from capital and labor services, denoted t_k^* and t_l^*, which maximize tax revenue collection under alternative values of the parameters in the model. In all of these calculations, we have assumed that capital's share in output, α, is equal to 0.25. In order to aid the interpretation of these results, we have included at the bottom of the table the relations among and restrictions on the different parameters implied by our model. It is apparent from these relations that given ε, differences between the own-price factor supply elasticities η_l and η_k imply differences in the cross-elasticity parameters $-\sigma_l$ and $-\sigma_k$. For a given value of ε, the smaller is a factor's own-price supply elasticity (e.g., η_l), the larger will be its elasticity of supply with respect to the price of the other factor (e.g., $-\sigma_l$). Since the model assumes that cross-price elasticities are nonnegative (i.e., σ_l and σ_k are nonpositive), it is apparent that an increase in the tax rate will reduce the equilibrium level of employment of both factors of production. The effect on revenue collection due to an increase in the tax rate of a factor, say, labor, holding constant the other tax rate, consists of three components. The first

---

[14] See Wales (1973).

TABLE 1

Revenue-Maximizing Tax Structures[a]

η_l	η_k	ε	t_l^*	t_k^*
0.1	0.4	0.5	0.91	-0.07
0.1	1.0	0.5	0.90	-0.04
0.1	1.0	1.0	0.91	-0.73
0.4	0.1	0.5	0.64	0.73
0.4	0.4	0.5	0.70	0.56
0.4	1.0	1.0	0.71	-0.14
0.4	1.5	1.5	0.71	-0.54
0.7	0.4	1.0	0.55	0.36
0.7	0.7	0.9	0.57	0.39
0.7	1.0	1.0	0.59	0.24
0.7	1.0	1.5	0.61	-0.23
0.7	1.5	1.5	0.59	-0.16
0.7	1.5	2.0	0.65	-0.61
1.0	0.1	1.0	0.36	0.91
1.0	0.4	1.0	0.43	0.71
1.0	0.6	1.0	0.46	0.63
1.0	0.6	1.5	0.47	0.18
1.0	1.0	1.0	0.50	0.50
1.0	1.0	1.5	0.49	0.13
1.0	1.0	2.0	0.56	-0.33
1.0	1.5	1.5	0.50	0.10
1.0	1.5	2.0	0.52	-0.22
1.5	0.1	1.5	0.23	0.91
1.5	0.4	1.5	0.30	0.71
1.5	0.6	1.5	0.33	0.63
1.5	1.0	1.5	0.37	0.50
1.5	1.5	1.5	0.40	0.40
1.5	1.5	2.0	0.39	0.17
1.5	1.5	3.0	0.50	-0.50

[a] The following relations are implied by the assumptions of the model:

$$\eta_l = \varepsilon + \sigma_l > 0, \qquad \sigma_l < 0$$

$$\eta_k = \varepsilon + \sigma_k > 0, \qquad \sigma_k < 0$$

$$\sigma_s = \eta_l + \eta_k - \varepsilon = \sigma_l + \sigma_k + \varepsilon < 0.$$

of these is the change in labor tax revenue due to a change in the labor income tax rate, given the amount of labor income. We have called this the direct effect. The second is the change in labor tax revenue resulting from a change in the amount of labor income. We have called this the indirect effect. The third is the change in capital tax revenue due to a change in the amount of capital income. We refer to this as the cross effect. The direct effect corresponds to the second and fourth terms of Eq. (22) and is unambiguously positive—the direct effect of, say, an increase in the labor income tax rate is to increase revenue from the labor tax. In our model, the signs of the indirect and cross effects depend upon the signs of the tax rates. The indirect effect of a change in a factor income tax rate has a sign opposite to that of the factor's tax rate, while the cross effect has a sign opposite to the other factor income tax rate. These effects are combined in the first and third terms of Eq. (22).

The cross effect depends critically on the magnitude of the various elasticity parameters, the shares of the two factors in national income, and the tax rate on the other factor. If sufficiently large, this effect will dominate the direct and indirect effects, and the tax structure that maximizes revenue may involve a negative tax rate (i.e., a subsidy) on one of the factors of production, as shown in Table 1. One must keep in mind that the relative magnitude of the direct, indirect, and cross effects depends in part on the relative size of each factor's taxable income base. Our assumption of constant relative factor shares, with labor's share being three times as large as capital's, makes it less likely that the cross effect of an increase in the labor income tax rate will dominate the other effects. The revenue-maximizing tax structure will entail a subsidy to a factor only if the cross effect of a change in that factor's tax rate is large in absolute value relative to the sum of the direct and indirect effects. (Remember that if a factor's tax rate is negative, both the direct and indirect effects are positive.) If this is the case, it is possible to maximize revenue by subsidizing that factor, thus stimulating its supply to the market sector and hence market output and the tax base. Since in our model labor's share of national output is three times as large as capital's, the direct and indirect effects of a change in the labor income tax rate tend to be large relative to the cross effect, while the cross effect of a change in the capital income tax rate tends to be large relative to the direct and indirect effects. This explains why negative tax rates are observed only for capital.

Another feature of the results in Table 1 is that for given values of ε and η_k, the higher is η_l, the larger will be the indirect and cross effects of a change in the labor income tax rate. Thus, the lower will be the revenue-maximizing tax rate on labor income, t_l^*, and the higher will be the tax rate on income from capital, t_k^*. Similarly, for given values of ε and η_k, the higher η_k, the higher will be the indirect and cross effects of a change in the tax rate on income from capital. Whether an increase in η_k, given η_l and ε, will lead to a higher or lower revenue-maximizing value of t_k depends upon whether t_k^* is positive or negative. If t_k^* is positive, then the results are analogous to those for the labor income tax—an increase in η_k will lead to an increase in t_l^* and a reduction in t_k^*. However, if t_k^* is negative, an increase in η_k will lead to a reduction in t_l^* and an *increase* in t_k^*. This seeming anomaly is easily understood if one remembers why the revenue-maximizing tax structure might entail a subsidy to capital. Such a tax structure can arise if the cross effect of a change in the capital income tax is sufficiently large relative to the direct and indirect effects. In such a case, revenue will be maximized by subsidizing capital, thereby stimulating its supply and hence market output and the tax base. The larger the supply elasticity of capital, the smaller the subsidy required to effect a given increase in the supply of capital. Upon inspection of Table 1, it is apparent that both cases result for the range of parameters considered. As is apparent from the numbers reported there, t_k^* is more likely to be negative the smaller is η_l for given η_k, the larger is η_k for given η_l, and the larger is ε for given η_l and η_k.

Finally, it is apparent that a higher value of ε, given η_l and η_k, implies higher values of the cross elasticities of factor supply. However, it also implies a lower value of σ_s, the elasticity of substitution in factor supply. It should be remembered that ε measures the common proportionate increase in *both* capital and labor supplied to the market sector when the after-tax wage and rental rates both increase in common proportion. It thus measures the overall responsiveness of factor supply to the market sector. An increase in ε, given η_l and η_k, thus increases this *overall* responsiveness while reducing the elasticity of *substitution* in factor supply. These two effects have different effects on the tax rate structure. Because of the former, an increase in ε, given η_l and η_k, tends to reduce the revenue-maximizing tax rate on both capital and labor. This is because, even though the own-price factor supply elasticities have not changed, the cross elasticities, and thus overall factor supply responsiveness, are increased by an increase in ε. Because of the second effect, however, an increase in ε, given η_l and η_k, reduces the elasticity of substitution in factor supply and thus tends to lead to a larger difference between the revenue-maximizing tax rates on capital and labor. Since our assumed parameter values generally result in t_l^* larger than t_k^*, this means that an increase in ε, given η_l and η_k, tends to reduce t_k^* relative to t_l^*. Combining these two effects, we see that an increase in ε, given η_l and η_k, unambiguously tends to reduce t_k^* but may either raise or lower t_l^*. These results are borne out by the data reported in Table 1.

It should be kept in mind that the figures reported in Table 1 do not indicate the point at which each tax rate considered separately crosses from the normal into the prohibitive range. These pairs of tax rates correspond to the revenue-maximizing point M in Fig. 5. At this point, both tax rates are on the verge of the prohibitive range. It is quite possible that, for example, the tax on labor will become prohibitive at a rate lower than indicated in Table 1 if the tax rate on capital is higher than indicated there. Similarly, the parameter values for which t_k^* is negative do not imply that any positive tax rate on income from capital constitutes prohibitive taxation. The tax rate on income from capital may not enter the prohibitive range until it surpasses some positive value if the tax on labor income is set at a rate lower than indicated in Table 1.

7. CONCLUSION

Our analysis shows that increases in tax rates on factor incomes reduce the after-tax returns to factors as well as factor employment and market output. Our analysis also indicates that increases in tax rates could as well reduce as increase government tax revenue. In fact, there exists a tax rate structure which maximizes government tax receipts. This tax structure depends on the supply and output elasticities of the factors of production. The set of tax rates for which increases in the rates are accompanied by increases in government revenue is referred to as the normal range. Tax rates for which increases in the rates are accompanied by decreases in tax revenue are said to be in the prohibitive range. In general, a reduction in tax rates does not reduce total revenue in the same proportion. The more elastic factor supplies are, the more likely it is that any given tax rates will fall into the prohibitive range. Also, the higher the level of tax rates, the more likely tax rates are to be in the prohibitive range.

Our simple static model shows that government tax policy affects the market-sector output which can be obtained from a given stock of resources. In particular, increases in tax rates reduce market employment and output. Such a tax rate increase, however, would also have long-term effects on the size of the resource stock. Both human and nonhuman capital are reproducible resources which can be augmented only at some cost. The stocks of such capital at any time depend upon past investment decisions, and the future stocks depend upon current investment decisions. A change in after-tax factor rewards will affect not only the intensity of utilization of currently existing factors, but also the decision to invest in new resources, and thus the size of the future stock of factors of production. A dynamic model is required to analyze such questions. We merely note in closing that increases in tax rates are likely to cause reductions in future output potential which reinforce the reductions in current output predicted by our static model.

We also discuss the tax structures which solve two constrained maximization problems. One of these maximizes market-sector output while raising a given amount of government revenue, and the other maximizes economic welfare while raising a given amount of revenue. We show that these tax structures are not in general the same.

ACKNOWLEDGMENTS

Portions of this material were presented at the annual meeting of the American Statistical Association, San Diego, California, August 14–17, 1978, and at the Washington University and Federal Reserve Bank of St. Louis Conference on the Supply-Side Effects of Economic Policy, St. Louis, Missouri, October 24–25, 1980. We wish to thank Alan Blinder for helpful comments. Any remaining errors are, of course, the responsibility of the authors. In addition, Section 4 is an expanded version of material that appeared in *Economic Inquiry*.

REFERENCES

Atkinson, A. B., and Stiglitz, J. E. (1972). "The Structure of Indirect Taxation and Economic Efficiency," *Journal of Public Economics* **1**, 97–119.

Becker, G. S., and Ghez, G. (1975). *The Allocation of Time and Goods over the Lifecycle.* Columbia Univ. Press for the National Bureau of Economic Research, New York.

Canto, V. A. (1977). "Taxation, Welfare and Economic Activity." Ph.D. Dissertation, Univ. of Chicago, Chicago, Illinois.

Canto, V., and Miles, M. (1981). "The Missing Equation: The Wedge Model Alternative," *Journal of Macroeconomics* **3**, 247–269.

Canto, V., Laffer, A., and Odogwu, O. (1978). "The Output and Employment Effects of Fiscal Policy in a Classical Model." Working Paper, Univ. of Southern California, Los Angeles, California.

Cooter, R. (1978). "Optimal Tax Schedules and Rates: Mirrlees and Ramsey," *American Economic Review* **68**, 756–768.

Feldstein, Martin (1974a). "Incidence of a Capital Income Tax in a Growing Economy with Variable Saving Rates," *Review of Economic Studies* **41**, 505–513.

Feldstein, Martin (1974b). "Tax Incidence in a Growing Economy with Variable Factor Supply," *Quarterly Journal of Economics* **88**, 551–573.

Harberger, A. C. (1964). "The Measurement of Waste," *American Economic Review* **54**, 58–76.

Harberger, A. C. (1974). *Taxation and Welfare.* Little, Brown, Boston, Massachusetts.

Joines, H. (1979). "Government Fiscal Policy and Private Capital Formation." Ph.D. Dissertation, Univ. of Chicago, Chicago, Illinois.

Mirrlees, J. (1971). "An Exploration in the Theory of Optimum Income Taxation," *Review of Economic Studies* **38**, 175–208.

Wales, T. J. (1973). "Estimation of a Labor Supply Curve for Self-Employed Business Proprietors," *International Economic Review* **14**, 69–80.

Willig, R. D. (1976). "Consumer Surplus without Apology," *American Economic Review* **66**, 589–597.

Chapter 2

Taxation in a Closed Economy Intertemporal Model with a Variable Supply of Labor to the Market Sector*

Victor A. Canto

INTRODUCTION

In the context of a two-sector growth model Schenone (1975) concluded that a constant proportioned tax rate on consumption goods will be neutral that a constant tax rate on income will have the same welfare cost as a constant tax rate on investment because the consumption component of the tax does not generate any welfare losses. Therefore, the welfare cost per dollar of revenue collected will be smaller for the income tax than for the investment tax; this is due to the larger tax base of the former.

The model developed in this chapter shows that if the supply of labor to the market sector is not completely inelastic, then, although a constant tax rate minimizes the welfare costs, taxation of consumption goods will no longer be neutral. It is also shown that the optimal investment tax rate is not necessarily a constant tax rate. In addition, since income taxation is

* Reprinted with permission of the original publisher, Foundation Journal Public Finance, from *Public Finance/Finances Publiques*, 1981, Vol. 36, No. 3, pp. 374–394.

equivalent to some combination of consumption and savings (investment) taxation, the optimal income tax will not be a constant tax rate either. These results indicate that Schenone's analysis is clearly biased against investment taxation. That is, the constant tax rate comparison of the welfare cost generated by the different tax alternative does not necessarily shed any light on the question of the superiority of one of the forms of taxation. The comparison should be conducted in terms of each of the alternative optimal tax schedules. To the extent that neither alternative is neutral, the superiority of direct versus indirect taxation cannot be established by theory alone, as Harberger (1974) and Little (1951) have correctly pointed out.

This chapter is organized as follows. In Section 1 the basic model is developed and a solution for the long-run, steady-state condition is developed. Section 2 discusses the role of the government sector. Section 3 analyzes and compares the long-run effects of different taxes on the economy's capital–labor ratio. In Section 4 the analysis focuses on a special case for which a closed form solution is obtained. Section 5 compares the welfare cost of different taxes when the different alternatives are constrained to collect a given amount of revenue over the life cycle.

1. THE MODEL

The next few paragraphs describe the structure of the model. Capital is an endogenous variable. Following the traditional two-sector model, two factors of production, capital K and labor H, are utilized in the production process. The production of market goods is separated into consumption C and investment I. In addition, following Becker (1965), it is assumed that a household commodity z is produced and consumed in the household by combining market purchased goods C and household (leisure) time L. Thus labor can be employed either in the market sector H_m or in the household L. All production functions are assumed to be linear homogeneous, twice differentiable with both inputs indispensable.

$$X_J = F_J(K_J, H_J) = H_J f_J(\Phi_J), \qquad J = \{i, c\} \tag{1}$$

$$Z = F_z(C, L) = L f_z(\Psi) \tag{2}$$

where $\Phi_i = K_i/L_i$ and $\Phi_c = K_c/L_c$ represent the capital–labor ratios in the production of the investment and consumption goods and Ψ the market intensity of the household commodity.

The economy's resource constraint will be

$$K = K_i + K_c \tag{3}$$

$$T = H_m + L \tag{4}$$

$$H_m = H_c + H_i \tag{5}$$

The household good capital intensity Φ_z can be expressed in terms of the consumption good capital intensity Φ_c:

$$\Phi_z = \frac{K}{H_c + H_L} = \frac{H_c}{H_c + H_L} \Phi_c = \gamma \Phi_c, \qquad 0 < \gamma < 1 \qquad (6)$$

Combining Eqs. (3)–(6), shows that the economy's factor employment conditions (market and nonmarket) can be written as

$$h_i \Phi_i + \Phi_z(1 - h_i) = K/T \qquad (7)$$

where $h_i = H_i/T$ is the proportion of time devoted to the production of the investment good.

Under competitive conditions with a positive quantity of each commodity produced, the relative cost of producing the investment good in terms of the household commodity P is easily derived from the ratio of average cost of producing each good:

$$P = \left[\frac{W + \Phi_i}{f_i(\Phi_i)}\right]\left[\frac{f_z(\Psi)}{W + P_c \Psi}\right] \qquad (8)$$

where W and R represent the marginal product of labor and capital respectively, and P_c the average cost of producing the consumption good.

Since the capital intensities Φ_i and Φ_z and the proportion of leisure time to total time devoted to the production of the household good γ are all functions of the wage-rental ratio,[1] the investment good to relative price P will also be a function of the wage–rental ratio. Whether the relation between these two variables is positive or negative will depend on the relative capital intensities of the household and investment goods.

To summarize, knowledge of the relative price P allows one to determine the wage–rental ratio, which, in turn, allows one to determine the capital

---

[1] Differentiating logarithmically ($E = d_{\log}$ operator) gives

$$E\Phi_z = E\gamma + E\Phi_c = (1 - \gamma)[E\Psi - \mu_c E\Phi_o] + E\Phi_c$$

However, since

$$E\Psi = \sigma_z E(P_c/w) = \mu_c \sigma_z E(W/R)$$

It follows that

$$E\Phi_z = \{(1 - \gamma)\mu_c \sigma_z + [1 - (1 - \gamma)\mu_c]\sigma_c\}E(W/R)$$

Similarly,

$$E\gamma = E\Phi_z - E\Phi_c = (1 - \gamma)\mu_c(\sigma_z - \sigma_c)E(W/R)$$

where the σ represent the input elasticity of substitution in production.

intensities of the different goods. With this information and Eq. (7) one can solve for the proportion of labor employed in, as well as for the production of, the investment sector [Eq. (1)]. Also, the wage–rental ratio allows one to solve for γ; thus one can solve for the production of household good Z, and the proportion of time devoted to leisure L. Clearly, enough relation have been accumulated to allow, at least in principle, the regulation of production by means of a single control, the relative price P.

It is important to point out at this time a basic difference between the model described in the previous paragraph and other two-sector models, such as the model developed by Kemp and Jones (1962), that allow for a variable supply of labor to the market sector. In the Kemp and Jones model, leisure is assumed to be an explicit argument of the utility function. One disadvantage of their formulation is that the supply of labor to the market sector cannot be described independently of the utility function; thus the production possibility frontier (the supply side) cannot be described independent of the demand (utility) considerations. In contrast, the model developed in this paper assumes a household production function; this assumption allows one to specify a derived demand for leisure time independent of the utility function. Thus a production possibility frontier that allows for a variable supply of labor to the market sector can be specified that is independent of the economy's preferences (utility).

Assuming no depreciation, the aggregate quantity of capital existing at any time is given by the accumulation of investment goods produced in past periods:

$$\dot{K} = I \tag{9}$$

For simplicity, the time subscript for each variable will be omitted and the dot is assumed to denote the time derivative. The economy–labor endowment is assumed to grow at a constant rate:

$$\dot{T}/T = n \tag{10}$$

Combining the two previous equations yields the rate of change of the economy's capital–labor ratio ($K/T = \Phi$) over time:

$$\dot{\Phi} = i(\Phi,P) - n\Phi \tag{11}$$

where the lowercase letters denote per capita variables.

Following Uzawa (1967), the economy is assumed to behave so as to maximize

$$\int_0^\infty G(z)e^{-\delta t}\, dt$$

The instantaneous utility $G(z)$ is assumed to satisfy the Inada conditions. Given the constraints,[2] the Hamiltonian becomes

$$H(\Phi, \lambda, P) = \{G[z(\Phi, P)] + \lambda[i(\Phi, P) - n\Phi]\}e^{-\delta t} \tag{12}$$

Under competitive conditions with something of each market good provided, the necessary optimality conditions are

$$0 = \left(G' - \frac{\lambda}{P}\right)\frac{\partial z}{\partial p} \tag{13}$$

$$(\lambda e^{-\delta t}) = -\frac{\partial H}{\partial \Phi} = (\lambda n - R)e^{-\delta t} \tag{14}$$

Differentiating Eq. (13) and subsituting Eq. (14) into it yield

$$\frac{\dot{P}}{P}\left(G' + \frac{G''}{P}\frac{\partial z}{\partial P}\right) = (n + \delta - f'_i(\Phi_i))G' - G''\dot{\Phi}\frac{\partial z}{\partial \Phi} \tag{15}$$

A phase diagram for P and Φ can be easily constructed. Formal derivation can be found in Hadley and Kemp (1971) or Intrilligator (1971).

The slope of the $\dot{P} = 0$ locus with derivatives evaluated at $\Phi = \dot{P} = 0$ will be

$$\left.\frac{dP}{d\Phi}\right|_{\dot{P}=0} = -\frac{G''(\partial z/\partial \Phi)[(\partial i/\partial \Phi) - n]}{f''_i(\partial \Phi_i/\partial P)G'P + G''P(\partial z/\partial \Phi)(\partial i/\partial P)} \tag{16}$$

The slope of the $\dot{\Phi} = 0$ [Eq. (11)] locus with derivatives evaluated at $\Phi = \dot{P} = 0$ will be

$$\left.\frac{dP}{d\Phi}\right|_{\dot{\Phi}=0} = -\frac{\partial\dot{\Phi}/\partial\Phi}{\partial\dot{\Phi}/\partial P} = \frac{\partial i/\partial\Phi - n}{\partial i/\partial P} \tag{17}$$

For some cases the slopes of Eqs. (16) and (17) are ambiguous, depending on whether $(\partial i/\partial \Phi - n) \gtreqless 0$. Upon inspection of the formulas one can see that both slopes will always have the same sign; the question, then, is which one will be steeper. Looking at Eq. (15); a point in both $\dot{\Phi} = 0$ and $\dot{P} = 0$ implies $n + \delta = f'_i$, a point on $\dot{P} = 0$ to the left of $\dot{P} - 0$ must imply $(n + \delta) < f'_i$. For the case where $\Phi_z > \Phi_i$ (shown in Fig. 1) the point to the left implies a value of P lower than the one which will make $(n + \delta)$ equal to f'_i. Therefore, $\dot{P} = 0$ intersects $\dot{\Phi} = 0$ from above. For the case where $\Phi_z < \Phi_i$ (shown in Fig. 2) the locus may be downward sloping; a point to the

---

[2] The constraints are $\chi_J = h_J f_J(\Phi_J)$ $(J = i, c)$, $z = lf_z(\Psi)$, $1 = l + h$, $h = h_i + h_c$, $\Phi = h_i\Phi_i + (1 - h_i)\Phi_z$, $R \geq P_J f'_J(\Phi_J)$ $(J = i, c)$, $W \geq P_J[f_J(\Phi_J) - \Phi_J f'_J(\Phi_J)]$, $W \geq P_z[f_z(\Psi) - \Psi f'_z(\Psi)]$, $P_c \geq P_z f'_z(\Psi)$, $\bar{\omega} = \max\{\omega_i, \omega_z\}$, $\underline{\omega} = \min\{\omega_i, \omega_z\}$, $\bar{P} = \max\{P(\omega), P(\bar{\omega})\}$, $\underline{P} = \min\{P(\underline{\omega}), P(\bar{\omega})\}$.

left of $\dot{\Phi} = 0$ implies a value of P higher than the one which will make $(n + \delta) = f'_i$. Therefore $\dot{P} = 0$ intersects $\dot{\Phi} = 0$ from below.

The curves $\dot{\Phi} = 0$ and $\dot{P} = 0$ intersect at the point (Φ^*, P^*). A glance at Figs. 1 and 2 suggests that most trajectories veer away from point $(\Phi < \Phi^*)$, and one from the right $(\Phi < \Phi^*)$. That this is so can be determined by linearizing Eqs. (11) and (15) and examining the characteristic roots.

The preceding discussion implicitly neglects the existence of any distortion or government intervention. The next part of the analysis discusses some of the effects of government expenditure on output and employment.

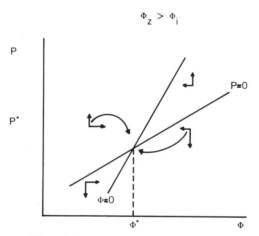

Figure 1. Long-run equilibrium, $\Phi_z > \Phi_i$.

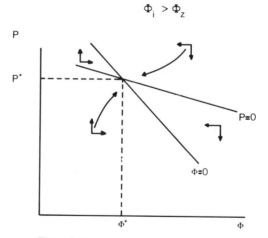

Figure 2. Long-run equilibrium, $\Phi_i > \Phi_z$.

2. THE GOVERNMENT SECTOR

The role played by the government in this model is very specific. It is assumed that for whatever reason the government decides to provide some transfer payments free of charge to some people in the economy. It is also assumed that no distribution costs or waste are associated with the provision of the services. The government budget is assumed to be balanced over the life cycle in order to finance the expenditure; taxes will have to be imposed, and the net present value of tax collection will be equal to the net present value of the government expenditure. Since the analysis implicitly assumes perfect foresight and certainty of all relevant variables, including knowledge of all future taxes and government expenditures, the government budget deficit at some time implies that at some other time a budget surplus will occur. In this model government bonds are not assumed to be net wealth. The conditions under which government bonds constitute net wealth or not can be found in Barro (1974). The substitution effects due to the government action, however, still remain to be analyzed.

To the extent that transfer receipts are uncorrelated with tax collections, the taxes will drive a wedge between the price paid by consumers and the price received by producers. The change in relative prices resulting from the imposition of the tax will generate substitution effects which may alter the consumption-goods–leisure choice (work–leisure decision) at a given time, the choice among consuming the household goods at a different time (the consumption–savings choice), or a combination of both.

Different financing alternatives for the transfer payments will be considered. For each tax alternative it is assumed that taxes are imposed in such a way as to minimize their welfare cost. The tax will induce changes in the relative price faced by consumers and producers and thus will affect the quantity produced at a given time. Once one knows how the economy's path is distorted, one can search for the welfare implications of these changes in the path. The analysis is analogous to the static procedure of evaluating welfare triangles once it is known how the instantaneous market equilibrium is affected by a change in taxation.

The estimation of the welfare cost of the different taxes will be an intertemporal generalization of Harberger's (1964, 1971) welfare indicator, which approximates the true change in welfare using a Taylor series expansion. The welfare indicator makes use of the same basic information which is used in the revealed preference theory developed by Samuelson (1974). Diewert (1976) has shown formally that Haberger's welfare indicator is consistent with the results of revealed preference when applied to a single individual. Willig (1976) also has shown that observed consumer's surplus can be rigorously utilized to estimate unobservable compensating and equivalent variations and that these are the correct theoretical measures of the welfare impact of changes in prices and income for the individual.

A remaining problem is the valid extension of Willig's and Diewert's results from individual persons to a group of consumers. This is accomplished by Harberger's third postulate: the adding up of benefits and costs across different members of the community for which the welfare economic analysis is undertaken produces an aggregate measure. Harberger advocates the use of the third postulate as a technical convention that permits the separation resource allocation from distributional effects in the analysis of the problem.

In the model developed in this chapter the economy is assumed to behave as a single individual. Therefore, Harberger's third postulate is implicit in the analysis. Distribution effects will be ignored completely.

3. LONG-RUN EFFECTS OF TAXES

3.1. Household Good Taxation

A household good tax increases the relative price of household consumption in the taxed period. The tax generates a substitution effect away from household consumption in the taxed period into other periods. The modified income constraint due to the imposition of the household good tax is

$$y_F = z + Pi = [W(\bar{P}) + R(\bar{P})\Phi + TR](1 - T) \tag{18}$$

when TR is the transfer payments, T the tax, and $\bar{P}$ is the relative price faced by suppliers.

In the neighborhood of equilibrium the change in demand price [Eq. (15)] and the modified equation for the rate of change in the economy's capital–labor ratio due to the household tax become

$$\dot{P}/P = 0 = (n + \delta) - f_i' = (n + \delta) - R(\bar{P}) \tag{19}$$

$$\dot{\Phi} = 0 = (n + \delta) - (1 - T)[R(\bar{P})/\bar{P}] \tag{20}$$

The shift of the $\dot{P} = 0$ locus and of the $\dot{\Phi} = 0$ locus will be

$$\varepsilon_{PT}\bigg|_{\dot{\Phi}=0} = \varepsilon_{PT}\bigg|_{\dot{P}=0} = -\frac{T}{1 - T}$$

Since both loci shift by the same amount, the steady-state capital–labor ratio remains unchanged and the net of tax relative price decreases by the same proportion as the tax rate increases. This is shown graphically in Fig. 3. The household good tax does not have any effect on relative prices, the consumption and savings schedules remains unchanged, and no welfare costs is generated by a transfer payment financed by a tax on household consumption. The household commodity tax is neutral.

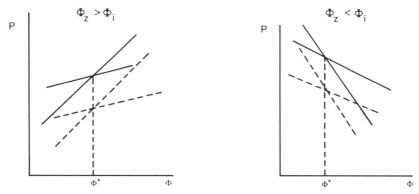

Figure 3. The effects of a consumption tax on long-run equilibrium.

3.2. Consumption Good Taxation

The household good tax implies that the consumption of good and leisure time is taxed at the same marginal rate. In general, leisure is never explicitly taxed; therefore, a more realistic assumption will be a government policy which does not tax leisure. The consumption good tax is such a policy.

While consumption good represents market output, taxation of a consumption good is equivalent to taxation of an input. The tax will shift the economy inside the production possibility frontier.

A consumption good tax increases the demand price of the consumption good and the household good. The tax distorts the input choices and thus induces a substitution which reduces the market goods intensity of the household good. If the economy is initially without distortions, the percentage increase in the price of the household good will equal the product of the share of consumption goods (μ) times the tax rate in percentage terms. The shift of the $\dot{\Phi} = 0$ and $\dot{P} = 0$ schedules around equilibrium will be qualitatively the same as that of household good taxation; the exact magnitude of the shifts will be $\mu \varepsilon_{PT}$. The household good tax does not change the economy's relative prices. Thus, no intertemporal substitution effects are generated, and the long-run capital labor ratio remains unchanged. In other words, the consumption good tax does not distort the savings–investment choices, and the economy's capital accumulation path remains unchanged. The consumption good tax will distort the labor–leisure choice, and the consumption commodity output decreases as a result of the inefficiency induced by the input tax. Given that the capital accumulation path (investment) remains unchanged, and that leisure tend to increase, market output will unambiguously fall.

The results are markedly different from those obtained in models of capital accumulation, which specify the savings as a fraction of income, as seen in Feldstein (1974a, b). These other models indicate that an increase in the consumption tax rates will lead to an increase in capital accumulation. The different implications of the two models are easily explained. The latter models implicitly treat savings as a good; that is, in addition to yielding future utility, through future consumption, the act of saving is also a source of utility. The consumption good tax will generate a substitution effect toward the least taxed commodity (savings).

Recent studies by Joines (1979) and Canto and Laffer (1979) tend to favor this chapter's implication that consumption goods–leisure distortions, measured as the economy's marginal tax rate on labor income, will have no effect on an economy's long-run capital accumulation. Joines's (1979) study analyzes the effect of government tax and spending policies on capital formation during the period 1929–1975. A transfer function model was fitted to private plant and equipment investment. Three independent variables were used; two were the weighted average of the marginal tax rate on income from capital and labor; the third independent variable attempted to approximate a measure of the government's total appropriation of economic resources. The empirical results indicate that an increase in the weighted average tax rate on capital exerts a statistically significant deterrent effect on investment, while the marginal tax rate on labor exerts no statistically significant effect. Similarly, Canto and Laffer (1979), in their analysis of the Puerto Rican economy for the period 1947–1975, find a negative and statistically significant relation between changes in the per capita output and changes in the marginal tax rate on labor income, while at the same time they fail to find a statistically significant relation between the marginal tax rate on labor income and savings.

The variability of the supply of labor to the market sector implies that the welfare cost of consumption taxation is positive. Clearly the magnitude of the welfare costs generated will depend on the magnitude of the marginal tax rate on labor and the magnitude of the goods–leisure substitution effects. Empirical studies such as that by Becker and Ghez (1975) report a nonzero elasticity of substitution between goods and leisure. Feldstein (1978) also reports a substantial effect of unemployment insurance on temporary (layoff) unemployment. Evans (1978) has estimated an elasticity of substitution between capital and labor in the market sector in excess of unity. Similar are studies by Joines (1979), Laffer (1978), Burkhauser (1976), Burkhasuer and Turner (1978), and Quinn (1977), Boskin (1977), and Feldstein (1978) suggest that significant tax-induced distortions exist on the U.S. labor market.

3.3. Investment Taxation

An investment tax will increase the price of the investment good. The modified income constraint will be

$$y_F = z + Pi = W(\bar{P}) + R(\bar{P})\Phi + TR. \tag{21}$$

The equation of motion for the demand price in the neighborhood of equilibrium will be

$$\dot{P} = 0 = R(\bar{P})/P - (n + \delta) \tag{22}$$

The shift of the demand price equation ($\dot{P} = 0$) around equilibrium becomes

$$\varepsilon_{PT} = \frac{T}{1 - T} \left[\frac{\varepsilon_{RP}}{\varepsilon_{RP} - 1} \right] \tag{23}$$

The term in the brackets will be greater or smaller than one depending on the relative intensity of z and i.[3] The shift of the capital–labor ratio equation of motion [Eq. (11)] will be

$$\varepsilon_{PT} = T/(1 - T) \tag{24}$$

The steady state capital–labor ratio unambiguously decreases. This is shown graphically in Fig. 4.

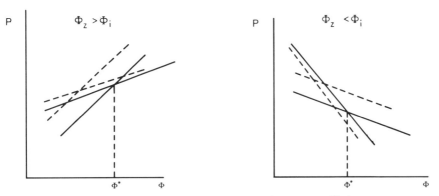

Figure 4. The effects of an investment tax on long-run equilibrium.

---

[3] Differentiating the numeraire logarithmically yields

$$EP_z = \mu_z \mu_c ER - (1 - \mu_z \mu_c)EW = 0$$

Differentiating the investment good relative price yields

$$EP = \mu_i ER - (1 - \mu_i)EW$$

Combining the two equations gives

$$EP = \frac{\mu_i - \mu_z \mu_c}{1 - \mu_z \mu_c} ER$$

$$\varepsilon_{RP} = \frac{1 - \mu_z \mu_c}{\mu_i - \mu_z \mu_c}$$

$$\frac{\varepsilon_{RP}}{\varepsilon_{RP} - 1} \gtrless 1 \qquad \text{as} \qquad \Phi_i \gtrless \Phi_z.$$

3.4. Income Taxation

Traditionally the income tax is assumed to be equivalent to an equal tax rate on both current consumption and savings. Implicitly this equivalence assumes that savings is part of the taxable base. To the extent that this is so, the income tax is equivalent to a joint consumption and investment (savings) tax. The effects of the income tax will be the net of the consumption and investment good components of the tax. The latter component will lead to a reduction of the economy's long-run capital accumulation.

Recently, the equivalence of the income tax to a joint tax on consumption and savings has been questioned. Miller and Scholes (1978) have argued that the deduction of interest payments from the taxable income base allows, at least in principle, for the elimination of the savings tax component of the income tax. Evidence supporting Miller and Scholes's hypothesis is provided by Joines (1979) in the study previously mentioned. He finds that the weighted average personal income tax rates on income from capital, beginning in the early 1950s, follow a downward path interrupted briefly by the Vietnam surcharge. Thus it appears that the personal income tax system is evolving into a consumption tax. However, to the extent that the savings component of the income tax is not completely eliminated, the long-run capital–labor ratio will be altered. Nevertheless, the effect will not be as strong as what the first interpretation suggests.

4. A SPECIAL CASE

The analysis presented in the previous section could have been easily presented in the context of a more general utility function for which the leisure and market good are incorporated directly as the argument of the instantaneous utility function. However, as is shown in this section, the consumption of a household commodity allows one to obtain a closed form solution to the model. Substitute per capita household production z in place of the instantaneous utility function; then the Hamiltonian optimality conditions become

$$0 = \left(1 - \frac{\lambda}{P}\frac{\partial z}{\partial P}\right) \tag{13'}$$

$$\dot{\lambda} = -R + (n + \delta)\lambda \tag{14'}$$

Since $\lambda = P$, the shadow price equation of motion becomes

$$\dot{P} = -R + P(n + \delta) \tag{15'}$$

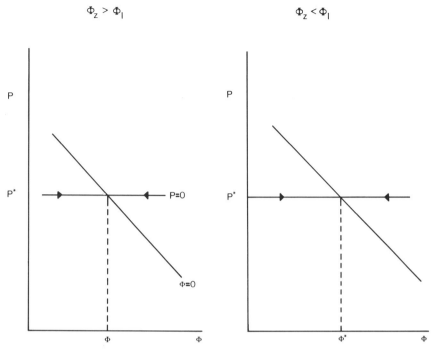

Figure 5. Long-run equilibrium.

Equation (15′) is independent of the economy's capital–labor ratio in the nonspecialization region; therefore, its slope will be horizontal in the (P, Φ) space. The slope of the other equation of motion is described by (17). Fig. 5 presents the phase diagrams.

Since P is constant along the path, the wage–rental ratio will also be constant, as will be factor proportions in the production of the different goods. By the Rybczynski theorem, the equilibrium level of investment and household goods produced will be linear functions of the economy's overall capital–labor ratio, the sign of the relation depending on the goods' relative capital intensity. From the factor employment condition [Eq. (7)], one can solve for the proportion of labor employed in the production of investment goods. The investment and household goods production will be

$$i = \frac{I}{T} = h_i f_i(\Phi_i) = \left(\frac{h\Phi_c - \Phi}{\Phi_c - \Phi_i}\right) f_i(\Phi_i) \tag{25}$$

$$z = \frac{Z}{T} = lf_z(\Psi) = \left(\frac{\gamma}{1 - \gamma}\right) h_c f_z(\Psi) = \left(\frac{\gamma}{1 - \gamma}\right)\left(\frac{\Phi - h\Phi_i}{\Phi_c - \Phi_i}\right) f_z(\Psi) \tag{26}$$

Substituting Eq. (25) into Eq. (11), one obtains a first-order differential equation. The solution of the equation will be

$$\dot{\Phi} = (\Phi - B)e^{-At} + B \tag{27}$$

where

$$A = \frac{f_i + n(\Phi_c - \Phi_i)}{\Phi_c - \Phi_i}$$

$$B = \frac{h\Phi_c f_i}{(\Phi_c - \Phi_i)} \frac{(\Phi_c - \Phi_i)}{[f_i + n(\Phi_c - \Phi_i)]} = \frac{h\Phi_c f_i}{f_i + n(\Phi_c - \Phi_i)} = \Phi_\infty$$

For the case in which the consumption good is the labor intensive good, $f_i > n(\Phi_c - \Phi_i)$ will be sufficient condition to guarantee stability ($A > 0$); and for the case in which consumption is the capital intensive good, the stability condition will be unambiguously satisfied.

Equation (27) describes a stock adjustment behavior. If $\Phi_0 > \Phi_\infty$, then Φ will decline steadily toward Φ_∞. But if $\Phi_0 < \Phi_\infty$, then Φ will increase steadily toward Φ_∞.

Substituting Eq. (27) into Eq. (26), one obtains the optimal path for the consumption of the household commodity.

The discounted sum of all consumption along the optimal path gives the welfare of the program:

$$\Omega = \int_0^\infty e^{-\delta t} z \, dt = \frac{z_\infty}{\delta} + \frac{z_0 - z_\infty}{A + \delta} \tag{28}$$

The welfare of the program will be the steady state (permanent commodity consumption) discounted at the rate of time preference plus an adjustment factor to take account of the fact that the economy need not start in the steady state.

5. WELFARE RANKING OF THE TAX POLICIES

The change in welfare due to the imposition of a tax will be

$$d\Omega = \frac{dz_\infty}{\delta} + \frac{dz_0 - dz_\infty}{A + \delta} - \frac{z_0 - z_\infty}{(A + \delta)^2} dA \tag{29}$$

The first term corresponds to the change in welfare generated by a change in the steady-state consumption; the second term corresponds to an adjustment factor allowing for the possibility that the economy may not be in the steady state when the tax is imposed; the third component represents the change in the rate of growth (speed of adjustment to the steady state).

A consumption tax does not alter the rate of capital accumulation; that is, the economy's speed of adjustment to the steady-state capital–labor ratio remains unchanged ($dA = 0$). In addition, the change in relative price due to the consumption good tax will be the same in every period; and since the savings path does not change, the change in the quantity of the household good is the same in every period. Therefore, no welfare cost is generated by the second component of the welfare equation (29). The total change in welfare due to an optimal consumption tax is the capitalized value of the change in the consumption commodity due to the tax, i.e., the first term of the welfare equation (29).

The investment good tax results in a change once and for all in the relative price of the investment good P and a reduced long-run capital–labor ratio that implies a reduction in the steady-state per capita consumption of the household good. The tax also leads to a change in the speed of adjustment to the new steady state and a change in initial per capita household consumption. Clearly all three components of the welfare cost in Eq. (29) will be different from zero.

Two possibilities have to be considered in the analysis of the welfare cost of an income tax. One possibility is that the income tax is equivalent to a joint consumption and savings (investment) tax, in which case the welfare cost of the tax will be the net of the consumption and savings (investment) tax components. However, as previously argued, to the extent that interest payments are deducted from the taxable income base, the income tax will be equivalent to a consumption tax. Therefore, the welfare cost will be the same as the consumption tax.

An issue of interest is whether the welfare rankings of the different tax alternatives could be equivalently measured through the use of the standard triangle analysis. The standard triangle analysis is "static"; it measures the welfare cost of a tax at a given time. If the tax in question is presumed to last for more than one period, obviously the analysis has to be appropriately modified to take account of this fact. In this case one will have to measure the welfare triangle at each time. Care must be exercised to ensure that no double counting of the welfare cost takes place; clearly once the dynamic considerations are incorporated, both alternatives should provide the same welfare cost estimate. The interesting question is whether by computing the welfare costs at a given time one could somehow estimate the welfare cost of the whole program without computing any of the future periods' welfare costs, that is, without taking into account dynamic consideration. This possibility is now examined.

In the case of a constant rate for the optimal consumption tax, as previously established, the economy's savings path remains unchanged, and the change in consumption is the same in every period. No triangle generated by the consumption good tax is a tax in an input; the instantaneous welfare cost will only result from the goods–leisure distortion, which, as Wisecarver (1976) has shown, can be measured either by measuring the welfare cost triangle under the demand for consumption goods or directly from the change in household production. Since the static welfare cost is the same in every period, the welfare cost of the whole program is the capitalized value of the instantaneous (static) welfare cost. Thus in this case the two alternatives are equivalent, and any any difference that may arise from using the capitalized value of the instantaneous (static) analysis must be attributed to implicit assumptions about the effects of consumption taxes on savings (i.e., on whether or not savings is implicitly treated as a good).

The investment (savings) tax only generates a triangle under savings which at a given time measures the loss of welfare resulting from reduced future consumption because the economy did not save enough. The question is whether the instantaneous triangle could be used as an approximation of future instantaneous triangles.

In this special case the economy is characterized by a stock adjustment behavior. Since the investment tax alters the economy's speed of adjustment A, the new savings path will differ from the undistorted savings path by a constant proportion (the change in speed of adjustment). Canto (1977) has shown in the case of a small open economy that the income tax rate declines over time at a constant rate. It implies that although the change in savings (the base of the welfare triangle) is not the same in every period, the optimal tax rate also changes over time so that the area of the instantaneous welfare triangle does not change.

The analysis in this section suggests that with appropriate modification the standard "static" analysis can be appropriately used to evaluate the welfare costs of the "optimal" tax programs.

6. CONCLUDING REMARKS

This chapter develops a two-sector model of production (consumption and investment goods) with a variable supply of labor to the market sector. The introduction of a household production function allows for the derivation of a demand function for leisure independent of a utility or preference function. In other words, the production possibility frontier, at a given time, can be described independently of demand considerations, and, given factor endowments, the relative price P is sufficient to regulate sectoral output and market employment of labor.

The solution to the general model with an instantaneous utility of the form $G(z)$ yields a time-varying relative price of the investment good in terms of the household good; as a result the wage–rental ratio will vary along the optimal path. This prevents one from obtaining a global solution and the change in the welfare cost of the different tax schemes. Only for the special case for which a closed form solution obtains are the global properties of the model unambiguously established. The inability to obtain a global solution for the general case restricts the analysis to the neighborhood of equilibrium where the local stability conditions are satisfied; as a result, only the long-run effects of taxes are unambiguously established. Nevertheless, this does not prevent one from being able to make inferences about the short- versus long-run incidence and welfare ranking of the alternative tax schemes.

It is apparent from the previous sections that neither of the tax alternatives considered will be neutral. The consumption good tax distorts the labor–leisure choice; however, it has no effect on the economy's capital accumulation path. To the extent that the magnitude of the substitution effects between goods and time remains unchanged over time, the optimal consumption tax will be a constant rate. Therefore, the long-run incidence of the tax will be the same as the short-run incidence. These implications are markedly different from the model of capital accumulation that specifies savings as a fraction of income, which yields the result that a consumption tax leads to higher capital accumulation and different long-run incidence effects.

The investment good tax distorts the economy's savings–investment choices and unambiguously reduces the economy's long-run capital–labor ratio. Alternatively stated, the investment tax reduces the net return to investment (savings). This generates an intertemporal substitution effect toward earlier periods' consumption in order to avoid the tax. In the process of avoiding the tax, welfare costs are generated. Clearly, the intertemporal substitution effects will in general also lead to different long- and short-run incidence of the tax. The analysis of the effects of the investment tax is not very different from that of other models, at least qualitatively.

The superiority of an investment tax over a consumption tax depends in part on the relative strength of the work–leisure and savings–investment substitution effects. Although the empirical results previously cited, with the exception of Joines (1979), do not provide explicit information on the dynamic effects of taxes on the work–leisure and savings–investment choices, the evidence suggests that substitution effects induced by the different taxes and their welfare costs may be sizable.

It must be emphasized that the substitution effects discussed are not the elasticity of substitution between goods and leisure or the elasticity of substitution between consumption in one period and consumption in another period. The substitution effects considered are the reduced form reaction coefficients of consumption generated by the taxes, which depend on demand

and supply conditions. Another point that must be mentioned is that the specific utility function assumed discounts consumption at a constant rate δ independent of taxes. In general, there is no reason for the social discount rates to be constant and independent of the tax rate. If the social discount rate is affected by the taxes, its effect should be incorporated in the change of welfare equation. Such changes in the social discount rate could be determined along the lines discussed by Harberger (1969a, b).

This chapter also analyzes the welfare costs of income taxation. Traditionally an income tax has been assumed to be equivalent to a joint consumption and savings tax. In this case, the effects of the income tax will be the net of the consumption and savings (investment) tax component. Whether the income tax is superior to a consumption or investment tax (subject to the constraint that each raises the same amount of revenue over the life cycle) cannot be determined without reference to the magnitudes of the substitution effects. Since the optimal income tax will not minimize the welfare cost of either the consumption or savings component individually, at best it will do as well as a combination of investment goods and consumption goods taxes that are not constrained to have the same rate at a given time; therefore, the income tax must be an inferior alternative.

The deduction of interest rate payments from the taxable income base suggests the possibility that the savings component of the income tax may be completely eliminated, in which case the income tax becomes a consumption tax. How much of the savings component of the tax is eliminated by the deduction of interest payment from the taxable base is an empirical issue. Joines (1979) estimates that, on income from capital, the U.S. income tax component of the marginal tax rates capital has steadily declined; this is consistent with the hypothesis that the U.S. income tax is evolving into a consumption tax, in which case the savings component of the income tax will be greatly reduced, if not completely eliminated. To the extent that the income tax is equivalent to a consumption tax, a progressive income tax under conditions of a fluctuating taxable base will be inferior to the constant rate optimal consumption good tax.

If this latter possibility regarding the equivalence of the income tax is taken seriously, contrary to Schenone's conclusions, it is the constant rate of consumption and income taxes, and not the income and investment taxes, that are equivalent in terms of the welfare cost generated. Furthermore, since in addition the taxable base of the income (consumption) and investment taxes are different, one cannot determine *a priori* which alternative yields the lower welfare cost per revenue collected.

Finally, the analysis of the special case, for which a closed form solution obtains, suggests that the use of the static triangle analysis correctly approximates the welfare ranking of the different optimal tax alternatives discussed.

REFERENCES

Barro, R. J. (1974). "Are Government Bonds Net Wealth?" *Journal of Political Economy* **82**, 1095–1117.

Becker, G. S. (1965). "A Theory of the Allocation of Time," *Economic Journal* **75**, 493–517.

Becker, G. S., and Ghez, G. (1975). *The Allocation of Time and Goods over the Life Cycle.* Columbia Univ. Press for National Bureau of Economic Research, New York.

Boskin, M. (1977). "Social Security Retirement Decisions," *Economic Inquiry* **15**, 1–25.

Burkhauser, R. (1976). "The Early Pension Decision and Its Effect on Exit from the Labor Markets," Ph.D. Dissertation, Univ. of Chicago, Chicago, Illinois.

Burkhauser, R., and Turner, J. (1978). "A Time-Series Analysis on Social Security and Its Effect on the Market Work of Men at Younger Ages," *Journal of Political Economy* **86**, 701–716.

Canto, V. (1977). "Taxation, Welfare and Economic Activity," Ph.D. Dissertation, Univ. of Chicago, Chicago, Illinois.

Canto, V., and Laffer, A. (1979). *Report to the Governor: Recommendations for Economic Reform in Puerto Rico.* Wainwright Economics, Boston, Massachusetts.

Diewert, W. E. (1976). "Harberger's Welfare Indicator and Revealed Preference Theory," *American Economic Review* **66** (2), 143–152.

Evans, P. (1978). "Fiscal Policy and the Labor Market," Mimeograph, Stanford Univ., Palo Alto, California.

Feldstein, M. (1974a). "Incidence of a Capital Income Tax in a Growing Economy with Variable Savings Rates," *Review of Economic Studies* **41**, 505–523.

Feldstein, M. (1974b). "Tax Incidence in a Growing Economy with Variable Factor Supply," *Quarterly Journal of Economics* **88**, 551–573.

Feldstein, M. (1978). "The Effect of Unemployment Insurance on Temporary Layoff Unemployment," *American Economic Review* **68**, 834–846.

Hadley, G., and Kemp, M. C. (1971). *Variational Methods in Economics.* American Elsevier, New York.

Harberger, A. C. (1964). "Taxation, Resource Allocation and Welfare," in *The Role of Direct and Indirect Taxes in the Federal Reserve System.* Princeton Univ. Press for the National Bureau of Economic Research and the Brookings Institution, Princeton, New Jersey.

Harberger, A. C. (1969a). "Professor Arrow on the Social Discount," in *Cost Benefit Analysis of Manpower Policies* (G. W. Somers and W. D. Wood, eds.), pp. 76–88. Queen's University, Kingston, Canada.

Harberger, A. C. (1969b). "On Measuring the Social Opportunity Cost of Public Funds," *Conference Proceedings of the Committee on the Economics of Water Resources Development*, pp. 1–24. Western Agricultural Economics Research Council, Report No. 17, Denver, Colorado.

Harberger, A. C. (1971). "Three Basic Postulates for Applied Welfare Economics," *Journal of Economic Literature* **9**, 785–797.

Harberger, A. C. (1974). *Taxation and Welfare.* Little, Brown, Boston, Massachusetts.

Intrilligator, M. D. (1971). *Mathematical Optimization and Economic Theory.* Prentice Hall, Englewood Cliffs, New Jersey.

Joines, D. (1979). "Government Fiscal Policy and Private Capital Formation." Ph.D. Dissertation, Univ. of Chicago, Chicago, Illinois.

Kemp, M. C., and Jones, R. (1962). "Variable Labor Supply and the Theory of International Trade," *Journal of Political Economy* **70**, (1), 30–36.

Laffer, A. B. (1978). "Prohibitive Tax Rates and the Inner City: A Rational Explanation of the Poverty Trap," in *Economic Study.* Wainwright Economics, Boston, Massachusetts.

Little, M. D. (1951). "Direct versus Indirect Taxes," *Economic Journal* **61**, 577–584.

Miller, M., and Scholes, M. (1978). "Dividends and Taxes," *Journal of Financial Economics* **6**, 333–364.

Quinn, J. (1977). "The Microeconomic Determinants of Early Retirement: A Cross Section View of White Married Men," *Journal of Human Resources* **12**, 329–346.

Samuelson, P. A. (1974). *Foundation of Economic Analysis.* Atheneum, New York, Massachusetts.

Schenone, O. H. (1975). "A Dynamic Analysis of Taxation," *American Economic Review* **65**, 101–114.

Uzawa, H. (1967). "Optimal Growth in a Two-Sector Model of Economic Growth," *Review of Economic Studies* **34**, (2).

Willig, R. D. (1976). "Consumer Surplus without Apology," *American Economic Review* **66**, 589–597.

Wisecarver, D. (1976). "The Social Cost of Input Market Distortions," *American Economic Review* **66**, (4), 589–597.

Chapter 3

A Neoclassical Model of Fiscal Policy, Employment, and Capital Accumulation

Douglas H. Joines

This chapter is concerned with the effects of government fiscal policy on equilibrium levels of market employment of factors of production. Economic intuition tells us that in a world inhabited by rational economic agents, taxation of an activity reduces the amount of that activity taking place. A general tax on market activity, for example, will result in a decrease in market activity in favor of nonmarket activity. A tax on the employment of a specific factor of production, say labor, will result in a reduction in the employment of that factor. The effect of a labor tax on the employment of other factors is unclear, however. An increase in the labor tax will cause any level of market production to be carried out utilizing more of the other factors and less labor. But since such a tax strikes market activity and not nonmarket activity, it will tend to reduce production in the market sector, and thus employment of all factors of production. The net effect on the level of factors other than labor is unclear.

These problems are here analyzed in terms of a theoretical model most aspects of which are to be found in the standard literature on neoclassical growth, saving, national debt, labor supply, and taxation of the past 20 years. The basic framework is a Solow-type one-sector growth model in which population grows at a constant, exogenously given rate and in which output is produced by labor and capital according to a neoclassical production function.[1] Unlike that model, however, this chapter does not assume labor supply to be strictly proportional to population or saving (investment) to be strictly proportional to income (output). The individual's behavior with regard to consumption and factor supply is derived as the result of an explicit utility maximization process. The labor-supply decision is analyzed within the household production framework of Becker (1965).[2] Explicit motivation for the individual's saving behavior derives from the standard two-period consumption problem dating back at least to Irving Fisher and here embedded in an overlapping-generations framework of the type used by Samuelson (1958). Following Diamond (1965), we reduce both the number of periods in an individual's life and the number of generations living at any point in time from three to two since production is admitted into the model.

The derivation of the individual's consumption and factor-supply decisions as the outcome of an explicit utility maximization process serves to highlight the simultaneous nature of these decisions. The quantity of one factor supplied to the market sector is seen to depend not just on the after-tax return to that factor, but on the return to the other factor as well. This finding is in contrast to those of most other models in the literature. Feldstein (1974c), for example, assumes that the quantity of each factor supplied is positively related to its own after-tax return, but that all cross effects on the supply side of the factor market are zero. The existence of nonzero cross effects on the supply side serves, within the context of the present model, to eliminate the ambiguity concerning the effect of a tax on one factor's income on the employment of the other factor. Taxation of either factor of production is found to reduce the market employment of *both* factors.

----

[1] See Solow (1956).

[2] In many static models of labor supply, market goods and leisure are treated as the only two arguments in the individual's utility function, and are thus substitutes. Many two-period saving-investment models similarly take current and future consumption of market goods as the only arguments in the utility function. It is here desired to build a two-period model with variable labor supply. If both leisure and market goods in each of the two periods were allowed to enter directly into the utility function, then all the arguments wouldn't necessarily be substitutes. One could always sign the various cross-price effects by making *a priori* assumptions. If possible, however, it would be desirable to impose additional structure on the model in a less arbitrary manner. An arguably reasonable means of doing so is to regard "satisfaction" in any period as the product of two inputs (market goods and own time) in that period and to regard current and future satisfaction as substitutes.

Within the context of a two-period overlapping-generations model such as that employed here, Diamond (1965) concluded that national debt reduces private capital formation. This result is applicable not only to national debt but also to an unfunded social security system or other government program of intergenerational income transfers. Recent work of Becker (1974) and Barro (1974) has cast doubt on these conclusions. Barro has demonstrated that if voluntary intergenerational transfers are taking place in the absence of such programs, then the programs will not affect private capital formation. In order to deal with these issues adequately, it is necessary to include a bequest motive in the individual's choice problem. By basing individual behavior upon utility maximization, it is possible to derive explicit conditions under which bequests will and will not take place.

1. THE MODEL

Consider a world in which all individuals, assumed homogeneous, live for two periods, being employed in the first and retired in the second. Let N_t be the number of individuals in generation t, where t denotes the first period of life, and suppose that population grows at a constant rate n, that is, $N_{t+1} = (1 + n)N_t$. In period t each member of generation t chooses to spend a fraction l_t of his time in the market sector and the remaining fraction $1 - l_t$ in the household sector.[3]

---

[3] The assumption that $l = 0$ in the second period of life is perhaps a bit extreme. It is introduced as a simple method of highlighting the intertemporal effects of a change in the after-tax wage rate. Except under equally stringent assumptions, a change in the after-tax wage rate will affect not only the price of leisure in terms of market goods, but also the price of current household commodities in terms of future household commodities. See Section 2, and especially footnote 10.

The present model differs from the standard formulation of Diamond (1965) and Samuelson (1967, 1968), not in assuming $l = 0$ in the second period of life, but in assuming l to be a variable rather than a constant in the first period. The assumptions of the present model are thus less restrictive than those of previous formulations. They are also sufficient to yield an aggregate supply of labor which is sensitive to, among other things, the after-tax wage rate.

One can present any number of scenarios to justify a zero labor supply in the second period of life. A simple one is that the government imposes such a high tax on employment in period 2 (such as the Social Security retirement test) that each member of the older generation maximizes his utility at the corner solution corresponding to zero market employment. Another scenario involves human capital. Suppose that each individual is born with a given stock of human capital which depreciates at a given rate. Suppose that the stock of human capital affects one's productivity in the market sector more than his productivity in the household sector. A sufficiently high rate of depreciation of the human capital stock would then result in the same corner solution. The model could be complicated by making the rate of depreciation depend on expenditures undertaken to maintain one's stock of human capital.

Assume there is a single market good which serves as both capital and consumption good. Let output of this good be given be the concave, linear homogeneous production function $Y_t = F(K_t, l_t N_t)$ where K_t, the capital stock at time t, is equal to aggregate saving in the previous period, S_{t-1}.[4] Output per worker can be written as $y_t = F(k_t, l_t)$.[5] The capital stock per worker is given by $k_t = s_{t-1}/(1 + n)$. It is assumed that $F(k, 0) = F(0, l) = 0$, $F_i > 0$, $F_{ii} < 0$, and $F_{ij} > 0$, where the subscripts i and j denote partial differentiation of the production function with respect to arguments i and j. It is also assumed that factors are paid their marginal products

$$r_t = F_k(k_t, l_t)$$

$$w_t = F_l(k_t, l_t)$$

where r_t and w_t denote the rental price of capital and the wage rate, respectively.

The lifetime utility of a member of generation t is assumed to depend upon the utility of his heirs in generation $t + 1$ as well as upon his own consumption in the two periods of his life of a homogeneous, nonstorable commodity z, which he produces:

$$U^t = U(z_{t,t}; z_{t,t+1}; U^{t+1}) \tag{1}$$

Here U^{t+1} is a utility index of each heir in the succeeding generation and is assumed to be anticipated without error. The utility of any one generation is thus seen to depend at least indirectly upon the utility of all future genera-

---

[4] Suppose that production takes place at the beginning of a period, and that consumption and investment occur at the end of a period. Since the consumption and capital goods are indistinguishable from each other, the total of this market good available for consumption and investment at the end of period t is equal to the capital stock as of the beginning of period t, plus the quantity of the good newly produced during the period, less the capital consumed in such production. The function $F(\ )$ could be defined in any of three ways: (1) as newly produced goods, (2) as newly produced goods less capital consumption, or (3) as newly produced goods plus beginning-of-period capital stock less capital consumption. Definitions 1 and 3 are of course equivalent if the entire capital stock is consumed during the production process, while definitions 1 and 2 are equivalent if the depreciation rate is zero. For most of this paper depreciation will be assumed to be zero and definitions 1 and 2 will apply to $F(\ )$. When a specific functional form is assumed for $F(\ )$ in appendix C, however, it will be more convenient to adopt definition 3. The main effect of these assumptions is on the exact form of the consumer's second-period budget constraint (5), but the definition of the production function has no effect on the signs of any of the income and substitution effects derived below.

[5] Small letters, when applied to quantity variables, denote per capita values. The normalization factor for variable x_t is N_t. For variables with double subscripts, the first subscript denotes the generation and the second denotes the time period. Thus the normalization factor x_{ij} is N_i.

tions.[6] The consumption commodity z is produced in the household according to a linear homogeneous production function:

$$z_{t,t} = z(c_{t,t}; 1 - l_t) \tag{2}$$

$$z_{t,t+1} = z(c_{t,t+1}; 1) \tag{3}$$

where $c_{t,t}$ and $c_{t,t+1}$ denote consumption of market goods by an individual of generation t in periods t and $t + 1$, respectively. All arguments in the utility function are assumed to be normal "goods" and to be substitutes.

Each individual chooses l_t, $c_{t,t}$, $c_{t,t+1}$, and b_{t+1}, a bequest to each of his heirs in the next generation, so as to maximize his lifetime utility subject to the constraints (2) and (3) as well as

$$c_{t,t} = g_{t,t} + (1 - \theta)b_t + w_t l_t(1 - \gamma) - s_t \tag{4}$$

$$c_{t,t+1} = g_{t,t+1} + [1 + r_{t+1}(1 - \tau)]s_t - (1 + n)b_{t+1} \tag{5}$$

Here $g_{t,t}$ and $g_{t,t+1}$ are lump-sum government transfer payments (if positive) or taxes (if negative) accruing to members of generation t in periods t and $t + 1$, respectively, and θ, γ, and τ are the tax rates on bequests, income from labor, and income from capital, respectively. All three of the market or interpersonal transactions in which an individual might engage are assumed to be taxed. For simplicity the tax rates are assumed constant. It is also assumed that r_{t+1} is forecast without error.

The first-order conditions for maximization of lifetime utility are

$$l_t: \quad U_1^t z_2(c_{t,t}; 1 - l_t) - \lambda_t w_t(1 - \gamma)[1 + r_{t+1}(1 - \tau)] = 0$$

$$c_{t,t}: \quad U_1^t z_1(c_{t,t}; 1 - l_t) - \lambda_t[1 + r_{t+1}(1 - \tau)] = 0$$

$$c_{t,t+1}: \quad U_2^t z_1(c_{t,t+1}; 1) - \lambda_t = 0$$

$$b_{t+1}: \quad U_3^t \lambda_{t+1}[1 + r_{t+2}(1 - \tau)](1 - \theta) - \lambda_t(1 + n) = 0$$

$$\lambda_t: \quad g_{t,t+1} + [1 + r_{t+1}(1 - \tau)][g_{t,t} + (1 - \theta)b_t$$
$$+ w_t l_t(1 - \gamma) - c_{t,t}] - (1 + n)b_{t+1} - c_{t,t+1} = 0$$

[6] For the sake of symmetry, one could also include U^{t-1} as an argument in the utility function. Since in this case U^{t-1} is increased by an increase in U^t, which in turn is raised by the increase in U^{t-1}, certain restrictions must be placed on the form of the utility function in order for utility to remain finite (see Becker 1974). Such conditions would presumably guarantee that intergenerational transfers would not take place in both directions simultaneously.

If U^{t-1} is an argument in U^t, then the utility of the current generation depends upon the utilities of all previous generations. Since only generation $t - 1$ remains alive at time t, however, there is no possibility of increasing the welfare of each generation by a transfer of resources infinitely far into the past unless there exists some family or social compact to effect such a transfer. See Barro (1976) and Appendix B. Since the implications of a bequest motive for the questions at hand depend on an unbroken stream of bequests extending infinitely far in either direction, and since in the absence of some social compact there is a finite "horizon" of one period into the past, inclusion of U^{t-1} as an argument in U^t gives rise to no implications over and above those flowing from a model based upon Eq. (1). See Appendix B and footnote 16.

where λ_t is a Lagrange multiplier equal to the marginal lifetime utility to a member of generation t of one unit of the market good received in the second period of life, and $z_i(\ )$ is the partial derivative of the household production function with respect to argument i.

The fourth of these equations deserves some explanation. The first term merely says that the marginal utility to a member of generation t of a gross-of-tax bequest of one unit of the market good received by each of his immediate heirs in period $t + 1$ is the product of four quantities:

(1) U_3^t, the marginal utility to a member of generation t of a unit increase in the utility index of each of his heirs,

(2) λ_{t+1}, the marginal utility to a member of generation $t + 1$ of one unit of the market good received in period $t + 2$, that is, the increase in his lifetime utility resulting from a one-unit relaxation of his lifetime budget constraint,

(3) $1 + r_{t+2}(1 - \tau)$, the after-tax discount factor between periods $t + 1$ and $t + 2$, and

(4) $1 - \theta$, the fraction of the bequest actually received by the heir after payment of inheritance taxes.

The coefficient on λ_t is the price, in terms of market goods in period $t + 1$, of a gross bequest of one unit of market goods to each heir in period $t + 1$ and is merely equal to the number of heirs.[7]

Assume that all members of generation t and all future generations maximize their utility so that conditions similar to those above hold for every generation. These conditions imply that

$$U_3^{t+j} = \frac{\lambda_{t+j}}{\lambda_{t+j+1}} (1 + n)/(1 - \theta)[1 + r_{t+j+2}(1 - \tau)], \qquad j = 1, 2, 3, \ldots$$

(6)

[7] It is analytically more instructive, but notationally more cumbersome, to regard the true object of choice as net bequests per heir, $b_{t+1}(1 - \theta)$, rather than gross bequests per heir, b_{t+1}. This is because we assume that the utility of a member of generation t is directly affected by the standard of living of his heirs and not by the magnitude of his sacrifice in improving their standard of living. His total sacrifice, or expenditure on bequests, is $b_{t+1}(1 + n)$. Thus the price of net bequests in terms of his own consumption of the market good in the second period of life is merely total expenditure on bequests divided by units of net bequests purchased,

$$b_{t+1}(1 + n)/b_{t+1}(1 - \theta) = (1 + n)/(1 - \theta).$$

For a given rate of growth of population, an increase in the inheritance tax rate raises the relative price of net bequests. If the proceeds of the tax are redistributed lump-sum to either generation there is no income effect (other than a welfare loss) from the tax change. Whether total expenditure on bequests increases or decreases as a result of the tax change is unclear. Since saving is directly affected by the amount of gross bequests rather than by units of net bequests purchased, the effect on desired saving of a change in the inheritance tax is ambiguous.

Note that the marginal utility to a member of generation t of one unit of the market good received in period $t + i$ by each of his heirs of generation $t + i$ is

$$U_3^t U_3^{t+1} U_3^{t+2} \ldots U_3^{t+i-1} \lambda_{t+i}[1 + r_{t+i+1}(1 - \tau)]$$

$$= \frac{U_3^t \lambda_{t+1}[(1 + n)/(1 - \theta)]^{i-1}}{\prod_{j=3}^{i}[1 + r_{t+j}(1 - \tau)]}, \qquad i = 3, 4, 5, \ldots \qquad (7)$$

At the initial values of $l_{t+j}, c_{t+j,t+j}, c_{t+j,t+j+1}$, and b_{t+j+1}, for $j = 1, 2, 3, \ldots$, one can normalize the utility index of generation $t + 1$ so that $\lambda_{t+1} = 1$. Thus for analyzing marginal changes, one could take the utility function of generation t as

$$U^t = U(z_{t,t}; z_{t,t+1}; h_{t+1})$$

where

$$h_{t+1} = g_{t+1,t+1} + w_{t+1}l_{t+1}(1 - \gamma) + (1 - \theta)b_{t+1}$$

$$- s_{t+1} + \sum_{i=1}^{\infty} v_{1,i}Q_{1,i} + \sum_{i=1}^{\infty} v_{2,i}Q_{2,i}$$

$$Q_{1,i} = g_{t+i,t+i} + w_{t+i}l_{t+i}(1 - \gamma) + (1 - \theta)b_{t+i} - s_{t+i} \qquad (8)$$

$$Q_{2,i} = g_{t+i,t+i+1} + [1 + r_{t+i+1}(1 - \tau)]s_{t+i} - (1 - n)b_{t+i}$$

$$v_{1,i} = \frac{[(1 + n)/(1 - \theta)]^{i-1}}{\prod_{j=2}^{i}[1 + r_{t+j}(1 - \tau)]}$$

and

$$v_{2,i} = \frac{[(1 + n)/(1 - \theta)]^{i-1}}{\prod_{j=2}^{i+1}[1 + r_{t+j}(1 - \tau)]}$$

The variable h_{t+1} has merely been defined in such a way that dU^{t+1}/dx_{t+i} is equal to dh_{t+1}/dx_{t+i} for any variable $x_{t+i}, i \geq 0$. It can be seen that h_{t+1} is just the present value as of period $t + 1$ of income accruing to generation $t + 1$ and all future generations, normalized by N_{t+1}. Note that the discount factors $v_{1,i}$ and $v_{2,i}$ involve more than the after-tax marginal product of capital. They depend on the rate of growth of population and the inheritance tax rate as well. The infinite sum h_{t+1} converges to a finite number only if the rate of growth of population and the rates of taxation of bequests and of the income from capital are "small" relative to the gross marginal product of capital.[8]

---

[8] It might thus appear necessary for U_3^t eventually to fall to zero as h_{t+1} increases in order for U^t to remain finite and for the consumer to have a meaningful maximization problem. Such a restriction on the form of the utility function is unnecessary as long as $U_3^{t+i}\lambda_{t+i+1} < \lambda_{t+i}$ when $b_{t+i+1} = 0$, that is, as long as the utility of a member of generation $t + i$ is increased more if he receives an additional unit of the market good in the second period of life than if his heirs each receive an additional unit of that good in the second period of life. See Appendix B for a discussion of this point.

2. COMPARATIVE STATICS OF THE INDIVIDUAL'S MAXIMIZATION PROBLEM

The comparative-static effects of changes in parameter values on the consumer's desired quantities of l_t, $c_{t,t}$, $c_{t,t+1}$, b_{t+1}, and s_t are easily determined and are quite intuitive. To an individual of generation t the relevant parameters are $w_t^* = w_t(1 - \gamma)$, $r_{t+1}^* = r_{t+1}(1 - \tau)$, $(1 - \theta_t)b_t$, $g_{t,t}$, $g_{t,t+1}$, n, θ_{t+1}, and $h_{t+1}^* = h_{t+1} - (1 - \theta)b_{t+1}$.[9] The income and substitution effects of changes in these parameters are shown in Table 1. It is assumed that s_t and l_t are positive. This assumption is necessary, at the individual level, for some of the income effects to be nonzero. The assumption is not unreasonable since, at the aggregate level, s_t and l_t must be positive in order for market output to be positive.

The income effects require little explanation. Any parameter change which results in an expansion of an individual's lifetime opportunity set, with no change in the relative prices of his ultimate objects of choice, $z_{t,t}$, $z_{t,t+1}$, and U^{t+1}, will result in increased demand for all of them. Thus the derived demands for $1 - l_t$, $c_{t,t}$, and $c_{t,t+1}$ all increase.

The substitution effects generally involve both substitution in consumption of the three ultimate objects of choice and substitution in household

TABLE 1

Comparative-Static Effects of Changes in Certain Parameters on an Individual's Desired Levels of Labor Supply, Saving, Bequests, and Consumption of Market Goods

Parameter	l_t	$c_{t,t}$	$c_{t,t+1}$	b_{t+1}	s_t
Income Effects					
w_t^*	−	+	+	+	+
r_{t+1}^*	−	+	+	+	−
n, θ_{t+1}	+	−	−	−	+
$(1 - \theta)b_t, g_{t,t}$	−	+	+	+	+
$g_{t,t+1}$	−	+	+	+	−
h_{t+1}^*	−	+	+	−	−
Substitution Effects					
w_t^*	+	?	+	+	+
r_{t+1}^*	+	−	+	+	+
n, θ_{t+1}	−	+	+	?	−
$(1 - \theta)b_t, g_{t,t}$	0	0	0	0	0
$g_{t,t+1}, h_{t+1}^*$	0	0	0	0	0

[9] See Appendix A for a discussion of the correct evaluation of changes in h_{t+1}^*.

production. As a result, a change in the after-tax wage rate will in general have a nonzero substitution effect on saving as well as on labor supply. Similarly, a change in the after-tax interest rate will have a nonzero substitution effect on labor supply as well as on saving.

Let the notation $p(x/y)$ denote the price of x in terms of y. Then

$$p(z_{t,t}/z_{t,t+1}) = p(z_{t,t}/c_{t,t})p(c_{t,t}/c_{t,t+1})p(c_{t,t+1}/z_{t,t+1})$$

$$= \frac{c_{t,t} + w_t^*(1 - l_t)}{z_{t,t}}[1 + r_{t+1}^*]z_1(c_{t,t+1}; 1)$$

A compensated increase in w_t^* raises $p(z_{t,t}/z_{t,t+1})$,[10] reducing demand for $z_{t,t}$ and thus for $c_{t,t}$ and own time. Furthermore, it will cause any amount of $z_{t,t}$ to be produced with more market goods and less own time. The effect on l_t is unambiguously positive, as are the effects on s_t, b_{t+1}, and $c_{t,t+1}$. The net effect on $c_{t,t}$ is unclear, however, since the substitution effects in consumption and production work in opposite directions.

A compensated increase in r_{t+1}^* also raises $p(z_{t,t}/z_{t,t+1})$, but causes no substitution in the production of $z_{t,t}$. Thus both saving and labor supply increase. The effects of changes in n and θ can be determined in a similar manner.[11]

3. GOVERNMENT FISCAL POLICIES

If government imposes a tax, it must in some way dispose of the proceeds of that tax. It will be assumed throughout the paper that any revenues collected from income or inheritance taxes are redistributed in lump-sum payments to the citizenry.[12] Given this assumption, there are only four

[10] This is true under the present specification that $l = 0$ in the second period of life. If l is positive in both periods, then the effect of a change in w_t^* on $p(z_{t,t}/z_{t,t+1})$ depends upon the elasticity of substitution of the household production function, upon the stock of human capital in the first period relative to that in the second, and upon the productivity of human capital in the household sector relative to its productivity in the market sector.

Neither w^* nor r^* affects the price of after-tax bequests in terms of $z_{t,t+1}$. Hence an increase in $p(z_{t,t}/z_{t,t+1})$ implies an increase in $p[z_{t,t}/(1 - \theta)b_{t+1}]$.

[11] The sign of the substitution effect on b_{t+1} of a change in θ is unclear for reasons given in footnote 7.

[12] It has long been recognized that within a closed general equilibrium system, a change in relative prices will not ordinarily entail any aggregate income effect [see Hicks (1946, p. 64)]. Whether a tax-induced change in relative prices entails an income effect (before economic agents have modified their behavior in response to the tax rate change) depends upon how the government disposes of the resulting incremental revenues. If the proceeds from taxation, or their equivalent in public services, are disbursed in a manner independent of how they are collected, then the *individual* income effects will generally cancel out, leaving only the substitution effect. If the government uses the tax revenues to produce public services which are either more or less valuable than the lost private consumption, then a tax rate change will entail a nonzero aggregate income effect.

possible independent government policies consistent with a balanced budget:

(1) a tax on labor income redistributed to the working generation,
(2) a tax on the income from capital redistributed to the retired generation;
(3) an inheritance tax redistributed to the working generation; and
(4) a government-enforced lump-sum intergenerational transfer.

All other government policies are just combinations of these four basic ones.[13]

If the government enforces the same balanced-budget policies period after period, then when the economy converges to long-run equilibrium the following steady-state relations will hold[14]:

$$g_{t,t} = f_{t,t} + \theta b_t + \gamma w_t l_t$$

$$g_{t,t+1} = f_{t,t+1} + \tau r_{t+1} s_t$$

Here $f_{t,t}$ and $f_{t,t+1}$ denote forced intergenerational transfers and $f_{t,t+1} = -(1 + n)f_{t,t}$. Even if the economy is not on a steady-state growth path, the following relations hold at any time t:

$$g_{t,t} = f_{t,t} + \theta b_t + \gamma w_t l_t$$

$$g_{t-1,t} = f_{t-1,t} + \tau r_t s_{t-1}$$

Now suppose that in period t the government gives a lump-sum transfer payment to generation t and finances this transfer with debt which must be repaid in period $t + 1$. Let the debt and transfer be d_t per member of generation t. Suppose the government must pay the market rate of return r_{t+1}, and let the resulting interest payments be taxed at the same rate as income from physical capital. Then saving s_t is equal to the sum of d_t and accumulation of

[13] Here the intensity of policies 1–3 is measured by the level of the relevant tax rate, with a higher tax rate denoting greater intensity. Given a set of tax rates and intergenerational transfers, a unique value of government revenue from each of the three taxes is implied. For some purposes it might seem desirable to measure policies 1–3 by the revenue raised by each, but such a measure would be ambiguous. This is because a given amount of revenue from a labor income tax, for example, can in general be raised at more than one level of the labor income tax rate or cannot be raised at all. Revenue is not a single-valued function of the tax rate because an increase in the rate tends to shrink the tax base while increasing the revenue raised from a given tax base. To complicate matters further, the revenue raised by a given labor income tax rate is not independent of the tax rates on bequests and income from capital.

[14] A steady state is here defined as constancy over time of all tax rates, prices, and per capita quantities. It is assumed that a stable steady-state equilibrium exists.

physical capital s_t'. The government's budget constraint in period $t + 1$ is given by

$$\tau r_{t+1} s_t - g_{t,t+1} - (1 + r_{t+1})d_t$$
$$+ (1 + n)[\theta b_{t+1} + \gamma w_{t+1} l_{t+1} - g_{t+1,t+1}] = 0$$

or

$$[1 + r_{t+1}(1 - \tau)]d_t = \tau r_{t+1} s_t' - g_{t,t+1}$$
$$+ (1 + n)[\theta b_{t+1} + \gamma w_{t+1} l_{t+1} - g_{t+1,t+1}]$$

Here $[1 + r_{t+1}(1 - \tau)]d_t$ is the amount required to pay the principal and interest (after taxes) on the government debt. Assuming the debt is repaid by a lump-sum tax on the retired generation gives a fifth basic government fiscal policy:

(5) a debt-financed lump-sum transfer to the working generation with the debt being repaid by a lump-sum tax on that generation during its retirement years.

A debt issue repaid in any other way is just a combination of this and one of the other four basic policies. This fifth basic policy, consisting as it does of lump-sum taxes and transfers, entails no substitution effects. The debt policy does not affect the resources available to generation $t + 1$ or any future generation. And since the lump-sum tax on generation t in period $t + 1$ is equal to $- [1 + r_{t+1}(1 - \tau)]$ times the lump-sum transfer in period t, there is no effect on the lifetime resources available to generation t. Thus policy 5 will result in no change in an individual's desired levels of l_t, $c_{t,t}$, $c_{t,t+1}$, or b_{t+1}. The entire lump-sum transfer in period t will be saved in order to pay the lump-sum tax in period $t + 1$. Thus accumulation of physical capital is also unaffected by policy 5. Table 2 shows the combined income and substitution

TABLE 2

Combined Income and Substitution Effects of Government Fiscal Policies on an Individual's Desired Level of Labor Supply and Saving

Policy	Bequests positive		Bequests zero	
	l_t	s_t	l_t	s_t
1	—	—	—	—
2	—	—	—	—
3	—	—	0	0
4	0	0	—	—
5	0	0	0	0

effects of the five basic policies on the individual's desired levels of labor supply and saving, given some values of w_t and r_t. These combined effects, which can be viewed as shifts in factor supply curves, are shown both for the case in which bequests are positive and for the case in which they are zero.[15]

To say that policy 5 has no effects on consumption, labor supply, or capital formation is not to say that a debt issue has no such effects, however. The extent of any such effects is determined by the method used to service the debt. A debt issue serviced by a lump-sum tax on generation $t + 1$ is a combination of policies 4 and 5[16]; a debt issue serviced by a tax on income from capital is a combination of policies 2 and 5; and a debt issue serviced by a labor income tax is a combination of policies 1, 4, and 5. The effects of a government debt issue thus depend not only on the effects of policy 5, but also on the effects of these other policies. In particular, a debt issue serviced by taxes on bequests or on the income from capital or labor will entail distortions which can be expected to affect the capital stock in the period when the distortions occur.

The concurrent effect of a debt issue on physical capital formation depends on the nature of any resulting distortions and on when they occur. To

[15] A change in policies 1–3 is taken to be an increase in the relevant tax rate. A change in policy 4 is taken to be an increase in the size of the forced transfer from the working generation to the retired generation, and a change in policy 5 is taken to be an increase in the size of the debt issue.

[16] This combination of policies, which can be shown to have no effects on consumption, labor supply, or capital formation, is the one assumed by Barro (1974). It would be possible, of course, to refinance the debt in period $t + 1$, which would also involve a combination of policies 4 and 5. But repeated application of these policies would also be neutral as long as bequests are positive at each step along the way. This neutrality depends on the existence of bequests not just in the period of issuance of the debt, but in every period during which the debt is outstanding. A single break in the chain of bequests means that the debt will have real effects on the behavior of every generation before the break.

Feldstein (1976) points out that no debt service payments need ever be made if $n > r(1 - \tau)$. As pointed out above, however, this condition implies that bequests are zero and thus invalidates the neutrality of a combination of policies 4 and 5. If $n < r(1 - \tau)$, however, and if the public imposes some upper limit on the ratio of national debt to national income, then issuance of debt implies that debt service payments will have to be made at some time in the future, and as Barro (1976) shows, they will have to be equal in present value to the debt issue.

Possibly because of the Keynesian tradition of focusing on income or wealth effects in explaining macroeconomic phenomena, the debate over the neutrality of national debt has concentrated on the question of whether some combination of policies 4 and 5 is neutral. Unfortunately, much of the literature leaves the impression, or even explicitly states, that given the neutrality of such a combination "it follows that neither government debt nor social security affects private capital accumulation" (Feldstein, 1976, p. 331). Such logic is, of course, faulty. A government debt issue which relies on policies 1–3 to finance the debt service payments will be nonneutral since all three of these policies entail substitution effects. As Miller and Upton (1974, p. 165) point out, the "question . . . is one of distortion now versus distortion later."

see this more clearly, assume that debt cannot be serviced by lump-sum taxes but must be either refinanced or serviced by distorting taxes. If a debt issue in period t entails an increase in the capital income tax rate in period $t + 1$, this will lower the return to savers below the marginal product of capital and will thus directly impinge upon the saving decision. If a debt issue in period t entails an increase in the labor income tax rate in period $t + 1$, there might be an indirect effect on saving in period t. This is because the labor income tax can be expected to affect the employment of labor, and thus the location of the marginal product of capital schedule, in period $t + 1$.

If a debt issue in period t is refinanced in period $t + 1$ and results in distortionary taxes only in period $t + 2$, there might be an even less direct effect on saving in period t. By the same argument given above, any distortionary tax in period $t + 2$ can be expected to affect saving in period $t + 1$. But as was seen in Section 1, the saving and labor supply decisions are not independent. Thus the distortions in period $t + 2$ can be expected to affect employment of labor and hence the marginal product of capital schedule in period $t + 1$, in turn affecting saving in period t. By straightforward extension of the argument, a debt issue resulting in a distortionary tax in any future period can be expected to affect current capital formation. This effect is in no way dependent upon the existence of bequests. It might be argued that if the debt is refinanced and the distortion pushed further into the future, its effect on current capital formation is reduced. Such a result is not obvious, however, since the size of the distortion is increased the longer it is postponed, assuming $n < r(1 - \tau)$, that is, assuming the distortion will have to be encountered at all.

There is yet another indirect route by which a debt issue might affect current capital formation, namely, through the effect of future distortions on h_{t+1}^*. The argument advanced by Barro (1974) is essentially that, if bequests are taking place, a debt issue serviced by lump-sum taxes on future generations will reduce h_{t+1}^* just sufficiently to cause saving to increase by the amount of the debt issue, leaving capital formation unaffected. Government bonds thus have no net wealth effect, and do not result in a decrease in private capital formation.

If the debt is serviced by distortionary taxes on future generations, however, these taxes will entail a welfare cost or excess burden in future periods and the reduction in h_{t+1}^* will be greater than if the taxes had been lump sums. If a lump-sum tax reduces h_{t+1}^* by an amount which leaves private capital formation unaffected, a distortionary tax, by reducing h_{t+1}^* even further, will tend to increase capital formation. This is because the current generation will find it optimal to bear part of the welfare cost of taxation itself rather than shift the entire burden to future generations. The current generation will consequently increase its bequest by more than the amount of the debt issue.

A debt issue serviced by distortionary taxes on future generations will thus not only always have a substitution effect (however indirect) on current capital formation; it will also always have a net wealth effect. If bequests are zero, the wealth effect will tend to reduce private capital formation. If bequests are positive, it will tend to increase private capital formation.

4. GENERAL EQUILIBRIUM

The purpose of this analysis is to determine the general equilibrium effects of changes in γ, τ, and θ on k and l. The comparative-static analysis of Section 2 yields three simultaneous equations for l_t, s_t, and b_{t+1} in terms of w_t, r_{t+1}, γ, τ, θ, h_{t+1}^*, and the gs. Combining these with the equations for w, s, and h^* gives a simultaneous system of six first-order difference equations in the six endogenous variables l, s, b, w, r, and h and the five exogenous variables γ, τ, θ, $g_{t,t}$, and $g_{t,t+1}$. A local linear approximation of this system can be written as

$$H(F)[l_t \; s_t \; b_t \; w_t \; r_t \; h_t]' = G(F)[\gamma_t \; \tau_t \; \theta_t g_{t,t} \; g_{t,t+1}]' \qquad (9)$$

where $H(F)$ and $G(F)$ are matrices whose elements are polynomials of at most order one in the operator F, defined by $Fx_t = x_{t+1}$ for any variable x. This system can in principle be solved for the contemporaneous effect on l and s of various government policy changes. Also of interest are the effects of permanent changes in government policies on the long-run values of l and s. These effects can be determined by noting that in long-run equilibrium $x_t = x_{t+1}$ for any variable x and solving system (9) as a static system of simultaneous equations, with F replaced by unity. Solution of this problem requires that the sign of $|H(1)|$ be known. It follows from the assumption that system (9) is stable that $|H(1)| > 0$.[17]

Analytical solution of this system with no restrictions on the form of the utility and production functions would, if possible at all, be exceedingly difficult. The signs of the general equilibrium effects of various fiscal policies on l and s depend on the elasticity of substitution of the market production function $F(k, l)$, on whether $e_{sr^*}e_{lw^*} > e_{sw^*}e_{lr^*}$,[18] where e_{ij} is the compensated elasticity supply of i with respect to j, and on the magnitude of e_{sw^*}.

If it is assumed that utility and production functions are of the Cobb–Douglas form, determination of the effects of various fiscal policies on the steady-state values of l and s becomes much more straightforward. The signs

---

[17] No proof is presented here, but the outline is as follows: stability of (9) requires that the roots of $|H(F)| = 0$ be less than unity in absolute value. This latter condition turns out to be equivalent to $|H(1)| > 0$ (see Samuelson, 1941).

[18] This condition can be shown to hold, given the present specification of the consumer's maximization problem.

TABLE 3

Steady-State Effects of Government Fiscal Policies in a Cobb–Douglas World[a]

Policy	Bequests positive		Bequests zero	
	l_t	s_t	l_t	s_t
1	−	−	−	−
2	−	−	−	−
3	?	−	0	0
4	0	0	+	−
5	0	0	0	0

[a] Appendix C contains derivations of these effects.

of these effects are shown in Table 3 for the case in which bequests take place and also for the case in which bequests are zero.

As can be seen from Table 3, an increase in the rate of taxation of income from either labor or capital will reduce the steady-state quantities of both labor and capital employed in the market sector. This applies regardless of whether bequests are positive or zero. An increase in the rate of taxation of bequests in a steady state in which bequests are positive also reduces the steady-state market employment of capital, but has an ambiguous effect on the employment of labor. A change in the rate of taxation of bequests has no effect on a steady state in which bequests are zero, however.[19] An increase in the forced lump-sum transfer from workers to retirees will increase the employment of labor and reduce the capital stock per head in a steady state in which bequests are zero, but will have no effect if bequests are positive. A change in policy 5 will have no effect on the employment of capital or labor regardless of whether bequests are zero or positive.[20]

5. SUMMARY

This chapter deals with the output and employment effects of taxation of factor income. In its emphasis on aggregate levels of employment, it differs from earlier papers which have used models somewhat similar to the one presented here to examine the incidence of income taxes and their effects on the economy's capital-labor ratio. It is seen that within the context of a model which makes reasonable assumptions about the utility-maximizing behavior

[19] Appendix C contains derivations of the signs of these effects.
[20] The question arises as to what government debt policies are consistent with a steady state in which bequests are zero. See Appendix B for a discussion of this issue.

of market participants and about the economy's production opportunities, taxation of market activity leads to a shift away from such activity in favor of nonmarket activity. An increase in the rate of the income from either labor or capital will in general reduce both capital formation and the employment of labor, while taxation of bequests will reduce capital formation.

By admitting government debt and a bequest motive into the model, this chapter also manages a synthesis of two heretofore separate strands of economic literature, one dealing with the effects of a capital income tax and the other dealing with the effects of national debt on capital formation. It is argued that the effects of these two policies are interrelated. A government debt issue is found to influence capital formation through both substitution and wealth effects, with the exact effect depending upon the nature of the taxes imposed to service the debt. In addition, an inheritance tax, by discouraging bequests, increases the likelihood that the wealth effect of a debt issue will be such as to reduce rather than to increase capital formation.

APPENDIX A. EVALUATION OF CHANGES IN h_{t+1}^*

A change in h_{t+1}^* is brought about by change in some future value of w, r, g, γ, τ, or θ. It is not affected by a change in any of the discount factors, denoted v. The reasoning behind this statement is as follows: h_{t+1}^* is a weighted sum of future values of incomes, where the weights are products of marginal utilities. The vs enter into h_{t+1}^* only because, around any sequence of equilibrium values of the control variables l, c_1, c_2, s, and b, the vs bear well-defined relations to expressions involving marginal utilities [see Eqs. (6)–(8)]. These marginal utilities are not affected by changes in θ, τ, and the r_{t+j}, which define the vs, but are affected only by changes in the future values of the control variables and thus of ultimate consumption of the household commodity denoted by z.

Taking the vs as constants, a change in h_{t+1}^* for an individual can result from either of two general causes: (1) a change in real lifetime resources of one of his heirs brought about by a change in some future value of w or r or (2) a change in the welfare costs of taxation brought about by a change in some future value of γ, τ, or θ. Bearing this in mind, one can evaluate a change in h_{t+1}^* as

$$
\begin{aligned}
dh_{t+1}^* &= \frac{\partial g_{t+1,t+1}}{\partial w_{t+1}} dw_{t+1} + \frac{\partial g_{t+1,t+1}}{\partial l_{t+1}} \frac{\partial l_{t+1}}{\partial \gamma} d\gamma + l_{t+1}(1-\gamma)\, dw_{t+1} \\
&\quad + \sum_{i=2}^{\infty} v_{1,i}\, dQ_{1,i} + \sum_{i=1}^{\infty} v_{2,i}\, dQ_{2,i} \\
&= l_{t+1}\, dw_{t+1} + \gamma w_{t+1} \frac{\partial l_{t+1}}{\partial \gamma}\, d\gamma + \sum_{i=2}^{\infty} v_{1,i}\, dQ_{1,i} + \sum_{i=1}^{\infty} v_{2,i}\, dQ_{2,i}
\end{aligned}
$$

where

$$dQ_{1,i} = \frac{\partial g_{t+i,t+i}}{\partial w_{t+i}} dw_{t+i} + \frac{\partial g_{t+i,t+i}}{\partial l_{t+i}} \frac{\partial l_{t+i}}{\partial \gamma} d\gamma + \frac{\partial g_{t+i,t+i}}{\partial b_{t+i}} \frac{\partial b_{t+i}}{\partial \theta} d\theta$$

$$+ l_{t+i}(1 - \gamma) dw_{t+i}$$

$$= l_{t+i} dw_{t+i} + \gamma w_{t+i} \frac{\partial l_{t+i}}{\partial \gamma} d\gamma + \theta \frac{\partial b_{t+i}}{\partial \theta} d\theta$$

and

$$dQ_{2,i} = \frac{\partial g_{t+i,t+i+1}}{\partial r_{t+i+1}} dr_{t+i+1} + \frac{\partial g_{t+i,t+i+1}}{\partial s_t} \frac{\partial s_t}{\partial \tau} d\tau + s_t(1 - \tau) dr_{t+i+1}$$

$$= s_t dr_{t+i+1} + \tau r_{t+i+1} \frac{\partial s_t}{\partial \tau} d\tau$$

Remembering that h_{t+1}^* is a proxy for the utility of future generations, dh_{t+1}^* can be interpreted as the sum of the changes in welfare induced by future changes in variables which are market or government policy parameters to the individual. The terms involving dw and dr are welfare gains from expansion of lifetime resources associated with increases in w and r. The terms involving $d\gamma$, $d\tau$, and $d\theta$ are welfare losses from the distortions associated with increases in tax rates. Notice that terms involving expressions such as

$$\frac{\partial l}{\partial w} dw \quad \text{and} \quad \frac{\partial s}{\partial r} dr$$

do not appear in dh_{t+1}^*. This is because such terms do not correspond to any welfare gains or losses as long as the changes in w and r are infinitesimal. Terms involving

$$w(1 - \gamma) \frac{\partial l}{\partial \gamma} d\gamma \quad \text{and} \quad r(1 - \tau) \frac{\partial s}{\partial \tau} d\tau$$

are excluded for similar reasons.

APPENDIX B. FURTHER ASSUMPTIONS BEHIND THE THEORETICAL MODEL AND RESULTING IMPLICATIONS CONCERNING THE EXISTENCE OF BEQUESTS

B.1. Restrictions on the Form of the Utility Function When h_{t+1} Does Not Converge

In the theoretical model presented above, the utility function of an individual of generation t is taken to be

$$U^t = U(z_{t,t}; z_{t,t+1}; h_{t+1})$$

The third argument, h_{t+1}, is a surrogate for the well-being of future generations and has the form of a per capita wealth variable. As such, it is the discounted sum of an infinitely long income stream, where the discount factors involve the rate of return to capital, the rate of population growth, and the rates of taxation of bequests and income from capital. This infinite sum converges to a finite number only if the rate of growth of population and the tax rates on bequests and the income from capital are sufficiently small relative to the marginal product of capital.

It might thus appear necessary for U_3^t eventually to fall to zero as h_{t+1} increases in order for U^t to remain finite and for the consumer to have a meaningful maximization problem. Such a restriction on the form of the utility function is unnecessary as long as $U_3^{t+i}\lambda_{t+i+1} < \lambda_{t+i}$ when $b_{t+i+1} = 0$, that is, as long as the utility of a member of generation $t + i$ is increased more if he receives an additional unit of the market good in the second period of life than if his heirs each receive an additional unit of that good in the second period of life. Whether $U_t^{t+i}\lambda_{t+i+1} < \lambda_{t+i}$ when bequests are zero depends not only upon the form of the utility function (assumed the same for generations $t + i$ and $t + i + 1$) but also upon the lifetime resource endowment of generation $t + i$ relative to that of generation $t + i + 1$. If the latter were sufficiently lower than the former, then one could reasonably assume $U_3^{t+i}\lambda_{t+i+1} > \lambda_{t+i}$ when $b_{t+i+1} = 0$. This reasoning will not yield a situation in which $U_3^{t+i}\lambda_{t+i+1} > \lambda_{t+i}$ indefinitely far into the future, however, unless one assumes a sufficiently large secular downtrend in per capita income extending indefinitely far into the future. And the assumption that $U_3^{t+1}\lambda_{t+i+1} > \lambda_{t+i}$ indefinitely in the absence of such a secular decline in income is even less plausible.

To see this, assume that the inheritance tax rate, the capital income tax rate, and the population growth rate are all zero and that $U_3^{t+j}\lambda_{t+j+1} > \lambda_{t+j}$ for all $j \geq i$. In this case a member of generation $t + i$ could give up one unit of the market good in the second period of life and increase the consumption of market goods by his heir in the second period of the heir's life by $1 + r_{t+i+2}$ units. The utility of the member of generation $t + i$ would be increased by this shift in resources, as would that of his heir in generation $t + i + 1$. But the utility of the person in generation $t + i + 1$ would be increased even further if he did not consume these $1 + r_{t+i+2}$ units, but instead passed them along to *his* heir in generation $t + i + 2$. This further increase in U^{t+i+1} would in turn increase U^{t+i}. In fact, U^{t+i} could be increased by any arbitrary amount simply by passing the bequest sufficiently far into the future, with the size of the bequest continually growing at the rate of interest. If the bequest were passed on forever and were never consumed, U^{t+i} would increase without bound. Thus a one-unit reduction in consumption of the market good by a member of generation $t + i$, with no change in the consumption of any of his heirs infinitely far into the future, would cause U^{t+i} to increase without bound.

The absurdity of such a result is compounded by noting that a member of generation $t + i + 1$ could increase his utility still further not merely by passing along the bequest from generation $t + i$, but by reducing his own period 2 consumption of the market good by one unit and adding this to his bequest to generation $t + i + 2$. The same situation applies to all future generations. Thus a permanent one-unit reduction in *every* generation's consumption of the market good from period $t + i$ to infinity results in an increase in the utility of every generation. Such an extreme degree of altruism (or puritanism) is ruled out by assumption, as is a persistent secular downward trend in per capita income.

It should be remembered that h_{t+1} is not truly an argument in the utility function, but is rather a proxy for U^{t+1}. If the behavior described in the two preceding paragraphs is ruled out by assumption, then U^{t+i} cannot be increased without bound by transferring resources to future generations. Thus even if $U_3^{t+i-1} > 0$ always, there is no need to worry about U^{t+i-1} becoming infinite. This argument can be extended backward to U^t.

Presumably the ratio $U_3^{t+1} \lambda_{t+i+1}/\lambda_{t+i}$ is smaller at $b_{t+i+1} > 0$ than at $b_{t+i+1} = 0$, so that if the ratio is less than unity at $b_{t+i+1} = 0$, then it is less than unity for $b_{t+i+1} > 0$. But $b_{t+i+1} > 0$ implies that

$$\frac{U_3^{t+1} \lambda_{t+i+1}}{\lambda_{t+i}} = \frac{(1 + n)/(1 - \theta)}{1 + r_{t+i+2}(1 - \tau)}$$

Thus, even though h_{t+1} is not really an argument in the utility function, the assumptions that $b_{t+i+1} > 0$ and $U_3^{t+i}\lambda_{t+i+1} < \lambda_{t+i}$ are sufficient to ensure that h_{t+1} is finite. Although h_{t+1} can always be mechanically computed according to (8), it will not be a proxy for U^{t+1} unless $b_{t+i+1} > 0$ for $i = 1, 2, 3, \ldots$. This is because derivation of h_{t+1} made use of the first-order condition corresponding to b_{t+i+1}, which will not in general hold if $b_{t+i+1} = 0$.

B.2. Barro, Feldstein, and Government Bonds as Net Wealth

Suppose, however, that bequests are always positive and that r is constant over time. This implies that $n + \theta < r(1 - \tau)(1 - \theta)$, which in turn implies that $n < r(1 - \tau)$. The condition that $n < r(1 - \tau)$ is central to the exchange between Feldstein (1976) and Barro (1974, 1976) concerning government bonds as net wealth. Barro's result that government debt does not affect private saving holds only if positive voluntary intergenerational income transfers occur in the absence of the debt. Barro argues that since a debt issue implies future tax liabilities, it constitutes a net transfer of resources from future generations to the current one unless it is offset by a voluntary transfer in the opposite direction. Barro (1974, p. 1103) states that

> if, prior to the government bond issue, a member of the old generation had already selected a positive bequest, it is clear that this individual already had the option of shifting resources from his descendant to himself, but he had determined that such shifting, at the margin, was nonoptimal. Since the change in [government debt] does not alter the relevant opportunity set in this sense, it follows that—through the appropriate adjustment of the bequest—the values of current and future consumption and attained utility will be unaffected.

Feldstein argues that if the growth rate of national income (here equal to n since the rate of technological change is assumed to be zero) is greater than the after-tax interest rate, a government debt issue implies no future tax liabilities. He writes (1976, pp. 332–33):

> In this circumstance, the government can create debt and yet never have to levy a future tax to repay the debt or to pay interest on the debt. Instead, the government merely issues new debt with which to pay the interest. The debt therefore grows at the rate of interest.... Since [the rate of interest is less than or equal to the growth rate of national income], the ratio of debt to national income will not increase. The first generation—that is, the generation that receives the debt as a transfer from the government—knows that no future generation will be called upon to pay the debt. There is no need, therefore, to increase the previously planned bequests. The first generation will therefore increase its own consumption and thus reduce capital accumulation.

The case where the after-tax rate of interest is less than the growth rate of national income corresponds to the case in which bequests do not take place, a point recognized by Barro (1976, p. 345, n. 6). [However, $n < r(1 - \tau)$ does not imply that bequests do take place.] His reply to Feldstein is based on an appeal to the implausibility of $n > r(1 - \tau)$ and on the possibility of "reverse bequests" from the younger generation to the older one. His conclusion that government debt does not affect private saving depends upon the existence, prior to the debt issue, of voluntary intergenerational transfers in *either* direction. He states (1976, p. 345) that

> when [the interest rate is less than or equal to the growth rate of national income] in a steady state, transfer payments from young to old ... that grow at a rate at least equal to [the interest rate] but not higher than [the growth rate of national income] would be feasible—in the sense that the ratio of transfers to income would not grow over time—and

would raise at least the present consumption level without reducing any future levels of consumption. . . . My main hesitancy about this conclusion is that I have been unable to demonstrate that the transfer scheme . . . would be consistent with utility maximization as viewed by each family member separately.

If such an inconsistency were to prevent private transfers from young to old, then it is conceivable that the old generation might collectively try to bring about such a transfer either by debt-financed government expenditures or by an unfunded social security system. The feasibility of such a policy would depend upon the willingness of the younger generation eventually to purchase and hold the government securities issued to the older generation, to pay off those securities with taxes, or to pay the social security benefits of the older generation, or upon the ability of the older generation to force them to do so. Such considerations are beyond the scope of this paper, however.

B.3. The Effect of Endogenous Population Growth

In this context, it is worth examining the sensitivity of the above results to the assumed exogeneity of the population growth rate. Suppose that people derive utility from their children and can control the number of children they have. There will then be an additional first-order condition corresponding to n_{t+1}. Suppose also that the only cost associated with having children is the bequest which will be made to them. If bequests are zero and the marginal utility of children is positive, then n_{t+1} will increase. This increase in n_{t+1} would at first glance appear to reduce even further the quantity $r_{t+1}(1 - \tau) - n_{t+1}$ and make it even less likely that bequests would take place. This, however, is not the case. As n_{t+1} increases, so does the labor–capital ratio which will prevail in the next period, given any current level of saving. This implies that r_{t+1} will increase and thus the quantity $r_{t+1}(1 - \tau) - n_{t+1}$ may become sufficiently positive for bequests to take place. The increase in r_{t+1} is accompanied by a fall in w_{t+1}, and thus in the standard of living of each member of the next generation. A sufficiently large decrease in w_{t+1} will bring forth positive bequests. In fact, it can be shown using a model similar to that in Appendix C, modified only to include n_{t+1} as an argument in the current generation's utility function, that bequests will always be positive in the steady state. This conclusion does not necessarily hold if there are costs of having children other than the bequests which will be made to them.

B.4. Government Debt Policies Consistent with Zero Bequests

It has been seen that an increment to the outstanding stock of government debt is not viewed as net wealth by the private sector if bequests take place in the absence of the incremental debt issue. In this regard, the question arises as to what government debt policies are consistent with a steady state in which bequests are zero. If bequests are zero, the rate of population growth may be either greater or less than the after-tax rate of return on capital, a distinction which is of some importance in answering this question. Assume an economy which is initially on a steady-state growth path with no outstanding government debt. For simplicity, also assume that debt is never serviced by distortionary taxes. It can be seen from Table 2 that a debt issue serviced by lump-sum taxes on future generations will, if bequests are zero, lower s, which will in turn raise r as long as l does not decrease by a larger percentage than s. This policy will also reduce h^*, making it more likely that bequests will occur.

Consider first a one-shot debt issue of d, with the principal being refinanced by another debt issue each period and the interest payment being financed by a lump-sum tax. For any positive rate of population growth, it is obvious that the ratio of outstanding debt to population approaches zero over time and that this policy has no long-run effect on the steady-state growth path, although, if the initial debt issue is sufficiently large, it may temporarily induce positive bequests. If interest payments are also financed by issuing additional debt and $n < r(1 - \tau)$, then the ratio of debt to population will grow over time, and will eventually lower h^* to the point where bequests become positive. If interest payments are financed by additional debt and initially $n > r(1 - \tau)$, however, the ratio of debt to population will approach zero unless the initial debt issue raises r to the point where $n < r (1 - \tau)$.

Now consider a policy under which government not only rolls over the maturing debt but also issues new debt equal to d per period. Interest payments are assumed to be financed by lump-sum taxes. In this case the ratio of outstanding debt to population converges to d/n (d itself being a per capita quantity). This policy will result in a new steady state with a lower per capita capital stock and a lower value of h^*. The reduction in h^* may or may not be sufficient to induce positive bequests in the new steady state. The larger d, the more likely it is that bequests will be positive in the new steady state. There is some value of d which will just cause bequests to become positive in the new steady state, and any increases in the size of the debt issue above this amount will exert no further depressing effect on the new steady-state capital stock.

Finally, consider a policy identical to the above but with interest payments also financed by additional debt rather than by lump-sum taxes. If $n < r(1 - \tau)$, then the ratio of outstanding debt to population will grow over time, lowering the steady-state capital stock and eventually inducing positive bequests. If $n > r(1 - \tau)$ initially, then the ratio of debt to population will, unless the initial debt issue raises r to the point where $n < r(1 - \tau)$, converge to $d[1 + r(1 - \tau)]/[n - r(1 - \tau)] > d/n$. This policy will result in lower steady-state values of s and h^*, and the reduction in h^* may or may not be sufficient to induce positive bequests in the new steady state.

It is thus seen that certain government debt policies are inconsistent with a steady state in which bequests are zero. Pursuit of such policies will eventually induce positive bequests, and beyond this point the policies will cease to depress capital formation via a wealth effect. Furthermore, it is possible that the public imposes an upper bound on the ratio of outstanding government debt to population and refuses to hold additional government bonds issued in excess of this limit. Certain government debt policies are seen to be inconsistent with a steady state in which such a limit on the ratio of debt to population is satisfied.

APPENDIX C. STEADY-STATE EFFECTS OF TAXATION ON FACTOR EMPLOYMENT IN A COBB–DOUGLAS WORLD

Specialize the model in the text by assuming that utility and production functions are of the Cobb–Douglas form:

$$U_t = z_{t,t}^\alpha z_{t,t+1}^\beta U_{t+1}^{1-\alpha-\beta}$$
$$z_{t,t} = c_{t,t}^\phi (1 - l_t)^{1-\phi}$$
$$z_{t,t+1} = c_{t,t+1}^\phi$$
$$y_t = k_t^\pi l_t^{1-\pi}$$

where $0 < \alpha,\ \beta,\ \phi,\ \pi < 1$. The production function is now defined according to definition 3 in footnote 4. This change in definition merely has the effect of simplifying the form of the budget constraint while changing none of the results. The consumer's period 2 budget constraint becomes

$$c_{t,t+1} = g_{t,t+1} + r_{t+1}(1 - \tau)s_t - (1 + n)b_{t+1}$$

where

$$g_{t,t+1} = \tau r_{t+1} s_t$$

The following conditions are necessary for utility maximization:

$$\alpha(1 - \phi)U_t - \lambda r_{t+1}w_t(1 - \gamma)(1 - \tau)(1 - l_t) = 0$$
$$\alpha\phi U_t - \lambda r_{t+1}(1 - \tau)c_{t,t} = 0$$
$$\beta\phi U_t - \lambda c_{t,t+1} = 0$$
$$\alpha\phi(1 - \theta)(1 - \alpha - \beta)\,U_t - \lambda(1 + n)c_{t+1,t+1} = 0$$

The last of these conditions holds if bequests are positive. Use will also be made of the following relations:

$$k_t = s_{t-1}/(1 + n)$$
$$c_{t,t} = b_t + w_t l_t - s_t$$
$$c_{t,t+1} = r_{t+1}s_t - b_{t+1}(1 + n)$$

Initially assume that bequests are positive and note that in a steady state $c_{t,t} = c_{t+1,t+1}$. Using the first-order conditions corresponding to these variables allows one to solve for r:

$$r(1 - \tau) = \frac{1 + n}{(1 - \theta)(1 - \alpha - \beta)} \equiv B$$

$$r = \frac{B}{1 - \tau}$$

Note that this last condition corresponds to a dynamically efficient growth path. Bequests would be zero along an inefficient steady-state growth path.

It can be seen that an increase in the capital income tax rate or in the rate of taxation of bequests increases r and lowers the capital–labor ratio, while a change in the labor income tax rate has no effect on r or on the capital–labor ratio

Using the first-order conditions for utility maximization, one can see that in a steady state

$$c_{t,t+1} = (\beta/\alpha)Bc_{t,t} \qquad \text{and} \qquad c_{t,t} = \frac{\phi}{1 - \phi}w_t(1 - \gamma)(1 - l_t)$$

Using the relations between r and the capital–labor ratio gives the steady-state relations

$$s_t = \left[\frac{B}{\pi(1 - \tau)}\right]^{1/(\pi - 1)}(1 + n)l_t$$

Solving for l gives

$$l = \frac{P(1 - \gamma)}{P(1 - \gamma) + 1 - \pi(1 + n)(1 - \tau)/B}$$

where

$$P \equiv \frac{\phi}{1 - \phi} \frac{(1 - \pi)}{(1 + n)} \frac{\beta}{\alpha} B + (1 + n)$$

It can be seen that an increase in either γ or τ results in a reduction in the steady-state employment of labor. An increase in γ results in equal percentage reductions in k and l in the steady state, while an increase in τ results in a greater percentage reduction in k than in l. An increase in θ has an ambiguous effect on l but reduces k.

Now assume that bequests are zero in the steady state. In general

$$\alpha\phi(1 - \phi)(1 - \alpha - \beta)U_t - \lambda(1 + n)c_{t+1,t+1} < 0$$

and

$$r < B/(1 - \tau)$$

Thus a zero-bequest steady state may or may not be dynamically efficient. Certain other relations which hold when bequests are positive must be modified:

$$c_{t,t} = w_t l_t - s_t$$
$$c_{t,t+1} = r_{t+1} s_t$$
$$c_{t,t+1} = \frac{\beta}{\alpha} r_{t+1}(1 - \tau)c_{t,t}$$

Solution for l now yields

$$l = \frac{[\phi/(1 - \phi)](1 - \gamma)[(\beta/\alpha)(1 - \tau) + 1]}{1 + [\phi/(1 - \phi)](1 - \gamma)[(\beta/\alpha)(1 - \tau) + 1]}$$

It can be seen that an increase in either γ or τ results in a reduction in the steady-state employment of labor, while a change in θ has no effect. Noting that

$$c_{t,t+1} = \pi y_{t+1}(1 + n)$$

and

$$c_{t,t} = (1 - \pi)y_t - s_t$$

one can determine through substitution that

$$r = \frac{\pi(1 + n)}{1 - \pi}\left[1 + \frac{\alpha}{\beta}\frac{1}{(1 - \tau)}\right]$$

Thus r is unaffected by changes in γ and θ, but is increased by an increase in τ. The steady-state value of k is reduced by an increase in either γ or τ and is unaffected by a change in θ.

ACKNOWLEDGMENTS

The helpful comments of John P. Gould, Arthur B. Laffer, Merton H. Miller, and R. David Ranson are gratefully acknowledged.

REFERENCES

Bailey, M. J. (1971). *National Income and the Price Level*, 2nd ed. McGraw-Hill, New York.

Barro, R. J. (1974). "Are Government Bonds Net Wealth?" *Journal of Political Economy* **82**, 1095–1117.

Barro, R. J. (1976). "Reply to Feldstein and Buchanan," *Journal of Political Economy* **84**, 343–349.

Becker, G. S. (1965). "A Theory of the Allocation of Time," *Economic Journal* **75**, 493–517.

Becker, G. S. (1974). "A Theory of Social Interactions," *Journal of Political Economy* **82**, 1063–1093.

Diamond, P. A. (1965). "National Debt in a Neoclassical Growth Model," *American Economic Review* **55**, 1126–1150.

Diamond, P. A. (1970). "Incidence of an Interest Income Tax," *Journal of Economic Theory* **2**, 211–224.

Feldstein, M. (1974a). "Social Security, Induced Retirement, and Aggregate Capital Accumulation," *Journal of Political Economy* **82**, 905–926.

Feldstein, M. (1974b). "Incidence of a Capital Income Tax in a Growing Economy with Variable Saving Rates," *Review of Economics Studies* **41**, 505–523.

Feldstein, M. (1974c). "Tax Incidence in a Growing Economy with Variable Factor Supply," *Quarterly Journal of Economics* **88**, 551–573.

Feldstein, M. (1976). "Perceived Wealth in Bonds and Social Security: A Comment," *Journal of Political Economy* **84**, 331–336.

Fisher, I. (1930). *The Theory of Interest*. Macmillan, New York.

Hicks, J. R. (1946). *Value and Capital*, 2nd ed. Oxford Univ. Press, London and New York.

Hirshleifer, J. (1958). "On the Theory of Optimal Investment Decision," *Journal of Political Economy* **66**, 329–352.

Miller, M. H., and Upton, C. W. (1974). *Macroeconomics: A Neoclassical Introduction*. Irwin, Homewood, Illinois.

Samuelson, P. A. (1941). "Conditions That the Roots of a Polynomial Be Less Than Unity in Absolute Value," *Annals Mathematical Statistics* **21**, 360–364.

Samuelson, P. A. (1958). "An Exact Consumption-Loan Model of Interest with or without the Social Contrivance of Money," *Journal of Political Economy*, **66**, 467–482.

Samuelson, P. A. (1967). "A Turnpike Refutation of the Golden Rule in a Welfare-Maximizing Many-Year Plan," in *Essays on the Theory of Optimal Economic Growth* (K. Shell, ed.). M.I.T. Press, Cambridge, Massachusetts,

Samuelson, P. A. (1968). "The Two-Part Golden Rule Deduced as the Asymptotic Turnpike of Catenary Motions," *Western Economic Journal* **2**, 85–89.

Schenone, O. H. (1975). "A Dynamic Analysis of Taxation." *American Economic Review* **65**, 101–114.

Solow, R. (1956). "A Contribution to the Theory of Economic Growth," *Quarterly Journal of Economics* **70**, 65–94.

Chapter 4

The Revenue Effects
of the Kennedy Tax Cuts

Victor A. Canto, Douglas H. Joines,
and Robert I. Webb

The proposition that increases in tax rates discourage market-sector production and hence, beyond a certain level, may be counterproductive in raising tax revenues is an old issue in the economic literature. Its recent revival has generated considerable controversy and interest among both economists and policymakers. The resolution of this controversy depends upon identifying the empirical relation existing between changes in tax rates and changes in economic activity and hence in tax revenues. As yet, however, this relation has been subjected to little systematic empirical analysis.

Section 1 of this chapter presents a simple model of tax rates, output, and revenues. Section 2 traces some of the historical antecedents of what is now commonly known as the Laffer curve. Section 3 presents a review of the limited empirical evidence on the influence of tax rates on revenues. In Sections 4–6, we empirically examine the 1962 and 1964 federal income tax cuts in order to determine their effect on revenues and economic activity.

1. A SIMPLE MODEL

In any serious examination of the influence of taxation on economic activity, it is of paramount importance to distinguish between tax revenues and tax rates. Tax revenues may influence economic activity through an income effect, while tax rates operate through a substitution effect. For example, a change in income tax rates generates a substitution effect by altering the relative rewards to market and nonmarket activity.

It has long been recognized that within a closed general equilibrium system, a change in relative prices will not ordinarily entail any aggregate income effect [see Hicks (1946, p. 64)]. Whether a tax-induced change in relative prices entails an income effect (before economic agents have modified their behavior in response to tax rate change) depends upon how the government disposes of the resulting incremental revenues. If the proceeds from taxation, or their equivalent in public services, are disbursed in a manner independent of how they are collected, then the *individual* income effects will generally, in the absence of collection costs or distribution effects, cancel out, leaving only the substitution effect. If the government uses the tax revenues to produce public services which are either more or less valuable than the lost private consumption, then a tax rate change will entail a nonzero aggregate income effect.

These ideas may be formally illustrated through the use of a simple static model of tax rates, output, and revenues. In this model, a single good is produced in the market sector using a production process which employs only a single factor of production, say, labor.[1] Per capita output of the market good is denoted q, while l denotes the number of units per capita of labor time employed in the market sector. The production function may thus be written $q = q(l)$. The additional assumption that the marginal product of labor is positive but decreasing implies that $q'(l) > 0$ and $q''(l) < 0$.[2]

As an alternative to market-sector employment, individuals may spend time in household production, wherein their own effort is combined with the market good to produce a single household commodity. Per capita output of the household commodity is denoted c, while per capita time spent producing it is denoted h. This yields the household production function $c = c(q, h)$, which is assumed to have the property that the marginal product of each factor is positive but decreasing. In addition, an individual's utility is

---

[1] The issue of capital accumulation is not central to the presentation. For our purposes, the quantity of capital may be regarded as fixed. The issue of capital accumulation has been considered elsewhere. See Canto (1977) and Joines (1980).

[2] The residual left after paying labor its marginal product presumably accrues to capital, the stock of which is fixed. For simplicity, we assume that income from capital is taxed at the same rate as labor income.

assumed to increase monotonically with his consumption of the household commodity and to depend only on his consumption of that commodity. For simplicity of exposition, all individuals are assumed to be identical. Finally, the fixed per capita endowment of time which is usable in either household or market production is denoted t^*.

The household and market-sector production opportunities of this simple economy are represented graphically in Fig. 1. The combinations of "leisure" time h and market output q that are feasible, given the economy's resource endowment and market production technology, lie within the area bounded by the two axes and the transformation curve connecting t^* and q_{max}. The concavity of this curve results from the assumption of decreasing returns in market-sector production. Household production technology is represented by a set of isoquants, each of which illustrates the different combinations of h and q which yield a given amount of the household commodity. Diminishing marginal productivity of h and q guarantees the convexity of these isoquants unless $\partial^2 c / \partial q\, \partial h$ is very negative, which we assume not to be the case. Inspection of Fig. 1 shows that among all feasible combinations of h and q, that given by point D corresponds to the largest output of the household commodity and hence to the maximum attainable utility. Figure 1 serves to highlight the fact that there is only one market transaction within the model—the exchange of labor for market output.

In the absence of external distortions, the allocation of resources (h and l) to the production of the different commodities (c and q) is uniquely determined by technology, tastes, and resource availability. In general, the resource allocation may be influenced by government policies. Of particular

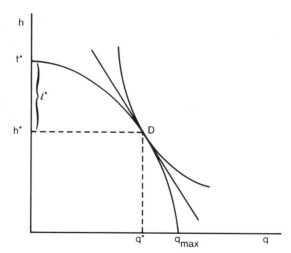

Figure 1. Undistorted equilibrium.

interest to this chapter are the effects of government taxation on the composition of employment between market and nonmarket sectors.

As with traditional economic analysis, it is assumed that only market activity and not leisure is subject to taxation.[3] If the tax is not lump sum in nature, then it distorts the work–leisure choice. If the proceeds from taxation are returned to the economy in a neutral and costless fashion, then the tax entails no income effects and only causes a movement along the production possibility frontier. The tax drives a wedge between the price of market output in terms of labor units paid by consumers (marginal rate of substitution, MRS) and the relative price faced by producers (marginal rate of transformation, MRT). This wedge can be represented graphically by the angle θ between the two rates of transformation at the new equilibrium, as shown in Fig. 2. If a tax is imposed on market-sector production, the net-of-tax relative price faced by producers decreases as compared to the undistorted situation considered earlier, while the gross-of-tax relative price faced by the consumers increases. The result is unambiguous; the equilibrium quantity of market production declines, as shown in Fig. 3. The higher the tax rate, the lower is the equilibrium level of output. The elasticity of output with respect to the tax rate is thus negative.

Examination of Fig. 3 indicates that a "corner" solution of zero output is associated with a sufficiently high tax rate.[4] As the tax rate is reduced, the

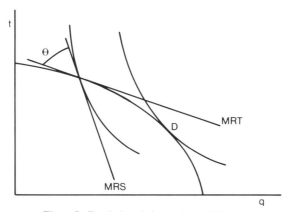

Figure 2. Tax-induced change in equilibrium.

---

[3] It should be noted that the assumption of only one variable input in the production of market goods implies that a product tax is equivalent to a factor tax. Since there is only one variable factor of production, taxation will never distort the input choice and will never push the economy inside the production possibility frontier.

[4] It is possible to have zero output associated with tax rates less than 100 percent. Similarly, it is also possible to have nonzero output associated with a tax rate in excess of 100 percent if individuals have an endowment of wealth and derive satisfaction from working.

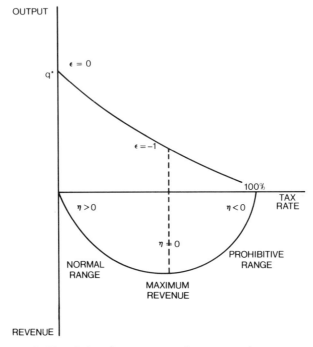

Figure 3. The relation of tax rates to market output and tax revenue.

incentive to produce market goods increases and the economy moves along the production possibility frontier away from the leisure axis. When the tax rate is zero, q^* units of output are produced. It is possible for market output to increase beyond this point if a subsidy to the production of market goods is admitted into the model. Such a subsidy could take the form of forced labor or a tax on leisure. In summary, the elasticity of market output with respect to the tax rate on such output is negative as long as the tax rate is positive, which we assume to be the case.

Tax revenues are a function of both the tax rate and the tax base. The tax base, in turn, is a function of economic activity (the production of market goods), which is itself a negative function of the tax rate.[5] For simplicity, we assume that the tax base is equal to market-sector output. If income effects

___

[5] It should be recognized that there is not necessarily a one-to-one correspondence between output and the taxable base. The reason for this is that at certain tax rates individuals may find it profitable to avoid taxation through the acquisition of expensive tax shelters. Lower marginal tax rates may discourage the acquisition of such tax shelters. Consequently, it is possible that a reduction in tax rates may lead to an increase in tax revenues even if output increases by a smaller percentage than the tax rate decreases.

cancel out across individuals, only the negative substitution effect generated by the wedge will be left.[6] Thus the impact of a change in tax rates on tax revenues depends on the empirical magnitude of the elasticity of tax revenues with respect to tax rates η. Since this elasticity is equal to one plus the elasticity of output with respect to the tax rate ε, it has an upper bound of unity and may be negative.

Tax rates, then, exert their influence on economic activity or the tax base through their effect on economic incentives. If individuals are concerned with after-tax income, then the imposition of a tax will discourage production of the taxed commodity. At some levels of tax rates, the induced decline in production may more than offset any gain in tax revenues resulting from the tax rate increases alone. Alternatively stated, the absolute value of the tax rate elasticity of output may exceed unity. Consequently, tax revenues may be lower than what would prevail at a lower tax rate. The notion that over some range higher tax rates lead to lower tax revenues is depicted by the prohibitive range of the Laffer curve. In the normal range, by contrast, tax revenues increase with tax rates, albeit at a decreasing rate. These concepts are illustrated in Fig. 3.

2. HISTORICAL ANTECEDENTS OF THE LAFFER CURVE

Although the empirical relation among tax rates, economic activity, and tax revenues is presently a matter of some controversy, the idea that excessive tax rates may be counterproductive in raising revenues was explicitly recognized in the early economic literature. For example, Adam Smith (1976, p. 414) asserted that

> High taxes, sometimes by diminishing the consumption of the taxed commodities, and sometimes by encouraging smuggling, frequently afford a smaller revenue than what might be drawn from more moderate taxes.

This view was shared by Smith's compatriot David Hume (1963, p. 332), who wrote,

> We ought, however, always to remember the maxim of Dr. Swift, that, in the arithmetic of the customs, two and two make not four, but often

---

[6] If the government were either more or less efficient in producing market goods than the private sector, then the production possibility frontier, which includes the government good, would change. This could conceivably reduce the production of private goods and leisure, thus weakening or strengthening the negative relation between the tax base and tax rate resulting from the substitution effect alone.

make only one. It can scarcely be doubted, but if the duties on wine were lowered to a third, they would yield much more to the government than at present....

Similarly, Say (1971, p. 449) stated that

Taxation, pushed to the extreme, has the lamentable effect of impoverishing the individual, without enriching the state.... Thus, the taxpayer is abridged of his enjoyments, the producer of his profits, and the public exchequer of its receipts.

Smith, Hume, and Say were thus aware of the substitution effect through which tax rate increases reduce the tax base. Furthermore, Say explicitly recognized that the elasticity of revenues with respect to tax rates, even when positive, is less than unity. He stated (p. 450) that the resultant decrease in economic activity

is the reason why a tax is not productive to the public exchequer, in proportion to its ratio; and why it has become a sort of apophthegm, that two and two do not make four in the arithmetic of finance. Excessive taxation .... extinguishes both production and consumption, and the taxpayer into the bargain.

It was apparent to Say that the full effect of taxation goes beyond the mere transfer of resources from the private sector to the public. He stated (p. 450),

A tax that robs the individual, without benefit to the exchequer, substitutes no public consumption whatever, in place of the private consumption it extinguishes.

These ideas were not universally accepted by economists of the period, however. Indeed, Ricardo (1973, pp. 155–156) openly disagreed with Say over this very point:

If a tax, however burdensome it may be, falls on revenue, and not on capital, it does not diminish demand, it only alters the nature of it. It enables government to consume as much of the produce of the land and labour of the country as was before consumed by the individuals who contribute to the tax, an evil sufficiently great without overcharging it. If my income is £1000 per annum, and I am called upon for £100 per annum for a tax, I shall only be able to demand nine-tenths of the quantity of goods which I before consumed, but I enable government to demand the other tenth.

Ricardo thus failed to recognize the negative effect of high tax rates on the tax base. He instead argued that an increase in income tax rates merely increases public consumption at the expense of private consumption, with the sum of the two remaining constant.

The purpose of the above discussion is not to provide an exhaustive survey of economic doctrine concerning the relation between tax rates and revenues, but merely to note that even early economists recognized that the relation might be a negative one if tax rates were sufficiently high.[7]

3. EXISTING EMPIRICAL EVIDENCE ON TAX RATES, ECONOMIC ACTIVITY, AND TAX REVENUES

Although the theoretical proposition that increases in tax rates above a certain level may actually reduce revenues is by now widely accepted, there is considerable disagreement over whether any real-world economies have been observed to operate in the prohibitive range of the Laffer curve. Some of the remarks cited in Section 2 indicate that at least some writers regarded prohibitive tax rates not merely as a theoretical possibility, but as an empirical reality. This might not be too surprising when one considers that governments in the eighteenth century relied much more heavily on import duties as a source of revenue than do governments today, and that the prohibitive tariff has long been regarded as something more than a theoretical curiosity. Modern governments rely for revenue primarily on broad-based taxes on economic activity, however, and the notion that such governments might be operating in the prohibitive range of the Laffer curve meets with considerable resistance.[8] The issue is essentially an empirical one, and comments of eighteenth- and nineteenth-century economists provide little systematic evidence on this point.

As was noted above, in order for a government to be in the prohibitive range of the Laffer curve, the elasticity of the tax base with respect to the tax rate must be less than -1. If one assumes for simplicity that the tax base is

[7] For such a comprehensive review, see Keleher and Orzechowski (1980).

[8] The notion that the prohibitive range might be empirically relevant has remained alive and well, however, even in our own century. See, for example, Bronfenbrenner (1942) and the references therein. Bonfenbrenner analyzes the short-run revenue effects of changes both in income tax rates and also in excise tax rates applied to specific commodities. He also notes that increased tax rates, by lowering saving and investment, may lower income enough to reduce revenue in the long run even if not in the short run.

proportional to market-sector output, the prohibitive range is the range over which $\varepsilon < -1$, where ε is the elasticity of output with respect to the tax rate τ.[9] As is shown in Fig. 3, ε is not in general a constant, but depends on τ. In general, ε takes a maximum value of zero at $\tau = 0$ and is negative for positive values of τ. For simplicity, we assume that ε decreases as τ increases for all values of τ between 0 and 1.

Let τ^* denote the tax rate which maximizes revenue. It follows that τ^* will be lower, and the prohibitive range will be encountered sooner, the more negative is the value of ε associated with any value of τ. We thus see that whether the economy is in the prohibitive range depends upon the tax rate τ and upon value of the elasticity ε associated with each value of τ.

This suggests that one can draw some inference as to whether an economy is in the prohibitive range by examining existing empirical evidence on the value of τ and on the shape of the function $\varepsilon(\tau)$. In our simple one-factor model, ε can be expressed in terms of the tax rate τ, the elasticity of labor demand with respect to the before-tax real wage rate, denoted ε^d, and the elasticity of labor supply with respect to the after-tax real wage rate, denoted ε^s.[10] It can shown that if ε^d and ε^s are constant, then $\varepsilon'(\tau) < 0$ for $0 < \tau < 1$. It is possible to have $\varepsilon'(\tau) > 0$ only if ε^d, ε^s, or both decrease sufficiently fast in absolute value as τ increases. If a real-world economy could be adequately represented by our simple one-factor model, then one could appeal to existing evidence on the value of the labor demand elasticity (or, preferably, on the form of the market-sector production function), the value of the labor supply elasticity (or the form of the utility function), and the value of τ. One could use this evidence to make inferences about the value of ε.[11]

While this approach can shed some light on the question of whether an economy is in the prohibitive range, there are sufficient difficulties with it that one would undoubtedly want additional evidence on the question. The first difficulty concerns measurement of the tax rate, of which there are many

---

[9] If increased tax rates, by encouraging the acquisition of the tax shelters and outright tax evasion, cause the tax base to fall as a percentage of output, then the prohibitive range will be encountered while $\varepsilon > -1$.

[10] The relation is

$$\varepsilon = -\left[\frac{\tau}{1-\tau}\right]\left[\frac{\varepsilon^d \varepsilon^s}{\varepsilon^d - \varepsilon^s}\right]\varepsilon_{q/l} < 0$$

where $\varepsilon_{q/l}$, the elasticity of market output with respect to labor, is assumed to be less than unity. The elasticity ε^d is determined by the shape of the transformation curve in Fig. 2, while ε^s is determined by the shape of the isoquants. Since the real wage rate is the reciprocal of the price of market output in terms of leisure (labor), we could have expressed ε in terms of aggregate demand and supply elasticities of market output.

[11] For a study conducted along these lines, see Fullerton (1980). For estimates of effective, economy-wide tax rates on income from labor and income from capital, see Joines (1981).

rather than just one. Effective tax rates vary across individuals and across types of economic activity. Some of these tax rates may be in the prohibitive range even though others are not. Another difficulty concerns measurement of the labor supply elasticity, of which there are also many. The numbers cited by Fullerton (1980) show how these estimated supply elasticities vary over different types of labor. If labor were the only productive factor, then aggregation of tax rates and supply elasticities over various types of labor probably would not cause serious problems if one were attempting to determine the revenue effects of a broad-based cut in labor income tax rates. If one found the overall labor income tax rate to be in the normal range, however, then one could not conclude that the tax rate facing *each* type of labor was in the normal range. It might still be possible to design selective tax rate cuts which would increase revenue.

A more serious difficulty with the above approach is that there are factors of production other than labor. In general, a tax on one factor will affect the employment and income of other factors and hence the revenue generated by taxing the income of such other factors.[12] For example, a reduction in the labor income tax could be expected to stimulate capital formation and would thus eventually exert an indirect effect tending to increase revenues from taxation of income from capital.[13]

One might argue that a one-factor model is adequate for analyzing the effects of a reduction in the labor income tax rate during the short run when the capital stock is fixed.[14] Even this is not true, however, since an increase

---

[12] Such indirect effects were recognized by Bronfenbrenner (1942, p. 701), who, in his discussion of excise taxes, observed that the notion of an inverse relationship between tax rates and revenues takes two forms:

> A direct form limits attention to the specific levy under consideration. As applied in direct form, the argument applied to the tax on beer states simply that an increased rate would decrease revenues from the tax on beer, and vice versa. An indirect form applies to the general . . . tax system. As applied to the beer tax, it states that even though an increased rate may increase receipts from beer, it will decrease receipts from other taxes by more than enough to offset the gross increase.

[13] See, for example, Joines (1980). Canto *et al.* (1978) analyze the relation between tax rates and revenue in a two-factor model in which the tax rates on the two factor incomes may differ. Not only does the tax rate on one factor affect the revenue generated by a given rate of taxation of the other factor, but whether one tax rate is in the prohibitive range depends on the level of the other tax rate. In general, it is possible to have combinations of tax rates in which one, both, or neither of the rates is in the prohibitive range.

[14] The short-run revenue effects are regarded as important by those who believe that tax rate deductions, even though they might lead to increased revenues in the long run, would not do so in the short run. In the absence of spending restraints more stringent than are likely to occur, the argument goes, this would result in increased deficits, money creation, and inflation during the interim.

in labor employment would in general increase the income of capital even if the capital stock were fixed. If one were careful to take account of these indirect effects and also of the effects of any reduction in capital income tax rates, an estimate of short-run revenue effects might be obtained.[15] Such an estimate would tend to overstate the short-run revenue loss, however, unless it took account of any tendency for a reduction in capital income tax rates to result in earlier realization of capital gains. Feldstein *et al.* (1978) present evidence that these effects can be significant.[16]

It thus appears that while the approach of using existing parameter estimates together with some theoretical model can provide useful insights into the likely revenue effects of broad-based income tax cuts, any readily tractable application of this approach must of necessity abstract from certain effects which many people would regard as significant. It seems that such an approach has distinct limitations in reducing the disagreement about the empirical question of how tax rate cuts would, in fact, affect revenues. This suggests that other approaches should also be employed to shed more, and perhaps different, light on this issue.

One approach which suggests itself is to examine the revenue effects of past instances of substantial changes in tax rates. The Kennedy tax cuts of 1962 and 1964 offer a natural experiment, and their revenue effects have been cited by both proponents and opponents of recently proposed broad-based tax cuts. Following the enactment of the Kennedy tax cuts, the economy experienced a greater-than-normal expansion of real economic activity. A comparison between measures of economic activity prevailing before (1961) and after (1966) the tax cuts were enacted indicates that (1) unemployment declined from 6.7 to 3.8 percent, (2) capacity utilization as measured by the Federal Reserve Board increased from 77.3 to 91.9 percent, and (3) the federal government deficit declined from \$4.3 billion to \$1.3 billion. During this period, real GNP grew at an average annual rate of 5.2%. The average annual growth rate of nominal GNP was 7.5 percent, while nominal federal government expenditures grew at a rate of 6.2 percent. Consequently, the ratio of government expenditures to GNP fell. It thus seems unlikely that

---

[15] Fullerton's general equilibrium simulation appears to take account of the indirect effect on revenue from taxation of income from capital caused by reducing the labor income tax, but not to consider the revenue effects of reducing the capital income tax rate itself.

[16] Roberts (1978) argues that even if revenues decline in the short run, the deficit need not increase if transfer payments and other government spending fall sufficiently. He also argues that saving may be stimulated sufficiently to finance any short-run deficit without increased money creation. Feldstein (1980) presents similar arguments as to why "the supply side tax-cut goal of increasing incentives without budget deficits can be achieved . . . without depending on a miraculous response of labor supply or productivity."

the increase in economic activity can be attributed entirely to the stimulus of increased government spending.

Another issue concerns whether the apparent expansion of economic activity was sufficiently large to offset the negative effect on tax revenues of the tax rate reductions themselves. Alternatively stated, the issue concerns whether the economy was in the normal or the prohibitive range of the Laffer curve. Some casual evidence on the revenue effects of the Kennedy tax cuts has appeared in the popular press, but there is considerable disagreement as to the interpretation of this evidence.

Evans's (1978) examination of revenue data for this time period indicates that federal personal income tax revenues from individuals with taxable incomes in excess of $100,000 increased from $2.3 billion in 1962 to $2.5 billion in 1963, $3.0 billion in 1964, and $3.8 billion in 1965. Total personal income tax revenues, however, declined between 1963 and 1964. Although high-income individuals would appear to have been in the prohibitive range of the Laffer curve, the evidence concerning overall personal tax revenue suggests that the weighted average of the individual personal income tax rates was in the normal range.

Representative Kemp and Senator Roth have asserted that federal tax revenues during the fiscal years 1963–1968 showed a cumulative increase of $54 billion over the 1962 level of annual receipts, whereas the Treasury Department had estimated a cumulative revenue loss of $89 billion over the same period as a result of the tax cuts.[17] Heller (1978) and others have pointed out that these two numbers are not comparable, however. The $54 billion refers to the increase in actual revenues between the earlier and later years. The $89 billion figure is the Treasury Department's estimate of the difference between actual revenues during the later period and what they would have been during the same period if the tax reduction had not occurred. That there is no necessary inconsistency between these two numbers can be seen by examining a similar set of estimates reported by Pechman (1965). Pechman forecast that actual individual income tax liability on returns filed for 1965 would be $46.4 billion, or $10.7 billion lower than his estimate of 1965 liability with no tax cut, but $1.6 billion higher than actual liability on 1962 returns. Furthermore, if the $89 billion figure cited by Kemp and Roth were adjusted to include similar Treasury estimates of the effects of the Tax Adjustment Act of 1966, the Treasury's cumulative revenue loss estimate for the Kennedy tax cuts alone would be only $83 billion.

[17] See, for example, Representative Kemp's statement in the *Congressional Record* of July 14, 1977.

It is quite possible that the Pechman and Treasury estimates overstate the size of the actual revenue loss resulting from the tax cuts of the early 1960s. These estimates are derived by comparing the revenues which would result from applying alternative tax structures to a *given* level of economic activity. Such "static" estimates thus ignore any feedback effects of tax rates on economic activity and revenues.[18] If these feedback effects are quantitatively important, then the static estimates may considerably overstate the true revenue loss.

It would be desirable to obtain an alternative set of revenue loss estimates which allow for any feedback of tax rates on economic activity. Such estimates would not be based on any prescribed level of economic activity. In the next section, we report such a set of estimates derived from time-series analysis of various revenue series.

Before reporting these estimates, it is probably worthwhile to clarify what alternative results can tell us about the empirical relevance of the prohibitive range of the Laffer curve. If our estimates show that revenues in the wake of the rate reductions were larger than they otherwise would have been, this is evidence that the prohibitive range is indeed empirically relevant. If our estimates show revenue losses comparable to the static estimates cited above, then this is evidence that any feedback effects were negligible and that the economy was operating well within the normal range. Revenue losses substantially smaller than the static estimates would provide evidence that even if the economy as a whole were in the normal range, the feedback effects were empirically important. Furthermore, such a result should not be taken as evidence that *all* tax rates were in the normal range. To increase revenues was not the primary goal of the Kennedy tax cuts, and such broad tax cuts are less likely to result in revenue increases than are selective cuts in those

---

[18] In computing a set of static revenue loss estimates based on actual income for 1964 and 1965, Okun (1968) recognized the existence of feedback effects but judged them to be unimportant in determining the size of such static estimates:

> In principle, we should calculate the dollar value of the tax cut by applying the lower rates to incomes as they would have been in the absence of the tax cut and not to incomes as they actually turned out. But this difference is minor, and there are enough big problems to justify compromises on the little ones.

This merely says that the size of the static revenue loss estimate is not greatly affected by whether the alternative tax structures are applied to actually realized income y_1 or to income as it would have been without the tax cuts, y_0. This does not mean that feedback effects are unimportant in determining the level of actual revenues, however. In the simple case where there is a single tax rate t, the two alternative static revenue loss estimates are $(\Delta t)y_1$ and $(\Delta t)y_0$. The difference between the two is $(\Delta t)(\Delta y)$, which Okun says is small. The actual revenue change, however, is $(\Delta t)y_0 + t_0(\Delta y) + (\Delta t)(\Delta y)$, and the feedback effect is $t_0(\Delta y) + (\Delta t)(\Delta y)$, which may be large even if $(\Delta t)(\Delta y)$ is not.

rates thought most likely to be in the prohibitive range. Even if total revenues did decline after the tax cuts, it might still have been possible to design selective rate reductions which would have increased revenues. The only way our estimates could provide strong evidence against such a possibility is if they reveal virtually no feedback effects, indicating that none of the rate reductions which were enacted resulted in a measurable increase in the tax base.

4. TIME-SERIES ESTIMATES

There are several ways of obtaining revenue estimates without first prescribing a level of aggregate economic activity. The desirability of these estimates rests on the belief that the true structure of the economy might be such that tax rate changes affect economic activity. An obvious way of incorporating any existing feedback effects would be to estimate a structural model which includes such effects. This model could be used to obtain forecasts of what revenues would have been in the absence of tax rate cuts, and these forecasts could in turn be compared with actual revenues. Alternatively, the model could be used to simulate the effects of various tax rate changes.

There are several difficulties with this approach, however. Aside from the sheer effort required to design and estimate a complete structural model, the resulting forecasts would be subject to certain sources of error in addition to the parameter estimation errors which affect all attempts at statistical inference. The most important of these sources is misspecification of the structural model, either through an incorrect choice of variables to be included in the model or through the imposition of incorrect identifying restrictions. In addition, Lucas (1976) points out that policy simulations based on the usual structural models (those consisting of decision rules such as consumption and investment functions) are inherently suspect because the parameters of the models are in general functions of policy variables and will change in response to shifts in those policy variables.

Zellner and Palm (1974) provide an exhaustive taxonomy of the various types of equations associated with dynamic simultaneous equation systems and discuss the uses and limitations of each. It is particular interest to note that the univariate time-series properties of the system's endogenous variables are implied by the structure of the model and the time-series properties of the exogenous variables. It is thus meaningful to fit time-series models to each of the endogenous series over periods when both the structure of the complete model and the time-series properties of the exogenous variables are stable. One of the primary uses of such a simple univariate model is in forecasting the series to which it is fit, and these models make much more modest demands in terms of data requirements and *a priori* knowledge of the system's structure than would full-blown structural estimation. Furthermore, as Nelson (1973) points out, univariate time-series models are not subject to errors in specifying the structure of the complete model and, in theory, need not yield less accurate forecasts than would structural estimation. The results reported in Nelson (1972) indicate that this conclusion holds in practice as well as in theory.

The period from 1950 to the early 1960s saw the most stable federal tax policy of any period of comparable length since the end of World War I. There were no important changes in personal or corporate income tax rates from 1951 to 1964. Compared to the fluctuations in tax rates during the Great Depression, World War II, and the Korean War, the stability during the 1950s and the early 1960s is quite striking.

In 1964, income tax rate cuts for both corporations and individuals were enacted. The corporate income tax rate was reduced to 48 from 52 percent, and personal income tax rates were reduced across the board, declining to 14 from 20 percent at the bottom and to 70 from 91 percent at the top. In addition, a minimum standard deduction of $200 plus $100 per exemption was introduced. This had the effect of removing from the tax rolls a substantial number of individuals. Thus the effective tax cut was somewhat larger than the reduction in the tax rates alone suggests. The 1964 tax cuts were phased in over two years, with about half of the reduction in tax rates taking effect in 1964. The full reduction in tax rates became effective in calendar year 1965. The corporate tax rate reductions had been preceded in 1962 by enactment of an investment tax credit and by liberalization of depreciation schedules used in computing taxable income.

Given the stability of economic policy during the 1950s and the early 1960s, it seems reasonable for our purposes to regard this period as one during which the underlying structure of the economy was fairly stable. Furthermore, the period of stability is long enough to provide a sufficient number of observations for identification and estimation of univariate time-series models. Consequently, we used this period to fit univariate models to various revenue series of interest and employed these models to forecast revenues into the mid-1960s under the assumption of no changes in tax rates or the underlying structure of the economy. The forecast errors from these models can be regarded as point estimates of the revenue changes resulting from the tax rate cuts of the early 1960s.

The two federal revenue series to which univariate models were fit are denoted FPR and FCR. They represent, respectively, quarterly federal personal income tax receipts and quarterly federal corporate income tax receipts, each deflated by the Consumer Price Index(CPI). The base period for the price deflation is the fourth quarter of 1963 (1963:4). None of these series has been seasonally adjusted.

The models which fit these two series are[19]

$$\nabla\nabla_4 \text{FPR}_t = 0.00256 + \varepsilon_t$$
$$(0.105)$$

$$\hat{\sigma}_\varepsilon = 0.602$$

$$t = 1956{:}1 - 1963{:}4$$

and

$$\nabla \text{FCR}_t = -0.317\delta_{1t} + 0.409\delta_{2t} - 0.240\delta_{3t}$$
$$(0.125) \qquad (0.119) \qquad (0.119)$$

$$+ 0.154\delta_{4t} + \frac{\varepsilon_t}{[1 + 0.199B^4]}$$
$$(0.119) \qquad\qquad (0.152)$$

$$\hat{\sigma}_\varepsilon = 0.473$$

$$\delta_{it} = \begin{cases} 1, & \text{quarter } i, \quad i = 1, \dots, 4 \\ 0, & \text{otherwise} \end{cases}$$

$$t = 1952{:}2 - 1962{:}4$$

[19] Standard errors appear in parentheses below parameter estimates. The model for FPR for the longer period 1952:2–1963:4 is slightly complicated due to an "intervention" which occurred in the first quarter of 1955. The Internal Revenue Code of 1954 moved the filing deadline for the federal personal income tax from March 15 to April 15 of each year. This change noticeably altered the seasonal pattern of personal income tax receipts, shifting revenues from the first quarter to the second quarter of each calendar year from 1955 onward. Such an intervention can be represented by the model in the differenced series

$$\nabla\nabla_4 \text{FPR}_t = \mu + [\omega_0 - \omega_1 B - \omega_2 B^2]I_t + \varepsilon_t$$

where

$$I_t = \begin{cases} 1, & t = 1955{:}1 \\ 0, & \text{otherwise.} \end{cases}$$

One would expect *a priori* to find $\omega_0, \omega_1 < 0$ and $\omega_2 > 0$. Estimation of this model yields the equation

$$\nabla\nabla_4\text{FPR}_t = -0.0489 + [-2.00 + 5.99B$$
$$(0.0910) \qquad (0.610)(0.610)$$

$$- 2.27B^2]I_t + \hat{\varepsilon}_t$$
$$(0.610)$$

$$\hat{\sigma}_\varepsilon = 0.603$$

Examination of the residuals $\hat{\varepsilon}_t$ gives no indication of model inadequacy. See Box and Tiao (1975) for a description of intervention analysis.

It was necessary to employ an additive seasonal model for FCR rather than the standard Box–Jenkins multiplicative seasonal model since seasonal differencing to induce stationarity resulted in a noninvertible model. For a discussion of this issue, see Plosser and Schwert (1977).

Examination of the residuals yields no indication of model inadequacy. The forecast errors which result from applying these models to the immediate postestimation observations may be regarded as point estimates of the revenue changes resulting from the 1962 and 1964 tax reductions. These estimates may then be compared with other published estimates of the revenue changes.

Table 1 contains our time-series estimates of the cumulative change in federal personal income tax receipts as well as several published static estimates. The Treasury estimates are for the cumulative change from the time the rate reductions became effective until the end of selected federal government fiscal years. Pechman's estimates are for the cumulative change in tax liability on returns filed for selected tax years and hence correspond more closely to calendar years than to fiscal years. The Okun and time-series estimates are available for both fiscal and calendar years.

Comparison of our time-series estimate with the various static estimates shows very little discrepancy for fiscal 1964. Furthermore, while our point estimate is similar to the various static estimates for that year, it is more than two standard errors below zero. This would seem to indicate that the initial feedback effects on the tax base were negligible.

Examination of Table 1 shows that for years after fiscal 1964, the time-series estimates show smaller revenue losses than do the static estimates, and by 1966 the difference between the time-series and Treasury estimates is considerable. It should be noted that the standard error associated with the time-series estimate for 1966 is quite large and that there consequently remains considerable uncertainty about the exact size of the true change in revenues. Nevertheless, our results, if taken at face value, indicate that there is only about a 20 percent probability that the cumulative change through 1966 was positive. They also indicate, however, that there is only about a 30 percent chance that the cumulative loss was as large as the Treasury estimated.[20]

Table 2 contains alternative estimates of the cumulative change in federal corporate income tax receipts resulting from the various corporate tax changes legislated in 1962 and 1964. Whereas the Treasury estimates show a steadily growing revenue loss between 1963 and 1966, the time-series estimates show a negligible revenue loss in 1963, followed by a steadily increasing revenue gain between 1964 and 1966. As was the case with federal personal income tax receipts, the standard error associated with the cumulative revenue change through 1966 is somewhat large. Nevertheless, our results indicate that there is only about a 20 percent chance that there was a cumulative

---

[20] These probabilities are approximately 0.21 and 0.32, respectively. Using forecasts based on the intervention model reported in footnote 19, the probability of a revenue gain increases to 0.28, while the probability of a revenue loss as large as the Treasury estimated falls to 0.25.

TABLE 1

Estimates of Cumulative Change in Federal Personal Income Tax Receipts[a,b]

Cumulative change through fiscal year	Fiscal years				Calendar years			
	Treasury[c]	Okun[d]	Time[e] series	Transfer[e] function	Pechman[f]	Okun[d]	Time[e] series	Transfer[e] function
1964	−2.4	−3.3	−2.93	−3.31	−9.8	−8.2	−7.03	−7.59
			(1.33)	(1.06)			(3.25)	(2.59)
1965	−11.0	−12.8	−9.31	−9.94	−20.3	−17.6	−13.01	−13.50
			(6.76)	(5.81)			(11.47)	(10.25)
1966	−22.8	—	−14.44	−15.17	—	—	—	—
			(18.02)	(16.72)				

[a] Billions of constant dollars.
[b] Price deflation is by the CPI with base period 1963:4.
[c] Source: Fowler (1967).
[d] Source: Okun (1968).
[e] Standard errors appear in parentheses below estimates.
[f] Cumulative change in tax liability on returns filed for relevant tax year. Source: Pechman (1965).

TABLE 2

Estimates of Cumulative Change in Federal Corporate Income Tax Receipts[a,b]

Cumulative change through fiscal year	Treasury[c]	Time[d] series	Transfer[d] function
1963	−2.4	−0.06	−0.81
		(1.06)	(1.04)
1964	−4.1	1.70	−2.45
		(4.34)	(4.16)
1965	−6.9	4.77	−2.60
		(8.47)	(7.79)
1966	−9.4	10.74	0.97
		(13.43)	(12.21)

[a] Billions of constant dollars.

[b] Base period for price deflation is 1963:4.

[c] Fowler (1967).

[d] Standard errors appear in parentheses below estimates.

revenue loss, and less than a 7 percent probability that there was a loss as great as the Treasury estimated.

Thus far, we have examined only federal government receipts from the taxes which were actually reduced in the early 1960s. If the federal personal and corporate income tax cuts did in fact expand economic activity, if the base for other taxes is positively related to economic activity, and if the rates of these other taxes remained constant, then one should observe higher-than-expected revenues from these other taxes during the years immediately following the federal income tax reductions. Furthermore, if such indirect effects do exist, they should be taken explicitly into account in estimating the revenue effects of proposed tax rate changes.

In order to determine whether any indirect revenue increases resulted from the federal income tax cuts, we fit a univariate time-series model to quarterly state and local income tax receipts deflated by the CPI, neither of which had been seasonally adjusted. The model appropriate to this variable, denoted SLR, is

$$\nabla_4 \text{SLR}_t = 0.114 + [1 + 0.249B + 0.540B^2]\varepsilon_t$$
$$\phantom{\nabla_4 \text{SLR}_t = }(0.0196) (0.109) (0.111)$$

$$\hat{\sigma}_\varepsilon = 0.0887$$

$$t = 1948:1 - 1963:4$$

TABLE 3

Time-Series Estimates of Cumulative Change in Selected Variables[a]

Cumulative change through fiscal year	State and local[b] income tax receipts (1)	GNP[b] (2)	Government[b] deficit (3)	Transfer[c] payments to persons (4)	CPI[d] (5)
1964	0.49	5.25	3.81	−0.0554	0.0005
	(0.14)	(4.81)	(3.89)	(0.0625)	(0.0101)
1965	1.48	29.05	9.67	−0.3130	0.0111
	(0.45)	(18.03)	(20.12)	(0.2664)	(0.0553)
1966	3.28	84.34	22.10	−0.5638	0.0012
	(0.87)	(33.68)	(52.48)	(0.5480)	(0.1364)

[a] Standard errors appear in parentheses below estimates.

[b] Billions of constant dollars. Price deflation is by CPI with base period 1963:4.

[c] Natural logarithm of billions of constant dollars. Price deflation is by CPI with base period 1963:4.

[d] Natural logarithm. Base period for CPI is 1963:4.

Examination of the residuals gives no indication of model inadequacy.

Column 1 of Table 3 contains estimates of the cumulative change in state and local income tax receipts for selected fiscal years. For each year the point estimate is positive and large relative to its standard error. It is possible that part of this increase could have arisen because state and local tax rates increased faster between 1964 and 1966 than they did during the period used to construct our forecasts. To check this possibility, we computed a weighted average of state personal income tax rates for years before and after the federal rate cuts.[21] This weighted average actually increased more slowly during the three years after the federal rate cuts than during the preceding three years. Our evidence thus suggests strongly that the federal tax cuts did entail the predicted indirect revenue increases.

[21] For each year, this average was computed by taking the marginal personal income tax rate in each state applicable to a return reporting taxable income equal to the U.S. median family income. The weight for each state was that state's share in total U.S. personal income. It should be noted that in 1966, New York City enacted an income tax which did bring in a substantial amount of revenue. However, this tax did not take effect until July 1, 1966, the day after our sample period ended. See the *Annual Report of the Comptroller of the City of New York for the Fiscal Year 1966–1967*. The other major local income taxes enacted during this period, notably those of Baltimore and Cleveland, took effect even later.

If the evidence of indirect revenue gains at the state and local level is to be believed, then it is quite likely that the numbers in Table 3 understate the true size of such gains. This is because they account only for increases in state and local income tax receipts and ignore any effects on indirect business tax receipts. In 1963, states and localities derived 62 percent of their revenue from indirect business taxes (largely sales and property taxes) and only 8 percent from income taxes. If the federal tax reductions stimulated income tax and indirect business tax receipts in the same proportion, this implies that the cumulative increase in total state and local revenues could have been in excess of $30 billion. It is unlikely that the actual figure was this large, however, since sales tax receipts probably have a somewhat lower income elasticity than do income tax receipts, and property taxes probably have an even lower income elasticity.

In summary, our analysis of the three types of revenues examined thus far yields a point estimate for the cumulative loss in the three types of revenues combined of $0.42 billion through 1966. Given the uncertainty attaching to this estimate, it is virtually indistinguishable from zero. Furthermore, it contrasts with the Treasury's estimate of the federal revenue loss of $32 billion. It thus seems quite likely that the static revenue estimates used by the Treasury greatly overstate the revenue effects of federal tax rate changes. In addition, it seems almost as likely that the federal tax cuts increased revenues as that they reduced them. All of these inferences are based on the assumption that state and local receipts from sources other than the income tax were unaffected by the federal rate cuts. If one imputes even a small increase in such receipts, then the point estimate of the combined federal, state, and local revenue change becomes positive, but it is still accompanied by substantial uncertainty about the exact size of the true revenue effects.

5. EFFECTS ON OTHER ECONOMIC VARIABLES

If the Kennedy tax cuts did result in revenue losses smaller than those implied by simple static calculations, this suggests that tax rate reductions may in fact be effective in stimulating economic activity. One qualification to this line of reasoning is in order, however. It was noted above that if tax shelters are expensive, a reduction in tax rates might result in an increase in tax revenues without necessarily being accompanied by an increase in economic activity. The expansion of the tax base might instead occur as people transfer economic activity from nontaxable to taxable forms. Examination of some variable such as Gross National Product (GNP) would allow a separate check on the influence of the Kennedy tax cuts on economic activity.

The following seasonal time-series model was identified and estimated for quarterly data on real GNP:

$$\nabla GNP_t = 9.358\delta_{1t} + 5.196\delta_{2t} + 0.095\delta_{3t} + 8.365\delta_{4t}$$
$$\quad (0.652) \quad\quad (0.627) \quad\quad (0.624) \quad\quad (0.626)$$
$$\quad + [1 - 0.350B^3]\varepsilon_t$$
$$\quad\quad (0.140)$$

$$\hat{\sigma}_\varepsilon = 2.150$$
$$\delta_i = \begin{cases} 1, & \text{quarter } i, \quad i = 1,\ldots,4 \\ 0, & \text{otherwise} \end{cases}$$
$$t = 1948{:}2 - 1963{:}4$$

The price index was the CPI, and the series was not seasonally adjusted. Diagnostic checks of the residuals did not indicate any significant departures from a white noise process.

This time-series model was used to develop forecasts of real output which were then compared with post sample realized values. The results are summarized in column 2 of Table 3. The point estimates reported there provide evidence that an unforecast expansion of economic activity followed the tax rate cuts, with most of the effect occurring in fiscal years 1965 and 1966. This is consistent with evidence from our analysis of tax revenues. The point estimate of the cumulative gain through 1966 is $84 billion and is about 2.5 times its standard error.

As was noted above, some of those expressing concern about recent tax cut proposals have done so because they fear that these proposals, if enacted, would result in larger government deficits and higher rates of inflation. Proponents of tax reduction counter that the deficit need not increase even if revenues fall, since the resulting increase in economic activity will lower government spending, particularly transfer payments to persons. They also argue that even if a deficit occurs, it need not be inflationary, since saving may be stimulated sufficiently to make the deficit self-financing and since the increased growth of economic activity may more than offset any increase in money growth which may occur in order to finance such a deficit.[22] In order to examine the empirical relevance of these arguments, we fit univariate time-series models to the combined real federal, state, and local government deficit, denoted DEF, to the natural logarithm of real transfer payments to persons, denoted LNTRP, and to the natural logarithm of the CPI, denoted LNCPI.[23]

[22] See the references in footnote 16.

[23] Deflation of transfer payments and the deficit was by the CPI, with base period 1963:4. The logarithmic transformation was necessary to render the transfer payments variable stationary. Since the base period for the CPI is 1963:4, the estimates in column 5 of Table 3 can be interpreted as cumulative percentage changes in the price level.

The models for these variables are, respectively,[24]

$$\nabla \nabla_4 \text{DEF}_t = [1 - 0.356B + 0.332B^2][1 - 0.211B^4]\varepsilon_t$$
$$\quad\quad (0.140) \quad (0.141) \quad\quad\quad (0.151)$$

$$\hat{\sigma}_\varepsilon = 2.021$$

$$t = 1952:2 - 1963:4$$

$$\nabla \text{LNTRP}_t = 0.08142\delta_{1t} + 0.00035\delta_{2t} - 0.02301\delta_{3t}$$
$$\quad\quad (0.00842) \quad\quad (0.00806) \quad\quad (0.00806)$$
$$\quad\quad + 0.02268\delta_{4t} + \varepsilon_t$$
$$\quad\quad (0.00806)$$

$$\hat{\sigma}_\varepsilon = 0.0279$$

$$\delta_{it} = \begin{cases} 1, & \text{quarter } i, \quad i = 1, \ldots, 4 \\ 0, & \text{otherwise} \end{cases}$$

$$t = 1952:2 - 1963:4$$

and

$$\nabla \text{LNCPI}_t = 0.00386 + [1 + 0.350B - 0.120B^2$$
$$\quad\quad (0.00134) \quad\quad (0.131) \quad (0.141)$$
$$\quad\quad + 0.489B^3][1 + 0.412B^4]\varepsilon_t$$
$$\quad\quad (0.126) \quad\quad\quad (0.126)$$

$$\hat{\sigma}_\varepsilon = 0.00394$$
$$t = 1951:2 - 1963:4$$

We used these models to forecast the variables in question and compared the resulting forecasts with subsequently realized values to obtain estimates of the changes brought about by the Kennedy tax cuts. The estimated cumulative changes, together with their standard errors, are shown in columns 3–5 of Table 3.

[24] Notice that the constant term has been suppressed in the equation for the deficit. If the constant is estimated, it turns out to be negative but less than half a standard error from zero. As was the case with the equation for federal personal income tax receipts, we find a negative constant term to be implausible both on economic grounds and also because it is inconsistent with the properties of the actual time series. Such a negative constant implies a secularly increasing government budget surplus. We find it difficult to believe that any real-world government would behave in such a manner. Furthermore, such a secular increase is inconsistent with the behavior of the actual series, which shows no trend. Although we differenced the raw series to induce stationarity, the observed nonstationary of the undifferenced series did not take the form of a trend. Rather, it was due primarily to seasonality and possibly also to long swings away from the mean. If a time series model is fitted to the differences of such a nontrended series, then the sign of the constant term is an artifact of the beginning and end points of the sample chosen.

The point estimates in column 4 indicate that transfer payments in the wake of the Kennedy tax cuts were probably lower than they otherwise would have been. The point estimate of the cumulative change through fiscal 1966 in the logarithm of transfer payments is about one standard error below zero.[25] The probability that the Kennedy tax cuts increased transfer payments is thus only 15 percent. In principle, it is possible that this unforeseen decline in transfer payments occurred not because of an unforeseen expansion of economic activity, but as a result of legislation tightening the criteria governing eligibility for benefits. In fact, however, it seems likely that any legislated changes worked so as to increase transfer payments (and, correspondingly, to understate the estimated decrease due to the tax cuts), since Great Society programs began to be enacted during the period covered by our forecasts. The evidence from transfer payments is thus consistent with the evidence from GNP and state and local income tax receipts. The behavior of all of these series suggests an unforeseen expansion of economic activity following the Kennedy tax cuts.

The point estimates in column 3 of Table 3 indicate that an unforeseen increase in the government deficit followed the Kennedy tax cuts. The point estimate of the cumulative increase in the deficit through fiscal 1966 is $22 billion. This figure is less than half its standard error, however, and there is a 34 percent probability that the deficit actually decreased. This weak evidence of an increase in the deficit conflicts somewhat with our earlier evidence on revenues. In order for all this evidence to be mutually consistent, revenues must actually have fallen by more than our point estimates indicate, transfer payments must have decreased by less, the deficit must have increased by less, or there must have occurred an unforeseen increase in some other component of government spending. The largest such component, purchases of goods and services, appears not to have increased at an unusually rapid rate after the Kennedy tax cuts. Point estimates derived from a univariate time-series model indicate a cumulative unforeseen increase in real government purchases of only $2.5 billion, which is small relative to its standard error.[26] Given the uncertainty surrounding our point estimates for all these variables, there is no strong evidence of inconsistency among them. The most likely scenario seems to be that the Kennedy tax cuts resulted in a significant increase in economic activity and modest reductions in revenues

[25] The point estimate of -0.5638 corresponds to a cumulative reduction in transfer payments of about $14.5 billion through fiscal 1966.

[26] This is consistent with the fact, reported above, that government spending as a fraction of GNP declined between 1961 and 1966 and with the numbers reported in Fowler (1967) which indicate that the Vietnam War did not have a substantial budgetary impact until fiscal year 1967.

and transfer payments to persons that, when combined with a small increase in government purchases of goods and services, resulted in a slight increase in the deficit. It seems unlikely, however, that the tax cuts resulted in revenue losses or deficits as large as those suggested by static estimates.

As concerns the price level, our time-series analysis is almost completely uninformative. The point estimate is that the Kennedy tax cuts resulted in an increase in the price level of about 1.2 percent spread over 10 calender quarters. The uncertainty surrounding the price level effect is so great, however, that an interval of 1.5 standard errors on either side of our point estimate encompasses the possibility that the Kennedy tax cuts increased the price level by 20 percent over this period. This could be true, however, only if the price level would have fallen by more than 20 percent during the same 10 quarters in the absence of the tax cuts. Such an event is unprecedented in recent history, and the possibility that it would have occurred if the tax cuts had not appears extremely unlikely. Our time-series model thus does virtually nothing to reduce our uncertainty about the inflationary effects of the Kennedy tax cuts.

6. TRANSFER FUNCTION ESTIMATES

In principle, it is possible to obtain more precise estimates of the changes induced by the Kennedy tax cuts by basing forecasts of the relevant variables on information in addition to that contained in the past history of the variables themselves. This can be done without resorting to structural estimation. If the structural system is stable during our estimation period, as we have assumed, then there will exist for each of the system's endogenous variables a transfer function relating the current value of that variable to its own lagged values, to current and lagged values of the system's exogenous variables, and to current and lagged error terms.[27]

We assume for purposes of estimation that the U.S. economy can be adequately represented by a simple structural system with only two exogenous variables. These two variables are two primary government policy variables—real purchases of goods and services and the growth rate of the nominal stock of high-powered money.[28] For each of the endogenous vari-

---

[27] See Zellner and Palm (1974) for a discussion of this point. See Box and Jenkins (1976) for a discussion of transfer function models.

[28] In principle, tax rates should also be regarded as exogenous variables. They were virtually constant during our estimation period, however, and therefore need not be included in the estimated equations.

TABLE 4

Transfer Function Estimates of Cumulative Change in Selected Variables

Cumulative change through fiscal year	State and local[b] income tax receipts (1)	GNP[b] (2)	Government[b] deficit (3)	Transfer[c] payments to persons (4)	CPI[d] (5)
1964	0.51	2.61	7.02	−0.1883	0.0029
	(0.14)	(4.58)	(3.57)	(0.0488)	(0.0099)
1965	1.48	14.47	26.00	−1.1194	0.0062
	(0.45)	(18.11)	(19.90)	(0.2083)	(0.0500)
1966	3.37	55.25	50.56	−2.7887	(0.0353)
	(0.87)	(35.33)	(54.77)	(0.4286)	(0.1170)

[a] Standard errors appear in parentheses below estimates.

[b] Billions of constant dollars. Price deflation is by CPI with base period 1963:4.

[c] Natural logarithm of billions of constant dollars. Price deflation is by CPI with base period 1963:4.

[d] Natural logarithm. Base period for CPI is 1963:4.

ables in Tables 1–3, we estimated a transfer function using these two policy variables as inputs.[29] We then used these equations to obtain forecasts of each endogenous variable, conditional on actual realized values of the input variables, for the same periods covered by our univariate forecasts. We took the difference between our transfer function forecast of each endogenous variable and its subsequently realized value as a point estimate of the change brought about by the Kennedy tax cuts, after controlling for changes in the government's other monetary and fiscal policy tools.[30]

The transfer function estimates of cumulative changes in real federal personal income tax receipts are shown in Table 1. Those for federal corporate income tax receipts are shown in Table 2, and those for other variables are shown in Table 4. Comparison of these estimates with our previous estimates reveals several interesting results. The first is that the gain in precision from using transfer functions as opposed to univariate models is minor for most of the variables under consideration. The second is that the point estimates of cumulative changes in federal personal income tax receipts and state and

[29] The specific transfer function models are reported in the Appendix.

[30] This procedure is valid only if the behavior of these other monetary and fiscal policy variables during the post estimation period was sufficiently similar to their behavior during the estimation period so as not in itself to have caused any shift in the structural model. Shifts caused by changes in the tax rates, however, do not invalidate our procedure.

local income tax receipts obtained from transfer function forecasts are very similar to those obtained from univariate time-series forecasts. For federal corporate income tax receipts, however, the point estimate of the cumulative revenue gain through fiscal 1966 obtained from the transfer function analysis is only about one-tenth the size of that obtained from univariate time-series analysis. The sum of the point estimates for these three types of revenues now shows a cumulative loss through fiscal 1966 of almost $10 billion, compared with the figure of less than $0.5 billion yielded by the univariate analysis. This figure includes no estimate of the change in state and local indirect business tax receipts, however. If the tax cuts did stimulate economic activity and hence such indirect business tax receipts, then the loss of combined federal, state, and local revenues is likely to have been less than $10 billion, and total revenues might even have increased.

The transfer function analysis does provide evidence that tax cuts stimulated economic activity. In addition to the evidence from state and local income tax receipts, the figures in column 4 of Table 4 indicate that a substantial and statistically significant reduction in transfer payments to persons occurred following the tax cuts. This evidence is much stronger than was the analogous evidence obtained from the univariate analysis. The evidence on GNP, however, is somewhat weaker than that obtained from univariate analysis. Nevertheless, the point estimate is that the cumulative change in GNP through fiscal 1966 was $55 billion. This figure is more than 1.5 times its standard error, and corresponds to a probability of only 6 percent that the tax cuts actually reduced GNP.

The transfer function estimate of the cumulative increase in the government deficit through fiscal 1966 is more than twice as large as the analogous estimate obtained from univariate analysis, but is still somewhat smaller than its standard error. This larger estimate of the increase in the deficit is consistent with larger estimate of the combined revenue loss and the smaller estimated increase in GNP obtained from the transfer function analysis as compared with the univariate analysis. Like the univariate analysis, the transfer function analysis is almost completely uninformative with regard to the price level effects of the tax cuts.

7. CONCLUSIONS

The proposition that increases in tax rates beyond a certain level may reduce market-sector output and hence tax revenues is an empirical issue. Data on tax revenues, real output, and other variables before and after the Kennedy tax cuts of 1962 and 1964 were examined in order to ascertain whether this proposition has empirical support. The most consistent evidence running through our analysis is that an unforeseen expansion of economic activity occurred after these tax cuts were enacted. This evidence comes directly from an examination of GNP and indirectly from an examination of state and local income tax receipts and transfer payments to persons.

Our evidence on revenues is much less conclusive. The point estimate of the combined revenue loss through fiscal 1966 from the three taxes we examined was about zero in the case of our univariate analysis and about $10 billion in the case of transfer function analysis. These estimates are considerably smaller than the published static revenue loss estimates (such as the Treasury estimate of $32 billion). Furthermore, neither of these estimates accounts for the possibly substantial increase in state and local indirect business and other tax receipts which would have resulted from the expansion of economic activity. Assuming a unit elasticity of such revenues with respect to GNP and using our point estimates of the change in GNP yields a point estimate of $4–6 billion for this gain. The combined point estimates for all taxes thus show a cumulative revenue gain of between $4 billion and $6 billion according to the univariate analysis and a cumulative revenue loss of between $4 billion and $6 billion according to the transfer function analysis. Given the uncertainty attaching to these numbers, they are virtually indistinguishable from zero. Our best evidence thus seems to indicate that it is almost as likely that the Kennedy tax cuts increased government revenues as that they reduced them. This conclusion must be tempered somewhat, however, by our evidence, albeit fairly weak, that the government deficit increased following the tax cuts. Finally, our analysis tells us virtually nothing about the behavior of the price level following the tax cuts.

It should be emphasized that the evidence we have presented concerns a specific historical episode. Even if we could determine with complete certainty the economic effects of the Kennedy tax cuts, it could not be inferred that tax cuts today, even cuts similar in form to the Kennedy cuts, would necessarily have the same effects. It is entirely possible that the economic environment, and hence the economy's structural relations (as that term is usually employed), have changed in such a way that a tax cut now would reduce revenues even if the Kennedy tax cuts increased them or that a tax cut now would increase revenues even if the Kennedy tax cuts reduced them. However, our evidence strongly suggests that the Kennedy tax cuts were followed by feedback effects which held any actual revenue losses to levels below the static estimates. This result would be inapplicable today only in the extreme case that the structure of the economy has shifted in such a way that tax cuts would have no expansionary effect on the level of economic activity or its allocation between taxable and nontaxable forms.

APPENDIX

The specific transfer function models are

$$\nabla\nabla_4 FPR_t = 0.0219 + [-2.09 + 5.41B - 2.33B^2]I_t$$
$$(0.108) \qquad (0.466)\ (0.457)\quad (0.456)$$
$$+\ [0.0346B + 0.0353B^3 - 0.0791B^6 + 0.0423B^8]MB_t$$
$$(0.0194) \qquad (0.0189) \qquad (0.0202) \qquad (0.0188)$$
$$+\ [1 + 0.450B^4]\varepsilon_t$$
$$(0.199)$$

$$\hat{\sigma}_\varepsilon = 0.0473$$

$$t = 1954{:}2{-}1963{:}4$$

$$\nabla FCR_t = -0.334\delta_{1t} + 0.431\delta_{2t} - 0.277\delta_{3t} + 0.167\delta_{4t}$$
$$(0.112) \qquad (0.111) \qquad (0.108) \qquad (0.105)$$
$$+\ [0.0277 + 0.0291B]MB_t - 0.125GP_t$$
$$(0.0210)\ \ (0.0215) \qquad\qquad (0.112)$$
$$+\ \frac{\varepsilon_t}{[1 + 0.344B^4]}$$
$$(0.173)$$

$$\hat{\sigma}_\varepsilon = 0.465$$

$$t = 1952{:}3{-}1962{:}4$$

$$\nabla_4 SLR_t = 0.113 - 0.0378GP_t + [1 + 0.304B + 0.589B^2]\varepsilon_t$$
$$(0.0197)\ (0.0125) \qquad\qquad (0.107)\quad (0.107)$$

$$\hat{\sigma}_\varepsilon = 0.0845$$

$$t = 1948{:}2{-}1963{:}4$$

$$\nabla GNP_t = -9.68\delta_{1t} + 5.40\delta_{2t} - 0.223\delta_{3t} + 8.65\delta_{4t}$$
$$(0.631) \qquad (0.602) \qquad (0.603) \qquad (0.602)$$
$$+\ 0.162MB_{t-2} - 0.737GP_{t-4} + [1 - 0.208B^3]\varepsilon_t$$
$$(0.0777) \qquad\qquad (0.388) \qquad\qquad (0.162)$$

$$\hat{\sigma}_\varepsilon = 2.05$$

$$t = 1952{:}2{-}1963{:}4$$

$$\nabla\nabla_4 DEF_t = 0.119 - 0.252MB_{t-2} + 1.34GP_t$$
$$(0.293)\ (0.0834) \qquad\qquad (0.431)$$
$$+\ [1 - 0.277B + 0.362B^2]\varepsilon_t$$
$$(0.155)\quad (0.150)$$

$$\hat{\sigma}_\varepsilon = 1.79$$

$$t = 1952{:}4{-}1963{:}4$$

$$\nabla \text{LNTRP}_t = 0.0885\delta_{1t} + 0.1804\delta_{2t} - 0.0233\delta_{3t} + 0.0251\delta_{4t}$$
$$(0.00702) \quad (0.00662) \quad (0.00679) \quad (0.00660)$$
$$+ [0.00272 - 0.00330B^2 - 0.00275B^3] \text{MB}_t$$
$$(0.000956) \, (0.000939) \quad (0.000968)$$
$$+ 0.0147\text{GP}_{t-4} + \varepsilon_t$$
$$(0.00534)$$

$$\hat{\sigma}_\varepsilon = 0.0218$$
$$t = 1953{:}2 - 1963{:}4$$

$$\nabla \text{LNCPI}_t = 0.00346 + 0.00153\text{GP}_{t-1} + [1 + 0.317B$$
$$(0.00101) \quad (0.000692) \qquad\qquad (0.151)$$
$$- 0.160B^2 + 0.328B^3] [1 + 0.289B^4]\varepsilon_t$$
$$(0.150) \qquad (0.145) \qquad\qquad (0.161)$$

$$\hat{\sigma}_\varepsilon = 0.00393$$

$$t = 1951{:}3 - 1963{:}4$$

In these equations, MB and GP denote stationary transformations of the discrete growth rate of the monetary base, expressed as an annualized percentage rate, and real federal, state and local government purchases of goods and services, respectively. In particular, the monetary growth rate has been seasonally differenced and the first differences of government purchases have been expressed as deviations from seasonal means. In addition, the terms I_t and δ_{it} are defined as

$$I_t = \begin{cases} 1, & t = 1955{:}1 \\ 0, & \text{otherwise} \end{cases}$$

and

$$\delta_{it} = \begin{cases} 1, & \text{quarter } i, \quad i = 1, \ldots 4 \\ 0, & \text{otherwise} \end{cases}$$

ACKNOWLEDGMENTS

This chapter incorporates some material presented at the annual meeting of the American Statistical Association in Washington, D.C., on August 13, 1979, under the title "Empirical Evidence on the Effects of Tax Rates on Economic Activity." We have benefitted from the comments of Paul Evans, Marc Reinganum, and the participants in the Modelling Workshop, Department of Economics, University of Southern California. We wish to thank Russell Fujii and Sin Poe Soh for computational assistance.

REFERENCES

Annual Report of the Comptroller of the City of New York for the Fiscal Year 1966–1967.

Box, G. E. P., and Jenkins, G. M. (1976). *Time Series Analysis: Forecasting and Control*, 2nd ed. Holden-Day, San Francisco.

Box, G. E. P., and Tiao, G. C. (1975). "Intervention Analysis with Applications to Economic and Environmental Problems," *Journal of the American Statistical Association* **70**, 70–79.

Bronfenbrenner, M. (1942). "Diminishing Returns in Federal Taxation?" *Journal of Political Economy* **52**, 699–717.

Canto, V. A. (1977). "Taxation, Welfare and Economic Activity," Ph.D. Dissertation, Univ. of Chicago, Chicago, Illinois.

Canto, V. A., Joines, D. H., and Laffer, A. B. (1978). "Taxation, GNP, and Potential GNP," *Proceedings of the Business and Economic Statistics Section*, American Statistical Association.

Evans, M. (1978). "Taxes, Inflation, and the Rich," *The Wall Street Journal*, August 7. Reprinted in *The Economics of the Tax Revolt* (A. B. Laffer and J. P. Seymour, eds.). Harcourt, New York, 1979.

Feldstein, M. (1980). "Tax Incentives without Deficits," *The Wall Street Journal*, July 25.

Feldstein, M., Slemrod, J., and Yitzhaki, S. (1978). "The Effects of Taxation on the Selling of Corporate Stock and the Realization of Capital Gains," NBER Working Paper No. 250.

Fowler, H. J. (1967). "Statement before the Committee on Banking and Currency," *Meetings with Department and Agency Officials: Hearings before the Committee on Banking and Currency, House of Representatives*. U.S. Government Printing Office, Washington, D.C., 1967.

Fullerton, D. (1980). "On the Possibility of an Inverse Relationship between Tax Rates and Government Revenues," NBER Working Paper No. 467.

Heller, W. (1978). "The Kemp–Roth Laffer Free Lunch," *The Wall Street Journal*, July 12. Reprinted in *The Economics of the Tax Revolt* (A. B. Laffer and J. P. Seymour, ed.). Harcourt, New York, 1979.

Hicks, J. R. (1946). *Value and Capital*, 2nd ed. Oxford Univ. Press, London and New York.

Hume, D. (1963). "Of the Balance of Trade," in *Essays Moral, Political, and Literary*. Oxford Univ. Press, London and New York.

Joines, D. H. (1980). "A Neoclassical Model of Fiscal Policy, Employment, and Capital Accumulation," Univ. of Southern California, Los Angeles, California.

Joines, D. H. (1981). "Estimates of Effective Marginal Tax Rates on Factor Incomes." *Journal of Business* **54**, 191–226.

Keleher, R. E., and Orzechowski, W. P. (1980). "Supply Side Effects of Fiscal Policy: Some Historical Perspectives." Unpublished manuscript, Federal Reserve Bank of Atlanta, Georgia.

Kemp, J. (1977). "The Roth–Kemp Tax Reduction Act of 1977 Parallels the Kennedy Tax Reductions of the Early Sixties," *Congressional Record*, July 14, H7156-58.

Lucas, R. E., Jr., (1976). "Econometric Policy Evaluation: A Critique," in *The Phillips Curve and Labor Markets* (K. Brunner and A. Meltzer, ed.). North-Holland, Publ., Amsterdam.

Nelson, C. R. (1972). "The Predictive Performance of the FRB–MIT–PENN Model of the U.S. Economy," *American Economic Review* **62**, 902–917.

Nelson, C. R. (1973). *Applied Time Series Analysis for Managerial Forecasting*. Holden Day, San Francisco, California.

Okun, A. M. (1968). "Measuring the Impact of the 1964 Tax Reduction," in *Perspectives on Economic Growth* (W. W. Heller, ed.). Random House, New York. Reprinted in *Readings in Money, National Income, and Stabilization Policy* (W. L. Smith and R. L. Teigen, ed.), 3rd ed. Irwin, Homewood, Illinois.

Pechman, J. (1965). "The Individual Income Tax Provisions of the Revenue Act of 1964," *Journal of Finance* **20**, 247–272.

Plosser, C. I., and Schwert, G. W. (1977). "Estimation of a Noninvertible Moving Average Process: The Case of Overdifferencing," *Journal of Econometrics* **6**, 199–224.

Ricardo, D. (1973). *The Principles of Political Economy*. Dutton, New York.

Roberts, P. C. (1978). "The Economic Case for Kemp–Roth," *The Wall Street Journal* August 1. Reprinted in *The Economics of the Tax Revolt* (A. B. Laffer and J. P. Seymour, ed.). Harcourt, New York.

Say, J. B. (1971). *A Treatise on Political Economy* (Transl. by C. R. Prinsep). M. Kelley, New York.

Smith, A. (1976). *An Inquiry into the Nature and Causes of the Wealth of Nations* (E. Canaan, ed.). Univ. of Chicago Press, Chicago, Illinois.

Zellner, A. and Palm, F. (1974). "Time Series Analysis and Simultaneous Equation Econometric Models," *Journal of Econometrics* **2**, 17–59.

Chapter 5

Fiscal Policy and the Labor Market

Paul Evans

1. INTRODUCTION

It has been standard practice in macroeconomics to assume that the effects of fiscal policy on aggregate demand dwarf its effects on aggregate supply. In the past few years, this assumption has come under increasing criticism. Feldstein (1974, 1976) has found that the social security system greatly reduces the supply of capital and that unemployment insurance raises the unemployment rate by a significant amount. The study of Boskin (1978) has suggested that the taxation of the income from capital substantially lowers the supply of capital. The studies in Cain and Watts (1974) have generally found that income maintenance programs have important effects on the supply of labor. If the view expressed by Klein (1978) is widespread among model builders, these supply-side effects will soon be incorporated into the large econometric models.

In this paper, we explore the general-equilibrium relation between fiscal policy and labor market activity. Our analysis takes explicit account of the ways in which the fiscal authorities dispose of their tax revenues.[1]

In Section 2, we develop a general-equilibrium model of the labor-supply decision. In this model, workers decide whether to work and, if they work, how many hours to work. We show that the fraction of potential workers who are employed and the average number of hours worked by each employed person depend on the real before-tax wage rate, the shares of each type of government spending in the national product, the marginal valuation of each type of spending, and the distribution of government benefits between workers and nonworkers.

In Section 3, we derive an aggregate demand function for private man-hours.

In Section 4, we estimate the supply and demand functions developed in Sections 2 and 3, using annual U.S. data that span the period 1931–1977. These estimated functions satisfy the theoretical restrictions derived in Sections 2 and 3.

In Section 5, we simulate the estimated model of Section 4. In most cases, increases in the shares of federal purchases, state and local purchases, and transfer payments in the net national product reduce employment and average hours of work both in the short run and in the long run. These effects are large enough to be economically important. Indeed, an increase in the share going to state and local purchases lowers total man-hours by so much in the long run that total government revenue actually falls. Our estimates therefore provide some evidence supporting the view of Laffer (1978).

In Section 6, we summarize our results.

In Section 7, we describe the data used in our empirical analysis and give their sources.

2. THE SUPPLY OF LABOR

The economy has a continuum of individuals, each of whom is indexed by a real number on the interval [0, 1]. The fraction of individuals with ns less than n^* is just n^*. Individual n has a utility function

$$U(c, h) - f(n)q$$

where c is his consumption, h is the number of hours that he works, and q is a dummy variable that equals one when h is positive and equals zero when h

---

[1] The analyses of Canto *et al.* (1978), Joines (1978), and Canto (1978) also take this into account.

is zero. The function $U(c, h)$ is increasing in c, decreasing in h, strictly concave, and twice continuously differentiable; consumption and leisure are normal goods. The function $f(n)$ is increasing and continuously differentiable with $f(0) = 0$ and $\lim_{n \to 1} f(n) = \infty$.

The government taxes wage income at the constant rate τ and spends the revenue from this tax in m different ways.[2] At the margin, the public values g_i, the expenditure per worker on the ith type of government activity, at $\gamma_i g_i$.[3] We follow Bailey (1962) in assuming that each γ_i is between zero and one even though it is conceivable that, at the margin, government spending might actually hurt the public or might be of more value to the public than their own spending. A fraction k_i of the ith type of government spending benefits only those individuals who work, while a fraction $1 - k_i$ benefits only those individuals who do not work.

Assuming that there is no property income, one can write the budget constraint of each worker as

$$c = (1 - \tau)wh + \sum_{i=1}^{m} k_i \gamma_i g_i \tag{1}$$

where w is the real before-tax wage rate. Each worker maximizes the function $U(c, h)$ subject to Eq. (1). Since no individual worker can influence $\sum k_i \gamma_i g_i$, the government's contribution to his disposable income, the necessary and sufficient conditions for a maximum of $U(c, h)$ are

$$(1 - \tau)wU_c + U_h = 0 \tag{2}$$

and Eq. (1). Total government spending per worker must equal total tax revenue per worker:

$$\sum g_i = \tau wh$$

Defining

$$\tau_i \equiv g_i/wh \tag{3}$$

we have

$$\tau = \sum \tau_i \tag{4}$$

Substituting Eqs. (3) and (4) into Eq. (1) then yields

$$c - [1 - \sum(1 - \gamma_i k_i)\tau_i]wh = 0 \tag{5}$$

---

[2] In this model, we are abstracting from all intertemporal considerations. We therefore assume that a deficit has exactly the same effect on behavior as an explicit tax on wage income.

[3] Thus, the γ_i are shadow prices.

Equations (2) and (5) imply that each worker consumes and works according to the equations

$$c = C(w; \tau_1, \ldots, \tau_m; \gamma_1 k_1, \ldots, \gamma_m k_m) \tag{6}$$

and

$$h = H(w; \tau_1, \ldots, \tau_m; \gamma_1 k_1, \ldots, \gamma_m k_m) \tag{7}$$

with

$$C_w = \frac{(1 - \tau)\mu w U_c - \mu h[U_{hh} + (1 - \tau)w U_{ch}]}{D} \tag{8}$$

$$C_{\tau_i} = \frac{-\mu w^2 U_c + (1 - \gamma_i k_i)[U_{hh} + (1 - \tau)w U_{ch}]}{D}, \qquad i = 1, \ldots, m \tag{9}$$

$$C_{\gamma_i k_i} = \frac{-\tau_i w h[U_{hh} + (1 - \tau)w U_{ch}]}{D}, \qquad i = 1, \ldots, m \tag{10}$$

$$H_w = \frac{(1 - \tau)U_c + \mu h[(1 - \tau)w U_{cc} + U_{ch}]}{D} \tag{11}$$

$$H_{\tau_i} = \frac{-w U_c - (1 - \gamma_i k_i)[(1 - \tau)w U_{cc} + U_{ch}]}{D}, \qquad i = 1, \ldots, m \tag{12}$$

$$H_{\gamma_i k_i} = \frac{\tau_i w h[(1 - \tau)w U_{cc} + U_{ch}]}{D}, \qquad i = 1, \ldots, m \tag{13}$$

where

$$\mu = 1 - \sum (1 - \gamma_i k_i)\tau_i$$

and

$$D = - U_{hh} - (1 + \mu - \tau)w U_{ch} - \mu(1 - \tau)w^2 U_{cc}$$

Since consumption and leisure are normal goods,[4] one can sign these derivatives as follows:

$$C_w > 0 \tag{14}$$

$$C_{\tau_i} < 0, \qquad i = 1, \ldots, m \tag{15}$$

$$C_{\gamma_i k_i} > 0, \qquad i = 1, \ldots, m \tag{16}$$

$$H_w \gtreqless 0 \tag{17}$$

$$H_{\tau_i} \gtreqless 0, \qquad i = 1, \ldots, m \tag{18}$$

and

$$H_{\gamma_i k_i} < 0, \qquad i = 1, \ldots, m \tag{19}$$

---

[4] Consumption is a normal good if $U_{hh} + (1 - \tau)w U_{ch} < 0$, and leisure is a normal good if $(1 - \tau)w U_{cc} + U_{ch} < 0$. These two conditions in turn imply that $D > 0$.

In general, the derivatives H_w and H_{τ_i} cannot be signed because the income and substitution effects work in opposite directions. If the substitution effect dominates, H_w is positive and H_{τ_i} is negative; and conversely. Note, however, that when $\gamma_i k_i$ is one, the income effect in Eq. (12) vanishes, so H_{τ_i} is unambiguously negative. As a general rule, the more g_i benefits the public and the larger the fraction of these benefits that accrue to workers, the more likely is H_{τ_i} to be negative.

Conditional on working, individual n maximizes his utility by consuming and working according to Eqs. (6) and (7). He attains the utility

$$V(w; \tau_1, \ldots, \tau_m; \gamma_i k_i, \ldots, \gamma_m k_m; n)$$

$$\equiv U[C(w; \tau_1, \ldots, \tau_m; \gamma_1 k_1, \ldots, \gamma_m k_m), H(w; \tau_1, \ldots, \tau_m; \gamma_1 k_1, \ldots,$$
$$\times \gamma_m k_m)] - f(n) \tag{20}$$

Conditional on not working, individual n consumes

$$\sum (1 - k_i)\gamma_i g_i = wh \sum (1 - k_i)\gamma_i \tau_i$$

attaining the utility

$$R(w; \tau_1, \ldots, \tau_m; \gamma_1, \ldots, \gamma_m; k_1, \ldots, k_m)$$

$$\equiv U[wH(w; \tau_1, \ldots, \tau_m; \gamma_1 k_1, \ldots, \gamma_m k_m) \sum (1 - k_i)\gamma_i \tau_i, 0] \tag{21}$$

Individual n chooses to work if V is greater than R, the reservation utility, and chooses not to work if V is less than R.

Now, suppose that

$$V(w^*; \tau_1, \ldots, \tau_m; \gamma_1 k_1, \ldots, \gamma_m k_m; n)$$

$$= R(w^*; \tau_1, \ldots, \tau_m; \gamma_1, \ldots, \gamma_m; k_1, \ldots, k_m) \tag{22}$$

so that individual n is indifferent between working and not working at the wage rate w^*. An increase in the wage rate makes work look more attractive because[5]

$$V_w = U_c C_w + U_h H_w = U_c[C_w - (1 - \tau)wH_w]$$

$$= \frac{U_c\{U_c \sum k_i \gamma_i \tau_i - \mu h[(1 - \tau)^2 w^2 U_{cc} + 2(1 - \tau)wU_{ch} + U_{hh}]\}}{D} > 0$$

$$\tag{23}$$

but also raises net transfers to nonworkers, thus making it more attractive not to work:

$$Rw = U_c(H + wH_w) \sum (1 - k_i)\gamma_i \tau_i$$

$$= \frac{U_c[(1 - \tau)wU_c - hU_{hh}] \sum (1 - k_i)\gamma_i \tau_i}{D} > 0 \tag{24}$$

---

[5] One can derive these results using Eqs. (2), (8), and (11).

In general, V may rise more or less than R when the wage rate rise. We assume, however, that the tax rates are low enough and workers get a high enough share of the benefits from government spending so that

$$V_w > R_w \tag{25}$$

In that case, individual n chooses to work if the wage rate exceeds w^*, for then $V > R$; and he chooses not to work if the wage rate falls short of w^*, for then $V < R$. Define w^* to be zero if $\lim_{w \to 0} (V - R) > 0$ and to be infinite if $\lim_{w \to \infty} (V - R) < 0$. It then follows that

$$w^* = W(\tau_1, \ldots, \tau_m; \gamma_1, \ldots, \gamma_m; k_1, \ldots, k_m; n) \tag{26}$$

is a well-defined function if the τ_is are not too large and if the k_is are not too small.

Equation (22) implies that

$$W_{\tau_i} = \frac{(R_{\tau_i} - V_{\tau_i})}{(V_w - R_w)}, \qquad i = 1, \ldots, m \tag{27}$$

$$W_{\gamma_i} = \frac{(R_{\gamma_i} - k_i V_{\gamma_i k_i})}{(V_w - R_w)}, \qquad i = 1, \ldots, m \tag{28}$$

$$W_{k_i} = \frac{(R_{k_i} - \gamma_i V_{\gamma_i k_i})}{(V_w - R_w)}, \qquad i = 1, \ldots, m \tag{29}$$

and

$$W_n = \frac{-V_n}{(V_w - R_w)} \tag{30}$$

It is straightforward to use Eqs. (20), (21), (2) and (8)–(13) to show that

$$V_{\tau_i} = \frac{U_c\{-w^2 U_c \sum \gamma_i k_i \tau_i + (1 - \gamma_i k_i)[(1 - \tau)^2 w^2 U_{cc} + 2(1 - \tau)w U_{ch} + U_{hh}]\}}{D}$$

$$< 0, \qquad i = 1, \ldots, m \tag{31}$$

$$V_{\gamma_i k_i} = -\frac{\tau_i w h U_c[(1 - \tau)^2 w^2 U_{cc} + 2(1 - \tau)w U_{ch} + U_{hh}]}{D}$$

$$> 0, \qquad i = 1, \ldots, m \tag{32}$$

$$V_n = -f'(n) < 0 \tag{33}$$

$$R_{\tau_i} = U_c[w H_{\tau_i} \sum (1 - k_i)\gamma_i \tau_i + w H (1 - k_i)\gamma_i] \gtreqless 0, \qquad i = 1, \ldots, m \tag{34}$$

$$R_{\gamma_i} = U_c[k_i w H_{\gamma_i k_i} \sum (1 - k_i)\gamma_i \tau_i + (1 - k_i)\tau_i w H] \gtreqless 0, \qquad i = 1, \ldots, m \tag{35}$$

and

$$R_{k_i} = U_c[w\gamma_i H_{\gamma_i k_i} \sum (1 - k_i)\gamma_i \tau_i - \gamma_i k_i w H] < 0, \qquad i = , \ldots, m \tag{36}$$

In general, it is not possible to sign the derivatives R_{τ_i} and R_{γ_i} because changes in τ_i and γ_i change the tax base wh and the effective transfer rate $\sum (1 - k_i)\gamma_i\tau_i$ in opposite directions. I assume that the tax rates $\{\tau_i\}$ are small enough so that the second term in the brackets in Eq. (34) dominates, resulting in

$$R_{\tau_i} > 0 \tag{37}$$

Note, however, that Laffer (1980) has argued forcefully that effective transfers may actually fall when the effective transfer rate rises. If he is right, then (37) would fail to hold.

Making use of (27)–(33) and (35)–(37), one can show that

$$W_{\tau_i} > 0, \qquad i = 1, \ldots, m \tag{38}$$

$$W_{\gamma_i} \gtreqless 0, \qquad i = 1, \ldots, m \tag{39}$$

$$W_{k_i} < 0, \qquad i = 1, \ldots, m \tag{40}$$

and

$$W_n > 0 \tag{41}$$

All individuals with reservation wages below the prevailing wage rate work; all individuals with reservation wages above the prevailing wage rate do not work. There is a unique demarcating value of n for which[5a]

$$w = W(\tau_1, \ldots, \tau_m; \gamma_1, \ldots, \gamma_m; k_1, \ldots, k_m; n^*) \tag{42}$$

It follows that any individual whose index is less than n^* works and that any individual whose index exceeds n^* does not work. Since the indices of workers are uniformly distributed on the interval $[0, 1]$, n^* is the fraction of the labor force employed. By the implicit function theorem, n^* — which we shall call the employment ratio—takes on the value

$$n^* = N(w; \tau_1, \ldots, \tau_m; \gamma_1, \ldots, \gamma_m; k_1, \ldots, k_m) \tag{43}$$

where the function $N(\ )$ has the derivatives

$$N_w = 1/W_n > 0 \tag{44}$$

$$N_{\tau_i} = -W_{\tau_i}/W_n < 0, \qquad i = 1, \ldots, m \tag{45}$$

$$N_{\gamma_i} = -W_{\gamma_i}/W_n \gtreqless 0, \qquad i = 1, \ldots, m \tag{46}$$

and

$$N_{k_i} = -W_{k_i}/W_n > 0, \qquad i = 1, \ldots, m \tag{47}$$

[5a] Since $f(0) = 0$ and $\lim_{n\to 1} f(n) = \infty$, $W(\tau_1, \ldots, \tau_m; \gamma_1, \ldots, \gamma_m; k_1, \ldots, k_m; 0) = 0$ and $\lim_{n\to 1} W(\tau_1, \ldots, \tau_m; \gamma_1, \ldots, \gamma_m; k_1, \ldots, k_m; n) = \infty$. The uniqueness of n^* follows from these properties of $W(\ )$.

In this section, we have shown that the employment ratio and average hours of work per employed person are functions of the real before-tax wage rate w and a set of fiscal variables $\tau_1, \ldots, \tau_m; \gamma_1, \ldots, \gamma_m;$ and $k_1, \ldots, k_m$. These fiscal variables are the shares of national income devoted to different types of government spending; the marginal valuations of these types of spending; and the distribution of the benefits from government spending between workers and nonworkers. [In Section 4, we fit Eqs. (7) and (43) to U.S. data and then test the restrictions (17), (18), (44) and (45).]

3. THE DEMAND FOR LABOR

We assume that the private sector produces output according to the CES technology

$$Y = [(Ehe^{at+v})^{(\sigma-1)/\sigma} + B(Ke^{bt})^{(\sigma-1)/\sigma}]^{\sigma/(\sigma-1)} \tag{48}$$

where Y is private-sector output, E is the number of workers employed in the private sector, h is the average hours worked by each worker employed in the private sector, K is the stock of physical capital, a and b are the technical rate of augmentation of Eh and K, t is an index of time, B is a constant, σ is the elasticity of substitution between man-hours and capital, and v is an error term. When competition prevails, the marginal product of man-hours is equated to the real wage rate:

$$w = \frac{\partial Y}{\partial EH} = (EH)^{-1/\sigma} \exp\left[\left(\frac{\sigma-1}{\sigma}\right)(at+v)\right][(EHe^{at+v})^{(\sigma-1)/\sigma}$$
$$+ B(Ke^{bt})^{(\sigma-1)/\sigma}]^{1/(\sigma-1)} \tag{49}$$

which may be written as

$$w = e^{at+v}\left\{1 + B\left[\frac{K}{EH}e^{(b-a)t-v}\right]^{(\sigma-1)/\sigma}\right\}^{1/(\sigma-1)} \tag{50}$$

Multiplying both sides of Eq. (50) by EH/Y and using Eq. (48), one has

$$\frac{wEH}{Y} = \left\{1 + B\left[\frac{K}{EH}e^{(b-a)t-v}\right]^{(\sigma-1)/\sigma}\right\}^{-1} \tag{51}$$

Eliminating the expression in braces between Eqs. (50) and (51) yields

$$\frac{wEH}{Y} = \left(\frac{w}{e^{at+v}}\right)^{1-\sigma}$$

or, equivalently,

$$\log\frac{wEH}{Y} = a(\sigma-1)t + (1-\sigma)\log w + (\sigma-1)v$$

Differencing both members of this equation then yields

$$\Delta \log \frac{wEH}{Y} = a(\sigma - 1) + (1 - \sigma)\Delta \log w + (\sigma - 1)\Delta v \qquad (52)$$

In the next section, we shall fit Eq. (52), which is the demand function for private-sector man-hours, to U.S. data.

4. EMPIRICAL IMPLEMENTATION OF THE MODEL

One can recast Eqs. (7) and (43) in the form

$$\Delta \log n^* = \alpha_0 + \alpha_1 \log w + \sum \alpha_{2i}\Delta \tau_i + \Delta X_n$$

and

$$\Delta \log h = \beta_0 + \beta_1 \Delta \log w + \sum \beta_{2i}\Delta \tau_i + \Delta X_h$$

where $\alpha_0, \alpha_1, \alpha_{21}, \ldots, \alpha_{2m}, \beta_0, \beta_1, \beta_{21}, \ldots, \beta_{2m}$ are parameters and $X_n + \alpha_0 t$ and $X_h + \beta_0 t$ are the remainder terms in the Taylor-series expansions of $\log n^*$ and $\log h$ about the sample means of $\log w$ and $\tau_1, \ldots, \tau_m$. We assume that X_n and X_h are random walks without drift, so ΔX_m and ΔX_h are identically distributed, serially uncorrelated error terms with zero means and finite variances. In empirically implementing these equations, we have disaggregated government spending into three types: federal purchases, state and local purchases, and transfer payments. We denote the shares of these types of spending in the net national product by τ^f, τ^{sl}, and τ^t and rewrite the above equations as follows[6]:

$$\Delta \log n^* = \alpha_0 + \alpha_1 \Delta \log w + \alpha_{21}\Delta \tau^f + \alpha_{22}\Delta \tau^{sl} + \alpha_{23}\Delta \tau^t + \varepsilon \qquad (53)$$

and

$$\Delta \log h = \beta_0 + \beta_1 \Delta \log w + \beta_{21}\Delta \tau^f + \beta_{22}\Delta \tau^{sl} + \beta_{23}\Delta \tau^t + \eta \qquad (54)$$

where $\varepsilon = X_n$ and $\eta = \Delta X_h$.

We also assume that the error term v defined in the previous section under Eq. (48) is a random walk without drift. Therefore, Eq. (52) may be rewritten as

$$\Delta \log \frac{weh}{y} = \lambda_0 + \lambda_1 \Delta \log w + u \qquad (55)$$

---

[6] Note that in formulating this theory we assumed that the average and marginal tax rates are equal and that property income is zero. We replace these assumptions with the following, less restrictive assumptions: the contributions of federal purchases, state and local purchases, and transfer payments to the marginal tax rate on labor income are proportional to their shares in the net national product; no potential worker receives any property income; and no net transfers pass from recipients of property income to potential workers.

where e is the fraction of the potential labor force that works in the private sector, y is private-sector output per employable person, $\lambda_0 = (\sigma - 1)a$, $\lambda_1 = 1 - \sigma$, and u, which equals $(\sigma - 1)\Delta v$, is an identically distributed, serially uncorrelated error term with a zero mean and a finite variance. We have fitted Eqs. (53)–(55) to annual U.S. data spanning the period 1931–1977.[7] The real wage rate w is endogenous. Furthermore, the fiscal authorities generally vary τ^f, τ^{sl}, and τ^t in response to changes in employment and hours. We have therefore used two-stage least squares in the estimation.[8] We have also investigated the possibility that the employment ratio and average hours do not respond completely to changes in w, τ^f, τ^{sl}, and τ^t within a single year. Only in the average hours equation was any lagged variable statistically significant at the 0.05 significance level.

The results of the estimation procedure are[9,10]

$$\Delta \log n^* = \begin{array}{c} -0.00176 \\ (0.00570) \end{array} + \begin{array}{c} 0.348 \ \Delta \log w \\ (0.170) \end{array} - \begin{array}{c} 0.311 \ \Delta \tau^f \\ (0.084) \end{array} - \begin{array}{c} 2.279 \ \Delta \tau^{sl} \\ (0.565) \end{array} - \begin{array}{c} 0.691 \ \Delta \tau^t \\ (0.495) \end{array}$$

$$\text{S.E.} = 0.1947, \qquad \text{D.W.} = 1.59 \tag{56}$$

$$\Delta \log h = \begin{array}{c} -0.00490 \\ (0.0046) \end{array} - \begin{array}{c} 0.211 \ \Delta \log w \\ (0.123) \end{array} + \begin{array}{c} 0.258 \ \Delta \log w_{-1} \\ (0.081) \end{array} + \begin{array}{c} 0.115 \ \Delta \tau^f \\ (0.059) \end{array}$$

$$\begin{array}{c} -0.873 \ \Delta \tau^{sl} \\ (0.391) \end{array} - \begin{array}{c} 0.225 \ \Delta \tau^t \\ (0.348) \end{array}$$

$$\text{S.E.} = 0.01349, \qquad \text{D.W.} = 2.26 \tag{57}$$

$$\Delta \log \frac{weh}{y} = \begin{array}{c} 0.0129 \\ (0.0043) \end{array} - \begin{array}{c} 0.327 \ \Delta \log w \\ (0.123) \end{array}$$

$$\text{S.E.} = 0.01923, \qquad \text{D.W.} = 1.62 \tag{58}$$

---

[7] See the Appendix for a detailed description of the data and their sources.

[8] The instruments used are the constant term; the growth rate of the relative wage between the federal and the private sector; the growth rate of the relative wage between the state and local and the private sectors; the growth rate of the total net national product per working-age person lagged one year; the growth rate of real federal purchases of goods and services per working-age person; the growth rate of real state and local purchases per working-age person; the growth rate of federal civilian employment per working-age person; the growth rate of state and local employment per working-age person; the growth rate of the MI money supply per working-age person; τ^f_{-1}; τ^{sl}_{-1}; and τ^t_{-1}. In fitting Eq. (54), we also included the instrument $\Delta \log w_{-1}$.

[9] The standard error of each estimated coefficient appears below it in parentheses.

[10] Note that in Eqs. (56) and (57) we have left in variables that have insignificant coefficients. We interpret these coefficients as imprecisely estimated, so the point estimates are the "best" estimates of the true parameters.

Equations (56) and (57) confirm the a priori restrictions (17), (18), (44), and (45). Moreover, Eq (56) shows that fiscal variables are important determinants of the supply of workers and the supply of hours per worker. A 10 percentage point increase in the share of federal purchases in the net national product would lower the supply of employment by 3.11 percent while raising the supply of hours by 1.15 percent. A 10 percentage point increase in the share going to state and local purchases would lower the supply of employment by 22.79 percent and would lower the supply of hours by 8.73 percent. A 10 percentage point increase in the share going to transfer payments would lower the supply of employment by 6.91 percent and lower average hours by 2.25 percent. These changes—especially the change resulting from the increase in the share going to state and local governments—are large effects.

The theory of this paper implies that the coefficient on τ_i in Eq. (54) is more negative, the greater the marginal valuation that the public puts on government spending of type i and the larger the portion of the benefits from this type of spending that accrue to those that work. The coefficients on τ^f, τ^{sl}, and τ^t in Eq. (57) are therefore consistent with the casual observation that the public attaches more value to state and local purchases than to federal purchases and that the benefits from state and local purchases are distributed more toward those that work than the benefits from transfer payments.[11]

Equation (56) implies that the elasticity of substitution between labor and capital is 1.327 (0.123).[12] Since it is larger than one, a reduction in the ratio of capital to private-sector man-hours resulting, say, from a reduced tax rate on labor income would increase the before-tax share of private-sector output going to labor.[13]

5. SIMULATION OF THE MODEL

Equations (56)–(58) do not constitute a complete model of the labor market. To complete the model, we make the following assumptions: (a) the fiscal authorities employ the fraction zn^* of the working-age population and z is proportional to $\tau^f + \tau^{sl} + \tau^t$; and (b) private-sector output y per working-age person is exogenous to this model. Later in this section, we shall replace assumption (b) by the assumption that (c) the ratio of capital to private-sector man-hours is exogenous.

---

[11] During the sample period, most federal purchases were for defense purchases, while a large portion of state and local purchases were for schooling.

[12] This elasticity of substitution is considerably larger than Boskin (1978) found. His findings, we believe, differ from ours because he did not take proper account of serial correlation in the error terms of the equation that he fitted.

[13] See Arrow *et al.* (1961).

Since y does not respond to any of the policy changes that we shall consider,[14] Eq. (54) implies that

$$\log \bar{w} - \log \underline{w} = -\frac{1}{1 + 0.327}(\log \bar{e}\bar{h} - \log \underline{e}\underline{h}) = -0.754 (\log \bar{e}\bar{h} - \log \underline{e}\underline{h})$$

(59)

where $\bar{w}$, $\bar{e}$, and $\bar{h}$ are the values of w, e, and h after the policy change and $\underline{w}$, $\underline{e}$, and $\underline{h}$ are the values of w, e, and h before the change. Assumption (a) implies that

$$e = n^*(1 - z)$$

(60)

so

$$\log \bar{e} - \log \underline{e} = \log \bar{n}^* - \log \underline{n}^* + \log (1 - \bar{z}) - \log(1 - \underline{z})$$

(61)

where $\bar{n}^*$ and $\bar{z}$ are the values of n and z after the policy change and n and z are the values before the change. Equations (56) and (57) imply that

$$\log \bar{n}^*\bar{h} - \log \underline{n}^*\underline{h} = 0.137 (\log \bar{w} - \log \underline{w}) + 0.258 (\log \bar{w}_{-1} - \log \underline{w}_{-1})$$
$$- 0.196 (\bar{\tau}^f - \underline{\tau}^f) - 3.152(\bar{\tau}^{sl} - \underline{\tau}^{sl}) - 0.916(\bar{\tau}^t - \underline{\tau}^t)$$

(62)

Substituting Eqs. (59) and (61) into Eq. (62) and rearranging then yields

$$\log \bar{e}\bar{h} - \log \underline{e}\underline{h} = -0.234 (\log \bar{e}_{-1}\bar{h}_{-1} - \log \underline{e}_{-1}\underline{h}_{-1}) + 0.906[\log(1 - \bar{z})$$
$$- \log(1 - \underline{z})] - 0.178(\bar{\tau}^f - \underline{\tau}^f)$$
$$- 2.856(\bar{\tau}^{sl} - \underline{\tau}^{sl}) - 0.830(\bar{\tau}^t - \underline{\tau}^t)$$

(63)

Equation (63) permits one to calculate how a policy change alters the time path of private-sector man-hours per working-age person. One can then use Eq. (59) to calculate the change in the time path of the real after-tax wage rate. Finally, plugging the changes in log w and the fiscal variables into

$$\log \bar{n}^* - \log \underline{n}^* = 0.348(\log \bar{w} - \log \underline{w}) - 0.311(\bar{\tau}^f - \underline{\tau}^f)$$
$$- 2.279(\bar{\tau}^{sl} - \underline{\tau}^{sl}) - 0.691(\bar{\tau}^t - \underline{\tau}^t)$$

(64)

and

$$\log \bar{h} - \log \underline{h} = -0.211(\log \bar{w} - \log \underline{w}) + 0.258(\log \bar{w}_{-1} - \log \underline{w}_{-1})$$
$$+ 0.115(\bar{\tau}^f - \underline{\tau}^f) - 0.873(\bar{\tau}^{sl} - \underline{\tau}^{sl}) - 0.225(\bar{\tau}^t - \underline{\tau}^t)$$

(65)

yields the changes in the time path of the employment ratio and average hours.

---

[14] We therefore assume that fiscal variables cannot effect aggregate demand. See Evans (1977) for an analysis of the relation between government purchases and aggregate demand.

TABLE 1

The Effects of Various Policy Changes When Private-Sector Output Remains Constant[a]

Variables	(1) $\Delta\tau^f = +0.10$	(2) $\Delta\tau^{sl} = +0.10$	(3) $\Delta\tau^t = +0.10$	(4) $\Delta z = +0.05$
eh	-6.36	-33.14	-12.88	-5.61
n^*	-1.44	-14.09	-3.53	$+1.47$
h	$+0.14$	-14.00	-4.30	-0.89
n^*h	-1.30	-28.09	-7.83	$+0.58$
w	$+4.80$	$+24.99$	$+9.71$	$+4.23$
$w(1-\tau)$	-13.67	$+6.52$	-8.76	$+4.23$
$n^*hw(1-\tau)$	-14.97	-21.57	-16.59	$+4.81$

[a] All changes in eh, n^*, h, n^*h, w, $w(1-\tau)$, and $n^*hw(1-\tau)$ are expressed as percentages. The calculations assume that the government initially claims 40.7 percent of the net national product and that its employment is 16.7 percent of the total. These values prevailed in 1977.

Table 1 reports the effects of various policy changes on private-sector man-hours, the employment ratio, average hours, the real before-tax wage rate, and the real after-tax wage rate in the year of the change. Since private-sector output is unlikely to remain constant for periods longer than a year, we have not used Eqs. (59), (61), (62), (64), and (65) to calculate the effects in later years. Columns (1)–(3) present the effects that result from raising the share of government spending in the net national product from 40.7 to 50.7 percent, while simultaneously raising the share of employment in the government from 16.7 to 20.8 percent ($= 16.7 \times 50.7/40.7$). In column (1) this increase goes entirely into federal purchases; in column (2), it goes entirely into state and local purchases; and, in column (3), it goes entirely into transfer payments. In column (4), the share of employment in the government rises from 16.7 to 21.7 percent, a 5 percentage point increase. Since the shares of federal purchases, state and local purchases, and transfer payments in the net national product remain unchanged, the induced increase in spending on services by both federal and state and local governments must be accompanied by a reduction in purchases of goods. Thus, column (4) gives the combined influences of an increase in the share of employment and a change in the composition of government purchases.

All of these policy changes lower total private-sector man-hours[15] and raise the real before-tax wage rate. In most cases, they also lower employment, average hours, and total man-hours. Real disposable wage income falls when the share claimed by the government rises, but rises when the government shifts its spending toward services.

[15] Since the working-age population is unaffected by these measures, changes in eh and n^* occur because total private man-hours and employment have changed.

Equation (50) shows that, at any given time, w depends only on the ratio of the capital stock to private-sector man-hours. Assumption (c), which states that this ratio is exogenous, is therefore equivalent to the assumption that w does not change in response to any policy change. Equations (56) and (57) then imply that

$$\log \bar{n}^* - \log \underline{n}^* = -0.311(\bar{\tau}^f - \underline{\tau}^f) - 2.279(\bar{\tau}^{sl} - \underline{\tau}^{sl}) - 0.691(\bar{\tau}^t - \underline{\tau}^t) \tag{66}$$

and

$$\log \bar{h} - \log \underline{h} = 0.115(\bar{\tau}^f - \underline{\tau}^f) - 0.873(\bar{\tau}^{sl} - \underline{\tau}^{sl}) - 0.225(\bar{\tau}^t - \underline{\tau}^t) \tag{67}$$

Since the ratio of capital to eh is constant, the ratio of private-sector output y to eh is also constant. Hence

$$\begin{aligned}\log \bar{y} - \log \underline{y} &= \log \overline{eh} - \log \underline{eh} \\ &= \log \bar{n}^* - \log \underline{n}^* + \log \bar{h} - \log \underline{h} + \log(1 - \bar{z}) - \log(1 - \underline{z})\end{aligned} \tag{68}$$

where $\underline{y}$ and $\bar{y}$ are the values of y before and after the policy change.

Table 2 reports the effects of the policy changes considered in Table 1 on the assumption that the ratio of capital to private-sector man-hours remains constant. It is clear from this table that an increase in the share claimed by the government decreases employment, total man-hours, private-sector man-hours, disposable income, and, with only a simple exception, average hours.

TABLE 2

The Effects of Various Policy Changes When the Ratio of Capital to Private-Sector Man-Hours Remains Constant[a]

Variable	$\Delta\tau^f = +0.10$	$\Delta\tau^{sl} = +0.10$	$\Delta\tau^t = +0.10$	$\Delta z = +0.05$
n^*	−3.11	−22.79	−6.91	0.00
h	+1.15	−8.73	−2.25	0.00
n^*h	−1.96	−31.52	−9.16	0.00
eh	−7.01	−36.57	−14.21	−6.19
w	0.00	0.00	0.00	0.00
$n^*hw(1 - \tau)$	−20.43	−49.99	−27.63	0.00
$\tau(y + zn^*hw)$	+18.71	−5.65	+11.35	−1.51

[a] All changes in n^*, h, n^*h, eh, w, $n^*hw(1 - \tau)$ and $\tau(y + zn^*hw)$ are expressed as percentages. The calculations assume that the government initially claims 40.7 percent of the net national product, that its employment is 16.7 percent of the total, and that private-sector output is 87.7 percent of the net national product. These values prevailed in 1977.

In most cases these reductions are substantial. Indeed, in one case, the reduction in total man-hours is so great that the increase in the share claimed by government actually reduces the total amount, $\tau(y + zn^*hw)$, that the government gets to spend. Thus, Table 2 provides some evidence to support Laffer's view that increased tax rates may actually lower tax revenue.

An increase in the share of workers employed in the government does not change total man-hours. It therefore shrinks the private-sector. Since less capital then exists, total income falls, lowering tax collections and hence government spending.

Tables 1 and 2 report the effects from four policy changes under two polar assumptions. In Table 1, private-sector output remains constant, so the changes in private-sector man-hours are accompanied by changes in the capital stock in the opposite direction. In Table 2, private-sector man-hours, the capital stock, and output are in fixed proportions to each other. The former assumption would hold in a Keynesian model, where output is determined by aggregate demand. In contrast, the latter assumption would hold in the standard neoclassical model when the economy is proceeding along a balanced growth path.[16] Which of these assumptions better characterizes the operation of the real world is an empirical question. In the absence of an empirical model of investment, we can only claim that the actual changes in employment, average hours, and the wage rate are bounded in the short run and interrun by those in Tables 1 and 2. In the long run, we should expect the effects of the policy changes to be those given in Table 2.

6. SUMMARY

There are good theoretical reasons to expect that the policy instruments of the fiscal authorities have important effects on the supply of labor services. Our empirical estimates confirm this theoretical conclusion. Increases in the share of government spending in the net national product generally reduce employment, average hours of work, and disposable wage income. For example, in the long run, an increase in the share claimed by state and local governments appears to reduce the supply of labor services by so much that the revenue collected by all branches of government actually declines. This finding provides some support for Laffer's views.

---

[16] If the marginal rate of substitution between consumptions in any two adjacent periods depends only on the ratio of these consumptions, if the rate of population growth is constant, and if technological progress is Harrod-neutral and occurs at a constant rate, then the steady-state capital–man-hours ratio depends only on the tax rate on capital. Therefore, this ratio will not change if the policies considered in Table 2 do not change this tax rate.

APPENDIX

The data used in the empirical analysis of this paper are presented in Tables 3 and 4.

The series n^* is the ratio of civilian employment to the working-age (18–64) population, including the military. The civilian employment series comes from *Long Term Economic Growth* (*LTEG*), papers 194 and 195, column A77; the *Handbook of Labor Statistics 1977*; and the *Survey of Current Business* (*SCB*). The population series comes from *Historical Statistics of the United States*, p. 10, columns 37 and 40, and *Current Population Reports*.

The series h is a normalization constant times the BLS index of private man-hours divided by private employment. Private employment is total civilian employment less civilian employment in the government. The normalization constant is private employment in 1967 divided by 100 times 1976, an estimate of the average annual hours for the private-sector in 1967.[17] The private manhours index comes from *LTEG*, pages 192 and 193, column A69, and the *Employment and Training Report of the president*, Table G-1.[18] The government employment series comes from *LTEG*, pages 196 and 197, column A91, the *Handbook of Labor Statistics 1977* and *SCB*.

The series w is private compensation divided by the GNP deflator, h, and e. Private compensation is total compensation less government compensation. The series e is $n^* - e^f - e^{sl}$, where the series e^f and e^{sl} are the civilian employments of the federal and state and local governments divided by the working-age population. Total compensation is row 2 of Table 1.13 of the National and Products Accounts (NIPA).[19] Government compensation is row 7 of Table 3.1 of the NIPA. The civilian employments of the federal and state and local governments come from *Employment and Earnings*, pp. 676, 677, 679, and 680. The GNP deflator is row 1 of Table 7.1 of the NIPA.

The series y is NNP less government compensation deflated by the GNP deflator. NNP is row 5 of Table 1.9 of the NIPA.

The series τ^f and τ^{sl} are the ratios of federal and state and local purchases—row 21 of Table 3.2 and row 39 of Table 3.4 of the NIPA—to NNP.

---

[17] According to the *SCB*, nonsupervisory workers in the manufacturing sector worked an average of 38 hours each week in 1967. An estimate of average annual hours worked in 1967 is 52 × 38, or 1976 hours.

[18] Starting in 1976, the *Employment and Training Report* stopped reporting the index of total private man-hours. In lieu of this series, it now reports private business man-hours. The 1976 and 1977 values of the index of total private man-hours were extrapolated from the index of private business man-hours by substracting 0.9.

[19] The NIPA for 1929–1972 are in the book entitled *NIPA*; the NIPA for 1973–1977 are in the July 1976, July 1977, and July 1978 editions of SCB.

TABLE 3

Principal Variables Used in the Empirical Analysis

Year	n^*	h	w	weh/y	τ^f	τ^{sl}	τ^l
1929	0.6602	2404	1.338	0.5232	0.0154	0.0788	0.0168
1930	0.6190	2363	1.329	0.5518	0.0191	0.0979	0.0208
1931	0.5700	2350	1.321	0.5619	0.0241	0.1169	0.0480
1932	0.5174	2289	1.267	0.5779	0.0312	0.1334	0.0487
1933	0.5091	2272	1.223	0.5698	0.0439	0.1267	0.0614
1934	0.5305	2109	1.329	0.5531	0.0543	0.1199	0.0778
1935	0.5418	2153	1.353	0.5334	0.0465	0.1109	0.0754
1936	0.5629	2199	1.424	0.5262	0.0671	0.0951	0.0616
1937	0.5805	2238	1.472	0.5456	0.0577	0.0890	0.0458
1938	0.5479	2159	1.501	0.5449	0.0719	0.1007	0.0578
1939	0.5600	2190	1.560	0.5436	0.0630	0.1014	0.0614
1940	0.5744	2209	1.593	0.5328	0.0668	0.0888	0.0564
1941	0.6005	2266	1.698	0.5249	0.1475	0.0695	0.0403
1942	0.6331	2310	1.807	0.5314	0.3534	0.0531	0.0346
1943	0.6336	2386	1.997	0.5420	0.4507	0.0416	0.0298
1944	0.6202	2376	2.106	0.5346	0.4498	0.0384	0.0349
1945	0.6011	2296	2.151	0.5319	0.3722	0.0408	0.0537
1946	0.6231	2183	2.045	0.5561	0.0900	0.0507	0.0978
1947	0.6370	2143	2.048	0.5654	0.0589	0.0592	0.0872
1948	0.6445	2106	2.103	0.5602	0.0699	0.0639	0.0859
1949	0.6299	2071	2.161	0.5625	0.0864	0.0762	0.0981
1950	0.6386	2068	2.283	0.5549	0.0714	0.0754	0.0947
1951	0.6454	2107	2.376	0.5581	0.1266	0.0720	0.0712
1952	0.6443	2116	2.500	0.5744	0.1649	0.0731	0.0660
1953	0.6502	2099	2.635	0.5871	0.1720	0.0747	0.0654
1954	0.6347	2066	2.673	0.5850	0.1439	0.0835	0.0725
1955	0.6523	2074	2.729	0.5783	0.1221	0.0839	0.0716
1956	0.6642	2063	2.821	0.5994	0.1202	0.0877	0.0744
1957	0.6622	2034	2.908	0.6004	0.1247	0.0926	0.0808
1958	0.6474	1993	2.974	0.5959	0.1332	0.1016	0.0944
1959	0.6585	2007	3.075	0.5943	0.1224	0.0992	0.0914
1960	0.6613	1994	3.152	0.6027	0.1172	0.1016	0.0931
1961	0.6522	1972	3.240	0.5973	0.1210	0.1071	0.1016
1962	0.6542	1989	3.338	0.5900	0.1242	0.1058	0.0982
1963	0.6576	1975	3.442	0.5880	0.1191	0.1088	0.0982
1964	0.6659	1969	3.568	0.5886	0.1122	0.1111	0.0979
1965	0.6699	1986	3.652	0.5843	0.1067	0.1127	0.0961
1966	0.6755	1998	3.809	0.5901	0.1140	0.1155	0.1002
1967	0.6779	1976	3.933	0.6004	0.1247	0.1224	0.1071
1968	0.6812	1979	4.056	0.6070	0.1233	0.1267	0.1117
1969	0.6880	1972	4.163	0.6240	0.1142	0.1294	0.1150
1970	0.6831	1935	4.231	0.6364	0.1073	0.1382	0.1318
1971	0.6762	1924	4.291	0.6254	0.0997	0.1425	0.1408
1972	0.6868	1922	4.397	0.6223	0.0958	0.1417	0.1457
1973	0.6983	1925	4.518	0.6252	0.0860	0.1408	0.1480
1974	0.6996	1900	4.515	0.6414	0.0871	0.1502	0.1564
1975	0.6789	1874	4.507	0.6332	0.0900	0.1576	0.1822
1976	0.6889	1853	4.692	0.6349	0.0853	0.1508	0.1787
1977	0.7015	1848	4.806	0.6371	0.0857	0.1471	0.1745

TABLE 4

Other Variables Used in the Empirical Analysis

Year	e^f	e^{sl}	s^f	s^{sl}	g^f	g^{sl}	M
1929	0.0074	0.0351	1.364	1.061	60.8	311	369
1930	0.0071	0.0357	1.284	1.104	66.4	340	351
1931	0.0075	0.0363	1.487	1.177	75.0	365	325
1932	0.0074	0.0354	1.645	1.292	81.6	349	281
1933	0.0074	0.0342	1.612	1.289	111.9	320	261
1934	0.0085	0.0343	1.584	1.194	148.6	328	284
1935	0.0097	0.0350	1.551	1.138	138.9	332	332
1936	0.0105	0.0360	1.617	1.195	228.3	324	375
1937	0.0105	0.0367	1.434	1.150	202.8	313	388
1938	0.0103	0.0378	1.504	1.209	237.5	333	378
1939	0.0111	0.0378	1.471	1.178	223.1	359	418
1940	0.0121	0.0388	1.471	1.166	252.4	336	479
1941	0.0160	0.0396	1.370	1.067	641.8	302	555
1942	0.0261	0.0385	1.302	0.931	1758.4	264	652
1943	0.0338	0.0369	1.353	0.882	2599.9	240	840
1944	0.0337	0.0358	1.220	0.864	2767.0	236	981
1945	0.0319	0.0357	1.206	0.894	2235.3	245	1129
1946	0.0254	0.0377	1.223	0.892	452.8	255	1201
1947	0.0211	0.0400	1.218	0.891	285.3	287	1249
1948	0.0206	0.0418	1.156	0.930	347.2	317	1241
1949	0.0209	0.0431	1.214	0.941	424.0	374	1215
1950	0.0209	0.0444	1.200	0.920	378.3	399	1237
1951	0.0248	0.0440	1.206	0.916	770.2	409	1285
1952	0.0259	0.0448	1.221	0.923	965.5	428	1339
1953	0.0245	0.0461	1.215	0.914	1038.4	451	1364
1954	0.0231	0.0482	1.211	0.935	848.0	492	1376
1955	0.0229	0.0496	1.226	0.919	764.9	526	1410
1956	0.0230	0.0528	1.216	0.914	760.7	554	1416
1957	0.0229	0.0558	1.212	0.927	794.2	590	1413
1958	0.0225	0.0580	1.301	0.938	838.0	640	1421
1959	0.0228	0.0596	1.254	0.927	813.2	659	1463
1960	0.0229	0.0612	1.264	0.945	786.3	681	1443
1961	0.0226	0.0626	1.307	0.958	821.4	727	1453
1962	0.0230	0.0642	1.298	0.976	886.1	755	1468
1963	0.0228	0.0667	1.319	0.975	876.1	800	1495
1964	0.0226	0.0696	1.349	0.962	861.8	854	1540
1965	0.0224	0.0725	1.364	0.968	852.9	901	1575
1966	0.0238	0.0762	1.361	0.976	951.7	964	1621
1967	0.0248	0.0791	1.327	1.014	1048.8	1030	1657
1968	0.0246	0.0817	1.360	1.021	1065.1	1094	1748
1969	0.0244	0.0834	1.369	1.017	992.6	1125	1825
1970	0.0235	0.0854	1.451	1.031	909.6	1172	1864
1971	0.0230	0.0871	1.470	1.043	856.5	1224	1956
1972	0.0225	0.0896	1.477	1.039	858.5	1269	2060
1973	0.0220	0.0916	1.484	1.045	799.0	1308	2178
1974	0.0222	0.0932	1.437	1.024	779.8	1344	2261
1975	0.0220	0.0959	1.425	1.019	774.8	1356	2318
1976	0.0215	0.0962	1.420	1.017	763.7	1350	2396
1977	0.0211	0.0966	1.425	1.001	795.4	1365	2527

The series τ^t is the ratio of total government expenditures — row 6 of Table 3.1 of the NIPA—to NNP less τ^f and τ^{sl}.

The series s^f and s^{sl} are the ratios of the full-time equivalent salaries in the federal and state and local governments to the average full-time equivalent salary in the private sector. The full-time equivalent salaries for the federal and state and local governments are rows 77 and 82 of Table 6.9 of the NIPA. The private-sector full-time equivalent salary is private employment divided into total employment times the full-time equivalent salary for all workers less federal civilian employment times the full-time equivalent salary in the federal government less state and local employment times the full-time equivalent salary in the state and local governments. The full-time equivalent salary for all workers is row 1 of Table 6.9 of the NIPA.

The series g^f and g^{sl} are federal and state and local purchases divided by the GNP deflator and the working-age population.

The series M is the M1 money supply divided by the working-age population. The money supply series comes from *LTEG*, pp. 230 and 231, column B109; *Business Statistics*, p. 101; and *SCB*.

REFERENCES

Arrow, K. J., Chenery, H. B., Minhas, B. S., and Solow, R. M. (1961). "Capital–Labor Substitution and Economic Efficiency," *Review of Economics and Statistics* 225–250.

Bailey, M. (1962). *National Income and the Price Level*. McGraw-Hill, New York.

Boskin, M. (1978). "Taxation, Saving, and the Rate of Interest," *Journal of Political Economy* **86**, S3–S28.

Bureau of Economic Analysis, Department of Commerce (1973). *Long Term Economic Growth*. U.S. Government Printing Office, Washington, D.C.

Bureau of Economic Analysis, Department of Commerce (1976). *National Income and Product Accounts*. U.S. Government Printing Office, Washington, D.C.

Bureau of Economic Analysis, Department of Commerce (1978). *Business Statistics*. U.S. Government Printing Office, Washington, D.C.

Bureau of Labor Statistics, Department of Labor (1976). *Employment and Earnings, United States, 1909–75*. U.S. Government Printing Office, Washington, D.C.

Bureau of Labor Statistics, Department of Labor (1978). *Handbook of Labor Statistics 1977*. U.S. Government Printing Office, Washington, D.C.

Bureau of the Census, Department of Commerce (1971–1978). *Current Population Reports*, Series P-20. U.S. Government Printing Office, Washington, D.C.

Bureau of the Census, Department of Commerce (1975). *Historical Statistics of the United States*. U.S. Government Printing Office, Washington, D.C.

Cain, G. and Watts, H., eds. (1974). *Income Maintenance and Labor Supply*. Academic Press, New York.

Canto, V. (1978). "Taxation in a Closed Economy Intertemporal Model with a Variable Supply of Labor to the Market Sector." University of Southern California, Los Angeles, California.

Canto, V., Joines, D., and Laffer, A. (1978). "An Income Expenditure Version of the Wedge Model." *Conference on Inflation*. Federal Reserve Bank of San Francisco, San Francisco, California.

Department of Labor (1978). *Employment and Training Report of the President*. U.S. Government Printing Office, Washington, D.C.

Evans, P. (1977). "The Timing and Duration of Fiscal Policy in a Neoclassical Model." Stanford Univ., Stanford, California.

Feldstein, M. (1974). "Social Security, Induced Retirement, and Aggregate Capital Accumulation," *Journal of Political Economy* **82**, 905–926.

Feldstein, M. (1976). "Temporary Layoffs in the Theory of Unemployment," *Journal of Political Economy* **84**, 937–958.

Joines, D. (1978). "A Neoclassical Model of Fiscal Policy, Employment and Capital Accumulation." Univ. of Southern California, Los Angeles, California.

Klein, L. (1978). "The Supply Side," *American Economic Review* **68**, 1–7.

Laffer, A. (1980). "Tax Cuts Would More Than Pay for Themselves," *Los Angeles Times*, May 27, Part 4, pp. 2, 7.

Chapter 6

Estimates of Effective Marginal Tax Rates on Factor Incomes*

Douglas H. Joines

1. INTRODUCTION

In recent years, there has been a resurgence of interest in the influence of tax policy on economic activity and, in particular, in the response of factor supply and employment to the taxation of factor income. These effects have been the subject of both theoretical and empirical investigations. Of particular importance are recent empirical studies which indicate that the elasticities of factor supply with respect to after-tax factor returns are larger than had previously been thought. Wright (1969) and Boskin (1977) have estimated nonnegligible interest elasticities of private saving. Joines (1979) found the equilibrium level of business fixed investment to be negatively related to tax rates on income from capital. Wales (1973) found important tax effects on the labor supply of self-employed business proprietors, and

* Originally published in the *Journal of Business*, 1981, Vol. 54, No. 2. © 1981 by The University of Chicago.

Rosen (1976) presented similar results for married women. These and other findings that factor supply is responsive to after-tax factor returns have important policy implications concerning the effects of tax policy on aggregate economic activity. The fact that nontrivial supply elasticities were estimated with respect to net-of-tax factor returns, whereas previous studies finding negligible elasticities had used gross returns, demonstrates the importance of tax considerations for both theoretical and empirical research, as well as for public policy.

At the same time that evidence of the empirical importance of tax rates has been mounting, several theoretical studies have appeared which have examined various aspects of tax policy in a growing economy. See, for example, Diamond (1970), Feldstein (1974a,b), and Miller and Upton (1974). An assumption common to all of these studies is that a single, economy-wide tax rate applies to income from capital and, where relevant, another uniform, economy-wide tax rate applies to income from labor. The magnitude of these tax rates has important implications for the amount of market-sector activity taking place and for the distribution of the burden of taxation.

If tax rates are as important as these theoretical and empirical studies would seem to indicate, some interesting questions arise as to the magnitude of the relevant tax rates. How high are effective factor income tax rates in the United States? How do current tax rates compare with rates which prevailed in the past? How do effective tax rates on income from labor compare with those on income from capital? Questions such as these might not appear amenable to ready answers in the absence of some summary measures of effective tax rates analogous to those in the theoretical studies cited above. This paper describes one method of distilling such summary measures from readily available U.S. data and reports the resulting calculations.

Summary measures of economy-wide tax rates such as those reported here have several potential uses. First, they may be of some descriptive use in answering questions like those posed above concerning the current state of the U.S. economy. The answers to these questions may in turn have important policy implications when combined with relevant parameter estimates such as factor supply elasticities. For example, estimates of effective tax rates and factor supply elasticities may be used in the theoretical models cited above to provide rough measures of the welfare loss from and the incidence of our current tax structure.

As mentioned above, one might be interested in the magnitude of the tax on labor income relative to that on income from capital. This comparison is of particular relevance in light of the recent conjecture of Miller and Scholes (1978) that the federal personal income tax is evolving into a pure consumption tax. If the Miller–Scholes hypothesis is correct, we should expect to observe the effective capital income tax rate decline over time relative to the labor income tax rate. In addition, recent papers by Feldstein and Summers (1979), Fama (1979), Holland and Myers (1980), and Gonedes (1981) provide conflicting evidence on whether the tax burden on the income from corporate-held capital has increased or decreased during the last quarter century. These questions will be examined in more detail later in the paper.

Finally, the measures of effective tax rates reported here might be useful in empirical research. The importance of incorporating tax rates into empirical work on factor supply is clear from the studies cited above. Many existing labor supply studies were conducted using disaggregated, cross-section data. Such gross, summary measures as those reported here would obviously be of no use in cross-section studies. They would be of use in studies employing aggregate time-series data, however. In fact, the tax rate measures reported here or measures similar to them have been successfully employed in several empirical investigations of time-series data. Wright's study, possibly the first to find an important effect of after-tax rates of return on saving, employed weighted-average marginal tax rates on income from capital similar in spirit to those reported here. In addition, Joines (1979) found a significant negative relation between business fixed investment and the capital income tax rates reported here.

2. SOME CAVEATS

The estimates of factor income tax rates reported below are intended to be empirically analogous to the corresponding analytical magnitudes which appear in the theoretical papers cited above. Any attempt at empirical measurement of such effective rates of income taxation will inevitably yield quantities which correspond only imperfectly to the theoretical magnitudes under consideration, and there are several factors which make the problem of measuring effective tax rates a particularly difficult one. The first of these problems is that some taxes are not levied directly on the employment of resources in the market sector but are levied indirectly, as, for example, on consumption. At the theoretical level, it is clear that individuals supply resources to the market in exchange for market output, but, at the empirical level, factor payments take the form of nominal income that must be exchanged for market output. At the theoretical level, it is clear that it makes no difference whether the government appropriates its share of national output when the owners of factors first receive nominal income or when they ultimately spend that income in the market. At the empirical level, however, the multiplicity of different taxes striking at different points in the production–expenditure cycle greatly complicates the task of measuring effective rates of income taxation.

Another complication is that, considering the income tax alone, there is only a very imperfect correspondence between nominal and effective tax rates. At both the individual and corporate levels, the impact of nominal tax rates is modified by a number of provisions concerning deductions, exemptions, and credits.

To complicate matters even further, there is also an imperfect temporal correspondence between certain acts of income generation and the tax consequences of those acts. One example is the taxation of capital gains only when they are realized rather than when they accrue.[1] Another is the investment tax credit, which reduces taxes in the year in which a capital good is acquired but might more properly be viewed as a reduction in the rate of taxation of the income stream produced by that capital good. Finally, neither nominal tax rates nor actual tax revenues incorporate the resources devoted to qualifying for the various deductions, exemptions, and credits.

Given the complexity of these issues, one might conclude that any attempt at measurement of effective tax rates is hopeless. It is obvious that no scheme for incorporating all the effects enumerated above into a single number representing *the* tax rate on income from labor or capital can be more than an approximation, and possibly a very rough one. This paper nevertheless describes such a scheme and reports the resulting numbers.

3. THE NATURE OF AVAILABLE DATA

The design of any method for quantifying effective tax rates must be influenced by the kinds of data available. The present method is obviously not unique, and no claim is made that, among measurement schemes which might be devised, the present one is optimal. Different readers can undoubtedly think of modifications they would regard as desirable, and it would probably be impossible to achieve a consensus as to which method is optimal. The absence of such a consensus should not, however, deter one from making any attempt at measurement. All that is claimed for the present method is that, given the limitations of existing data, it makes reasonable use of the information at hand.

Two major sources of data on income and taxes were used—the *National Income and Product Accounts of the United States* (henceforth NIPA) and the *Statistics of Income* series published by the Internal Revenue Service. The NIPA provide aggregate values for income from various sources and for taxes of various kinds. The *Statistics of Income* provide more detailed

---

[1] As Bailey (1969) points out, this deferral lowers the effective tax rate on capital gains.

data compiled from individual income tax returns. The data compiled from individual returns include (1) number of returns, (2) federal personal income tax liability, and (3) income from various sources, all of which are classified by adjusted gross income.

The classification of income by source in the *Statistics of Income* is consistent with that in the NIPA. Each type of income in the *Statistics of Income* falls within one of the types given in the NIPA, the income categories in the latter generally being broader than those in the former.

Each type of income was classified as deriving from labor or from capital. For each of these, the aggregate figure reported in the NIPA is larger than the total income of that type reported in the *Statistics of Income*, which merely indicates that total income subject to the personal income tax is less than national income.

4. A HYPOTHETICAL TAX STRUCTURE

It is desired, for each year, to condense the information from these sources into two numbers, one representing the effective economy-wide marginal tax rate on income from capital and another representing an analogous tax rate on income from labor. The economy-wide marginal tax rate on income from capital is the fraction of an incremental dollar of income earned by the economy's capital stock which is taken by the government in taxes. It thus depends upon the marginal tax rates of the individuals receiving the incremental dollar and upon the distribution of that dollar among those individuals. If we assume that each individual's share in an incremental dollar of income produced by the capital stock is equal to his share in existing capital income, then the economy-wide marginal tax rate is equal to a weighted average of the individual marginal tax rates, with the weights being the shares in existing capital income. A similar calculation will give the economy-wide marginal rate of taxation of labor income.

It is assumed that all taxes are ultimately taxes on the utilization of productive resources in the market sector and can thus be regarded as taxes on the income produced by those resources. All resources are aggregated into two categories—physical capital and labor. Real property is regarded as physical capital. Taxes on the income of these factors are of various types. Some apply to both types of income, while others are specific to one or the other; some are strictly proportional to income and others are progressive.

The specific tax structure is taken to be as follows: let the income of individual i be given by

$$y_i = y_{li} + y_{ki}$$

where

y_{li} = income from labor of individual i, and
y_{ki} = income from capital of individual i.

The tax liability of individual i is taken to be

$$t_i = \tau_i y_i + \tau_{li} y_{li} + \tau_{ki} y_{ki} + f_{li}(\gamma_{li} y_{li}) + f_{ki}(\gamma_{ki} y_{ki}) \tag{1}$$

where

τ_i = proportional tax rate on all income of individual i,
τ_{li} = proportional tax rate on labor income of individual i,
τ_{ki} = proportional tax rate on capital income of individual i,
$f_{li}(\ )$ = a function describing a nonproportional tax on labor income of individual i,
γ_{li} = the fraction of such labor income subject to the nonproportional tax,
$f_{ki}(\ )$ = a function describing a nonproportional tax on capital income of individual i, and
γ_{ki} = the fraction of such capital income subject to the nonproportional tax.

The functions $f_{li}(\ )$ and $f_{ki}(\ )$ and the constants τ_{li} and τ_{ki} need not be identical for all individuals. It can be assumed without loss of generality, however, that the fraction γ_{li} is equal to a constant γ_l, identical for all individuals. Any differences among individuals in the fraction of labor income subject to the nonproportional tax can be incorporated into the effective tax rate schedule $f_{li}(\ )$. The fraction γ_{ki} can similarly be assumed constant across individuals. It is also assumed that the proportional tax rate τ_i is equal to a constant τ which is identical for all individuals.

Given these assumptions, the marginal tax rates (MTR) on the income from labor and capital for individual i are

$$\text{MTR}_{li} = \frac{dt_i}{dy_{li}} = \tau + \tau_{li} + \gamma_l f'_{li}$$

$$\text{MTR}_{ki} = \frac{dt_i}{dy_{ki}} = \tau + \tau_{ki} + \gamma_k f'_{ki}$$

The marginal tax rates on the income from labor and capital for the entire economy are

$$\text{MTRK} = \frac{dR}{dY_L} \quad \text{and} \quad \text{MTRL} = \frac{dR}{dY_K}$$

where

$$Y_L = \sum_{i=1}^{N} y_{li} \quad \text{and} \quad Y_K = \sum_{i=1}^{N} y_{ki}$$

are economy-wide incomes from labor and capital, respectively,

$$R = \sum_{i=1}^{N} t_i$$

is total government tax revenue, and N is the number of taxpayers. Solving for MTRK in terms of the MTR_{ki} gives

$$\text{MTRK} = \frac{dR}{dY_K} = \frac{d \sum_{i=1}^{N} t_i}{dY_K}$$

$$= \sum_{i=1}^{N} \frac{dt_i}{dY_K}$$

$$= \sum_{i=1}^{N} \frac{dt_i}{dy_{ki}} \frac{dy_{ki}}{dY_K} = \sum_{i=1}^{N} \text{MTR}_{ki} \frac{dy_{ki}}{dY_K}$$

The assumption that the personal distribution of each additional dollar of capital income in the economy is the same as the personal distribution of existing capital income means that

$$\frac{dy_{ki}}{dY_K} = \frac{y_{ki}}{Y_K} = w_{ki}$$

so that

$$\sum_{i=1}^{N} w_{ki} = 1$$

Then

$$\text{MTRK} = \sum_{i=1}^{N} w_{ki}(\tau + \tau_{ki} + \gamma_k f'_{ki}) = T + TK + \gamma_k \sum_{i=1}^{N} w_{ki} f'_{ki} \qquad (2)$$

Here

$$T = \sum_{i=1}^{N} w_{ki}\tau = \tau \sum_{i=1}^{N} w_{ki} = \tau$$

is just total receipts from proportional taxes which are neither labor- nor capital-specific expressed as a ratio to total income ($Y_L + Y_K$). In addition,

$$TK = \sum_{i=1}^{N} w_{ki}\tau_{ki}$$

is the ratio of total receipts from capital-specific proportional taxes to income from capital, Y_K. A similar formula can be derived for MTRL:

$$MTRL = T + TL + \gamma_l \sum_{i=1}^{N} w_{li} f'_{li} \qquad (3)$$

where

$$TL = \sum_{i=1}^{N} w_{li} \tau_{li}$$

is the ratio of total receipts from labor-specific proportional taxes to total income, Y_L.

MTRL will in general differ from MTRK for several reasons:

1. Labor income and capital income may be subject to different proportional tax rates ($TL \neq TK$).

2. Different fractions of the two types of income may be subject to the nonproportional tax ($\gamma_l \neq \gamma_k$).

3. The personal distribution of labor income subject to the nonproportional tax may be different from that for capital income ($w_{li} \neq w_{ki}$).

4. The nonproportional tax rate schedules may be different for the two types of income ($f'_{li} \neq f'_{ki}$).

5. RELATION OF HYPOTHETICAL TAX STRUCTURE TO AVAILABLE DATA

The nonproportional tax on income from capital is identified with the federal personal income tax. The nonproportional tax on labor income is identified with the federal personal income and Social Security taxes.

All other taxes are taken to be proportional to income. For some taxes, this assumption may be reasonably accurate. For example, sales taxes, which are one of the larger of the remaining taxes, are proportional to expenditure. Property taxes, another of the most important taxes, are proportional to property values, which are in turn roughly proportional to the income from the property. Corporate income taxes are roughly proportional to corporate income and apply uniformly on a per share basis to all shareholders, rather than varying among shareholders on the basis of the shareholders's income. For other taxes, such as state and local income taxes (which are small relative to the three taxes discussed above), the assumption may be less reasonable. It must nevertheless be made, since the only readily available data on these taxes are total tax receipts.

The tax schedule represented by $f_{ki}(\ )$ is taken to be the effective federal personal income tax schedule, after taking into account deductions, exemptions, and credits, rather than the schedule listed in the tax codes. An attempt was made to measure this schedule by using data on actual income and tax payments gathered from individual tax returns and reported in the *Statistics of Income*.[2] Since the *Statistics of Income* gives only aggregate data for adjusted gross income classes, all individuals within an income class were assumed to be homogeneous. The subscript i now denotes income class rather than individual.

The marginal federal income tax rates f'_{ki} are computed as follows: let

R_i = total personal income tax liability of members of income class i,

Y_i = total income subject to personal income tax of members of income class i and

N_i = number of returns in income class i.

Then

$$f'_{ki} = \frac{(R_i/N_i) - (R_{i-1}/N_{i-1})}{(Y_i/N_i) - (Y_{i-1}/N_{i-1})}$$

The marginal nonproportional tax rates on labor income, f'_{li}, are obtained by adding the appropriate marginal Social Security tax rate to the marginal federal personal income tax rate applicable to income from capital, f'_{ki}. For adjusted gross income classes for which wage and salary income per return is less than the Social Security wage base, the marginal Social Security tax rate is taken to be equal to the average rate and is calculated as

$$\text{SST} = 2\left(\frac{V_1}{V_3}\right)\left(\frac{\text{SSE}}{1 + \text{SSE}}\right) + \left(\frac{V_2}{V_3}\right)\text{SSS} \qquad (4)$$

where

SST is the effective Social Security tax rate,

SSE the Social Security tax rate applicable to both the employee and the employer,

SSS the Social Security tax rate applicable to the self-employed,

V_1 the total number of employees contributing to the Social Security system during the year,

---

[2] The practice of taking weighted averages of marginal tax rates was also used by Wright (1969). Wright considered only the federal personal income tax in his calculations, and he took the marginal tax rate of each income bracket to be that listed in the tax code. To represent the marginal tax rate on income from capital, Wright took two weighted averages of these legislated rates. One average took the weight on the tax rate for each income bracket to be interest income accruing to people in that bracket as a fraction of total interest income. The other used similar weights constructed from dividend incomes. Wright found that changes in the after-tax interest rate had a significant negative substitution effect on consumption.

V_2 the total number of self-employed contributing to the Social Security system during the year, and

V_3 equals V_2 plus the larger of V_1 or average civilian employment during the year.

Equation (4) merely expresses the employer–employee tax rate as a rate on gross-of-tax wages and takes a weighted average of the resulting number and the tax rate on the self-employed. During the early years of Social Security, a substantial fraction of employees were not covered by the system, and hence (V_1/V_3) was substantially less than unity. The self-employed were exempt altogether. That exemption ended in 1951. In addition, coverage was gradually extended to a larger number of employees, until by 1957 the total number of employees contributing to the system during each year exceeded average civilian employment for the year, and the weights (V_1/V_3) and (V_2/V_3) summed to unity. This extension of coverage is a major factor in the upward drift of the effective Social Security tax rate over time. For adjusted gross income classes with labor income per return greater than the Social Security wage base, the marginal Social Security tax rate is taken to be zero, and hence f'_{li} is equal to f'_{ki}.[3]

TABLE 1

Classification of Proportional Taxes[a]

General taxes		Taxes specific to capital	
Federal	State and local	Federal	State and local
Personal taxes	Personal taxes	Corporate profits	Personal taxes
Estate and gift taxes	Income taxes	taxes	Property taxes
Indirect business taxes	Death and gift taxes		Corporate profits
	Motor vehicle		taxes
	licenses		Indirect business
	Other taxes		taxes
	Indirect business taxes		Property taxes
	Sales taxes		
	Motor vehicle licenses		
	Other taxes		

[a] General taxes are used in computing the proportional tax rate T and taxes specific to capital are used in computing the proportional tax rate TK.

[3] For the first income class, j, for which labor income per return exceeds the wage base, the marginal Social Security tax rate is taken to be a fraction of SST. The numerator of this fraction is the difference between the wage base and labor income per return in income class $j - 1$. The denominator is the difference between labor income per return in income class j and that in class $j - 1$.

The proportional taxes are categorized in Table 1. Some are assumed to apply generally to all income and some are assumed to be specific to capital. No proportional taxes specific to labor were found.

6. SOME REMAINING ISSUES

Before proceeding further with the tax rate calculations, it is necessary to resolve certain remaining issues. These issues concern

1. the treatment of income which is not readily attributable to either capital or labor,
2. the income base used—either national income or net national product—and
3. whether net capital gains are included in that portion of capital income subject to the personal income tax.

6.1. Treatment of Miscellaneous Income

The various types of income reported in the NIPA and the *Statistics of Income* were classified as either labor income, capital income, or miscellaneous income.[4] The classification is contained in Table 2.

The items classified as miscellaneous consist of labor income and income from capital in proportions that are far from obvious. The problem of allocating miscellaneous income between labor and capital was "solved" by computing different tax rate series under each of two extreme assumptions. Miscellaneous income was treated as pure labor income under one assumption and as pure capital income under the alternative assumption. Only these two polar cases were considered, and there seems no overwhelming reason for preferring one to the other. As will be seen below, the results of the calculations are not very sensitive to the treatment of miscellaneous income.

---

[4] Income from capital includes gross rather than net corporate profits, since the corporate profits tax rate applicable to a firm is in general positive if its profits are positive and zero otherwise. It is desired to measure TK in such a way that it is affected by changes in the positive component of the effective corporate tax schedule, which suggests including gross corporate profits in income from capital. If net corporate profits were used instead, TK would rise with a decrease in the difference between gross corporate profits and coporate losses, even if the positive component of the corporate tax schedule remained unchanged. This would induce a spurious negative association between MTRK and many broad measures of economic activity and could lead to incorrect inferences concerning relationships between the two. In particular, the resulting bias would be in the direction of overstating any apparent deterrent effect of tax rates on economic activity. Empirical work performed using both the tax rate series reported here and earlier series computed without this correction suggests that the bias could be severe. I am indebted to Paul Evans for pointing out the potential seriousness of this source of error.

TABLE 2

Classification of Income

National income accounts	Statistics of income
Labor income	Labor income
Compensation of employees	Wages and salaries
Capital income	Capital income
Rental income of persons	Dividends
Corporate profits with inventory valuation	Interest
and capital consumption adjustments	Rents
Net interest	Royalties
	Estates and trusts
	Fiduciary
	Capital gains[a]
Miscellaneous income	Miscellaneous income
Business and professional	Business and professional
Farm	Partnership
	Farm
	Annuities
	Small business corporations
	Other

[a] In some calculations. See the discussion in Section 6.

6.2. Income Base

A tax rate is merely a ratio of tax liability to income, either on average or at the margin. The tax rate thus depends on the income base chosen. Since it was desired to calculate general, economy-wide tax rates, an attempt was made to include all taxes in the numerator and to use a comprehensive measure of national income in the denominator. Initially, two such measures seemed reasonable, national income (NI) and net national product (NNP). NI measures national income (product) at factor cost, whereas NNP measures it at market prices. The approximate relation between the two is

$$NNP = NI + IBT$$

where IBT denotes indirect business taxes.

Two procedures were used to deal with the income base. The first excluded IBT from both the income base and proportional taxes (NI basis), and the second included them in both (NNP basis). In going from the NI basis to the NNP basis, indirect business taxes must be allocated to capital and labor. This was done in two steps. First, general indirect business taxes were allocated between labor and capital in proportion to total national income attributable to labor and capital. Then, indirect business taxes attributable to capital were allocated to capital. The choice of income base affects only the proportional tax rates T, TL, and TK and the fractions γ_l and γ_k. It does

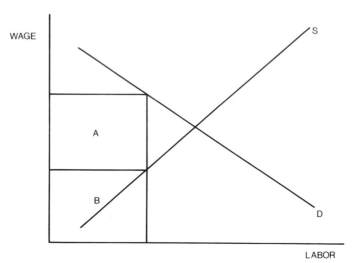

Figure 1. Alternative methods of treating indirect business taxes in computing effective tax rates.

not affect the weights w_{li} and w_{ki} or the marginal personal income tax rates f'_{li} and f'_{ki}.

The NI basis, as defined here, seems less sensible than the NNP basis, and it definitely understates the size of the wedge which taxes drive between gross- and net-of-tax values. To see this, assume there is only one factor of production, say labor, which is paid for working in the market sector. The wage rate is denominated in terms of market goods. Assume that the only taxes in the economy are indirect business taxes. The market for labor is shown in Fig. 1.

In Fig. 1, national income is given by area B, indirect business taxes by area A, and NNP by A + B. According to the NNP basis, the size of the wedge is given by A/(A + B), whereas according to the NI basis, the wedge is zero.

The ratio A/B would seem to have some meaning, so using this as the NI basis might be worthwhile. One possibly unappealing feature of this revised NI method is that taxes and after-tax income sum to more than national income. Thus, it is theoretically possible for the wedge to be greater than 100 percent. For these reasons, the NNP basis seems to provide the best measure of the size of the wedge and is used in the calculations reported below.

6.3. Treatment of Capital Gains

Excluding net capital gains from income subject to the personal income tax will not affect total national income attributable to either capital or labor.

It will merely reduce capital income subject to the personal income tax (assuming total net capital gains are positive). In addition, it will alter the weights γ_k and w_{ki} and the computed marginal nonproportional tax rates f'_{li} and f'_{ki}, while leaving the proportional tax rates T, TL, and TK unaffected.

Capital gains can result from at least three causes:

1. inflation,
2. relative price changes,
3. appreciation of equity securities due to retention of earnings by firms.

Inflation-induced capital gains do not constitute real income and should be excluded. Relative price changes result in offsetting capital gains and losses. Unless such changes are biased so as to benefit some income classes at the expense of others, net capital gains of the various income classes should not be greatly affected by price fluctuations of this sort. The third type of capital gain does reflect real income, but the income need not be earned in the year that the capital gains are realized. This timing problem does not shift national income from one year to another, however.

If the effects of relative price changes do net approximately to zero, and if one makes the assumption that capital gains of the third type are more important than those induced by inflation during most of the sample period, then it seems preferable to include net capital gains in income subject to the personal income tax. Nevertheless, since the case for including capital gains is far from overwhelming, separate tax rate series were calculated with capital gains excluded from income subject to the personal income tax.

7. ALTERNATIVE TAX RATE SERIES

The above discussion thus suggests four methods of calculating marginal tax rates, each differing in its treatment of miscellaneous income and capital gains. The four methods of calculation are summarized in Table 3. The results of these calculations are presented in Tables 4 and 5.

TABLE 3

Alternative Methods of Calculating
Weighted-Average Marginal Tax Rates

Method	Capital gains	Miscellaneous income attributed to
1	Included	Labor
2	Included	Capital
3	Excluded	Labor
4	Excluded	Capital

TABLE 4

Weighted-Average Marginal Tax Rates on Income from Labor

Year	MTRL1	MTRL2	MTRL3	MTRL4	Year	MTRL1	MTRL2	MTRL3	MTRL4
1929	3.51	3.34	3.88	3.55	1953	20.83	20.78	21.12	21.01
1930	3.60	3.54	3.63	3.57	1954	19.20	19.13	19.66	19.48
1931	3.82	3.79	3.81	3.78	1955	19.76	19.66	20.38	20.14
1932	4.89	4.85	4.91	4.86	1956	20.31	20.08	20.83	20.48
1933	6.79	6.63	6.90	6.70	1957	22.19	22.16	22.62	22.53
1934	7.47	7.33	7.49	7.34	1958	21.47	21.39	21.90	21.72
1935	7.44	7.29	7.51	7.34	1959	22.34	22.15	22.96	22.64
1936	8.03	7.75	8.16	7.86	1960	22.84	22.75	23.33	23.15
1937	8.06	7.92	8.10	7.95	1961	23.05	22.86	23.79	23.44
1938	8.25	8.13	8.30	8.16	1962	23.14	22.86	23.68	23.30
1939	8.25	8.09	8.28	8.12	1963	23.33	23.06	23.87	23.49
1940	9.05	8.70	9.06	8.71	1964	22.08	21.71	22.64	22.13
1941	11.78	11.21	11.76	11.18	1965	22.20	21.84	22.84	22.31
1942	15.37	14.65	15.45	14.69	1966	21.70	21.34	22.25	21.75
1943	17.83	16.80	18.09	16.93	1967	22.12	21.79	22.92	22.41
1944	18.84	17.94	19.16	18.14	1968	24.20	23.71	25.27	24.51
1945	19.71	18.52	20.39	18.92	1969	25.02	24.71	25.77	25.28
1946	18.79	17.63	19.55	18.15	1970	24.79	24.30	25.21	24.62
1947	19.25	18.47	19.71	18.81	1971	23.34	23.11	23.86	23.50
1948	16.13	15.77	16.48	16.04	1972	25.06	24.71	25.82	25.32
1949	16.15	15.91	16.39	16.10	1973	25.81	25.54	26.44	26.05
1950	17.95	17.40	18.74	17.95	1974	27.24	26.82	27.70	27.20
1951	19.69	19.54	20.14	19.86	1975	27.35	26.90	27.78	27.26
1952	20.50	20.47	20.86	20.74					

TABLE 5

Weighted-Average Marginal Tax Rates on Income from Capital

Year	MTRK1	MTRK2	MTRK3	MTRK4	Year	MTRK1	MTRK2	MTRK3	MTRK4
1929	29.45	20.22	29.51	20.59	1953	59.92	43.87	59.42	43.82
1930	27.76	20.03	27.98	20.19	1954	54.93	40.78	54.29	40.77
1931	28.59	21.16	28.74	21.26	1955	55.38	42.32	54.58	42.31
1932	33.12	26.32	33.25	26.42	1956	56.52	43.36	55.80	43.32
1933	41.08	31.09	41.13	31.21	1957	55.23	42.80	54.65	42.73
1934	41.00	29.78	40.98	29.78	1958	54.00	41.41	53.27	41.31
1935	41.44	27.86	41.37	27.85	1959	54.29	43.28	53.37	43.17
1936	46.20	31.37	46.01	31.36	1960	54.89	44.08	54.29	44.03
1937	44.43	28.96	44.53	29.05	1961	54.55	43.96	53.62	43.92
1938	41.36	28.13	42.17	28.64	1962	51.45	42.68	50.93	42.71
1939	42.55	28.99	42.87	29.19	1963	51.69	43.29	51.07	43.24
1940	45.12	31.91	45.34	32.05	1964	49.80	42.13	49.02	42.02
1941	55.81	39.13	56.06	39.29	1965	48.91	41.54	47.97	41.41
1942	59.96	41.76	59.93	41.85	1966	48.39	41.19	47.68	41.12
1943	61.99	43.95	61.68	44.10	1967	49.25	41.99	48.20	41.86
1944	59.96	42.70	59.35	42.74	1968	53.60	46.21	52.22	46.11
1945	62.89	43.43	61.50	43.61	1969	53.76	46.16	52.87	46.15
1946	61.71	40.09	60.42	40.34	1970	51.55	45.10	50.86	44.97
1947	59.21	40.65	58.45	40.71	1971	51.15	44.13	50.32	43.95
1948	52.90	35.79	52.35	35.80	1972	51.41	44.99	50.23	44.68
1949	49.92	34.99	49.72	35.07	1973	52.51	45.05	51.40	44.73
1950	62.03	43.99	62.05	44.77	1974	53.43	47.06	52.52	46.74
1951	64.05	45.21	63.41	45.24	1975	49.31	44.47	48.47	44.12
1952	60.23	43.07	59.59	43.03					

Table 6 shows a correlation matrix of the eight marginal tax rates. Since all the tax rates appear to have a common upward trend, the high correlations among them are probably the result of this common trend. Table 7 shows a correlation matrix of the first differences of the tax rates. The relevant correlations are in general still quite high. The first differences of the labor income tax rate computed by one method are very highly correlated with those computed by other methods, and the same situation holds for the capital income tax rates. The correlations of the first differences of the labor and capital income tax rates computed by any one method are between 0.66 and 0.72.

For reasons outlined above, tax rates which include capital gains in income subject to the personal income tax seem preferable to those which do not. Methods 1 and 2 meet this criterion and differ only as to whether miscellaneous income is attributed to capital or to labor. There seems little reason to prefer one of these two methods over the other. Furthermore, it is unlikely that the choice between method 1 and method 2 will materially affect the conclusions drawn from any statistical analysis performed using these tax rates. As all of the estimated tax rates exhibit mean nonstationarity, the differenced series should probably be used in statistical work. Since the correlation between the first differences of the labor income tax rates computed by methods 1 and 2 is 0.999 and the correlation between the first differences of the two capital income tax rates is 0.929, there is little reason to believe that any empirical results will be very greatly affected by the choice. Not only are the year-to year movements in the alternative tax rate series very similar, as evidenced by these high correlations, but the levels of the labor income tax rate computed by one method are very close to the levels computed by the other methods. The same cannot be said of the capital income tax rates, however. The level of the capital income tax rate is higher according to methods 1 and 3, which attribute miscellaneous income to labor, than according to methods 2 and 4, which attribute miscellaneous income to capital.

The reason for this phenomenon is that the proportional tax rate TK is substantially higher according to methods 1 and 3 than according to methods 2 and 4. TK is the capital-specific proportional tax receipts listed in Table 1 expressed as a fraction of income from capital. The numerator of this fraction is the same for all methods of calculating the tax rates. The denominator is larger, however, and the tax rate is correspondingly smaller when miscellaneous income is attributed to capital. Since no labor-specific proportional taxes were found, the allocation of miscellaneous income has no such effect on the labor income tax rates. This allocation merely affects the weights w_{li} used in constructing the weighted-average nonproportional tax rate on labor income. The fact that MTRL1 is slightly greater than MTRL2 (and MTRL3 is greater than MTRL4) indicates that, on average, miscellaneous income accrues to people in somewhat higher tax brackets

TABLE 6

Correlation Matrix of Tax Rates

	MTRL1	MTRL2	MTRL3	MTRL4	MTRK1	MTRK2	MTRK3	MTRK4
MTRL1	1.000	—	—	—	—	—	—	—
MTRL2	0.999	1.000	—	—	—	—	—	—
MTRL3	1.000	0.999	1.000	—	—	—	—	—
MTRL4	0.999	1.000	0.999	1.000	—	—	—	—
MTRK1	0.704	0.689	0.702	0.687	1.000	—	—	—
MTRK2	0.944	0.938	0.943	0.937	0.862	1.000	—	—
MTRK3	0.677	0.662	0.675	0.660	0.999	0.845	1.000	—
MTRK4	0.940	0.933	0.939	0.932	0.869	1.000	0.853	1.00

TABLE 7

Correlation Matrix of First Differences of Tax Rates

	ΔMTRL1	ΔMTRL2	ΔMTRL3	ΔMTRL4	ΔMTRK1	ΔMTRK2	ΔMTRK3	ΔMTRK4
ΔMTRL1	1.000	—	—	—	—	—	—	—
ΔMTRL2	0.991	1.000	—	—	—	—	—	—
ΔMTRL3	0.989	0.968	1.000	—	—	—	—	—
ΔMTRL4	0.992	0.994	0.986	1.000	—	—	—	—
ΔMTRK1	0.669	0.624	0.708	0.655	1.000	—	—	—
ΔMTRK2	0.706	0.664	0.734	0.689	0.929	1.000	—	—
ΔMTRK3	0.663	0.619	0.697	0.647	0.997	0.933	1.000	—
ΔMTRK4	0.693	0.647	0.726	0.675	0.929	0.998	0.935	1.000

than does labor income. This effect is small, however, since the difference between MTRL1 and MTRL2 is generally less than half a percentage point, except during and immediately after World War II. It thus appears that miscellaneous income is taxed at the personal level in a manner quite similar to labor income.

One curious fact apparent from Tables 6 and 7 is that the correlation between ΔMTRK1 and ΔMTRK2 is higher than that between MTRK1 and MTRK2, and similarly for the levels and first differences of MTRK3 and MTRK4. Also, the levels of the capital income tax rates computed by methods 2 and 4 are more highly correlated with the labor income tax rates than with MTRK1 and MTRK3. This curiosity has a simple explanation. Since miscellaneous income is becoming less important over time relative to other types of income, the difference between, for example, MTRK1 and MTRK2 is also diminishing over time. This imparts a sharper upward trend to the latter than to the former. Both of these series increased dramatically between 1929 and 1951. Since then, MTRK2 has increased slightly and has remained above its mean value for the 47-year sample of 38.78. MTRK1, on the other hand, has declined from its 1951 peak. As a result of this decline, MTRK1 has been below its mean of 50.82 during 5 of the 15 years between 1961 and 1975, and has barely been above the mean in 5 other years. This has served to reduce the computed correlation between MTRK1 and MTRK2. The labor income tax rates have exhibited a positive trend over the entire sample period and are thus highly correlated with MTRK2. Because of the common trends, however, these correlations are probably spurious in the sense discussed by Granger and Newbold (1974). The first differences of MTRK2 are more highly correlated with ΔMTRK1 than with the first differences of the labor income tax rates.

Since miscellaneous income appears to be taxed at the personal level in a manner so similar to labor income, and since most of the capital-specific nonproportional taxes listed in Table 1 do not apply to miscellaneous income, it is probably more appropriate to attribute such income to labor than to capital when discussing the levels of the tax rate series. Consequently, only the series computed by method 1 will be discussed in the remainder of the paper. Since most of the income to which MTRK1 applies derives from residential and corporate capital, this tax rate can be interpreted as a weighted average of the rates applicable to those two types of income.

8. BEHAVIOR OF TAX RATES OVER TIME

It is worthwhile to examine the behavior over time of the tax rate series and their components to see whether this behavior is broadly consistent with the major changes in tax policy which occurred during the sample period.

Figure 2 is a time-series plot of MTRK1 and MTRL1 (henceforth referred to as MTRK and MTRL, respectively). MTRK is greater than MTRL throughout the entire 47-year period. The two series follow similar patterns from 1929 until the early 1950s. Both exhibit noticeable upward movements during the 1930s, a period of increasing federal income tax rates, and reach unprecedented levels during World War II. They decline after the war, but not to prewar levels, and then rise sharply again during the Korean conflict.

Since the early 1950s, the two tax rates have moved much less closely together. MTRL has followed an irregular upward trend whose only major interruption occurred in the years immediately following the federal income tax rate cuts of 1964. This hiatus ended with the Vietnam surcharge, which was in effect from 1969 to 1970. The steady rise in MTRL from 1971 until 1975 appears to be largely the result of increased Social Security taxes and of taxpayers being pushed into higher nominal income brackets by inflation rather than by any readily identifiable change in statutory personal income tax rates.

In contrast to this behavior, MTRK exhibited an overall downward movement from the early 1950s until the impositon of the Vietnam surcharge in 1968. This downward trend was aided by the 1964 income tax cuts but was well under way before then. The two largest yearly decreases in MTRK during

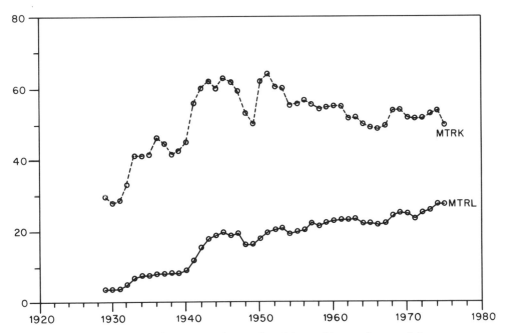

Figure 2. Marginal tax rates on income from labor and income from capital.

this entire period occurred in 1954, when accelerated depreciation was first permitted for tax purposes, and in 1962, when the federal investment tax credit was enacted and new service lives were adopted for calculating depreciation.[5]

More insight into the behavior of MTRL and MTRK can be gained by examining the components of each tax rate. A common component of both series is the general proportional tax rate T. A second component of MTRK is the capital-specific proportional tax rate TK The analogous quantity TL is equal to zero, since no labor-specific proportional tax rates were identified. The third component of MTRK is the contribution of the federal personal income tax to the overall tax rate on income from capital, defined as

$$\text{PCK} = \gamma_k \sum_{i=1}^{N} w_{ki} f'_{ki}$$

This is merely the third term in Eq. (2). A similar designation could be made for the third term in Eq. (3), which defines MTRL. This term, however, includes the contributions to MTRL of both the federal personal income tax and the Social Security tax. These two contributions may be isolated by noting that the marginal federal personal income tax rate applicable to labor income is equal to that applicable to income from capital, f'_{ki} and f'_{li} differing only by the relevant marginal Social Security tax rate. The contribution of the federal personal income tax to the overall tax rate on labor income is thus defined as

$$\text{PCL} = \gamma_l \sum_{i=1}^{N} w_{li} f'_{ki}$$

The contribution of the Social Security tax is defined as

$$\text{SSC} = \gamma_l \sum_{i=1}^{N} w_{li} \text{SST}_i$$

where SST_i is equal to the constant SST for adjusted gross income classes with labor income per return less than the Social Security wage base and is equal to zero otherwise.

Figure 3 shows MTRL as the sum of its components, which are listed in Table 8. By far the largest component is PCL, although SSC has become increasingly important since the late 1950s and is the source of roughly half of the increase in MTRL from that time until 1975. These increases in the contribution of Social Security to the tax rate on labor income at the margin are due to increases in both the Social Security tax rate and the wage base. In fact, the latter is, if anything, a more important factor than the former.

---

[5] The investment tax credit did not take effect until 1963.

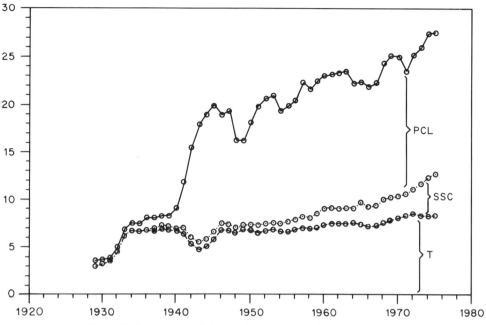

Figure 3. Components of the marginal tax rate on income from labor.

This can be seen by noting that the largest single year-to-year increase in SSC occurred between 1964 and 1965, a period during which the employer–employee tax rate was constant but the wage base was increased from \$4,800 to \$6,600.

The behavior of the proportional tax rate T is somewhat unusual and deserves comment. This rate is made up almost entirely of state and local taxes, the largest of these being sales taxes. After rising sharply in the early 1930s, T has remained fairly stable except for a noticeable decrease during World War II. Part of this wartime decline might be due to actual reductions in state and local tax rates. It is almost certain, however, that this decrease in T was at least in part induced by federal tax policy. Assume for the moment that T consists entirely of sales taxes and that taxable sales are proportional to disposable income. If the federal government were suddenly to institute large increases in personal and corporate income tax rates, as it did during the war, this would reduce disposable income, and hence sales and sales taxes, as fractions of national product. It seems quite likely that at least part of the reduction in T during World War II can be attributed to such a pre-emption of the tax base by the federal government.

Figure 4 shows **MTRK** as the sum of its components, which are listed in Table 9. The largest of these, TK, is made up entirely of property and

TABLE 8

Components of the Marginal Tax Rate on Income from Labor

Year	T	SSC	PCL	MTRL	Year	T	SSC	PCL	MTRL
1929	2.96	0.00	0.55	3.51	1953	6.81	0.65	13.37	20.83
1930	3.20	0.00	0.41	3.60	1954	6.60	0.78	11.82	19.20
1931	3.54	0.00	0.28	3.82	1955	6.64	1.00	12.12	19.76
1932	4.39	0.00	0.51	4.89	1956	6.88	0.92	12.51	20.31
1933	6.08	0.00	0.71	6.79	1957	6.96	1.17	14.06	22.19
1934	6.71	0.00	0.76	7.47	1958	6.89	1.13	13.45	21.47
1935	6.60	0.00	0.85	7.44	1959	7.02	1.47	13.85	22.34
1936	6.78	0.00	1.25	8.03	1960	7.28	1.65	13.91	22.84
1937	6.62	0.25	1.19	8.06	1961	7.44	1.61	14.00	23.05
1938	6.96	0.27	1.03	8.25	1962	7.42	1.52	14.20	23.14
1939	6.77	0.32	1.16	8.25	1963	7.44	1.63	14.26	23.33
1940	6.62	0.29	2.15	9.05	1964	7.52	1.49	13.07	22.08
1941	6.30	0.63	4.85	11.78	1965	7.36	2.29	12.55	22.20
1942	5.26	0.71	9.40	15.37	1966	7.12	2.08	12.50	21.70
1943	4.71	0.78	12.34	17.83	1967	7.20	2.02	12.90	22.12
1944	5.06	0.71	13.07	18.84	1968	7.54	2.42	14.24	24.20
1945	5.81	0.72	13.19	19.71	1969	7.81	2.32	14.89	25.02
1946	6.83	0.67	11.30	18.79	1970	8.01	2.29	14.49	24.79
1947	6.73	0.65	11.86	19.25	1971	8.27	2.24	12.84	23.34
1948	6.50	0.43	9.19	16.13	1972	8.47	2.54	14.06	25.06
1949	6.84	0.42	8.88	16.15	1973	8.24	3.27	14.30	25.81
1950	6.78	0.56	10.61	17.95	1974	8.21	4.02	15.01	27.24
1951	6.42	0.80	12.47	19.69	1975	8.27	4.28	14.79	27.35
1952	6.71	0.70	13.10	20.50					

corporate profits taxes. Its movement largely determines that of MTRK. The contribution of the federal personal income tax, PCK, is fairly stable (at roughly between 6 and 8 percentage points) during the postwar period.

Miller and Scholes (1978) have advanced the argument that the federal personal income tax is evolving into a pure consumption tax. If this were the case, one would expect to see the tax on income from capital become less important relative to that on income from labor. As was noted above, Fig. 2 provides some evidence that this has in fact occurred since the early 1950s. Since the Miller–Scholes hypothesis is expressed in terms of the federal personal income tax, however, more insight into its applicability can be gained by examining the contribution of this tax to MTRL and MTRK. Figure 5, a time-series plot of PCL and PCK, provides even more striking evidence in support of Miller and Scholes than did Fig. 2. While PCK is larger than PCL before World War II, the reverse is true thereafter. Furthermore, the difference between PCL and PCK becomes quite large by 1951 and seems to grow during the remainder of the sample period.

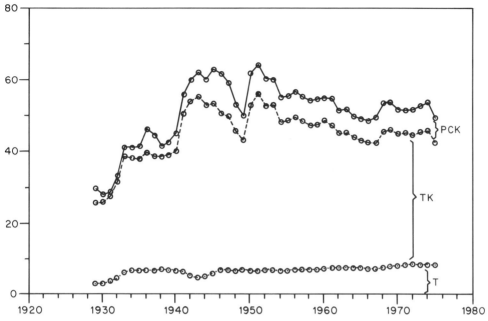

Figure 4. Components of the marginal tax rate on income from capital.

It should be noted that the behavior of PCL and PCK is determined not only by the weighted-average federal personal income tax rates, but also by the fractions (γ_l and γ_k) of labor and capital income subject to that tax. It is thus possible that the pattern in Fig. 5 is due entirely to movements in γ_l and γ_k. To examine this question, it is necessary to isolate movements in PCL and PCK due to γ_l and γ_k from those due to the weighted-average personal income tax rates on labor and capital themselves. These rates are defined as

$$\text{PTL} \equiv \sum_{i=1}^{N} w_{li} f'_{ki}$$

and

$$\text{PTK} \equiv \sum_{i=1}^{N} w_{ki} f'_{ki}$$

respectively.

Figure 6 is a time-series plot of γ_l and γ_k, which are listed in Table 10. The most striking feature of this graph is the sharp increase in γ_l over time and the relative constancy of γ_k. Starting from levels comparable to γ_k, γ_l rose dramatically during World War II and has continued to increase since then,

TABLE 9

Components of the Marginal Tax Rate on Income from Capital

Year	T	TK	PCK	MTRK	Year	T	TK	PCK	MTRK
1929	2.96	22.64	3.85	29.45	1953	6.81	46.17	6.94	59.92
1930	3.20	22.64	1.91	27.76	1954	6.60	41.40	6.93	54.93
1931	3.54	23.90	1.14	28.59	1955	6.64	41.86	6.88	55.38
1932	4.39	27.13	1.61	33.12	1956	6.88	42.52	7.12	56.52
1933	6.08	32.46	2.53	41.08	1957	6.96	41.40	6.87	55.23
1934	6.71	31.35	2.94	41.00	1958	6.89	40.19	6.91	54.00
1935	6.60	31.29	3.55	41.44	1959	7.02	40.34	6.93	54.29
1936	6.78	32.81	6.60	46.20	1960	7.28	41.31	6.30	54.89
1937	6.62	32.04	5.77	44.43	1961	7.44	39.82	7.29	54.55
1938	6.96	31.49	2.91	41.36	1962	7.42	37.67	6.36	51.45
1939	6.77	32.04	3.75	42.55	1963	7.44	37.75	6.50	51.69
1940	6.62	33.57	4.94	45.12	1964	7.52	36.36	5.92	49.80
1941	6.30	44.30	5.21	55.81	1965	7.36	35.71	5.84	48.91
1942	5.26	48.71	6.00	59.96	1966	7.12	35.47	5.80	48.39
1943	4.71	50.57	6.71	61.99	1967	7.20	35.24	6.82	49.25
1944	5.06	47.83	7.07	59.96	1968	7.54	37.98	8.09	53.60
1945	5.81	47.56	9.52	62.89	1969	7.81	38.13	7.83	53.76
1946	6.83	43.88	11.00	61.71	1970	8.01	36.88	6.67	51.55
1947	6.73	43.11	9.37	59.21	1971	8.27	36.75	6.14	51.15
1948	6.50	39.16	7.23	52.90	1972	8.47	35.96	6.98	51.41
1949	6.84	36.20	6.88	49.92	1973	8.24	37.13	7.15	52.51
1950	6.78	46.04	9.21	62.03	1974	8.21	37.62	7.60	53.43
1951	6.42	49.62	8.01	64.05	1975	8.27	34.03	7.01	49.31
1952	6.71	45.80	7.72	60.23					

rising to a level of roughly 0.8 by 1975. During the entire postwar period, by contrast, γ_k remained at levels comparable to those of the 1930s, and was approximately 0.3 in 1975. It thus appears that part of the upward drift in PCL since 1950 may be due to a similar upward drift in γ_l. It also appears that there has been an upward drift in γ_k since the early 1950s that would tend to increase PCK.[6] Thus, the relative movements of PCL and PCK cannot be explained entirely in terms of γ_l and γ_k.

Figure 7 shows the behavior of the weighted-average personal tax rates PTL and PTK over time. These tax rates are listed in Table 11. PTK is

---

[6] It should be noted that while a decrease in γ_k tends to decrease PCK, it will not necessarily be associated with a decrease in MTRK. In fact, it may be the result of an increase in TK, and thus in MTRK. For example, if the government increases corporate income tax rates, TK will increase. However, since a smaller fraction of income from capital remains to be subjected to the personal income tax, γ_k will fall. The increase in γ_k since the early 1950s might well be due to the fall in TK during that period.

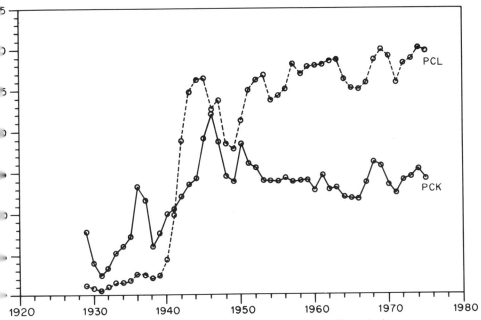

Figure 5. Contribution of the federal personal income tax to overall marginal tax rates.

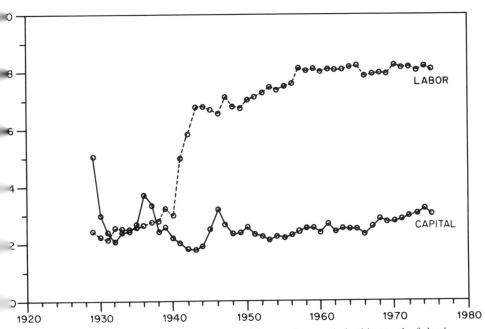

Figure 6. Fractions of income from labor and income from capital subject to the federal personal income tax.

TABLE 10

Fractions of Income Subject to Federal Personal Income Tax

Year	Labor	Capital	Year	Labor	Capital
1929	0.243	0.505	1953	0.745	0.211
1930	0.223	0.298	1954	0.735	0.225
1931	0.214	0.238	1955	0.748	0.220
1932	0.255	0.207	1956	0.757	0.231
1933	0.251	0.240	1957	0.809	0.242
1934	0.247	0.241	1958	0.801	0.253
1935	0.256	0.269	1959	0.808	0.252
1936	0.265	0.370	1960	0.799	0.236
1937	0.276	0.334	1961	0.806	0.267
1938	0.279	0.242	1962	0.804	0.241
1939	0.323	0.256	1963	0.805	0.253
1940	0.298	0.219	1964	0.817	0.248
1941	0.499	0.204	1965	0.817	0.250
1942	0.582	0.179	1966	0.785	0.231
1943	0.677	0.177	1967	0.790	0.262
1944	0.679	0.190	1968	0.793	0.284
1945	0.669	0.250	1969	0.791	0.275
1946	0.654	0.319	1970	0.819	0.277
1947	0.712	0.264	1971	0.811	0.284
1948	0.677	0.235	1972	0.814	0.293
1949	0.673	0.239	1973	0.802	0.304
1950	0.702	0.258	1974	0.814	0.319
1951	0.712	0.232	1975	0.805	0.301
1952	0.728	0.226			

greater than PTL in the early years of the sample, and the difference between the two generally increases until the end of World War II. Beginning in 1950, PTK follows a downward path, interrupted briefly by the Vietnam surcharge. During the same period PTL exhibits an irregular upward drift, until by 1975 it is, for the first time, greater than PTK. This figure again provides suggestive support for the Miller–Scholes hypothesis.

As a final check on the reasonableness of the computed tax rates, various components of these rates are compared with readily available summary measures of federal tax policy. Figure 8 is a time-series plot of PCL and the statutory minimum-bracket federal personal income tax rate, denoted $TMIN$. Figure 9 is a similar time series plot of PCK and $TMIN$. Even though the minimum-bracket rate provides a very incomplete summary of the entire federal personal income tax structure, it is striking how closely $TMIN$ tracks both PCL and PCK. Furthermore, the two most noticeable discrepancies can be explained in terms of rates applicable to higher brackets. One of these occurs during the Vietnam surcharge of 1968 to 1970. Another

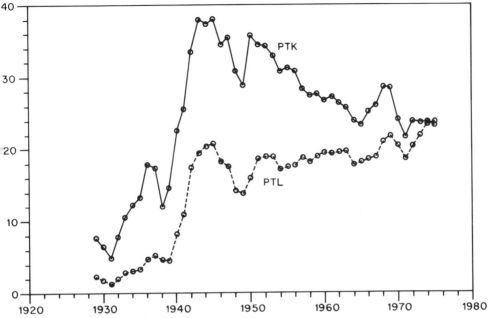

Figure 7. Federal personal income tax rates on income from labor and income from capital.

occurs during the mid-1930s, when the maximum-bracket rate rose from 25 to 79 percent even though the minimum-bracket rate remained roughly constant.

Figure 10 shows TK plotted along side the maximum-bracket federal corporate profits tax rate, denoted $TCORP$. The two move reasonably closely together until 1951 and again after the 1964 federal income tax cuts. The major discrepancy occurs between 1952 and 1963, during which period TK shows a steady downward movement while $TCORP$ is constant. As was noted above, however, this was the period when liberalized depreciation rules and the investment tax credit were instituted. Those modifications, together with the subsequent statutory rate reductions, give rise to the overall downward drift in TK over the last 25 years of the sample period. It thus appears that the Miller–Scholes hypothesis might be extended to include taxes other than the federal personal income tax.

In this connection, it is interesting to note that several recent studies have presented evidence that the corporate tax burden has decreased since the 1950s. Among these are Fama (1979), Holland and Myers (1981), and Gonedes (1981). Holland and Myers compute effective corporate tax rates using data on actual tax payments. They take the effective rate to be the ratio of total federal, state, and local profits tax payments to net operating income,

TABLE 11

Federal Personal Income and Social Security Tax Rates

Year	SST	PTL	PTK	Year	SST	PTL	PTK
1929	0.00	2.27	7.63	1953	2.74	18.83	32.87
1930	0.00	1.79	6.41	1954	3.61	17.14	30.76
1931	0.00	1.31	4.81	1955	3.69	17.55	31.29
1932	0.00	1.99	7.78	1956	3.72	17.74	30.84
1933	0.00	2.82	10.57	1957	4.28	18.82	28.41
1934	0.00	3.07	12.22	1958	4.29	18.20	27.34
1935	0.00	3.31	13.23	1959	4.73	18.96	27.53
1936	0.00	4.70	17.87	1960	5.67	19.47	26.68
1937	1.41	5.22	17.29	1961	5.67	19.37	27.26
1938	1.43	4.64	12.02	1962	5.89	19.55	26.35
1939	1.46	4.58	14.61	1963	6.77	19.75	25.73
1940	1.47	8.17	22.57	1964	6.78	17.83	23.91
1941	1.61	10.99	25.55	1965	6.83	18.17	23.32
1942	1.71	17.38	33.50	1966	7.85	18.58	25.15
1943	1.73	19.39	37.93	1967	8.20	18.89	26.04
1944	1.70	20.31	37.31	1968	8.21	21.00	28.49
1945	1.74	20.79	38.03	1969	9.04	21.75	28.50
1946	1.75	18.31	34.50	1970	9.04	20.50	24.08
1947	1.70	17.58	35.49	1971	9.76	18.59	21.58
1948	1.66	14.21	30.73	1972	9.76	20.40	23.81
1949	1.61	13.83	28.85	1973	10.89	21.92	23.55
1950	2.42	15.92	35.74	1974	10.89	23.38	23.84
1951	2.67	18.65	34.49	1975	10.89	23.70	23.26
1952	2.72	18.96	34.22				

defined as the sum of interest payments and before-tax profits with capital consumption and inventory valuation adjustments. Holland and Myers compute effective tax rates for manufacturing corporations and for all non-financial corporations for the years 1947–1978. Both tax rate series peak in the early 1950s, decline until the late 1960s, and rise somewhat thereafter. They do not in general, however, return to the levels of the 1950s.

Fama (1979) discusses a similar tax rate series for nonfinancial corporations, also computed using actual tax payments, for the period 1946–1977. He takes the effective tax rate to be the ratio of total federal, state, and local profits tax payments to net corporate cash flows, defined as the sum of monetary net interest payments, depreciation charges, and before-tax corporate profits. Gonedes computes an analogously defined tax rate series for all corporations.

The tax rates estimated by Fama and Gonedes are lower than those estimated by Holland and Myers since net operating income is less than net corporate cash flows. However, the year-to-year movements in these tax

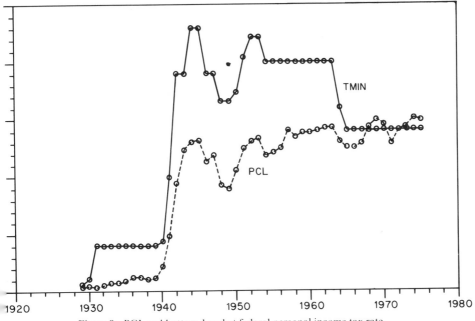

Figure 8. PCL and bottom-bracket federal personal income tax rate.

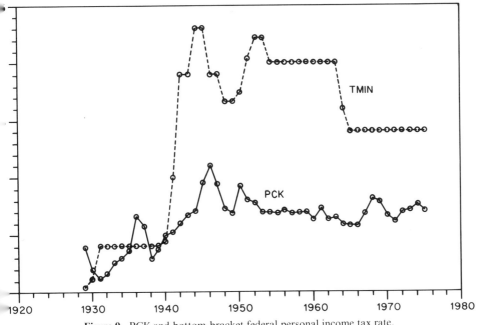

Figure 9. PCK and bottom-bracket federal personal income tax rate.

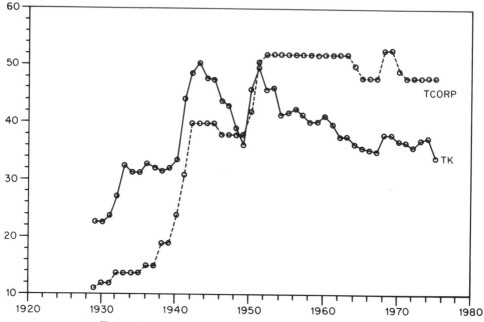

Figure 10. *TK* and top-bracket federal corporate income tax rate.

rates are quite similar to each other and to the year-to-year changes in the series *TK* reported above. Table 12 lists *TK*, the Fama and Gonedes series, the Holland and Myers series for nonfinancial corporations, and other tax rate series to be discussed shortly. As the table reveals, *TK* and the estimates of Holland and Myers and Fama all reach a postwar high in 1951, while the Gonedes series peaks in 1950. Following a sharp decline in 1954, the year accelerated depreciation was first permitted for tax purposes, *TK* and the Holland–Myers and Fama series exhibit a continued irregular decrease, reaching a trough in 1967 in the wake of the Kennedy tax cuts. From that point on, there is some discrepancy in the behavior of the various series. *TK* and the Holland–Myers series both generally remain above the 1967 level throughout the remainder of their respective sample periods. The Fama series, on the other hand, exhibits only a temporary upturn coincident with the Vietnam surcharge of the late 1960s. By 1970, it is below its 1967 value and remains there throughout the rest of the sample period. The Gonedes series behaves in a similar manner. All of the series (except that of Gonedes, which ends in 1974) exhibit a sharp drop in 1975. Although this is the final year of the sample for *TK*, the subsequent behavior of the other series indicates that this drop was a temporary phenomenon. The extraordinary sharpness of the drop in the Holland–Myers series in 1975 is due in part to the fact that this series had reached a relatively high level of 47.9 percent in 1974. All of these series, however, remain throughout the 1970s at levels below those of the 1950s.

The fact that the Fama and Gonedes series remain at such low levels during the 1970s, even when compared with those of the late 1960s, may appear somewhat surprising. The decade of the 1970s was a time when inflation was high by historical standards, and inflation has the effect of creating illusory inventory profits and understating true economic depreciation. These two factors result in an overstatement of real corporate profits and thus raise the effective tax rate on the true income of corporations. On the other hand, inflation raises nominal interest rates and increases the real tax shield associated with a given amount of real interest payments by corporations. This is because corporations can deduct for tax purposes the inflation premium as well as the real component of nominal interest payments. Fama and Gonedes interpret their series as evidence that the increased tax shield on interest payments, along with liberalized depreciation rules and the investment tax credit, have more than offset the tendency of inflation to increase effective corporate tax rates.

This contention is not universally shared, however. Feldstein and Summers (1979) argue that any apparent decline in the rate of taxation of the income from corporate capital in the 1970s is illusory and that effective tax rates on such income have in fact risen markedly since the late 1960s. They argue that the income from corporate-held capital is taxed not only at the corporate level, but also at the personal level, and that personal taxation of such income has increased more than enough to offset any decreases in rates of taxation at the corporate level.

Feldstein and Summers report estimates of the effective corporate tax rate for the period 1954–1977 which are similar to the estimates of Holland and Myers, Fama, and Gonedes. Like those estimates, the Feldstein–Summers series is computed from actual tax payments. Specifically, it is defined as the ratio of federal, state, and local corporate profits tax payments to a modified version of net operating income. The modification consists of deducting from net operating income as defined by Holland and Myers an amount equal to the inflation-induced reduction in the real value of certain nominal assets of the corporate sector. The nominal assets in question are liabilities of the government or of the corporations' customers. This series, shown in column 5 of Table 12, behaves in a manner quite similar to the series reported in columns 1–4. In particular, it reaches a trough in 1967 and generally remains in the 1970s at levels below those prevailing before the Kennedy tax cuts. It exhibits a sharp drop in 1975, but, as with the Holland–Myers series, this drop is from the very high level reached in 1974. Since 1974 was a year of severe recession, and since both the Holland–Myers and Feldstein–Summers series use some modification of net rather than gross profits of the

TABLE 12

Alternative Measures of the Effective Tax Rate on Capital

Year	TK (1)	Holland and Myers (2)	Fama (3)	Gonedes (4)	Feldstein and Summers corporate (5)	PCK (6)	Feldstein and Summers noncorporate (7)	MTRK (8)	Feldstein and Summers total (9)
1947	43.1	52.1	30.0	29.4	—	9.4	—	59.2	—
1948	39.2	44.2	29.2	27.5	—	7.2	—	52.9	—
1949	36.2	38.7	27.0	34.9	—	6.9	—	49.9	—
1950	46.0	55.4	34.6	41.7	—	9.2	—	62.0	—
1951	49.6	61.5	41.6	38.4	—	8.0	—	64.1	—
1952	45.8	56.5	37.7	37.6	—	7.7	—	60.2	—
1953	46.2	59.3	36.9	33.1	—	6.9	—	59.9	—
1954	41.4	51.7	31.7	33.5	51.6	6.9	11.9	54.9	63.5
1955	41.9	50.8	32.7	32.6	51.1	6.9	10.9	55.4	61.9
1956	42.5	53.2	31.6	31.5	54.8	7.1	13.5	56.5	68.4
1957	41.4	51.3	30.0	29.8	53.4	6.9	15.2	55.2	68.5

1958	40.2	49.4	27.3	30.9	50.6	6.9	16.3	54.0	67.0
1959	40.3	48.4	29.4	30.1	49.2	6.9	13.6	54.3	62.8
1960	41.3	46.9	27.9	29.7	47.7	6.3	15.1	54.9	62.8
1961	39.8	47.2	27.7	27.9	47.4	7.3	14.9	54.6	62.2
1962	37.7	41.7	26.0	28.4	42.4	6.4	14.7	51.5	57.1
1963	37.8	41.6	26.4	27.6	42.4	6.5	14.7	51.7	57.1
1964	36.4	38.7	25.2	26.7	39.1	5.9	14.2	49.8	53.3
1965	35.7	37.6	25.0	26.7	38.3	5.8	14.3	48.9	52.5
1966	35.5	37.5	25.0	25.5	38.7	5.8	15.2	48.4	53.9
1967	35.2	36.5	23.2	28.0	37.5	6.8	16.7	49.3	54.2
1968	38.0	40.9	25.6	27.2	42.7	8.1	18.0	53.6	60.8
1969	38.1	41.9	24.3	24.4	44.5	7.8	21.5	54.8	66.0
1970	37.9	39.8	20.7	24.1	42.5	6.7	25.4	51.6	67.8
1971	37.8	39.0	20.5	23.3	40.5	6.1	21.8	51.2	62.3
1972	36.0	36.8	20.0	23.7	38.0	7.0	20.0	51.4	58.0
1973	37.1	40.0	20.4	22.9	43.9	7.2	26.1	52.5	70.0
1974	37.6	47.9	19.5	21.1	56.0	7.6	38.7	53.4	94.9
1975	34.0	37.7	18.0	—	40.8	7.0	28.5	49.3	69.3
1976	—	40.0	20.2	—	42.5	—	22.4	—	64.9
1977	—	39.8	20.4	—	42.5	—	23.8	—	66.3

corporate sector in the denominator, both probably overstate the positive part of the effective corporate tax rate schedule for that year. Such an over-statement can occur for reasons outlined in Section 6.[7]

Column 7 of Table 12 shows the Feldstein–Summers estimates of the effective federal personal tax rate on the income of corporate-held capital. Unlike the effective tax rates discussed up to now, these estimates are not based primarily on actual tax payments. Instead, Feldstein and Summers attribute certain noncorporate tax rates to corporate income. These rates depend upon the form in which the income accrues to the noncorporate sector and upon who receives that income. The effective noncorporate tax rate on corporate income is just a weighted average of these various rates. For example, the weighted average tax rates on dividends and capital gains are taken to be 28.7 percent and 4.7 percent, respectively.

The numbers shown in column 7 are the Feldstein–Summers estimates of the total contribution of noncorporate taxes to the overall tax rate on the income of corporate capital. Unlike the effective corporate rate, this non-corporate rate increased markedly in the late 1960s and the 1970s. Its average level during the last five years of the sample was approximately twice the average during the first five years. Column 9 of Table 12 shows the Feldstein–Summers estimates of the total effective tax rate on corporate income, which is the sum of the corporate and noncorporate contributions in columns 5 and 7. As can be seen from the table, the increase in the noncorporate con-tribution more than outweighs the decline in the corporate contribution, and by 1969 the overall tax rate had returned to the levels prevailing before the Kennedy tax cuts. Of particular interest is the extreme value of 94.9 percent in 1974.

Table 12 also shows the overall capital income tax rate MTRK, which incorporates the effects of personal as well as corporate taxes. As can be seen from the table, there is a discrepancy between the behavior of MTRK and that of the Feldstein–Summers combined tax rate series in column 9. In particular, MTRK never returns after the 1964 tax cuts to the levels it had reached during the 1950s. There are two readily apparent explanations for the discrepancy between MTRK and the Feldstein–Summers series. The first is that MTRK is an estimate of the average tax rate on all income from capital, from both corporate and noncorporate sources. If MTRK is regarded as a weighted average of the effective tax rates on the incomes of corporate and noncorporate capital, then it is quite possible that the tax rate on the income from corporate capital could increase over time even if the weighted average rate did not. This could occur if the tax rate on income from noncorporate capital decreased over time or if the share of corporate capital income in total capital income decreased over time (assuming

---

[7] See specifically footnote 4.

income from corporate capital is taxed more heavily than income from noncorporate capital).

In fact, both of these effects appear to have been at work. During the first five years for which both MTRK and the Feldstein–Summers series exist (1954–1958), the Feldstein–Summers measure of the income of corporate capital averages 56.5 percent of total income from capital relevant for computing MTRK. During the last five years for which both series exist (1971–1975), this share falls to 45.7 percent. Using such shares, one can calculate for each year the implied tax rate on that portion of national income accruing to noncorporate capital required to make MTRK and the Feldstein–Summers series mutually consistent. This implied tax rate averages 13.0 percent between 1954 and 1958 and only 5.1 percent between 1971 and 1974. It is curious that this implied tax rate could fall dramatically during the same period when the Feldstein–Summers noncorporate tax rate on the income of corporate capital roughly doubled. A decline in effective rates of taxation of income from residential capital might have contributed to such a result, but it is difficult to believe that this factor alone could have accounted for a drop in the taxation of noncorporate capital income of the magnitude required to make MTRK and the Feldstein–Summers series mutually consistent.

A second explanation of the discrepancy between MTRK and the Feldstein–Summers series is that the various noncorporate tax rates which Feldstein and Summers impute to the income of corporate capital may be higher than the effective rates faced by taxpayers. This could occur if taxpayers are able to use certain of the devices discussed by Miller and Scholes to shelter ordinary income from taxation. For example, Feldstein and Summers assume that dividends are taxed at a weighted-average marginal rate of 28.7 percent. However, Miller and Scholes suggest mechanisms by which taxpayers can convert dividends into capital gains for tax purposes. According to Feldstein and Summers, the effective tax rate on capital gains is only 4.7 percent. If taxpayers are in fact successful in converting a substantial amount of ordinary income into capital gains for tax purposes, then actual tax payments would be lower than implied by the rates assumed by Feldstein and Summers. Consequently, effective tax rates computed from actual tax payments, like MTRK, would be lower than the rates assumed by Feldstein and Summers, who rule out by assumption any "clientele effects" operating to reduce effective rates of taxation at the noncorporate level.[8]

---

[8] It is interesting to note that the evidence reported in Fama (1975) is consistent with the hypothesis that the marginal personal tax rate on interest income relevant for pricing U.S. Treasury bills is in fact zero. A zero tax rate for the marginal investors in Treasury bills does not imply that all individuals face marginal tax rates of zero on ordinary income, however. The weighted average of such tax rates would thus in general be positive, even if they are lower than those assumed by Feldstein and Summers.

9. USES OF COMPONENTS OF TAX RATES

As was discussed in Section 4, the overall tax rate on income from capital can be written as

$$\text{MTRK} = T + TK + \text{PCK}$$

where T is treated as a proportional tax on all income, TK is a proportional tax striking only income from capital, and PCK is the contribution of the federal personal income tax to the overall tax rate. Empirically, T can be identified largely with sales taxes, while TK is composed entirely of property and corporate profits taxes. The overall tax rate on income from labor can be written as

$$\text{MRTL} = T + \text{SSC} + \text{PCL}$$

where SSC and PCL are the contributions of the Social Security tax and the federal personal income tax, respectively, to the overall tax rate. The question arises as to what the uses of these components of the overall tax rates might be. Unfortunately, their use is probably largely descriptive, and extreme caution should be exercised in employing any of these components in statistical analysis.

To see why this is so, consider a hypothetical economy in which all capital is held by firms, in which all income of such firms is taxed at a constant rate τ_c, in which all of a firm's after-tax earnings are distributed to its shareholders and are taxed at a constant rate τ_p, and in which there is a flat-rate sales tax equal to τ_s. In such a world, the overall tax rate on income from capital is

$$\tau_k = 1 - (1 - \tau_c)(1 - \tau_p)(1 - \tau_s) \tag{5}$$

which can be rewritten

$$\tau_k = \tau_c + (1 - \tau_c)\tau_p + (1 - \tau_c)(1 - \tau_p)\tau_s \tag{6}$$

The three terms on the right-hand side of Eq. (6) can be defined as the contributions of the corporate income tax, the personal income tax, and the sales tax, respectively, to the overall tax rate τ_k. One may think of these terms as theoretical analogues of TK, PCK, and T, respectively, although the empirically defined tax rate T incorporates some taxes other than the sales tax discussed here. Since the three individual tax rates enter Eq. (5) in identical fashion, the arrangement of terms on the right-hand side of Eq. (6) is arbitrary. For example, that equation could have been written so as to include a term equal to τ_p, and this term could have been defined as the contribution of the personal income tax to the overall tax rate τ_k. The effect of a multiplicity of taxes striking at different points in the income–expenditure cycle is thus to obscure the individual impact of each tax. Nevertheless, using the definitions embodied in Eq. (6) makes it obvious that the change in τ_k resulting from a change in any individual tax rate is equal to neither the change in the tax rate nor, except for τ_s, the change in its "contribution" to τ_k. It is also obvious that, except for τ_s, a change in an individual tax rate may induce changes in the "contribution" of the other tax rates, even though those rates remain constant. It was argued in Section 8 that this interaction of tax rates was largely responsible for the drop in the proportional tax rate T during World War II.

Since the contributions of the individual tax rates to the overall rate are defined in such an arbitrary manner, one should exercise extreme caution in employing them in statistical analysis. This applies both to the components of MTRK and to the components of MTRL.

Even if one were to identify empirical analogues to the individual tax rates τ_c, τ_p, and τ_s, however, it would still be impossible to identify the effect on most economic decisions of a change in any of these individual rates. This is because the effect of any one tax rate depends upon its interaction with all other rates.[9] If the interaction of the different rates is as in Eq. (5), and if the overall tax rate τ_k is relevant for economic decisions (for example, investment in physical capital), then empirical analysis should proceed using only the empirical analogue for τ_k, rather than any attempted measures of τ_c, τ_p, and τ^s. Similar considerations apply to the tax rate on income from labor.

10. SUMMARY

This paper describes a method of calculating summary measures of effective factor income tax rates in the United States using readily available data. The numbers resulting from application of this method are reported, and some of their possible uses are discussed. The estimated factor income tax rates behave over time in a manner quite consistent with the behavior of other broad measures of federal tax policy. The postwar movement in the tax rate on income from labor relative to that on income from capital (or, more accurately, the relevant components of these tax rates) provides suggestive support for the Miller–Scholes hypothesis that the federal personal income tax has been moving in the direction of a pure consumption tax. The tax rates reported here are consistent with other studies that show a decrease since the 1950s in rates of taxation at the corporate level of income from

---

[9] The effect of the interaction among different tax rates has been emphasized in a different context by Miller (1977) and Miller and Scholes (1978).

corporate-held capital. They are also consistent with the view that rates of taxation of such income at the noncorporate level have risen, but not quite sufficiently to offset the decline in the corporate tax burden.

ACKNOWLEDGMENTS

This paper is excerpted from my doctoral dissertation at the University of Chicago. I wish to thank the members of my committee: John P. Gould, Robert Hamada, Roger Kormendi, Robert Lucas, Merton Miller, and Arnold Zellner. Special thanks are due to Merton Miller for comments on the present draft. In addition, I am grateful to Paul Evans, Arthur Laffer, David Ranson, and Marc Reinganum for helpful suggestions and to Eugene Fama and Nicholas Gonedes for furnishing unpublished data.

REFERENCES

Bailey, M. J. (1969). "Capital Gains and Income Taxation," in *The Taxation of Income from Capital* (Arnold C. Harberger and Martin J. Bailey, eds.). Brookings Institution, Washington, D.C.

Boskin, M. J. (1978). "Taxation, Saving, and the Rate of Interest," *Journal of Political Economy* **86**, S3–S28.

Diamond, P. A. (1970). "Incidence of an Interest Income Tax," *Journal of Economic Theory* **2**, 211–224.

Fama, E. F. (1975). "Short-Term Interest Rates as Predictors of Inflation," *American Economic Review* **65**, 269–282.

Fama, E. F. (1979). "Stock Returns, Real Activity, Inflation and Money." Working Paper No. WP 24, Center for Research in Security Prices, Graduate School of Business, Univ. of Chicago, Chicago, Illinois.

Feldstein, M. (1974a). "Incidence of a Capital Income Tax in a Growing Economy with Variable Saving Rates," *Review Economic Studies* **41**, 505–523.

Feldstein, M. (1974b). "Tax Incidence in a Growing Economy with Variable Factor Supply," *Quarterly Journal of Economics* **88**, 551–573.

Feldstein, M., and Summers, L. (1979). "Inflation and the Taxation of Capital Income in the Corporate Sector," *National Tax Journal* **32**, 445–470.

Gonedes, N. J. (1981). "Evidence of the 'Tax Effects' of Inflation under Historical Cost Accounting Methods." *Journal of Business* **54**, 227–270.

Granger, C. W. J., and Newbold, P. (1974). "Spurious Regressions in Econometrics." *Journal of Econometrics* **2**, 111–120.

Holland, D. M., and Myers, S. C. (1980). "Profitability and Capital Costs for Manufacturing Corporations and All Nonfinancial Corporations." *American Economic Review Papers and Proceedings* 320–325.

Joines, D. H. (1979). "Government Fiscal Policy and Private Capital Formation." Ph.D. dissertation, Univ. of Chicago, Chicago, Illinois.

Miller, M. H. (1977). "Debt and Taxes," *Journal of Finance* **32**, 261–275.

Miller, M. H., and Scholes, M. S. (1978). "Dividends and Taxes," *Journal of Financial Economics* **6**, 333–364.

Miller, M. H., and Upton, C. W. (1974). *Macroeconomics: A Neoclassical Introduction*. Irwin, Homewood, Illinois.

Rosen, H. S. (1976). "Taxes in a Labor Supply Model with Joint Wage-Hours Determination," *Econometrica* **44**, 485–507.

Wales, T. J. (1973). "Estimation of a Labor Supply Curve for Self-Employed Business Proprietors," *International Economic Review* **14**, 69–80.

Wright, C. (1969). "Saving and the Rate of Interest," in *The Taxation of Income from Capital* (A. C. Harberger and M. J. Bailey, eds.). Brookings Institution, Washington, D.C.

Chapter 7

Government Fiscal Policy and Private Capital Formation—Some Aggregate Time-Series Estimates

Douglas H. Joines

1. INTRODUCTION

This chapter reports empirical estimates of the effects of government fiscal policy on real, private-sector investment in plant and equipment. The magnitude of any such effects has important implications for public policy. During the 1970s, the real wage rate of workers in the United States grew at a noticeably slower rate than during the earlier post–World War II period. This slow growth of real wages seems partly attributable to the unusually rapid growth of the working-age population which began in the mid-1960s as the postwar "baby boom" generation started to reach maturity. This "worker boom" would in itself have tended to slow the growth of the capital stock per worker, and hence of real wages. The widespread impression persists, however, that the slow growth rate of capital per worker was in part also an unintended side effect of government policy—in particular, large deficits, rapidly growing government spending, and high tax rates on income from capital. In light of this perception, it is extremely important to measure the size of these postulated effects in order to determine whether they were a significant cause of the phenomena in question and whether changes in policy might bring about an increase in the rates of capital formation and economic growth.

The notion that fiscal policy can exert a significant effect on fixed investment is not new. It was responsible for earlier attempts to use federal tax policy to stimulate such investment. These measures included the investment tax credit and provisions allowing for accelerated depreciation for tax purposes. In fact, attempts at measuring the effects of these policy changes constitute an important segment of previous empirical work on fiscal policy and capital formation. The present study differs from most previous empirical analyses in two major respects: the methodology employed and the use of new measures of tax rates on factor incomes.

The paper is organized as follows: Section 2 summarizes some of the implications of economic theory which are tested later in the paper. Sections 3 and 4 describe the methodology to be employed. Sections 5 and 6 describe the data used, while Section 7 reports univariate time-series models for the exogenous variables. Sections 8 and 9 report equations estimated for investment in nonresidential structures and producers' durable equipment, respectively. These equations are compared in Section 10, and results for selected subperiods are examined in Section 11. Section 12 summarizes the conclusions which can be drawn from this analysis.

2. THE HYPOTHESES TO BE TESTED

There are many instruments of fiscal policy which economic theory suggests may affect private capital accumulation. One of the most frequently analyzed is some form of taxation of income from capital. One strand of theoretical analysis traces the effects on capital accumulation of a capital income tax through its effects on desired saving. Notable among these studies are Wright (1969), Diamond (1970), Feldstein (1974a, b), and Miller and Upton (1974). Other studies examine the effect of a capital income tax on the investment behavior of the firms which acquire capital goods [see, in particular, Jorgenson (1963, 1967)]. Since saving provides the financial resources to support business investment, these two strands of analysis really deal with the same phenomenon, merely examining different sides of the same market.[1] The analyses are thus complementary, and both lead to the

---

[1] This phenomenon is analogous to examining the effects of an excise tax by shifting either the supply curve (saving function) or the demand curve (investment function).

testable hypothesis that taxation of income from capital deters capital formation.

Taxation of labor income might also affect capital formation. Viewed from the demand side of the factor market, a tax on the employment of labor would encourage firms to substitute capital for labor in the production of any given level of output. By raising the cost of production, however, this tax might also lead to a contraction in output, with the net effect on the demand for capital goods being ambiguous. There is also some reason for believing that a tax on labor income will affect capital formation through the supply side of the factor market. For example, Joines (1979) has developed a life-cycle model of saving and labor supply in which an increase in the labor income tax rate depresses both the supply of saving and the equilibrium level of capital formation. This implication, then, forms the second hypothesis to be tested.

The fraction of total income allocated to private capital formation is determined by many economic agents, not just by those who acquire the physical assets. The individual recipient of income must decide how much of that income to consume and how much to save, subject to his budget constraint. Of the amount saved, he must decide how much to invest for himself in household capital and how much to supply to the market sector through his purchases of securities. The firm must decide how much physical capital to acquire in order to maximize its market value subject to a production function and market factors such as the demand for its product and the cost of financial capital. Finally, government sets its fiscal program, which includes some value for its deficit. It is the effect of the deficit, or some other measure of the government's aggregate appropriation of economic resources, which constitutes the third hypothesis to be tested.

A simple diagramatic representation of the simultaneous nature of the various decisions affecting capital formation consists of a saving schedule which is upward sloping with respect to the interest rate and an investment schedule which is downward sloping, as in Fig. 1. Equilibrium occurs when saving exceeds private investment by an amount equal to the government deficit.[2] The importance of the deficit in the analysis concerns the question whether an increase in the deficit will result in a reduction in investment, an increase in saving, or both.

Some writers have argued that by going to the capital market to finance its expenditures, government increases the supply of securities, bidding up

---

[2] This is true regardless of the fraction of the deficit the government chooses to monetize. The issue of monetization concerns the proportion of the deficit which is financed by noninterest-bearing government debt. Although it is possible that the two forms of debt issue have different effects on capital formation, this question is not examined in the empirical tests which follow.

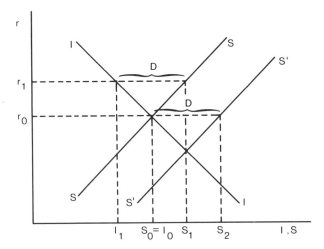

Figure 1. Effect on equilibrium saving and investment of a government debt issue to be serviced by lump-sum taxes.

interest rates, crowding out private borrowers, and reducing private capital formation. According to this view, the private sector regards government securities as net wealth and consequently lowers its accumulation of alternative assets, specifically, physical capital. Assuming that the government spending program is given, that a change in the deficit results from a change in tax receipts, and that such a change causes no shifts in either the saving schedule or the investment schedule, the argument is represented in Fig. 1. In the initial situation, the deficit is zero and the saving and investment schedules are given by SS and II, respectively. The equilibrium interest rate is r_0 and equilibrium saving and investment are $S_0 = I_0$. If the deficit is increased to D, the interest rate rises to r_1, saving increases to S_1, and private investment falls to I_1.

An alternative argument advanced by Barro (1974) and others contends that as long as voluntary intergenerational income transfers are taking place, the public does not regard government bonds as net wealth. This is because the issuance of debt implies future tax liabilities equal in present value to the debt issue. The public foresees these taxes and increases its saving, and thus its demand for securities, by an amount equal to the present value of the liabilities, that is, by an amount equal to the government debt issue. An increase in the supply of government securities thus creates an equal increase in the quantity demanded at any rate of interest and leaves unchanged the accumulation of physical capital. In terms of Fig. 1, the saving schedule shifts rightward to $S'S'$, the interest rate remains at r_0, and investment is constant at I_0. This increase in saving requires no reduction in consumption, since, for a given level of government expenditure, disposable income rises by the amount of the deficit.

If there are no intergenerational income transfers, then the saving schedule will remain at SS. If only part of the population engages in such transfers, then the saving schedule will shift rightward by an amount less than D, and an intermediate solution will result. The interest rate will be between r_0 and r_1, saving will be between S_1 and S_2, and investment will be between I_1 and I_0. Unless the saving schedule shifts all the way to $S'S'$, the deficit results in an increase in consumption and an increase in saving, the sum of which equals the deficit, which in turn equals the increase in disposable income.

The above discussion concerns only the wealth effects of a debt issue. Joines (1979) argues that a debt issue also entails substitution effects similar to those of a capital income tax. This is because a government deficit, to the extent that it implies future income taxes, makes it less profitable to acquire assets which will earn income in the future. A deficit thus causes the investment schedule to shift to the left in Fig. 2. The shift of the schedule to $I'I'$ implies a reduction in capital formation, regardless of whether the saving schedule remains at SS, shifts to $S'S'$, or settles somewhere in between. If the saving schedule does not shift, investment falls to I_3 as a result of the deficit. If the saving schedule shifts to $S'S'$, investment falls by a smaller amount to I_4. If the new saving schedule lies between SS and $S'S'$, investment will be between

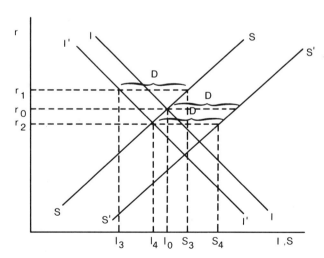

Figure 2. Effect on equilibrium saving and investment of a government debt issue to be serviced by distortionary taxes.

I_3 and I_4. The third hypothesis to be tested thus concerns whether there is a negative relation between the government deficit (or some proxy for it) and private capital formation. Unfortunately, if such a relation is found, it will not be possible to state conclusively whether it results from a wealth effect (the standard crowding-out argument) or an intertemporal substitution effect.[3]

3. METHODOLOGY

This Chapter differs from most of the previous studies of fiscal policy and capital formation in the methodology employed. Most previous studies of tax incentives and capital formation have been conducted within the investment function framework. The investment function literature has been primarily concerned with compiling evidence relating to the form of one equation of a simultaneous macroeconomic model—specifically, the function representing the demand for certain types of physical assets.[4] This task should be distinguished from that of explaining the equilibrium quantity of capital formation in the economy. Knowledge of the form of a single structural equation of a simultaneous system is usually not sufficient to allow one to determine the effects of changes in exogenous variables on the value of the endogenous variable described by that equation. The present study attempts to determine the influence of various fiscal policy variables on the equilibrium quantity of capital formation and is not directly concerned with structural estimation of investment functions.

An aggregate investment function can be viewed as one element of a small equilibrium macroeconomic model. It reflects society's opportunities for the intertemporal allocation of consumption. A complete model would also include a relation representing preferences and a market-clearing condition. In such a simple model, the choice faced by a consumer is between current and future consumption. His preferences are represented by a consumption function, more properly called a current consumption function. The market-clearing condition is that consumption and investment sum to national income.

The simple model outlined above could be expanded in several directions. Both investment and current consumption could be disaggregated, yielding

---

[3] If the government's monetary liabilities are in fact liabilities only in an accounting sense and do not imply any future taxes, then the monetized portion of the deficit would not entail either a wealth or a substitution effect.

[4] See, for example, Jorgenson (1963), Hall and Jorgenson (1971), and other papers contained in Fromm (1971).

separate equations for different types of consumption and investment. Government and foreign sectors could also be added to the model. It is here assumed that the aggregate U.S. economy can be represented by a linear dynamic simultaneous equation system. This system is taken to include equations for several types of consumption and investment and to include a government sector.

Dynamic simultaneous equation models (SEMs) and the various relations between the variables which follow from such models have been extensively analyzed by Zellner and Palm (1974). They show how various types of equations, such as final equations, reduced form equations, and final form equations, are derived from the SEM. They also enumerate the uses of and the requirements for using each type of relation.

Of particular interest are the transfer functions associated with an SEM. One transfer function will exist for each of the model's endogenous variables and will express the current value of that variable as a function of its own past values and of current and lagged values of all exogenous variables of the system. A dynamic SEM may be written as

$$H(L)\mathbf{y}_t = G(L)\mathbf{x}_t + F(L)\mathbf{e}_t \tag{1}$$

where $H(L)$, $G(L)$, and $F(L)$ are matrices whose elements are finite-order polynomials in the lag operator, $\mathbf{y}_t$ is the vector of variables endogenous to the system, $\mathbf{x}_t$ is the vector of exogenous variables, and $\mathbf{e}_t$ is a vector of error terms with the properties $E\mathbf{e}_t = \mathbf{0}$ and $E\mathbf{e}_t\mathbf{e}_t' = \delta_{tt'}I$, where I is an identity matrix and $\delta_{tt'}$ is the Kronecker delta.

Multiplying both sides of (1) by $H^{-1}(L)$ yields the transfer functions

$$\mathbf{y}_t = H^{-1}(L)G(L)\mathbf{x}_t + H^{-1}(L)F(L)\mathbf{e}_t \tag{2}$$

There is one transfer equation for each endogenous variable in $\mathbf{y}_t$. In (2) the coefficients multiplying the exogenous variables and the error term are ratios of finite-order polynomials in the lag operator.[5] Thus a single equation

---

[5] Multiplication of (2) by $|H(L)|$, the determinant of $H(L)$, yields

$$|H(L)|\mathbf{y}_t = H^*(L)G(L)\mathbf{x}_t + H^*(L)F(L)\boldsymbol{\varepsilon}_t \tag{3}$$

where $H^*(L)$ is the adjoint matrix associated with $H(L)$. Both systems (2) and (3) are representations of the transfer functions associated with the dynamic SEM (1). Each transfer equation in (3) relates the current value of an endogenous variable to a finite number of its own past values (via $|H(L)|$), to the current value and a finite number of lagged values of the exogenous variables, and to the current error term and a finite number of lagged error terms. The equivalent system (2) expresses the current value of each endogenous variable as a function of the current values of the exogenous variables, an infinite number of lagged values of the exogenous variables, the current disturbance term, and an infinite number of past disturbance term, and an infinite number of past disturbance terms.

from this system can be written as

$$y_t = \mu + \frac{\omega_1(L)}{\delta_1(L)} x_{1t} + \frac{\omega_2(L)}{\delta_2(L)} x_{2t} + \cdots + \frac{\omega_m(L)}{\delta_m(L)} x_{mt} + \frac{\theta_u(L)}{\phi_u(L)} u_t \quad (4)$$

It can be assumed without loss of generality that the input variables x_{it} and the output variable y_t have been differenced to induce stationarity. The white-noise process u_t by definition has the properties

$$E(u_t) = 0 \quad \text{for all} \quad t$$
$$E(u_t^2) = \sigma_u^2 \quad \text{for all} \quad t$$
$$E(u_t, u_{t+k}) = 0 \quad \text{for all} \quad t \text{ and for all } k \neq 0$$

An alternative form for Eq. (4) is

$$y_t = v_1(L)x_{1t} + v_2(L)x_{2t} + \cdots + v_m(L)x_{mt} + \frac{\theta_u(L)}{\phi_u(L)} u_t$$

where $v_i(L) = \delta_i^{-1}(L)\omega_i(L) = v_{i0} + v_{i1} L + v_{i2} L^2 + \cdots$. The weights v_{i0}, $v_{i1}, v_{i2}, \ldots$ are called the impulse response function associated with input i and describe the deviations in the output $y_t, y_{t+1}, y_{t+2}, \ldots$ resulting from a one-unit deviation in the input x_i at time t. The summation

$$\sum_{j=0}^{\infty} v_{ij} = g_i$$

is called the steady-state gain associated with input i and denotes the change in the equilibrium level of the output variable y resulting from a one-unit change in the level at which the input variable x_{it}, $t = 0, 1, 2, \ldots$, is fixed.

The uses of the transfer functions are more limited than those of the structural equations of system (1), and their requirements in terms of prior information and availability of data are correspondingly more modest. Both the structural equations and the transfer functions require that data be available on all the exogenous variables of the system. Structural analysis of the complete SEM generally requires that data be available on all endogenous variables as well, whereas transfer function analysis requires data only on those endogenous variables being analyzed. Estimation of either type of equation requires that the variables of the model be classified as endogenous or exogenous. However, estimation of the structural equations requires much more information about the form of the structural model than does transfer function estimation. It requires knowledge of which variables enter into each structural equation and possibly other information on restrictions which might be needed to identify the structural parameters. Transfer function analysis is thus considerably simpler than structural estimation, but is well-suited to answering the types of questions posed in Section 2.

4. IDENTIFICATION, ESTIMATION, AND DIAGNOSTIC
CHECKS OF TRANSFER FUNCTION MODELS

Box and Jenkins (1970) discuss the identification, estimation, and diagnostic checking of transfer function models similar to Eq. (4). When there is a single input variable, x_{it}, Box and Jenkins suggest using the estimated cross-correlation function between the prewhitened values of x_{it} and y_t to obtain estimates of the impulse response weights, and thus to identify a tentative form for the transfer function. The first step in this procedure is to find a linear filter $\phi_i(L)\theta_i^{-1}(L)$ such that

$$\alpha_{it} = \phi_i(L)\theta_i^{-1}(L)x_{it} \tag{5}$$

is approximately white noise. Apply the same filter to the output variable to obtain

$$\beta_t = \phi_i(L)\theta_i^{-1}(L)y_t \tag{6}$$

Then the original single-input model may be written as

$$\beta_t = v_i(L)\alpha_{it} + \varepsilon_t$$

where $\varepsilon_t = \phi_i(L)\theta_u(L)\theta_i^{-1}(L)\phi_u^{-1}(L)u_t$. Let $\rho_{\alpha\beta}(k)$ denote the correlation between $\alpha_{i,t-k}$ and β_t. Then the impulse response function is related to the cross-correlation function by[6]

$$v_{ik} = \frac{\rho_{\alpha\beta}(k)\sigma_\beta}{\sigma_\alpha}$$

If there is more than one input, the impulse response weights cannot in general be obtained merely by multiplying the bivariate cross correlations by a constant.[7] These estimated cross-correlation functions nevertheless provide a convenient starting point for exploring the relation which might exist between the output variable and the potential inputs.

---

[6] The impulse response function is estimated by

$$\hat{v}_{ik} = \frac{r_{\alpha\beta}(k)s_\beta}{s_\alpha},$$

where $r_{\alpha\beta}(k)$ is an estimate of $\rho_{\alpha\beta}(k)$ and s_α and s_β are estimates of σ_α and σ_β obtained by fitting (5) and (6), respectively.

[7] See Beveridge (1975) for one suggestion for identifying the form of a multiple-input transfer function.

If the model (4) has been fitted adequately, then the residuals $\hat{u}_t$ should be serially uncorrelated and should be uncorrelated with lagged values of the input variables. Model inadequacy may thus be suggested by nonzero values of the residual autocorrelation function $r_{\hat{u}\hat{u}}(k)$ and the cross-correlation function $r_{\alpha_i\hat{u}}(k)$ between prewhitened input α_{it} and residuals $\hat{u}_t$. If the transfer function model $\omega_i(L)\delta_i^{-1}(L)$ is incorrect, then the residuals will in general be both autocorrelated and also cross correlated with the prewhitened input. If the transfer function model is correct but the noise model $\theta_u(L)\phi_u^{-1}(L)$ is incorrect, then the residuals will be autocorrelated but will not be cross correlated with the prewhitened input.

To judge whether individual values of $r_{\hat{u}\hat{u}}(k)$ and $r_{\alpha_i\hat{u}}(k)$ are non zero, they may be compared with their approximate standard error $1/\sqrt{n}$, where n is the number of observations after differencing to achieve stationarity. A "portmanteau" test of the joint significance of the first M autocorrelations can be performed using the statistic

$$Q^*(M) = n(n + 2) \sum_{k=1}^{M} (n - k)^{-1} r_{\hat{u}\hat{u}}^2(k)$$

which is approximately distributed as χ^2 with $M - p - q$ degrees of freedom, where p is the order of the polynomial $\phi_u(L)$ and q is the order of the polynomial $\theta_u(L)$. A similar test of the concurrent and M lagged cross correlations can be performed using the statistic

$$S_{\alpha_i}^*(M) = n^2 \sum_{k=0}^{M} (n - k)^{-1} r_{\alpha_i\hat{u}}^2(k)$$

which is approximately distributed as χ^2 with M-h degrees of freedom. Here h is the number of parameters estimated, exclusive of those in the noise model but including the constant term [see Haugh (1976) and Ljung and Box (1976)]. Notice that the number of degrees of freedom of the Q^*-statistic is affected by the number of parameters of the noise model, but not by the number of transfer function parameters.

Given a value of Q^* or S^*, it is possible to determine the area in the upper tail of the relevant χ^2-distribution. Denote this value by P. A high value of Q^* or S^*, which is evidence of correlation, thus corresponds to a low value of P.

5. CHOICE OF A GOVERNMENT SPENDING VARIABLE

Analysis of the transfer functions associated with a dynamic simultaneous equation model requires that the variables appearing in the model be classified as either endogenous or exogenous. There will be a transfer function for each endogenous variable. This paper reports on the estimation of transfer functions for several measures of private capital formation; the transfer functions associated with the other endogenous variables in the system are not estimated.

Two types of exogenous variables are employed. One of these is a measure of tax rates on factor incomes. These estimated tax rates include weighted averages of effective marginal federal personal income tax rates. They also treat other taxes as ultimately falling on market-sector income and incorporate these taxes into the estimated tax rates. These series are described in detail in Joines (1981). The other exogenous variable is a measure of the aggregate appropriation of economic resources by the government.

Recent theoretical papers pose the question of whether a government debt issue will affect private capital formation. The size of the government's debt issue in any period is determined by the size of its budget deficit. If the deficit were regarded as an exogenous variable, it could be used along with the tax rates in a transfer function to explain investment. Together, the tax rates and the deficit would also determine some level of government spending and some level of revenues, these two variable being endogenous to the system.

Some readers might object to the treatment of the government deficit as an exogenous variable. It is equally reasonable to regard tax rates and total spending as exogenously determined policy variables, with revenues and the deficit being endogenous. If this view is correct, it would be inappropriate to include the deficit as an explanatory variable in the transfer function for private investment, even though the theoretical propositions discussed in Section 2 are formulated in terms of the deficit. Instead, total government spending should be regarded as the relevant explanatory variable.

It is also possible to argue that even though certain items of government spending are exogenously determined, other items, and thus total spending, are endogenous. One major component of total spending which could reasonably be regarded as endogenous is transfer payments to persons.[8] If this be the case, it is necessary that the explanatory variable used in the transfer functions be some subset of total government spending which is more nearly exogenous than are transfer payments. One reasonable candidate for inclusion is purchases of goods and services, which is far and away the largest item of government spending. The empirical tests reported below employ

---

[8] The government might be thought of as setting criteria governing eligibility for transfer payments rather than total expenditures on transfers. In this sense, the eligibility criteria are analogous to a tax rate schedule and total transfer payments are analogous to tax revenues. For completeness, one should also include as exogenous variables the criteria governing eligibility for transfer payments, just as the tax rates are included. This has not been done, however, in part because no method of summarizing these criteria with few parameters is readily apparent.

this variable as a measure of the government sector's aggregate appropriation of economic resources.[9]

6. THE DATA

The statistical analysis reported in this chapter employs annual time-series data for the United States covering the period 1929–1975, a total of 47 observations. Three investment series were used in the analysis. The first of these is real gross private domestic nonresidential fixed investment per capita, denoted INV. This series is derived by dividing gross private non-residential fixed investment in 1972 dollars by the total population aged 18–64, inclusive.[10]

[9] Most of the equations reported below were also estimated using either the deficit or total government spending, rather than purchases of goods and services, as an explanatory variable. In addition, if transfer payments are regarded as exogenous, it is possible that they affect investment differently than do purchases of goods and services. The approximate effect of using total spending as an explanatory variable is to constrain the effects of purchases and transfer payments to be the same. (The effect is approximate since these two items do not completely exhaust government spending. They do, however, make up by far the major share throughout the entire sample period used here and constituted more than 95 percent of total spending in 1975, the last year of the sample.) In order to relax this constraint, most of the equations were also estimated using both purchases and transfer payments as exogenous variables in the same equation.

The conclusions drawn from these alternative equations are quite similar to those drawn from the equations reported in the text. One should exercise some caution in interpreting the results of equations employing the deficit and transfer payments, however, since the diagnostic checks described above are not completely satisfactory for such equations and indicate that these models may be misspecified. The inability to estimate well-specified equations employing the deficit and transfer payments is informative, nevertheless. It suggests that these variables should probably be regarded as endogenous.

The diagnostic checks of equations employing total government spending as an explanatory variable are quite satisfactory. In fact, these equations are almost identical to those which employ purchases of goods and services.

[10] The three real investment series used here were obtained from the *National Income and Product Accounts of the United States, 1929–74* (NIPA), Table 1.2, lines 8, 9, and 10. These figures are based on the revised deflator for structures described in the August 1974 issue of the *Survey of Current Business*. The government purchases variable was obtained from line 21 of the same table. The NIPA contains finally revised data only for the years 1929 to 1972. Revised NIPA data for 1973 were obtained from the July 1977 issue of the *Survey of Current Business*. Revised NIPA data for 1974 and 1975 were obtained from the July 1978 issue of the *Survey of Current Business*. Each series is identified by the same table and line numbers in all these publications.

Population figures for the period 1929–1970 were obtained from *Historical Statistics of the United States, Colonial Times to 1970*, Series A37 and A40. Population data for the years 1970–1975 were obtained from the Census Bureau's *Current Population Reports*, Series P-25, No. 614, "Estimates of the Population of the United States, by Age, Sex, and Race: 1970 to 1975," and No. 721, "Estimates of the Population of the United States, by Age, Sex, and Race: 1970 to 1977."

The Bureau of Economic Analysis disaggregates fixed nonresidential investment into two exhaustive components: structures and producers' durable equipment. Each of these series was divided by the population figures described above to yield a per capita investment series comparable to INV. Real gross private domestic investment in nonresidential structures is denoted INVS, and real gross private domestic investment in producers' durable equipment is denoted INVE.

The measures of factor income tax rates used in the following empirical analysis are the weighted-average marginal tax rates on the incomes from capital and labor described above and denoted MTRK and MTRL, respectively.

As was discussed in Section 5, a number of variables related to government spending suggest themselves for inclusion in the transfer functions. The variable actually used in the tests reported below is real per capita government purchases of goods and services, denoted GXP. This variable is calculated by dividing real government purchases of goods and services by population aged 18–64.

A listing of these six variables appears in the appendix. Each of the series exhibits evidence of nonstationarity, specifically, a distinct upward trend. Further evidence of nonstationarity is provided by the autocorrelation functions, shown in Table 1. The autocorrelations are high at the first lag and, except for GXP, die out slowly as the lag increases. The differenced series give more evidence of stationarity. In general, neither the time-series plots nor the estimated autocorrelation functions, shown in Table 2, give any

TABLE 1

Estimated Autocorrelation Functions of Investment and Fiscal Policy Variables, 1929–1975

	Investment variables			Fiscal policy variables		
Lag	INV	INVE	INVS	MTRK	MTRL	GXP
1	0.95	0.94	0.95	0.86	0.92	0.84
2	0.87	0.85	0.86	0.67	0.83	0.56
3	0.79	0.76	0.78	0.52	0.74	0.30
4	0.72	0.69	0.72	0.41	0.66	0.14
5	0.66	0.62	0.67	0.36	0.61	0.07
6	0.60	0.56	0.60	0.29	0.55	0.07
7	0.53	0.49	0.55	0.22	0.48	0.09
8	0.47	0.35	0.49	0.21	0.43	0.10
Standard error	0.15	0.15	0.15	0.15	0.15	0.15

TABLE 2

Estimated Autocorrelation and Partial Autocorrelation Functions of First Differences of Investment and Fiscal Policy Variables, 1930–1975

Lag	Investment variables			Fiscal policy variables		
	ΔINV	ΔINVE	ΔINVS	ΔMTRK	ΔMTRL	ΔGXP
	Autocorrelation functions					
1	0.34	0.20	0.34	0.20	0.28	0.44
2	−0.15	−0.23	0.02	−0.20	0.06	−0.07
3	−0.18	−0.16	−0.12	−0.14	−0.30	−0.38
4	−0.02	0.03	−0.05	−0.08	−0.18	−0.38
5	−0.05	−0.11	0.06	0.12	−0.18	−0.23
6	−0.07	−0.04	−0.10	−0.05	−0.05	−0.08
7	0.05	0.05	0.02	−0.14	−0.10	0.00
8	−0.04	0.00	−0.03	0.18	0.13	0.11
Standard error	0.15	0.15	0.15	0.15	0.15	0.15
	Partial autocorrelation functions					
1	0.34	0.20	0.34	0.20	0.28	0.44
2	−0.30	−0.28	−0.11	−0.25	−0.03	−0.32
3	−0.01	−0.05	−0.11	−0.04	−0.34	−0.28
4	0.02	0.01	0.04	−0.09	0.00	−0.11
5	−0.13	−0.20	0.06	0.13	−0.11	−0.15
6	0.00	0.04	−0.19	−0.17	−0.07	−0.15
7	0.07	−0.01	0.15	−0.05	−0.13	−0.15
8	−0.17	−0.07	−0.09	0.22	0.13	−0.01

evidence that the first differences are nonstationary. Estimated partial auto-correlation functions for the differenced series are also shown in Table 2.

Table 3 shows sample means and standard deviations for the first differences of all six variables during the entire sample period and during selected subperiods. Examination of this table will reveal that several of the series exhibit less variability after 1950 than during the earlier years. For MTRL and GXP, however, the greater volatility during 1930–1949 than during 1950–1975 is associated with the war years rather than with the prewar period. It thus appears that for these series, a large part of the variability of the sample is directly attributable to World War II. For the investment series INV, INVS, and INVE, and the tax rate MTRK, a large part of the sample variability occurs in the 1930–1949 period rather than during the postwar years.

TABLE 3

Sample Means and Standard Deviations of First Differences of Investment and Fiscal Policy Variables for Selected Subperiods, 1930–1975

	Investment variables			Fiscal policy variables		
	ΔINV	ΔINVE	ΔINVS	ΔMTRK	ΔMTRL	ΔGXP
1930–1975						
Mean	8.63	8.37	0.251	0.432	0.518	33.4
Standard						
deviation	71.5	44.6	33.1	3.59	1.18	382
1930–1941						
Mean	−12.6	−0.557	−12.0	2.20	0.689	48.1
Standard						
deviation	78.4	42.2	38.1	4.13	0.856	105
1930–1949						
Mean	−0.513	4.04	−4.55	1.02	0.632	24.2
Standard						
deviation	86.6	49.7	44.6	4.07	1.40	574
1950–1975						
Mean	21.6	15.7	5.83	0.135	0.427	40.3
Standard						
deviation	47.0	33.5	17.6	3.07	1.01	110

7. UNIVARIATE TIME-SERIES MODELS FOR EXOGENOUS VARIABLES

Before proceeding with the identification and estimation of transfer function models, it is necessary to represent each input variable in terms of a linear univariate time-series model or filter which renders the input white noise. These filters have two uses in transfer function analysis. First, the filter is applied to the corresponding input variable and also to the output before cross correlations are computed between the two. Later, cross correlations are computed between the residuals from the transfer function and those from the univariate model in order to check the adequacy of the transfer function model.

A linear time series model for the variable z_t may be written as

$$\phi(L)z_t = \mu + \theta(L)a_t$$

where a_t is a white-noise process, μ is a constant term, and $\phi(L) = [1 - \phi_1 L - \phi_2 L^2 - \cdots - \phi_p L^p]$ and $\theta(L) = [1 - \theta_1 L - \theta_2 L^2 - \cdots - \theta_q L^q]$ are polynomials of orders p and q, respectively, in the lag operator L. It is assumed that z_t has been differenced sufficiently to achieve stationarity. $\phi(L)$

is termed the autoregressive (AR) polynomial and $\theta(L)$ is referred to as the moving-average (MA) polynomial.

If a univariate time series model has been adequately fitted, the residuals $\hat{a}_t$ from the estimated model should be approximately white noise. One property of a white noise process is a lack of autocorrelation at every lag. To test for autocorrelation at lag k, one can compare the sample autocorrelation of the $\hat{a}_t$ at lag k with its approximate standard error $1/\sqrt{n}$, where n is the number of observations. To test for the joint significance of the first M autocorrelations, one can compute the Q^* statistic described in Section 4 and compare this to a χ^2-distribution with $M - p - q$ degrees of freedom.

The marginal tax rate on income from capital, MTRK, can be represented as a second-order moving average in the first differences[11]:

$$\Delta MTRK_t = 0.422 + [1 + 0.226L - 0.250L^2]a_t$$
$$\quad\quad\quad (0.518) \quad\quad (0.150) \quad (0.149)$$

This $(0, 1, 2)$ model[12] does an adequate job of removing serial correlation from MTRK. None of the autocorrelations of residuals up to lag 6 is as large as its standard error, and $Q^*(6)$ corresponds to a P value of approximately 0.89. The autocorrelations between lags 7 and 12 are somewhat larger, and the P value associated with $Q^*(12)$ is only about 0.33. This figure, however, is not so small as to cause serious concern about model inadequacy.

The marginal tax rate on income from labor MTRL is represented as a third-order autoregressive process in the first differences, with the second-order coefficient constrained to equal zero[13]:

$$[1 - 0.306L + 0.328L^3]\Delta MTRL_t = 0.520 + a_t$$
$$\quad (0.138) \quad\quad (0.138) \quad\quad\quad\quad\quad (0.190)$$

This $(3, 1, 0)$ model does extremely well in removing serial correlation from MTRL. None of the residual autocorrelations up through lag 4 is larger than 0.03 in absolute value, and $Q^*(6)$ and $Q^*(12)$ correspond to P values of approximately 0.98 and 0.90, respectively.

---

[11] Throughout the paper, standard errors are reported in parentheses below parameter estimates. For this model, the standard error of the regression is 3.47. The approximate F-statistic of 2.62, with 2 and 43 degrees of freedom, indicates that the coefficient vector is not significantly different from zero at the 0.05 level. This is of no consequence, however, since the purpose of the filter is to render the series MTRK white noise, a task which it successfully performs.

[12] A nonseasonal univariate time series model may be categorized by the three parameters (p, d, q) denoting, respectively, the number of autoregressive parameters, the degree of differencing, and the number of moving-average parameters.

[13] The standard error of the regression is 1.09. The approximate F-statistic of 4.90, with 2 and 43 degrees of freedom, is significant at the 0.025 level.

The government spending variable GXP can also be represented as a third-order autoregressive process in the first differences[14]:

$$[1 - 0.483L + 0.155L^2 + 0.285L^3] \Delta GXP_t = 33.3 + a_t$$
$$\quad (0.148) \quad (0.164) \quad (0.148) \qquad\qquad (48.9)$$

This (3, 1, 0) model does quite well in removing serial correlation from GXP. None of the first six autocorrelations is as large as its approximate standard error of 0.15. $Q^*(6)$ and $Q^*(12)$ correspond to P values of approximately 0.57 and 0.87, respectively.

8. TRANSFER FUNCTION MODELS FOR INVS

Table 4 shows estimated cross correlations between ΔINV, $\Delta INVS$, and $\Delta INVE$, and the various prewhitened input series. The most striking pattern in Table 4 is the negative contemporaneous relation between ΔINV and the government spending variable ΔGXP. This correlation is more than twice its standard error in absolute magnitude, and there is little evidence of cross correlation at leads or lags. This pattern does not apply equally well to $\Delta INVS$ and $\Delta INVE$, however. The negative contemporaneous relation is much stronger for $\Delta INVS$ than for $\Delta INVE$. In fact, the contemporaneous relation between $\Delta INVE$ and ΔGXP could well be zero, while there is a hint of a negative relation between $\Delta INVE(t)$ and $\Delta GXP(t - 1)$. These correlations, combined with a weak positive relation between $\Delta INVS(t)$ and $\Delta GXP(t - 1)$, lead to an apparent lack of association between ΔINV and the lagged spending variable.

With regard to the two tax rates, there is some evidence of correlation between current values of each investment series and future values of one or both of $\Delta MTRK$ and MTRL. The strongest and most consistent of these is a negative association between $\Delta MTRK(t + 1)$ and the current value of each of the investment series. There may also be a negative relation between $\Delta MTRK(t + 3)$ and current investment, between $\Delta MTRL(t + 2)$ and $\Delta INVS$, and between $\Delta MTRL(t + 1)$ and $\Delta INVE$. In addition, there may be some association between current investment and lagged tax rates.

There are several possible explanations for the large sample cross correlations between current investment and future tax rates. First, current investment decisions might in some way affect future tax rates. Alternatively, expectations concerning future tax rates might be highly correlated with actual future tax rates, and these expectations might affect current investment

---

[14] The standard error of the regression is 324. The approximate F-statistic of 6.91, with 3 and 42 degrees of freedom, is significant at the 0.001 level.

TABLE 4

Estimated Cross-Correlation Functions between Investment Variables and Prewhitened Values of Potential Exogenous Variables[a]

	ΔGXP			ΔMTRK			ΔMTRL		
	ΔINV	ΔINVS	ΔINVE	ΔINV	ΔINVS	ΔINVE	ΔINV	ΔINVS	ΔINVE
Lead 4	0.233	0.127	0.253	0.206	0.275	0.112	0.043	0.153	-0.035
Lead 3	0.003	0.028	-0.017	-0.292	-0.351	-0.187	-0.011	-0.049	0.015
Lead 2	-0.052	0.021	-0.092	-0.129	-0.157	-0.080	-0.216	-0.366	-0.073
Lead 1	-0.025	0.103	-0.098	-0.377	-0.279	-0.376	-0.128	0.147	-0.281
Concurrent	-0.326	-0.664	-0.020	0.127	-0.055	0.240	0.060	-0.166	0.196
Lag 1	-0.050	0.269	-0.251	-0.150	-0.016	-0.222	-0.107	-0.048	-0.124
Lag 2	0.042	-0.016	0.067	-0.134	-0.254	0.015	-0.286	-0.256	-0.245
Lag 3	0.215	0.079	0.255	0.063	0.171	-0.031	0.154	0.133	0.136
Lag 4	-0.019	0.088	-0.085	0.163	0.052	0.206	0.278	0.303	0.200
Lag 5	0.040	-0.053	0.093	0.289	0.375	0.173	0.076	0.079	0.062
Lag 6	0.096	0.064	0.093	0.002	-0.113	0.083	0.105	-0.005	0.155
Lag 7	-0.095	-0.017	-0.126	-0.114	-0.040	-0.142	-0.142	-0.058	-0.170
Lag 8	0.193	0.057	0.241	-0.141	-0.123	-0.127	-0.028	0.051	-0.070
Standard error	0.152	0.152	0.152	0.147	0.147	0.147	0.152	0.152	0.152

[a] "Lead k" denotes the correlation between $\Delta I(t)$ and $\hat{a}(t+k)$, where $\Delta I(t)$ denotes the relevant differenced investment series and the $\hat{a}(t)$ are the prewhitened values of the relevant exogenous variable. "Lag k" denotes the correlation between $\Delta I(t)$ and $\hat{a}(t-k)$. The sample period is 1930–1975 for cross correlations with MTRK and is 1933–1975 for the other cross correlations.

decisions, thus producing large correlations between current values of investment and subsequent realized values of ΔMTRK and ΔMTRL. Finally, it is possible that these sample cross correlations, even though they are twice their standard errors, might have occurred purely by chance.

As concerns the first of these explanations, it seems quite plausible that current investment decisions, by affecting future income, will also influence future tax payments. It is not obvious that they would have any effect on future tax rates, however. Consequently, the possibility of causality running from investment to tax rates, which would imply that future tax rates should not be included in a transfer function for investment, will be dismissed for now. It will be taken up again later in this chapter.

The second explanation is the most attractive from the point of view of agreement with the theoretical propositions of Section 2. It becomes less and less plausible, however, the greater the lead at which the cross correlation occurs. It is reasonable to believe that, other things being equal, a given increase in the rate of taxation of the income from either labor or capital will have a smaller effect on current investment decisions, the further into the future the increase is expected to occur. Furthermore, it is plausible that predictions of future tax rates become less and less precise, the further into the future one tries to forecast. For these reasons, the cross correlation between investment and ΔMTRK at lead 3 will be ignored for the purpose of transfer function model identification, while that at lead 1 will be considered. Since much tax legislation works its way through Congress and state legislatures in the year before it is to take effect, it is plausible to think that economic agents can make reasonably accurate forecasts of tax rates one year into the future, but that forecasts further into the future are considerably less precise. For these reasons, ΔMTRK is shifted forward one period in the transfer function models reported below. The cross correlations between current investment and future values of ΔMTRL will be ignored in the initial models, since it is desired to keep these models relatively simple and since economic theory less strongly suggests a relation between investment and the labor income tax rate than one between investment and the capital income tax rate. Any indication that these restrictions are inappropriate should show up in nonzero cross correlations between the residuals from the transfer function models and future values of the prewhitened tax rates. In none of the models reported below, however, do the cross correlations suggest that any further forward shifting of the input variables is called for.

Examination of Table 4 suggests that INVS and INVE behave sufficiently differently that one should estimate separate transfer function models for each of them rather than a single model for their sum, INV. Such differences in behavior are also suggested by a comparison of the autocorrelation functions in Table 2 and by the fact that, as can be seen in Table 3, the sample standard deviation of ΔINVE drops by about one third during the post-1950 period as compared with the pre-1950 period, while the sample standard deviation of ΔINVS drops much more dramatically.

Transfer function models for ΔINVS are reported in Table 5. Examination of the model reported in the first column reveals that the coefficient on the marginal tax rate on income from labor is imprecisely estimated. Its standard error is about three times as large as that of the coefficient on the capital income tax rate. The coefficient occurs at lag 2 and is positive in sign, yielding a negative steady-state gain which is substantially larger in magnitude than that associated with ΔMTRK.

In deciding whether to restrict the coefficient on ΔMTRL to equal zero, it is useful to examine the likelihood ratio. Consider the two hypotheses

$$H_0 : \omega_{22} = 0 \quad \text{and} \quad H_a : \omega_{22} \neq 0$$

Let λ denote the ratio of the value of the likelihood function under H_0, maximized with respect to its parameters, to the value of the likelihood function under H_a, similarly maximized with respect to its parameters. This ratio of maximized likelihood functions is given by

$$\lambda = (\hat{\sigma}_a / \hat{\sigma}_0)^n$$

where $\hat{\sigma}_0$ denotes the standard error of the regression under H_0, $\hat{\sigma}_a$ denotes the standard error of the regression under H_a, and n is the number of observations.[15] A low value of λ is evidence against the restriction incorporated in H_0. In Table 5, the model in the second column is nested within the model in the first column; that is, none of the parameters in column (2) is restricted to equal zero in column (1), while at least one of the parameters in column (1) is restricted to equal zero in column (2). Given a nested model, λ must lie between zero and unity. In addition, the quantity $-2 \ln \lambda$ has a χ^2-distribution in large samples, with degrees of freedom equal to the number of restrictions imposed to obtain the nested model, here equal to one. One can use the P value, or area under the upper tail of the χ^2-distribution, to make inferences concerning the validity of the restriction. In the case of Table 5, λ assumes a value of 0.197, which corresponds to a P value of approximately 0.08, indicating that one should probably exercise some caution in imposing this

---

[15] In performing these likelihood ratio tests, it is necessary that the sample period for the dependent variable be the same in both of the models being compared. It should be understood that all likelihood ratio tests reported in this paper have been conducted using models estimated over strictly comparable sample periods, and that this sample period may be slightly shorter than that for one or the other of the models reported in the tables. In no case are the coefficients or diagnostic test statistics significantly affected when the model is estimated over the shorter sample period.

It should also be noted that the standard error reported in the tables is computed using the number of degrees of freedom as the divisor, whereas the standard error used in the likelihood ratio tests is computed using the number of observations as the divisor.

restriction. It thus appears that the data allow one to make no strong inference with regard to the true effect of taxation of labor income on investment in nonresidential structures. Fortunately, however, the inference made with regard to the labor income tax rate has no material effect on the inferences made with regard to the other input variables.

Turning to the marginal tax rate on income from capital, the results are fairly consistent between the two models reported in Table 5. The only apparent relation is a negative one between $\Delta INVS(t)$ and $\Delta MTRK(t + 1)$. The coefficient, which has a standard error of about 0.9, is more precisely estimated than that for $\Delta MTRL$.

The evidence concerning the effect of the government spending variable on INVS is also insensitive to the exclusion of $\Delta MTRL$. There is a negative contemporaneous relation between $\Delta INVS$ and ΔGXP which is partially offset by a positive relation at lag 1. The steady-state gain is negative, either -0.0325 or -0.0357. These numbers are quite small in economic terms, probably much smaller than most discussions of crowding out would lead one to believe. They indicate that if crowding out does occur, a \$1 increase in GXP

TABLE 5

Transfer Function Models for $\Delta INVS(t)$ 1931–1974[a]

	(1)	(2)
Constant Term	7.59	2.79
	(4.47)	(5.11)
$\Delta GPX(t)$		
$\hat{\omega}_{10}$	−0.0589	−0.0610
	(0.00896)	(0.0101)
$\hat{\omega}_{11}$	−0.0262	−0.0254
	(0.00898)	(0.0102)
Gain	−0.0325	−0.0357
	(0.0119)	(0.0141)
$S^*(6)$	4.43	1.64
P value[b]	0.11	0.66
$S^*(12)$	7.29	4.77
P value	0.51	0.85
$\Delta MTRL(t)$		
$\hat{\omega}_{22}$	4.50	—[c]
	(2.65)	
Gain	−4.50	—
	(2.65)	
$S^*(6)$	2.65	—
P value	0.27	—
$S^*(12)$	8.29	—
P value	0.42	—

(*continues*)

TABLE 5 (*continued*)

ΔMTRK($t + 1$)		
$\hat{\omega}_{30}$	−1.99	−2.06
	(0.889)	(0.992)
$S^*(6)$	1.05	2.87
P value	0.61	0.43
$S^*(12)$	7.42	6.64
P value	0.49	0.67
Noise model		
$\hat{\theta}_1$	−0.406	−0.486
	(0.168)	(0.152)
Summary statistics		
R^2	0.678	0.554
F	15.6[d]	12.1[e]
Standard error of		
regression	19.9	22.9
Autocorrelation of residuals		
$Q^*(6)$	1.82	1.52
P value	0.87	0.91
$Q^*(12)$	5.18	8.21
P value	0.92	0.69

[a] The form of the transfer function is
$$\Delta \text{INVS}_t = \mu + (\omega_{10} - \omega_{11}L)\Delta \text{GXP}_t - \omega_{22}\Delta \text{MTRL}_t$$
$$+ \omega_{30}\Delta \text{MTRK}_{t+1} + (1 - \theta_1 L)\varepsilon_t$$
where Δ is the difference operator, L is the lag operator, and $\varepsilon(t)$ is a white-noise process. Standard errors appear in parentheses below parameter estimates. The sample period for the model in column (1) is 1932–1974.

[b] The P value is the approximate area under the upper tail of the relevant χ^2-distribution.

[c] Parameter suppressed.

[d] This approximate F-statistic has 5 and 37 degrees of freedom and is significant at the 0.01 level.

[e] This approximate F-statistic has 4 and 39 degrees of freedom and is significant at the 0.01 level.

crowds out only about 3.5¢ worth of investment in structures. Though small in absolute magnitude, however, the gain is quite significant statistically.[16]

To summarize the results with respect to investment in nonresidential structures, the evidence is inconclusive with regard to the effect of the taxation of labor income on such investment. Although the true effect appears not to be zero, it is imprecisely estimated. Taxation of income from capital, however, exerts an economically strong and statistically significant effect on investment in structures. The effect appears to be concentrated at a lead of one year. The evidence indicates that a permanent 1 percentage point increase

[16] The models in Table 5 were estimated with the gain of GPX constrained to equal zero. Likelihood ratio tests were performed, and each test yielded a P value of 0.01 or less, thus contradicting the validity of the restrictions.

in the tax rate on income from capital will lead to a permanent reduction in annual investment in structures of about $2 per person of working age, measured in 1972 prices. Using 1981 prices and population, this translates into approximately $690 million of investment per year. An increase in GXP causes a contemporaneous reduction in INVS which is partially offset in the following year. The gain is statistically quite significant but economically fairly small.

9. TRANSFER FUNCTION MODELS FOR INVE

Table 6 reports transfer function models for investment in producers' durable equipment. Since the cross correlation function between ΔINVE and prewhitened values of MTRK indicates a strong relation at lead 1, MTRK is shifted forward one period.

Examination of column (1) of Table 6 reveals that the numerator polynomial on the labor income tax rate has a positive contemporaneous coefficient and a positive coefficient of similar magnitude at lag 1, thus yielding a negligible steady-state gain. Furthermore, these coefficients are imprecisely

TABLE 6

Transfer Function Models for ΔINVE(t) 1930 1974[a]

	(1)	(2)	(3)
Constant Term	16.0	13.9	15.4
	(4.77)	(4.32)	(3.66)
ΔGXP(t)			
$\hat{\omega}_{10}$	-0.0278	-0.0248	-0.0296
	(0.0173)	(0.0155)	(0.0148)
$S*(6)$	2.85	3.97	2.73
P value[b]	0.24	0.42	0.45
$S*(12)$	6.03	10.9	5.94
P value	0.64	0.38	0.75
ΔMTRL(t)			
$\hat{\omega}_{20}$	6.43	—[c]	7.20
	(5.26)		(3.71)
$\hat{\omega}_{21}$	7.76	—[c]	7.20[d]
	(4.59)		
Gain	-1.33	—	0.00[d]
	(6.33)		
$S*(6)$	5.16	—	5.02
P value	0.08	—	0.19
$S*(12)$	7.02	—	6.88
P value	0.54	—	0.65

(continues)

TABLE 6 (*continued*)

ΔMTRK($t + 1$)			
$\hat{\omega}_{30}$	-4.56	-3.98	-4.56
	(1.61)	(1.68)	(1.59)
$S*(6)$	3.98	6.41	3.92
P value	0.15	0.19	0.28
$S*(12)$	5.12	8.95	5.23
P value	0.74	0.54	0.81
Noise model			
$\hat{\theta}_2$	0.344	0.263	0.346
	(0.164)	(0.158)	(0.162)
Summary statistics			
R^2	0.357	0.226	0.356
F	4.22[c]	3.98[f]	5.40[g]
Standard error of			
regression	35.9	38.0	35.5
Autocorrelation of residuals			
$Q*(6)$	3.22	2.95	3.22
P value	0.67	0.71	0.67
$Q*(12)$	7.16	4.26	6.90
P value	0.78	0.95	0.80

[a] The form of the transfer function is

$$\Delta\text{INVE}_t = \mu + \omega_{10}\,\Delta\text{GXP}_t + (\omega_{20} - \omega_{21}L)\,\Delta\text{MTRL}_t$$
$$+ \omega_{30}\,\Delta\text{MTRK}_{t+1} + (1 - \theta_2 L^2)\varepsilon_t$$

where Δ is the difference operator, L is the lag operator, and $\varepsilon(t)$ is a white-noise process. Standard errors appear in parentheses below parameter estimates. The sample period for the models in columns (1) and (3) is 1931 to 1974.

[b] The P value is the approximate area under the upper tail of the relevant χ^2-distribution.

[c] Parameter suppressed.

[d] This value is implied by the constraint that the gain equal 0.

[e] This approximate F-statistic has 5 and 38 degrees of freedom and is significant at the 0.01 level.

[f] This approximate F-statistic has 3 and 41 degrees of freedom and is significant at the 0.01 level.

[g] This approximate F-statistic has 4 and 39 degrees of freedom and is significant at the 0.01 level.

estimated, neither being much more than 1.5 times its standard error. Constraining both ω_{20} and ω_{21} to equal zero causes no material change in the coefficient on the spending variable, but reduces the absolute magnitude of the coefficient on the capital income tax rate. One should be cautious about imposing this constraint, however, since a likelihood ratio test of the hypothesis that $\omega_{20} = \omega_{21} = 0$ against the alternative that at least one of the coefficients is nonzero yields a value of λ of 0.121. This likelihood ratio provides little support for the restriction and corresponds to a P value of only

0.13. Even though there is reasonable probability that either ω_{20} or ω_{21} is nonzero, it is not possible to reject the hypothesis that the steady-state gain $\omega_{20} - \omega_{21}$ is zero. This hypothesis yields a likelihood ratio of approximately 0.975, which corresponds to a P value of approximately 0.84.

Table 6 shows a negative relation between $\Delta INVE(t)$ and $\Delta MTRK(t + 1)$. The coefficient is -4.56 for the models which include $\Delta MTRL$ and -3.98 for the model which excludes $\Delta MTRL$. Each coefficient is between 2.3 and 2.8 times its standard error in absolute magnitude. There thus seems to be an economically substantial and statistically significant negative relation between the tax rate on income from capital and investment in producers' durable equipment.

Table 6 also provides evidence of a negative contemporaneous relation between investment in producers' durable equipment and the spending variable GXP, the coefficients being between -0.025 and -0.03.

In summary, it seems that an increase in government spending exerts a slight negative contemporaneous effect on investment in producers' durable equipment, while a change in the marginal tax rate on income from labor exerts no long-run effect. Using the point estimate from column (3) indicates that a permanent increase of 1 percentage point in the rate of taxation of income from capital leads to a permanent drop in annual investment in producers' durable equipment of about \$4.56 per person of working age, measured in 1972 dollars. Using 1981 prices and population, this translates into approximately \$1.26 billion of investment per year.

10. COMPARISON OF RESULTS FOR INVS AND INVE

A comparison of the results for investment in nonresidential structures reported in Table 5 with those for investment in producers' durable equipment reported in Table 6 reveals that quite similar inferences can be drawn from the two tables. Both $\Delta INVS(t)$ and $\Delta INVE(t)$ are negatively related to $\Delta MTRK(t + 1)$, although the coefficient on $\Delta MTRK(t + 1)$ in the models for $\Delta INVE(t)$ is quite a bit larger in absolute value than that in the equation for $\Delta INVS(t)$. This difference in magnitude occurs in part because the sample standard deviation of $\Delta INVE$ is about one third larger than that for $\Delta INVS$, but it is due mainly to the fact that the correlation between $\Delta INVE(t)$ and $\Delta MTRK(t + 1)$ is stronger than that between $\Delta INVS(t)$ and $\Delta MTRK(t + 1)$.

Another point of overall similarity between the results for INVS and those for INVE concerns the effects on investment of the labor income tax rate. In no case is a coefficient on $\Delta MTRL$ estimated very precisely. Furthermore, models which include $\Delta MTRL$ as an input variable have somewhat less acceptable diagnostic test statistics than do models which exclude $\Delta MTRL$. While it is highly unlikely that both ω_{20} and ω_{21} are zero in the models for

ΔINVE, it is impossible to reject the hypothesis that changes in the labor income tax rate exert no long-run effect on investment in producers' durable equipment.

All models estimated for both ΔINVS and ΔINVE show a negative contemporaneous relation between the change in investment and the spending variable ΔGXP. This contemporaneous effect is partially offset by a positive relation at lag 1 in models for ΔINVS.[17] In addition, the point estimate of the steady-state gain is more negative, and its standard error smaller, in the models for ΔINVS than in those for ΔINVE. It is thus more likely that the true effect is negative in the former models than in the latter.

It is tempting to venture an explanation for the apparent fact that the negative relation between ΔINVE(t) and ΔMTRK($t + 1$) is stronger than that between ΔINVS(t) and ΔMTRK($t + 1$). It has been noted that the investment decision should be influenced by expectations with regard to the tax rates which will prevail during the life of the asset being acquired. Since equipment typically has a shorter useful life than do structures, the decision to invest in equipment should be influenced by tax rates expected to prevail over a shorter time horizon than is relevant for investment in structures. It is possible that economic agents can forecast the capital income tax rate one year into the future with reasonable accuracy, and that MTRK($t + 1$) is a much better proxy for the tax rates which will exist over a relatively short horizon than for rates which will exist further into the future. This effect might be reinforced by the lag between the decision to undertake an investment project and the actual investment expenditures resulting from that decision. These expenditures will generally be distributed over some period of time after the investment decision has been made. If a larger portion of the expenditures on equipment occurs during the first year after the investment decision is made than is the case for investment in structures, then a change in MTRK in year $t + 1$ might have a stronger effect on the former

---

[17] When the government deficit rather than purchases of goods and services is used as an explanatory variable, it has a coefficient of about -0.08 in models for INVS and -0.07 in models for INVE. These effects are stronger than those estimated using GPX as an input. In addition, the coefficient on the capital income tax rate is only about -0.7 (with a standard error of about 0.9) in models for INVS using the government deficit as an input variable, compared with a coefficient of about -2.00 in models using GXP as an input. If government transfers to persons are included as an input variable in addition to GXP, the coefficient on transfer payments is between -0.2 and -0.3 (with a standard error of about 0.09) in models for INVS and is about 0.17 (with a standard error of about 0.17) in models for INVE. If taken at face value, these coefficients indicate that transfer payments exert a stronger crowding-out effect, at least on investment in structures, than do purchases of goods and services. These results are probably less reliable than those reported in the text, however, since equations using the deficit or transfer payments as input variables generally have poorer diagnostic test statistics than do equations using as inputs only those variables more likely to be exogenous.

type of expenditure in year t than on the latter, even if it has no differential effect on the two types of investment decision made in year t.

The above explanation can also be linked to the result that aggregate government spending appears to have a stronger deterrent effect on investment in structures than on investment in equipment. The standard explanation of this deterrent effect is that public spending or borrowing crowds out private spending or borrowing. The observed coefficients on government spending variables are much smaller than one would have been led to believe by discussions of crowding out, however. An alternative hypothesis advanced in Section 2 suggests that an increase in current government spending or borrowing may convey information that tax rates will be higher in the future than they otherwise would have been. It is possible that the government spending variables used in this chapter do convey such information and are in fact better proxies than $\Delta MTRK(t + 1)$ for the course of the capital income tax rate over a long horizon. The government spending variable might thus be a fairly good proxy for the tax rates relevant to investment in structures, while $MTRK(t + 1)$ might be the better proxy for tax rates relevant to investment in equipment. This line of reasoning is highly speculative, however, and there are undoubtedly other explanations for the empirical results reported here.

One alternative explanation as to why $\Delta MTRK(t + 1)$ affects investment in equipment more strongly than investment in structures concerns the investment tax credit. In 1962, Congress enacted a tax credit equal to 7 percent of a firm's investment in producers' durable equipment with a useful life of eight years or more. A reduced credit was granted for equipment with a useful life of four to eight years, and no credit was given for equipment with a useful life of less than four years. The credit applicable to utilities was 3 percent rather than 7 percent. Except for a few lapses (specifically, October 1966 to March 1967 and April 1969 to August 1971), and with minor modifications, the investment tax credit has been in effect ever since.

The estimated tax rate $MTRK$ is calculated using actual tax payments rather than legislated tax rates. The investment tax credit and other such provisions of the tax code affect $MTRK$ by affecting total tax payments. Because $MTRK$ is calculated for calendar years, which typically do not correspond to firms' fiscal years, and because there are provisions limiting the size of the tax credit which may be taken in any year but allowing the taxpayer to carry the unused portion forward to future tax years, it is possible that an increase in investment in equipment in calendar year t might reduce tax payments in calendar year $t + 1$. In other words, $INVE(t)$ might "cause" $MTRK(t + 1)$, rather than the other way around. Since the tax credit applied only to investment in equipment during the sample period, however, $INVS(t)$ would not affect $MTRK(t + 1)$.

In order to determine whether the relation between $\Delta INVE(t)$ and $\Delta MTRK(t + 1)$ is purely the result of the investment tax credit, the models reported in columns (1) and (2) of Table 6 were estimated for the period 1930–1960, before the investment tax credit took effect. The results, reported in Table 7, are almost identical to those for the full sample period, thus allowing rejection of the hypothesis that the observed relation is solely the result of causality running from $\Delta INVE(t)$ to $\Delta MTRK(t + 1)$ via the investment tax credit.[18]

There is some evidence in the data, however, to indicate that the enactment of the investment tax credit did affect the pattern of investment. The ratio of INVE to INVS, shown in Fig. 3, follows a very erratic path over time, starting from values of less than unity in the early years of the sample, rising above two during the war years, and remaining well within these bounds during the postwar period. Beginning in 1947, this ratio declined fairly steadily (only 4 of the 14 year-to year changes, also shown in Fig. 3, being positive) until 1961. Beginning in 1962, the year the tax credit on investment in equipment was enacted, the ratio increased almost steadily (only 3 of the 14 year-to-year changes being negative) until the end of the sample period in 1975. An alternative way of expressing this phenomenon is in terms of annual growth rates of INVS and INVE. From 1947 to 1961, INVS grew at a compound annual rate of 2.7 percent, while INVE grew at a rate of 0.1 percent. From 1961 to 1974, however, INVS grew at an annual rate of only 1.2 percent, while the growth rate of INVE increased to 4.9 percent.

The autocorrelation functions shown in Table 8 indicate that the ratio of INVE to INVS is probably nonstationary, while the first differences of this ratio are approximately serially uncorrelated. If the first differences of the ratio are in fact serially uncorrelated, then the ratio may be represented by the random-walk model

$$\Delta \frac{INVE(t)}{INVS(t)} = \mu + \varepsilon(t)$$

[18] It should be noted that some of the cross correlations between residuals from the transfer functions and lagged values of the prewhitened input MTRK are larger for the models reported in Table 7 than was the case for models estimated over the full sample period. The high S^*-statistic for each model results in large part from a spike in the autocorrelation function at a lag of five years. In addition, the model in column (1) of Table 7 has a positive cross correlation at lag 1, while that in column (2) has a negative cross correlation at lag 2. It seems unlikely that these blemishes are sufficient to reverse the conclusion that the association between $\Delta INVE(t)$ and $\Delta MTRK(t + 1)$ is not due solely to a relation created by the investment tax credit in 1962. In fact, results reported in Section 11 indicate that the relation may well be apparent only until the early 1950s.

No model analogous to that reported in column (3) of Table 6 is reported since constraining ω_{20} and ω_{21} to be equal results in large cross correlations between the residuals from the transfer function and lagged values of the prewhitened MTRL series.

where μ is a constant and $\varepsilon(t)$ is serially uncorrelated. Suppose that for $t = 1948, \ldots, 1961$, the ratio of $INVE(t)$ to $INVS(t)$ can be represented by the model

$$\Delta \frac{INVE(t)}{INVS(t)} = \mu_1 + \varepsilon_1(t)$$

and that for $t = 1962, \ldots, 1975$, it can be represented by the model

$$\Delta \frac{INVE(t)}{INVS(t)} = \mu_2 + \varepsilon_2(t)$$

TABLE 7

Transfer Function Models for $\Delta INVE(t)$, 1930–1960[a]

	(1)	(2)
Constant Term	9.13	9.68
	(5.68)	(5.74)
$\Delta GXP(t)$		
$\hat{\omega}_{10}$	−0.0423	−0.0273
	(0.0183)	(0.0156)
$S*(6)$	2.14	4.33
P value[b]	0.36	0.38
$S*(12)$	4.95	12.7
P value	0.76	0.24
$\Delta MTRL(t)$		
$\hat{\omega}_{20}$	15.0	—[c]
	(6.24)	
$\hat{\omega}_{21}$	7.86	—[c]
	(4.80)	
Gain	7.19	—
	(7.25)	
$S*(6)$	5.63	—
P value	0.06	—
$S*(12)$	6.17	—
P value	0.63	—
$\Delta MTRK(t + 1)$		
$\hat{\omega}_{30}$	−5.22	−3.85
	(1.69)	(1.82)
$S*(6)$	7.03	7.98
P value	0.03	0.09
$S*(12)$	9.55	8.93
P value	0.31	0.54
Noise model		
$\hat{\theta}^2$	0.457	0.205
	(0.206)	(0.198)

(continues)

TABLE 7 (*continued*)

Summary statistics		
R^2	0.482	0.279
F	4.47^d	3.49^e
Standard error of regression	34.4	38.3
Autocorrelation of residuals		
$Q*(6)$	6.49	3.90
P value	0.27	0.57
$Q*(12)$	8.09	7.54
P value	0.70	0.75

[a] The form of the transfer function is

$$\Delta INVE_t = \mu + \omega_{10} \Delta GXP_t + (\omega_{20} - \omega_{21}L) \Delta MTRL_t$$
$$+ \omega_{30} \Delta MTRK_{t+1} + (1 - \theta_2 L^2)\varepsilon_t$$

where Δ is the difference operator, L is the lag operator, and $\varepsilon(t)$ is a white-noise process. Standard errors appear in parentheses below parameter estimates. The sample period for the model in column (1) is 1931–1960.

[b] The P value is the approximate area under the upper tail of the relevant χ^2-distribution.

[c] Parameter suppressed.

[d] This approximate F-statistic has 5 and 24 degrees of freedom and is significant at the 0.01 level.

[e] This approximate F-statistic has 3 and 27 degrees of freedom and is significant at the 0.05 level.

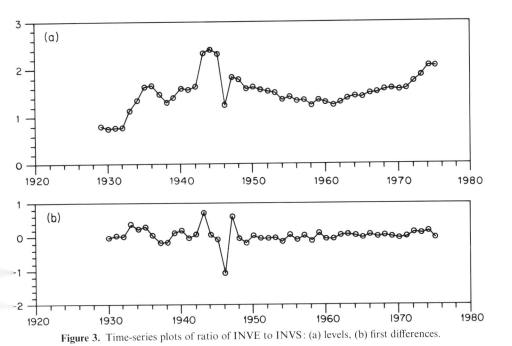

Figure 3. Time-series plots of ratio of INVE to INVS: (a) levels, (b) first differences.

TABLE 8

Autocorrelation Functions for the Ratio of INVE(t) to INVS(t) and for Its First Difference

	$\dfrac{INVE(t)}{INVS(t)}$ (1929–1975)	$\Delta\,\dfrac{INVE(t)}{INVS(t)}$ (1930–1975)
Lag 1	0.72	−0.13
Lag 2	0.48	−0.09
Lag 3	0.29	−0.19
Lag 4	0.19	0.13
Lag 5	0.08	−0.02
Lag 6	0.01	−0.16
Lag 7	0.04	0.04
Lag 8	0.06	0.25
Lag 9	−0.04	0.05
Lag 10	−0.19	0.06
Standard error	0.15	0.15
$Q^*(10)^a$	47.1	9.50
P value	0.00	0.49

[a] $Q^*(10)$ is distributed approximately χ^2 with 10 degrees of freedom.

where $\varepsilon_1(t)$ and $\varepsilon_2(t)$ are normally distributed white-noise processes with common variance σ^2. Now consider two alternative hypotheses:

$$H_0 : \mu_2 - \mu_1 \leq 0 \qquad \text{and} \qquad H_a : \mu_2 - \mu_1 > 0$$

Under these assumptions, and if H_0 is true, the quantity

$$t = (\hat{\mu}_2 - \hat{\mu}_1)\left[\left[\frac{N_1 s_1^2 + N_2 s_2^2}{N_1 + N_2 - 2}\right]\left[\frac{N_1 + N_2}{N_1 N_2}\right]\right]^{-1/2}.$$

has a Student t-distribution with zero mean and $N_1 + N_2 - 2$ degrees of freedom. Here N_1 and N_2 are the sizes of the two samples, $\hat{\mu}_1$ and $\hat{\mu}_2$ are the sample means, and s_1^2 and s_2^2 are the estimates of σ^2 computed using the sample size as divisor. In the present case $\hat{\mu}_1 = -0.0420$, $\hat{\mu}_2 = 0.0588$, and $t = 2.498$. This t-statistic has 26 degrees of freedom and is significant at the 0.01 level in a one-tailed test, providing strong evidence that the ratio of INVE to INVS behaved differently after enactment of the investment tax credit than during the earlier part of the postwar period.

Finally, one other item is worthy of note in comparing the models for investment in structures with those for investment in producer's durable equipment. The models for ΔINVS have considerably higher explanatory power, as measured by R^2, than do models for ΔINVE. The R^2 for ΔINVS models is in the neighborhood of 0.55–0.70, while that for ΔINVE models is around 0.20–0.35.

11. RESULTS FOR SELECTED SUBPERIODS

It was noted in Section 6 that most of the time series under consideration were much less volatile during the period after 1950 than during the earlier years. Since most of the variation in the data occurs during the earlier years, it is possible that the results for the entire sample are due to the relation which held during that earlier period. Not only is it possible that the postwar observations exert only a minor influence on the coefficients estimated for the entire sample period, it is even conceivable that the models appropriate to the postwar period are inconsistent with those appropriate to the earlier years and that the data for these earlier years, because of their greater variability, dominate the results for the entire sample period. In order to check this possibility, models for ΔINVS and ΔINVE were estimated using data only from 1950 or later. The same models were also estimated using data only from the earlier period. The results are summarized in Tables 9 and 10.

Examination of Table 9 reveals that the models for ΔINVS estimated for the earlier periods are generally similar to those estimated over the full sample. The coefficients on ΔGXP are negative, similar in size to those for the full sample, and more than twice their standard errors in absolute value. The coefficients on ΔMTRK$(t + 1)$ are more negative, but less precisely estimated, than those for a full sample. The major discrepancy concerns the coefficient on ΔMTRL, which in the earlier period is close to zero and opposite in sign to that for the full sample.

In models estimated over the post-1950 period, the small negative steady-state gain associated with ΔGXP becomes still less negative, or even positive. The coefficients on ΔMTRK$(t + 1)$ remain negative, that in column (6) being the most negative in the entire table, but are not very precisely estimated. The coefficient on ΔMTRL is very large and positive, but also quite imprecisely estimated. The influence of ΔMTRL in fact constitutes the most apparent discrepancy between the models estimated for the two subsamples.[19] The effects of ΔMTRK$(t + 1)$ are, by comparison, much more uniform across time periods.

Since the three-input models are identical in form for all estimation periods, it is possible to test the hypothesis that the true coefficient vectors

---

[19] Even this discrepancy is more apparent than real. Joines (1981) describes not only the overall factor income tax rates MTRK and MTRL, but also their components. One component of MTRL which has become increasingly important since the mid-1950s is that associated with the Social Security tax. Although it is probably inappropriate to use the individual components of MTRL as input variables in a transfer function analysis, crude correlations reveal that the positive relation between ΔINVS and ΔMTRL is due almost entirely to a positive association between ΔINVS and the contribution of the Social Security tax to ΔMTRL. Since this contribution was close to or equal to zero during the entire pre-1950 period, such a relation would show up only during the later subsample.

TABLE 9

Summary of Models for ΔINVS(t) for Selected Subperiods[a]

			Period			
	(1) 1932–1974	(2) 1932–1952	(3) 1953–1974	(4) 1931–1974	(5) 1931–1951	(6) 1952–1974
ΔGXP(t)						
$\hat{\omega}_{10}$	−0.0587	−0.0627	−0.0238	−0.0610	−0.0618	−0.00675
	(0.00896)	(0.0113)	(0.0582)	(0.0101)	(0.0127)	(0.0577)
$\hat{\omega}_{11}$	−0.0262	−0.0267	−0.0360	−0.0254	−0.0270	0.00673
	(0.00898)	(0.0107)	(0.0490)	(0.0102)	(0.0130)	(0.0467)
Gain	−0.0325	−0.0359	0.0122	−0.0357	−0.0349	−0.0135
	(0.0119)	(0.0153)	(0.0645)	(0.0141)	(0.0181)	(0.0459)
ΔMTRL(t)						
$\hat{\omega}_{22}$	4.50	−0.633	8.11	—[b]	—[b]	—[b]
	(2.65)	(4.34)	(4.34)			
ΔMTRK(t + 1)						
$\hat{\omega}_{30}$	−1.99	−2.73	−1.27	−2.06	−2.37	−2.78
	(0.889)	(1.30)	(2.16)	(0.992)	(1.38)	(2.39)
Summary statistics						
R^2	0.678	0.781	0.214	0.554	0.661	0.071
F	15.6	10.7	0.874	12.1	7.81	0.481
P value	0.00	0.00	0.52	0.00	0.00	0.70
Standard error of regression	19.9	23.5	17.4	22.9	28.4	19.3
Number of observations	43	21	22	44	21	23

[a] Standard errors appear in parentheses below parameter estimates.
[b] Parameter suppressed.

196

TABLE 10

Summary of Models for ΔINVE(t) for Selected Subperiods[a]

	Period					
	(1) 1933–1974	(2) 1933–1953	(3) 1954–1974	(4) 1933–1974	(5) 1933–1953	(6) 1954–1974
ΔGXP(t)						
$\hat{\omega}_{10}$	−0.0267 (0.0178)	−0.0350 (0.0226)	0.0811 (0.101)	−0.0293 (0.0149)	−0.0267 (0.0151)	0.0524 (0.155)
ΔMTRL(t)						
$\hat{\omega}_{20}$	6.12 (5.17)	11.2 (8.86)	−5.54 (7.58)	7.12 (3.38)	7.69 (4.97)	8.82 (5.17)
$\hat{\omega}_{21}$	7.83 (4.41)	6.88 (5.30)	24.5 (8.29)	7.12[b]	7.69[b]	8.82[b]
Gain	−1.71 (6.65)	4.35 (8.61)	−30.0 (13.4)	0.00[b] —	0.00[b] —	0.00[b] —
ΔMTRK(t + 1)						
$\hat{\omega}_{30}$	−4.24 (1.70)	−6.09 (1.82)	0.356 (4.85)	−4.21 (1.68)	−6.05 (1.78)	0.378 (5.20)
Summary statistics						
R^2	0.451	0.671	0.300	0.450	0.665	0.238
F	4.79	4.76	0.999	5.89	5.97	0.937
P value	0.00	0.01	0.47	0.00	0.00	0.49
Standard error of regression	34.6	33.5	37.1	34.1	32.6	37.4
Number of observations	42	21	21	42	21	21

[a] Standard errors appear in parentheses below parameter estimates.
[b] This value is implied by the constraint that the gain equal 0.

197

for those models are in fact equal during the two subsamples.[20] This test yields a likelihood ratio of 0.105, which corresponds to a P value of approximately 0.61. It is thus impossible to reject the hypothesis that the coefficient vectors are equal. Examination of the summary statistics, however, indicates that it is also impossible to reject the hypothesis that the entire coefficient vector is zero during the second subperiod. It thus seems that most of the explanatory power found in the full sample comes from the earlier subperiod, that little in the way of a strong or reliable relation can be estimated for the later subperiod, and that whatever relation exists during this second subsample is not inconsistent with that which exists during the first.

Table 10 contains models for ΔINVE estimated over different sample periods.[21] It can be seen that models estimated over the first subperiod are generally similar to those estimated for the full sample, while those for the later subperiod appear quite different. The coefficient on ΔGXP is negative in the first subperiod, but it becomes positive in the second subperiod. These coefficients are small in absolute value and are generally not very large relative to their standard errors. The coefficients of ΔMTRL are quite similar across sample periods when ω_{20} is constrained to equal ω_{21}. When the constraint is relaxed, however, this pattern changes from the earlier sample period, where the gain is positive but statistically insignificant, to the later period, where the gain becomes negative and large both in economic terms and relative to its standard error. The coefficient of ΔMTRK$(t + 1)$ is even more negative in the first subperiod than in the full sample, and is large relative to its standard error. This coefficient is close to zero in the later subperiod, however.

Using likelihood ratio tests, it is impossible to reject the hypothesis that the coefficient vectors in columns (2) and (3) of Table 10 are equal, or that those in columns (5) and (6) are equal. For the models in columns (2) and (3), the likelihood ratio is 0.023, which corresponds to a P value of approximately 0.38. For the models in columns (5) and (6), the likelihood ratio is 0.070, which corresponds to a P value of approximately 0.50. As was the case with models for ΔINVS, however, it is also impossible to reject the hypothesis that the true coefficient vector is equal to zero during the second subperiod.

In attempting to explain this apparent anomaly, it is worth examining the summary statistics reported in Table 9. It can be seen that models esti-

---

[20] This test is not performed for the two-input equations since the form of the noise model appropriate to the 1952–1974 subperiod is different from that appropriate to the earlier subperiod.

[21] The models reported in columns (1) and (4) differ slightly from those reported in Table 6, since each equation in Table 10 has an AR(2) noise model rather than an MA(2) model as in Table 6. AR(2) models performed almost as well as MA(2) models for the equations in columns (1), (2), (4), and (5), but MA(2) models proved inadequate for those columns (3) and (6). It was desired to keep the noise models identical in form across sample periods so that likelihood ratio tests could be performed.

mated over the earlier subperiod have both higher explanatory power, as measured by R^2, and larger standard errors of regression than do models estimated over the later subperiod. This result is due to the fact that, as was apparent from Table 3, ΔINVS is considerably more variable during the first subperiod than during the second. In fact, this difference in variability is so great that, despite the relatively high R^2, the models estimated over the earlier subperiod have a standard error of regression which is larger than the sample standard deviation of ΔINVS during the post-1950 period. Furthermore, not only are the investment series more variable during the earlier years, but the input series are more variable then as well. It thus seems that one explanation for the weakness of the relation estimated over the post-1950 period is that there was so little movement in the input series as compared with the variability of the noise process that it is impossible to estimate the relation very precisely. As Kormendi (1978) argues, identification of such relations may require a "natural experiment" during which there is substantial movement in the exogenous variables. While such an experiment, or experiments, may have occurred during the 1930s and 1940s, none has occurred since. Cagan (1956) makes a similar argument concerning the estimation of money demand functions during periods of hyperinflation.

If a transfer function of the form of Eq. (1) actually describes the relations between the investment series and the input series used here, a reduction in the variability of investment between the earlier and later subperiods must be the result of a similar reduction in the variability of one or more of the input series, of the noise process, or of both. Such a reduction in the variability of the inputs has already been pointed out. The transfer function is not based on particular assumptions about the relative variability of the inputs during different subsamples. It is explicitly based, however, on the assumption that the noise process has a constant variance over the entire sample. This suggests that in judging whether a single model estimated over an entire sample of data is valid for each of the relevant subsamples, one should determine whether the model fits the data equally well during each of those subperiods. It also suggests that the relevant criterion for judging goodness of fit should be some measure of the dispersion of the residuals and not the more commonly used R^2, changes which could be brought about by changes in the variability of the input series.

Table 11 contains measures of variability of the residuals, by decade, from models for ΔINVS and ΔINVE estimated for the full sample period and reported in column (1) of Tables 5 and 6. The sample standard deviation appears reasonably uniform over time in the model for ΔINVE. In the model for ΔINVS, the sample standard deviation of residuals is noticeably larger during the 1930s than during any of the subsequent periods, and there is a negative residual in the first year of the estimation period which is more than two standard errors from zero. If this initial residual is ignored, the sample

TABLE 11

Variability of Residuals from Transfer Function Models by Decade

Decade	Sample standard deviation of residuals[a]		Number of large residuals[b]	
	ΔINVS[c]	ΔINVE[d]	ΔINVS[c]	ΔINVE[d]
1930s	24.9	35.9	1	0
1940s	17.7	35.2	0	0
1950s	14.0	24.5	0	0
1960s	16.1	33.5	0	0
1970s	20.0	39.7	0	0

[a] The sample standard deviation of residuals is computed using zero as the mean in all subperiods and using the number of residuals as the divisor.

[b] A large residual is defined as being at least two standard errors from zero.

[c] Model reported in Table 5, column (1).

[d] Model reported in Table 6, column (1).

standard deviation for the 1930s falls to 15.0, which is very much in line with the other numbers in the table. It thus appears that, except for the initial observation in the model for ΔINVS, the residuals exhibit reasonably uniform variability over time.

The evidence presented here thus seems consistent with the following line of reasoning. The true error terms for each investment series are drawn from the same distribution throughout the entire sample period; a single transfer function model also applies to each of the investment series throughout the entire sample period, and the only major difference between the earlier and the later years concerns the variability of the input series. Because of the small variability of the inputs in the later years relative to their variability during the earlier period, the explanatory power of equations fit over the full sample comes almost entirely from the pre-1950 period. Because of the small variability of the input series relative to the noise process during the post-1950 period, it is difficult to measure the relations which existed during that subsample, but those relations were no different from the ones which existed during the earlier years.

It is also possible that the economic structure shifted sometime after World War II and that no relation existed between investment and the input series over the post-1950 period. The question arises as to what factors could have led to such a shift. Lucas (1976) has pointed out that the behavioral relations normally incorporated into structural economic models may change as a result of changes in the "economic environment." More specifically, changes in government policy may induce shifts in the parameters of the structural equations of the system, and hence in the parameters of the transfer functions as well. One major change in government policy during the post-war period as compared with the earlier years is a noticeable reduction in the variability of the three input variables used in this paper. It is conceivable that the government's adoption of less volatile fiscal policy altered the economic structure in such a way as to reduce the impact of those fluctuations which did occur. The evidence in the data, however, does not enable one to distinguish this view from the alternative one presented above.

12. CONCLUSION

This empirical results reported in this paper are supportive of several conclusions. First, investment in nonresidential structures and investment in producers' durable equipment appear to behave sufficiently differently that aggregating the two is inappropriate for the types of analysis performed here. These differences are apparent both in the univariate time-series properties of the two series and also in the form of the transfer functions relating them to the various measures of government fiscal policy. The transfer functions for INVS and INVE differ with respect to the form of lag distribution associated with the government spending variable and the marginal tax rate on income from labor, and with respect to the magnitude of the effects of these variables and of the marginal tax rate on income from capital. As to the signs of these effects, however, there is considerable consistency between models for INVS and those for INVE, both during the full sample period and during that portion of the sample which extends up through the early 1950s.

Equations estimated over the full sample period provide fairly convincing evidence that an increase in government purchases of goods and services is associated with a reduction in investment in nonresidential structures. This negative relation is consistent with both the traditional crowding-out effect and the tax-anticipation effect discussed in previous sections. While statistically significant, however, the coefficients are smaller than the usual crowding-out argument would seem to suggest. There is also evidence that an increase in government purchases is associated with a decrease in investment in producers' durable equipment. This relation is even smaller than that between INVS and purchases, however.

There is little evidence of a relation between investment and the marginal tax rate on income from labor. The relation between INVE and MTRL, as measured by the steady-state gain, is statistically insignificant at any reasonable level of significance, while the relation between INVS and MTRL is of marginal significance at most. This lack of statistical significance is due not to the small absolute size of the point estimates but rather to the lack of precision of those estimates. The point estimates of the coefficients in equations for both INVS and INVE are generally larger in absolute value than the coefficients on MTRK; they are much less precisely estimated, however.

The most powerful message in the full sample of data, however, is that taxation of the income from capital discourages capital formation. This negative relation is a consistent feature of all the models estimated and is quite robust with respect to the specification of the relation between investment and the other exogenous variables.

One might legitimately inquire as to the policy implications of these results. For example, by how much would a given reduction in the capital income tax rate stimulate business fixed investment? Unfortunately, one's answers to such questions depend on one's explanation of the weak statistical results of the post-1950 subperiod.

As noted in Section 11, it is possible that the reduction in the volatility of the economy after World War II as compared with the earlier years led the economic structure to change in such a way that fiscal policy had little effect on investment. If this is the case, then one would predict that fluctuations in fiscal policy of the magnitude experienced from the early 1950s to the early 1970s would have little effect on business fixed investment. On the other hand, major policy changes, such as a dramatic reduction in the capital income tax rate, would probably cause further changes in the economic structure with effects which would be difficult to predict based solely on the evidence reported here.

It is also possible that the economic structure was stable during the entire sample period and that lack of variability during the post-1950 period makes it impossible to measure the effects of fiscal policy on investment using post-war data only. If this is the case, then some policy conclusions can be drawn. In particular, the results reported here indicate that capital is currently being taxed in the United States at rates which significantly reduce market-sector activity. A few rough calculations might suggest at least approximately the magnitude of these effects. Assume the economy can be represented by an aggregate Cobb–Douglas production function with capital's share of national income being 25 percent. The empirical results of Sections 8 and 9 indicate that, using 1981 population and prices, a 1 percentage point increase in the marginal tax rate on income from capital reduces private investment by about $1.95 billion, or about 0.56 percent of 1981 gross private nonresidential fixed investment. Taking this 0.56 percent as a constant means that a permanent reduction in the capital income tax rate from 50 percent (its value in 1975) to 40 percent would result in a long-run increase in the capital stock of about 5.6 percent. If there were no response in labor employment, this would yield a permanent 1.4 percent increase in national income and a 6.3 percent reduction in government revenues (assuming average tax rates are reduced by the same proportion as marginal rates). If labor employment increased enough to keep the capital–labor ratio constant, it would yield a 5.6 percent increase in national income and a 2.4 percent decrease in government revenues. The welfare effects of such changes in tax rates and economic activity would depend upon the elasticities of the labor supply and saving schedules and upon how the government alters its spending programs in the face of changes in revenues. The results reported here thus indicate that changes in the rate of taxation of income from capital can be a powerful tool of public policy.

APPENDIX

Tables 12 and 13 list the data for fiscal policy and investment series, respectively.

TABLE 12

Fiscal Policy Series

Year	GXP[a]	MTRL	MTRK	Year	GXP[a]	MTRL	MTRK
1929	566.9	3.51	29.45	1953	1806.8	20.83	59.92
1930	607.9	3.60	27.76	1954	1635.7	19.20	54.93
1931	622.0	3.82	28.59	1955	1583.2	19.76	55.38
1932	585.5	4.89	33.12	1956	1586.6	20.31	56.52
1933	562.9	6.79	41.08	1957	1654.7	22.19	55.23
1934	632.7	7.47	41.00	1958	1738.8	21.47	54.00
1935	639.3	7.44	41.44	1959	1739.3	22.34	54.29
1936	742.7	8.03	46.20	1960	1738.2	22.84	54.89
1937	707.1	8.06	44.43	1961	1813.3	23.05	54.55
1938	760.9	8.25	41.36	1962	1894.0	23.14	51.45
1939	782.4	8.25	42.55	1963	1917.6	23.33	51.69
1940	791.7	9.05	45.12	1964	1947.6	22.08	49.80
1941	1143.7	11.78	55.81	1965	1975.1	22.20	48.91
1942	2188.3	15.37	59.96	1966	2124.9	21.70	48.39
1943	3116.2	17.83	61.99	1967	2263.2	22.12	49.25
1944	3434.2	18.84	59.96	1968	2325.7	24.20	53.60
1945	3007.6	19.71	62.89	1969	2267.2	25.02	53.76
1946	1049.9	18.79	61.71	1970	2173.9	24.79	51.55
1947	842.1	19.25	59.21	1971	2131.6	23.34	51.15
1948	929.0	16.13	52.90	1972	2127.7	25.06	51.41
1949	1051.1	16.15	49.92	1973	2088.9	25.81	52.51
1950	1058.9	17.95	62.03	1974	2098.0	27.24	53.43
1951	1428.3	19.69	64.05	1975	2102.7	27.35	49.31
1952	1705.6	20.50	60.23				

[a] Units are constant dollars per person of working age. The base period for price deflation is 1972.

TABLE 13

Investment Series[a]

Year	INV	INVS	INVE	Year	INV	INVS	INVE
1929	512.9	285.5	227.3	1953	598.4	239.1	359.2
1930	414.4	237.2	177.2	1954	585.0	248.2	335.8
1931	263.9	149.4	114.4	1955	642.1	265.4	376.6
1932	151.7	85.2	65.2	1956	678.8	292.5	386.2
1933	136.8	64.4	72.3	1957	682.1	290.4	391.7
1934	161.1	68.9	92.2	1958	604.9	271.1	333.8
1935	199.0	75.7	123.2	1959	640.9	273.1	367.8
1936	270.4	101.6	168.9	1960	663.5	289.5	374.0
1937	322.8	130.6	192.2	1961	650.7	290.6	360.1
1938	232.1	101.8	131.6	1962	695.4	302.1	393.3
1939	253.8	105.5	148.4	1963	713.3	298.9	414.4
1940	310.6	119.7	191.0	1964	778.3	319.9	458.3
1941	361.4	141.9	220.6	1965	900.9	373.2	527.7
1942	207.3	78.9	128.4	1966	983.2	393.8	589.4
1943	162.8	48.9	114.0	1967	943.4	374.6	568.8
1944	214.9	63.2	151.7	1968	969.0	376.9	593.1
1945	314.1	94.4	218.5	1969	1009.5	388.6	620.9
1946	473.7	212.0	261.6	1970	955.8	371.9	583.9
1947	546.1	193.2	352.9	1971	923.1	356.4	566.7
1948	563.4	203.3	361.2	1972	981.9	357.3	624.6
1949	502.6	194.5	308.1	1973	1083.7	376.4	707.3
1950	541.9	207.0	334.9	1974	1063.3	346.0	717.3
1951	569.4	221.7	347.6	1975	909.6	297.1	612.6
1952	557.1	220.3	336.8				

[a] Units are constant dollars per person of working age. The base period for price deflation is 1972.

ACKNOWLEDGMENTS

This chapter excerpted from my doctoral dissertation at the University of Chicago. Thanks are due to the members of my committee: John P. Gould, Robert Hamada, Roger Kormendi, Robert Lucas, Merton Miller, and Arnold Zellner. In addition, I am grateful to Paul Evans, Arthur Laffer, and Robert Webb for helpful suggestions.

REFERENCES

Barro, R. J. (1974). "Are Government Bonds Net Wealth?" *Journal of Political Economy* **82**, 1095–1117.

Beveridge, S. (1975). "An Evaluation of the St. Louis Model," Ph.D. Dissertation, Univ. of Chicago, Chicago, Illinois.

Box, G. E. P., and Jenkins, G. M. (1970). *Time Series Analysis: Forecasting and Control.* Holden-Day, San Francisco, California.

Cagan, P. (1956). "The Monetary Dynamics of Hyperinflation," in *Studies in the Quantity Theory of Money* (M. Friedman, ed.). Univ. of Chicago Press, Chicago, Illinois.

Diamond, P. A. (1965). "National Debt in a Neoclassical Growth Model," *American Economic Review* **55**, 1126–1150.

Diamond, P. A. (1970). "Incidence of an Interest Income Tax," *Journal of Economic Theory* **2**, 211–224.

Feldstein, M. (1974a). Incidence of a Capital Income Tax in a Growing Economy with Variable Saving Rates," *Review of Economic Studies* **41**, 505–523.

Feldstein, M. (1974b). "Tax Incidence in a Growing Economy with Variable Factor Supply," *Quarterly Journal of Economics* **88**, 551–573.

Fromm, G. (ed.) (1971). *Tax Incentives and Capital Spending.* Brookings Institution, Washington, D.C.

Hall, R. E., and Jorgenson, D. W. (1971). "Application of the Theory of Optimal Capital Accumulation," In *Tax Incentives and Capital Spending* (G. Fromm, ed.). Brookings Institution, Washington, D.C.

Haugh, L. D. (1976). "Checking the Independence of Two Covariance-Stationary Time Series: A Univariate Residual Cross-Correlation Approach," *Journal of the American Statistical Association* **71**, 378–385.

Joines, D. H. (1979). "Government Fiscal Policy and Private Capital Formation," Ph.D. Dissertation, Univ. of Chicago, Chicago, Illinois.

Joines, D. H. (1981). "Estimates of Effective Marginal Tax Rates on Factor Incomes," *Journal of Business* **54**, 191–226.

Jorgenson, D. W. (1963). "Capital Theory and Investment Behavior," *American Economic Review* **53**, 247–259.

Jorgenson, D. W. (1967). "The Theory of Investment Behavior," in *Determinants of Investment Behavior* (R. Ferber, ed.). Columbia Univ. Press, New York.

Kormendi, R. C. (1978). "Government Debt, Government Spending and Private Sector Behavior," Center for Mathematical Studies in Business and Economics Report no. 7863, Univ. of Chicago, Chicago, Illinois.

Ljung, G. M., and Box, G. E. P. (1976). "A Modification of the Overall χ^2 Test for Lack of Fit in Time Series Models," Department of Statistics Technical Report no. 477, University of Wisconsin.

Lucas, R. E., Jr. (1976). "Econometric Policy Evaluation: A Critique," in *The Phillips Curve and Labor Markets* (K. Brunner and A. Meltzer, eds.). North-Holland Publ., Amsterdam.

Miller, M. H., and Upton, C. W. (1974). *Macroeconomics: A Neoclassical Introduction*. Irwin, Homewood, Illinois.

"Revised Deflators for New Construction, 1947–73" (1974). *Survey Current Business* **54**, 18–27.

Wright, C. (1969). "Saving and the Rate of Interest," in *The Taxation of Income from Capital* (A. C. Harberger and M. J. Bailey, eds.). Brookings Institution, Washington, D.C.

Zellner, A., and Palm, F. (1974). "Time Series Analysis and Simultaneous Equation Econometric Models," *Journal of Econometrics* **2**, 17–54.

Chapter 8

What Does a Tax Cut Do?

Paul Evans

1. INTRODUCTION

There is much disagreement among economists about what a tax cut does. Just to illustrate the extent of this disagreement, we shall discuss four rather divergent positions that economists have taken.

The first position, which is enshrined in most textbooks on macroeconomics [for example, Dornbusch and Fischer (1978) and Gordon (1978)], is that a tax cut raises real income in the short run and the price level in the long run. It does not raise real income in the long run because there is a "natural" level of output that is independent of government policy.

A second position is that a tax cut has no effects unless the government can convince the public that it will change its future purchases of goods and services. This position derives from two postulates. First, the tax cut does not directly affect aggregate supply. Second, consumption is affected only if the present value of net taxes, which equals the present value of government purchases, changes. Consumption is not affected by any measure that merely changes how or when taxes will be raised. For further discussion, see Bailey (1971), Barro (1974), and Friedman (1957).

A third position, which a growing number of economists have accepted, is that a tax cut which reduces marginal tax rates raises real income somewhat in the long run. The national debt rises, eventually forcing the government to curtail its spending. This position is based on the belief that the more factor services are supplied and the more investment in factors is forthcoming, the lower marginal tax rates are. The augmented supply of factor services spells a larger real income in the long run. The national debt rises because tax revenues fall, and tax revenues fall because the rise in real income does not suffice to offset of the effect of the fall in tax rates on tax revenues. Feldstein (1980) takes this position.

A fourth position, which Laffer (1980) and almost no other economist takes, is that a tax cut spurs production by so much that tax revenues rise and the national debt falls in the long run. The government need never curtail its spending. See also Friedman (1980), who argues that a selective reduction in marginal tax rates may actually raise tax revenues.

In this paper, we analyze annual U.S. data for the period 1951–1978 in order to find out how tax cuts affect the U.S. economy. Our findings are detailed below:

> A reduction in autonomous net taxes[1] raises the price level in both the short run and the long run. It raises real income only in the short run.
>
> The size of the effects is fairly small—a reduction in autonomous net taxes that initially raises the real federal debt by 1 percent never raises real income by more than 0.23 percent and eventually raises the price level by only 1.36 percent.
>
> A reduction in the marginal tax rate on labor lowers real income and raises the price level in the short run; it raises both in the long run.
>
> These effects are fairly small—for each percentage point reduction in the marginal tax rate on labor, the long run effects are increases of 0.6 percent and 4.12 percent in real income and the price level.
>
> A reduction in the marginal tax rate on capital raises real income and lowers the price level in both the short run and the long run.
>
> The effects on real income and the price level are large—for each percentage point reduction in the marginal tax rate on capital, the long-run effects are an increase of 1.25 percent in real income and a decrease of 4.32 percent in the price level.
>
> In both the short run and long run, reductions in the marginal tax rate on labor reduce tax revenues and raise the national debt.

---

[1] Three methods by which the federal government can lower autonomous net taxes are to raise transfer payments, to raise tax credits or deductions in the tax code, and to rebate taxes to the public.

In the short run, a reduction in the marginal tax rate on capital lowers tax revenues and raises the national debt. In the long run, it does the opposite.

It is possible in the long run for the government to collect the same real net tax revenue with lower marginal tax rates on labor and capital and the same level of autonomous taxes. To achieve this result, the government must reduce the marginal tax rate on capital by much more than the marginal tax rate on labor.

These findings suggest that the second position is invalid and that the first, second and fourth positions are valid at least to some extent. Specifically, the first position holds for changes in autonomous net taxes, the third position holds for changes in the marginal tax rate on labor, and the fourth position holds for changes in the marginal tax rate on capital.

The plan of this paper is as follows. Section 2 discusses the econometric specification of our model. Section 3 briefly takes up some econometric issues relevant to our empirical analysis, which appears in Section 4. Section 5 discusses the properties of our estimated model. Finally, Section 6 provides estimates of how tax cuts affect the U.S. economy.

2. ECONOMETRIC SPECIFICATIONS OF THE MODEL

In each period t, the government purchases G_t in goods and services, and the public holds the real stock D_t of interest-bearing government debt and the nominal stock B_t of base money. We define NT_t, real taxes net of transfer payments and interest payment on the government debt, by the equation

$$G_t = NT_t + D_t - D_{t-1} + B_t/P_t - B_{t-1}/P_{t-1} \qquad (1)$$

where P_t is the price level in period t. Equation (1), the budget constraint of the government, says that government purchases must be financed by net taxes, by sales of interest-bearing government securities to the public, or by the issue of additional base money. Note that we have defined net taxes to include not only explicit taxes but also any capital losses the public may suffer on the liabilities of the government. For example, if the price level should rise from P_{t-1} to P_t between period $t - 1$ and period t, the public suffers the capital loss

$$\frac{P_t - P_{t-1}}{P_t}(D_{t-1} + B_{t-1}/P_{t-1})$$

which we include in NT_t. This definition implies that the real deficit $G_t - NT_t$ equals the real increase in the liabilities of the government.

We assume that NT_t is a function of E_t, a vector of variables that describe the state of the economy; T_t, a vector of marginal tax rates; and V_t, autonomous net taxes:

$$NT_t = F(E_t, T_t, V_t), \qquad dF/dV_t > 0 \qquad (2)$$

For example, if all net taxes were levied on total income and the net tax schedule were linear, Eq. (2) would take the form

$$NT_t = V_t + T_t y_t$$

where the marginal tax rate T_t is a scalar and y_t is real national income.

We assume that each entry of E_t, the vector that describes the state of the economy, depends only on the current and lagged values of log G_t, T_t, log B_t, log D_t, V_t, and the other entries of E_t, on its own lagged values, and on X_t, a vector of unobserved exogenous variables. Since Eqs. (1) and (2) imply that V_t is determined once E_t, log G_t, T_t, and the current and past values of log B_t and log D_t are given, each entry of E_t depends only on the current and lagged values of log G_t, T_t, log B_t, log D_t, and the other entries of E_t, on its own lagged values, and on X_t.

We further assume that the government has stable reaction functions that relate each policy variable to current and lagged values of E_t and the other policy variables, to its own lagged values, and to I_t, a vector of unobserved exogenous variables. Therefore, the vector Z_t, which includes E_t and the values of the policy variables at time t, depends only on lagged values of itself and on X_t and I_t. If this relation is linear, it can be written as

$$A_0 Z_t = \sum A_k' Z_{t-k} + Q_t \qquad (3)$$

where Q_t is a vector of unobserved exogenous influences (X_t and I_t) and $A_0, A_1', A_2', \ldots$ are matrices of parameters.

Finally, we assume that Q_t, the vector of exogenous influences, has the integrated, autoregressive representation[2]

$$\Delta Q_t = \sum B_k \Delta Q_{t-k} + U_t \qquad (4)$$

where Δ is the difference operator; $B_1, B_2, B_3, \ldots$ are matrices of parameters; and U_t is an independently and identically distributed error vector with a zero mean and a positive definitive symmetric covariance matrix S. Combining (3) and (4) then yields

$$A_0 \Delta Z_t = \sum_1^q A_k \Delta Z_{t-k} + U_t \qquad (5)$$

---

[2] We have assumed that one must difference Q_t to induce stationarity. We thereby hope to avoid some of the problems that Granger and Newbold (1974) and Plosser and Schwert (1978) claim arise when one estimates levels equations.

where

$$A_i = A_i' + \sum_1^i B_j A_{i-j}$$

and q, the maximal lag length, is assumed to be finite.

By estimating Eq. (5), we can assess what effects tax cuts have on the U.S. economy. We do so in Sections 4 and 5. First, however, it is necessary to take up some econometric issues.

3. SOME ECONOMETRIC ISSUES[3]

In this section, we argue that structural general-equilibrium models are hard to identify. We then discuss one alternative to fitting structural models, the fitting of simple vector autoregressions.

The usual procedure in identifying a model of the form (5) is to impose a large number of zero restrictions on the entries of $A_0, \ldots, A_q$. This procedure may be reasonable in a model of a single small market in a large economy because economic theory can then tell one what the "important" determinants of some economic decision are and because setting the effect of the "unimportant" determinants equal to zero is often a good approximation. In general-equilibrium macromodels, however, what the "unimportant" determinants are in some structural equation depends not only on the relative sizes of coefficients in that equation but also on the coefficients in every other equation. Thus, even when there is a widely accepted economic theory available to suggest reasonable zero restrictions, there is still no reason to believe that they will in fact yield an econometric model with good systems properties.

Agreement on economic theory is not universal, however. One economist, guided by his understanding of economic theory, will impose one set of zero restrictions, while another economist, guided by a different understanding, will impose quite a different set of zero restrictions.

Sargent (1979) has shown that, when agents form rational expectations about the future, there are rarely any zero restrictions to impose. If the structure can be identified at all, it can be identified only by imposing nonlinear restrictions on the covariance matrix.

Economic theory rarely has any clear-cut implications for the length of lag structures, so one does not know before estimation what q is or which entries of $A_q, A_{q-1}, \ldots$ to set equal to zero. This problem puts a further roadblock in the way of identification, as Hatanaka (1975) has shown.

---

[3] The analysis in this section draws heavily on Sims (1980).

Sims (1980) has suggested that economists give up on identifying general-equilibrium, structural macromodels. He has suggested that one should instead fit vector autoregressions to the data that one wishes to explain or predict. Implicit in his suggestion are still three *a priori* restrictions. One must still decide what are the important variables to include in the analysis. Since the number of parameters in a vector autoregression goes up as the square of the number of variables included in the model, one must severely restrict the number of variables in the model to obtain reasonable power in one's estimates. Second, one must choose the maximum lag length q by some *a priori* procedure. Third, and most important, one must choose an appropriate order for the variables since Sims's crucial identifying restriction is that A_0 be lower triangular with ones along the diagonal and S be diagonal.[4]

Imposing the restriction that A_0 be lower triangular enables one to rewrite the equation system (5) as

$$Z_{it} = \sum_{j=t}^{i-1} a_{ij0} Z_{jt} + \sum_{j=1}^{n} \sum_{k=1}^{q_{ij}} a_{ijk} Z_{jt-k} + U_{it}, \qquad i = 1,\dots,n \qquad (6)$$

---

[4] Let F_0 be the lower triangular matrix with units on the diagonals that diagonalizes the matrix $A_0^{-1}S(A_0')^{-1}$. Multiplying both members of Eq. (5) by $F_0 A_0^{-1}$ yields

$$F_0 Z_t = F_1 Z_{t-1} + \cdots + F_q Z_{t-q} + V_t$$

where

$$F_i = F_0 A_0^{-1} A_i, \qquad i = 1, \dots, n$$

and

$$V_t = F_0 A_0^{-1} U_t$$

The vector V_t is normally distributed since U_t is. It is independently and identically distributed with a zero mean vector and the diagonal covariance matrix Σ since

$$EV_t = EF_0 A_0^{-1} U_t = F_0 A_0^{-1} EU_t - 0$$

and

$$EV_t V_s' = E[(F_0 A_0^{-1} U_t)(F_0 A_0^{-1} U_s)'] = E[F_0 A_0^{-1} U_t U_s'(A_0')^{-1} F_0']$$
$$= F_0 A_0^{-1}(EU_t U_s')(A_0')^{-1} F_0' = F_0[A_0^{-1} S\delta_{ts}(A_0')^{-1}]F_0' = \Sigma\delta_{ts}$$

where δ_{ts} equals 1 when $t \neq s$ and equals 0 when $t \neq s$. Note that Σ is diagonal since it is the result of diagonalizing $A_0^{-1}S(A_0')^{-1}$.

The above manipulations show that there is no loss in generality in restricting A_0 to be lower triangular and S to be diagonal if there is no entry above the diagonal of A_0 that is known to be nonzero. This is true since no set of data can ever disprove this restriction. On the other hand, if economic theory tells one that some of the entries of A_0 are nonzero, one should attempt to arrange the variables in such a way that these nonzero entries of A_0 are below the diagonal.

where a_{ij0}, $j < i$, is the entry in the ith row and jth column of A_0; a_{ijk}, $k > 0$, is the entry in the ith row and jth column of A_k; q_{ij} is the k for which $a_{ijk} \neq 0$ and $a_{ijm} = 0$, $k < m \leq q + 1$; and n is the number of entries in Z_t. Note that the equation system (6) is fully recursive. Consequently, the full information maximum likelihood estimator for the system when all of the qs are known is ordinary least squares applied to each equation *seriatim*. In reality, one does not know the qs. Thus, some pretesting becomes inevitable in order to keep the qs reasonably small.

4. AN EMPIRICAL MODEL OF THE U.S. ECONOMY

Using annual data from the sample period 1951–1978, we have estimated the model given by (6). We chose to include seven variables in the vector Z and to order them as follows[5]: log G, TL, TK, log B, log Y, log y, and log D, where G is real federal[6] purchases of goods and services, TL and TK are the marginal tax rates on labor and capital,[7] B is the monetary base as measured by the St. Louis Fed, Y is nominal GNP, y is real GNP, and D is the real interest bearing federal debt held by the public.[8] Note that the price level P is simply Y/y.

The ordering of these variables deserves some comment. We place log G, TL, and TK before the other variables because Congress has difficulty in rapidly responding to monetary policy (B) and the state of the economy (Y and y). We place G before TL and TK because variations in G mainly reflect wars and other international crisis that do not occur because Congress wants to change marginal tax rates. We place TL before TK because taxes on labor raise much more revenue than taxes on capital.

In principle, it is possible for B, the monetary base, to be changed rapidly in response to changes in the state of the economy. Nevertheless, we place B before Y and y, thus requiring that B not respond within a single year to the Y and y while permitting it to respond immediately to G, TL and TK.

---

[5] We shall drop the subscript t wherever no confusion will result.

[6] For the most part, we treat state and local governments as if they are a part of the private sector.

[7] These tax rates take into account the taxes of state and local governments. We treat all revenues of the state and local governments, whether from their own taxes or from federal grants-in-aid, as if they are transfer payments to the public.

[8] We obtained the series G, Y, and y from the *National Income and Product Accounts* and the *Survey of Current Business*. The San Francisco Fed furnished the series B. We calculated the series D from data in the *Treasury Bulletin*. The series TL and TK, which are plotted in the appendix, come from Laffer *et al.* (1979).

We assume that it takes time for changes in the real income to affect nominal income. These assumptions require the ordering Y, y.

Equations (1) and (2) make D a function of Y and y unless Congress changes autonomous net taxes in such a way as to offset the effects of these variables on real tax revenues, real transfer payments, and the real servicing costs of the federal debt. Since it is implausible that Congress will make these adjustments, we place the variable D after the variables Y and y.

Rational economic agents do not suffer from money illusion. Therefore, an equiproportional increase in all nominal magnitudes in the U.S. economy should have no effect on the behavior of any economic agent. Applying this implication of economic theory to model (6) yields the restrictions

$$\sum_{j=4}^{5} \sum_{k} A_{ijk} = \begin{cases} 0, & i = 1, 2, 3, 6, 7 \\ 1, & i = 5 \end{cases} \tag{7}$$

In words, the sum of the coefficients of the current and lagged values of $\log B_t$, $\log Y_t$, and $\log P_t$ should be zero in the equations for the real variables G, TL, TK, y, and D and should be one in the equation for the nominal variable Y.

The estimation of model (6) entailed some pretesting because we did not know the qs *a priori*. First, we assumed that in each equation the distributed lag on each variable extends to length 3. Next we estimated model (6) and found the least significant variable at lag 3 in each equation. We then dropped this variable and reestimated the model. Again we found the least significant variable at lag 3, dropped it, and reestimated. We continued this procedure until all of the remaining variables at lag 3 were sinificant at the 0.05 level. We then found the least significant variable at lag 2, dropped it unless this variable was significant at lag 3, and reestimated. We continued this procedure until all of the remaining variables at lag 2 were significant at the 0.05 level. We applied this procedure to the variables at lag 1 and again to the variables at lag 0. At each stage, we imposed the restrictions given by (7), all of which could not be rejected at any reasonable significance level. The final result was seven regression equations, each of which has statistically significant coefficients at the end of each distributed lag.

In writing model (6) as we have written it, we have made the implicit assumption that none of the variables in the model has any deterministic time dependence. In reality, this assumption is unlikely to hold. We have therefore included a constant term and a time trend in each equation.

By examining plots of the residuals versus time, we found that a dummy variable should be included in the equation for G and two dummy variables should be included in the equations for TL and TK. The first dummy, which is 1 in 1951 and 0 in all future years, captures the effects of the cold war. The other two dummy variables capture the effects of the Kennedy–Johnson tax cut in 1964 and 1965 and the surtax in 1968–1970.[9] The first of these dummy variables is $\frac{2}{3}$ in 1964, $\frac{1}{3}$ in 1965, and 0 in all other years; the second is $\frac{3}{4}$ in 1968, $\frac{1}{4}$ in 1969, $-\frac{3}{4}$ in 1970, $-\frac{1}{4}$ in 1971, and 0 in all other years. Note that the cold war permanently raised G in 1951, that the Kennedy–Johnson tax cut permanently lowered TL and TK, and that the surtax only temporarily raised TL and TK.

Our estimates of model (6) appear below[10,11]:

$$\Delta \log G_t = 3.564 - 0.00181t + 0.607 \text{ COLDWAR}_t + 0.475 \, \Delta \log G_{t-1}$$
$$ (2.445) \quad (0.00124) \quad (0.048) \quad\quad\quad\quad (0.072)$$
$$ -0.205 \, \Delta \log G_{t-2} - 0.250 \, \Delta \log G_{t-3} \tag{8}$$
$$ (0.072) \quad\quad\quad\quad (0.070)$$
$$R^2 = 0.9119, \quad \text{S.E.} = 0.04313, \quad F = 45.55$$

$$\Delta TL_t = -0.850 + 0.000436t - 0.0246 \text{ TAXCUT}_t$$
$$ (0.397) \quad (0.000202) \quad (0.0112)$$
$$ +0.0196 \text{ SURTAX}_t +0.0325 \, \Delta \log G_t \tag{9}$$
$$ (0.0072) \quad\quad\quad (0.0128)$$
$$R^2 = 0.4989, \quad \text{S.E.} = 0.008039, \quad F = 5.72$$

$$\Delta TK_t = -0.860 + 0.000440t - 0.0287 \text{ TAXCUT}_t + 0.0284 \text{ SURTAX}_t$$
$$ (0.520) \quad (0.000265) \quad (0.0147) \quad\quad\quad\quad (0.0095)$$
$$ +0.041 \, \Delta \log G_t \tag{10}$$
$$ (0.0168)$$
$$R^2 = 0.4901, \quad \text{S.E.} = 0.01054, \quad F = 5.53$$

$$\Delta \log B_t = -3.202 + 0.00164t + 0.0566 \, \Delta \log G_t + 0.554 \, \Delta \log B_{t-1}$$
$$ (0.839) \quad (0.00043) \quad (0.0134) \quad\quad\quad (0.124) \tag{11}$$
$$R^2 = 0.9159, \quad \text{S.E.} = 0.008489, \quad F = 87.18$$

$$\Delta \log Y_t = 2.924 - 0.00148t + 0.112 \, \Delta \log G_t - 0.102 \, \Delta \log G_{t-1} + \Delta \log B_t$$
$$ (0.866) \quad (0.00044) \quad (0.027) \quad\quad\quad (0.027)$$
$$ + 0.179 \, \Delta \log D_{t-1}, \tag{12}$$
$$ (0.068)$$
$$R^2 = 0.7658, \quad \text{S.E.} = 0.01636, \quad F = 18.80$$

---

[9] We also tried including in the TL and TK equations a dummy variable for 1954, a year in which taxes were cut. This variable did not add any explanatory power.

[10] The standard error of each coefficient appears below it in parentheses.

[11] None of the standard tests for misspecification indicated any problems with these equations.

$$\Delta \log y_t = -0.055 + 0.000035t + 0.0218 \Delta \log G_t + 0.0757 \Delta \log G_{t-1}$$
$$\quad\quad\; (0.401) \;\; (0.000205) \;\; (0.0180) \quad\quad\quad (0.0221)$$
$$+ 0.221 \Delta TL_t + 0.193 \Delta TL_{t-1} - 0.682 \Delta TL_{t-2} - 0.480 \Delta TK_t$$
$$\quad (0.184) \quad\quad\quad (0.162) \quad\quad\quad\;\; (0.281) \quad\quad\quad\;\; (0.145)$$
$$- 0.525 \Delta TK_{t-1}$$
$$\quad (0.132)$$
$$+ 0.446 \Delta TK_{t-2} + 0.819 \Delta \log Y_t - 0.662 \Delta \log Y_{t-1} \quad\quad\quad (13)$$
$$\quad (0.200) \quad\quad\quad\; (0.065) \quad\quad\quad\;\; (0.081)$$
$$- 0.157 \Delta \log Y_{t-2}$$
$$\quad (0.061)$$
$$+ 0.554 \Delta \log y_{t-1}$$
$$\quad (0.135)$$

$$R^2 = 0.9606, \quad\quad \text{S.E.} = 0.006773, \quad\quad F = 30.47$$

$$\Delta \log D_t = -1.952 + 0.00103t - 0.057 \Delta \log G_t + 0.281 \Delta \log G_{t-1}$$
$$\quad\quad\quad\; (1.010) \;\; (0.00051) \;\; (0.056) \quad\quad\quad (0.052)$$
$$+ 0.314 \Delta TL_t - 0.982 \Delta TL_{t-1} - 3.714 \Delta TL_{t-2} - 1.715 \Delta TK_t$$
$$\quad (0.489) \quad\quad\quad (0.514) \quad\quad\quad\;\; (0.680) \quad\quad\quad\;\; (0.329)$$
$$+ 1.140 \Delta TK_{t-1} + 0.953 \Delta TK_{t-2} + 1.529 \Delta \log B_t$$
$$\quad (0.461) \quad\quad\quad\;\; (0.404) \quad\quad\quad\;\; (0.461) \quad\quad\quad\quad\quad (14)$$
$$- 1.529 \Delta \log B_{t-1}$$
$$\quad (0.461)$$
$$- 0.268 \Delta \log y_t - 1.230 \Delta \log y_{t-1} + 0.863 \Delta \log D_{t-1}$$
$$\quad (0.202) \quad\quad\quad\; (0.199) \quad\quad\quad\;\; (0.130)$$

$$R^2 = 0.9500, \quad\quad \text{S.E.} = 0.01598, \quad\quad F = 20.45$$

5. DISCUSSION OF THE ESTIMATES[12]

Equation (8) implies that G does not depend on any of the other variables. Equations (9)–(11) show that changes in real federal purchases result in changes in the marginal tax rates on labor and capital and the monetary base, but that these three variables do not respond to the state of the economy or the real federal debt.

Equation (12) shows that an increase in real federal purchases raises nominal income in the first year, but has essentially no effect by the second

---

[12] Throughout this discussion, we treat the equations reported above as if they were levels equations, that is, Eqs. (8)–(14) without the Δs. It is permissible to do so as long as one recognizes that the error terms are then random walks rather than white noise.

year. A change in the monetary base produces an equiproportional change in nominal income in the first year. An increase in the real federal debt raises nominal income with a one-year lag. The marginal tax rates on labor and capital do not directly affect nominal income. Furthermore, nominal income appears to be independent of past values of real income. This last finding is similar to that of Nelson (1979) for quarterly data. It is tempting to give a structural interpretation to Eq. (12) even though one is probably not justified in doing so. According to this interpretation, the aggregate demand schedule (the locus of real incomes and price levels supported by any given levels of real federal purchases, monetary base, etc.) is a rectangular hyperbole. It is shifted temporarily by an increase in government spending, but is not shifted at all by changes in the marginal tax rates. It is also shifted by current changes in the monetary base and past changes in the debt.

According to Eq. (13), 81.9 percent of any given increase in nominal income takes the form of an increase in real income in the first year, while only 18.1 percent takes the form of an increase in the price level ($\equiv Y/y$). In the second and third years, 61.1 percent and 33.8 percent of this increase in nominal income take the form of increases in real income, while 38.9 percent and 62.2 percent take the form of increases in the price level. Ultimately, all of the increase in nominal income is manifested as an increase in the price level; none goes into real income.[13]

One possible structural interpretation that can be given to these results is that the aggregate supply schedule (the locus of real incomes and price levels consistent with the availability of factors of production, technology, the expectations of economic agents, etc.) is flatter, the shorter the run, and is vertical in the long run. If this interpetation is valid, there is a "natural" level of output, as Friedman (1968) has argued.

Equation (13) also shows that the division of a change in nominal income between changes in real income and the price level is independent of the monetary base and the real federal debt. In contrast, real federal purchases and the marginal tax rates on labor and capital do affect this division as Fair (1979) has argued. An increase in real federal purchases or a reduction in

---

[13] In the second and third years, the effects are

$$0.611 = 0.819 - 0.662 + 0.554 \times 0.819$$

and

$$0.338 = 0.819 - 0.662 - 0.157 + 0.554 \times 0.611 = 0.554 \times 0.611$$

In the ith year, the effect is

$$0.611 \times 0.554^{i-2}, i > 2$$

This effect converges to zero as i approaches infinity.

either tax rate eventually raises real income relative to nominal income. If Eq. (13) is indeed an aggregate supply schedule, these policy changes shift both the short-run and long-run schedules toward higher real incomes. Presumably, this effect arises because an increase in purchases lowers the disposable wealth of the public and thus induces a larger factor supply and because a reduction in marginal tax rate induces the public to substitute toward market activity and to save more.[14]

Equation (14) implies that the real federal debt falls in the long run if federal purchases fall, the marginal tax rate on labor rises, real income rises, or the growth rate of the monetary base ($\log B_t - \log B_{t-1}$) falls. It also implies that an increase in the marginal tax rate on capital reduces the real federal debt in the short run, but has little effect in the long run. Only this last implication is remarkable. One would normally think that increasing the marginal tax rate on capital while keeping federal purchases, the federal tax rate on labor, real income, and the monetary base constant would raise net taxes and thus reduce the real debt. Apparently, the owners of capital can very easily move into tax shelters when the marginal tax rate on capital rises, a point that Friedman (1980) has made.

6. POLICY ANALYSIS

In this section, we use the estimated model given by (8)–(14) to analyze three types of tax cuts: a reduction in autonomous net taxes; a reduction in the marginal tax rate on labor; and a reduction in the marginal tax rate on capital.

Table 1 reports the effects of a reduction in autonomous net taxes that raises the error term of Eq. (14) by 1 percentage point for one year. Real income rises for three years and then converges to its original value.[15] At its peak, it is only 0.23 percent higher than its original value, implying that the multiplier for this tax cut is substantially less than 1 at the sample means. The price level rises slowly, converging ultimately to a value 1.36 percent larger than its original value. The real federal debt rises steadily, converging eventually to a value 7.58 percent higher than its original value.

Table 2 reports the effects of reducing the marginal tax rate on labor by 1 percentage point. Real income falls for the first two years, but eventually

[14] Increasing G while keeping TL, TK, and D constant leads to an increase in net autonomous taxes and thus lowers the disposable wealth of the public if the public attaches a lower value at the margin to federal purchases than to private purchases. Decreasing TL or TK while keeping G, D, and hence real net taxes constant has no wealth effect.

[15] To simplify the exposition, we treat each series as if it has no trend.

TABLE 1

*The Effects of a Reduction in Autonomous
Net Taxes*

Years in effect	Percentage changes in		
	y	P	D
1	0.00	0.00	1.00
2	0.15	0.03	1.83
3	0.23	0.10	2.35
4	0.23	0.19	2.69
6	0.16	0.38	3.33
8	0.14	0.52	3.95
10	0.12	0.64	4.48
∞	0.00	1.36	7.58

TABLE 2

*The Effects of a Reduction in the Marginal Tax
Rate on Labor*

Years in effect	Percentage changes in		
	y	P	D
1	−0.22	0.22	−0.3
2	−0.57	0.53	0.9
3	0.11	0.05	5.8
4	1.09	−0.04	9.0
6	1.39	0.49	11.3
8	1.08	1.09	13.2
10	1.03	1.52	15.2
∞	0.60	4.12	26.4

rises by 0.60 percent. The price level ends up 4.12 percent higher. In the long run, the real federal debt rises by nearly 26.4 percent, which is a lot.

Table 3 reports the effects of reducing the marginal tax rate on capital by 1 percentage point. Real income immediately rises, hitting its peak in the second year. In the long run, it rises 1.25 percent. Both the short-run and long-run effects on real income are rather large. The inflation rate falls by about half a percentage point in the first two years; in most future years, the inflation rate is reduced. Ultimately, the price level falls 4.32 percent. The real federal debt rises in the first year, but falls thereafter. Ultimately, it falls 17.1 percent.

TABLE 3

The Effects of a Reduction in the Marginal Tax Rate on Capital

Years in effect	Percentage changes in		
	y	P	D
1	0.48	−0.48	1.6
2	1.50	−1.22	1.0
3	1.35	−1.17	−1.8
4	0.89	−1.20	−3.8
6	0.71	−1.59	−5.7
8	0.88	−2.03	−7.2
10	0.93	−2.35	−8.6
∞	1.25	−4.32	−17.1

Laffer (1980) has asserted that a reduction in marginal tax rates in the United States would spur production by so much that revenue would actually rise. In order to analyze this assertion, we assume that

$$dTR = [bTL + (1 - b)TK] \, dy + y [b \, dTL + (1 - b) \, dTK] \quad (15)$$

where b, which is the marginal propensity for income to accrue to labor, is a constant and dTR is the change induced in total real tax revenues by the infinitesimal changes dy, dTL, and dTK in real income and the marginal tax rates on labor and capital. Tables 2 and 3 imply that in the long run

$$dy/y = -0.60 \, dTL - 1.25 \, dTK \quad (16)$$

Eliminating dy between Eq. (15) and 16), dividing both members of the resulting equation by y and collecting terms yields

$$dTR/y = \{b - 0.60[bTL + (1 - b)TK]\} \, dTL$$
$$+ \{1 - b - 1.25[bTL + (1 - b)TK]\} \, dTK \quad (17)$$

Therefore, Laffer's assertion would be borne out if

$$b - 0.60[bTL + (1 - b)TK] < 0 \quad (18)$$

and

$$1 - b - 1.25[bTL + (1 - b)TK] < 0 \quad (19)$$

In 1978, TL and TK were 0.443 and 0.419, respectively. The most reasonable values for b are between 0.6 and 0.8. Given these values of TL, TK, and b, condition (18) cannot be satisfied while condition (19) can be easily satisfied. Thus, Laffer's assertion is not borne out by the empirical analysis.

It may, however, be unfair to attribute to Laffer the view that reducing any marginal tax rate will raise tax revenue. His position may be that selective reductions in marginal tax rates can raise tax revenues. If so, his position, which Friedman (1980) shares, is borne out by our empirical analysis. Since condition (19) is easy to satisfy, it is clear that reducing the marginal tax rate on capital actually raises real tax revenues.[16]

A clear implication of this finding is that the marginal tax rate on capital is too high. By lowering TK, the government can raise its spending or lower the marginal tax rate on labor. For example, we estimate that real tax revenues would have been approximately the same in 1978 if the marginal tax rate on capital had always been zero and the marginal tax rate on labor had been 0.34 instead of 0.443.[17]

If reductions in the marginal tax rate on capital from its 1978 level would actually permit the government to raise spending and to lower the marginal tax rate on labor, one might wonder why the government has raised TK by nearly 7.5 percentage points in the past decade (see the appendix). In our opinion, the government has not lowered TK because it has failed to notice the inverse relations between TK and tax revenues. This inverse relation has not been clearly noticeable because the typical tax cut lowers the marginal tax rates on labor and capital by roughly the same amount.[18] Such a tax cut lowers tax revenues.[19]

One *caveat* is in order before concluding this paper. Lucas (1976) has argued persuasively that the *a*s in the equation of model (6) that describe the behavior of private economic agents depend on the *a*s in the reaction functions of the government of these agents base their behavior upon a rational assessment of how the actions of the government will affect them. In a stable policy regime, changes in government policy take the form of nonzero error terms in one or more of the reaction functions, but do not change any of the *a*s. One can readily predict the effects of such a change in policy by using an econometric model fitted to data generated by this stable policy regime. In contrast, a change in policy that affects the *a*s in the reaction functions is likely

---

[16] Actually, since TL and TK include state and local taxes, part of the change in TR accrues to state and local governments. Therefore, if grants-in-aid to state and local governments remained unchanged, federal net taxes might well fall. We assume that the federal government would reduce grants-in-aid in order to redistribute the increased tax revenues of the state and local governments to itself.

[17] These estimates assume that b, the marginal propensity for income to accrue to labor, is constant at 0.7. They also assume that the fitted model is an exact description of the U.S. economy. If instead it is an approximation that is close only near the sample means, these estimates could be grossly inaccurate since the reduction of TK to zero is certainly not a small change.

[18] For example, Eqs. (8) and (9) show that the Kennedy–Johnson tax cut lowered the marginal tax rates on labor and capital by 2.46 and 2.87 percent.

[19] Using Eq. (17), one can easily show that the condition for such a tax cut to lower tax revenue is

$$bTL + (1 - b)TK < 0.40 + 0.43b,$$

which is easily satisfied.

to change the *a*s in the rest of the model. Unless one can predict how these *a*s will change, it is impossible to predict the effects of this change in policy.

Lucas's critique of policy analysis weakens our conclusions in two ways. First, if the policy regime change between 1951 and 1978, our fitted model (8)–(14) may describe something like the average response of the economy to tax cuts over the sample period, but may not describe how the economy would respond at the present time. In order to test whether model (8)–(14) was stable, we fitted it over several subsamples and performed Chow tests. We found no evidence of instability in the model. Second, if the three types of tax cuts analyzed above had required the *a*s to change in Eqs. (8)–(11) or (14), the conclusions reached above would have been shaky. Examining these equations, however, reveals that these three types of tax cuts are produced by changing the error terms in Eqs. (9), (10), and (14) for one year. In other words, the tax cuts analyzed above are not changes in the policy regime. Therefore, one can predict their effects using standard econometric methodology.

APPENDIX

Figure 1 plots the measures of the marginal tax rates on labor and capital used in this paper.

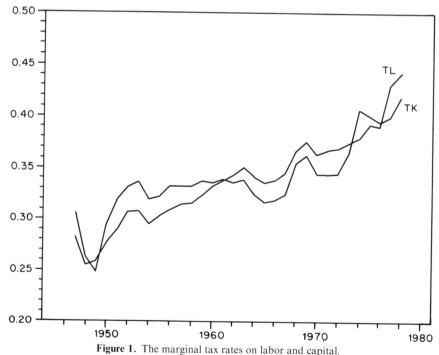

Figure 1. The marginal tax rates on labor and capital.

REFERENCES

Bailey, M. J. (1971). *National Income and the Price Level*, 2nd ed. McGraw-Hill, New York.

Barro, R. J. (1974). "Are Government Bonds Net Wealth?" *Journal of Political Economy* **82**, 1095–1118.

Dornbusch, R., and Fischer, S. (1978). *Macroeconomics*. McGraw-Hill, New York.

Fair, R. C. (1979). "On Modelling the Effects of Government Policies," *American Economic Review* **69**, 89–91.

Feldstein, M. (1980). "Tax Incentives without Deficits," *Wall Street Journal*, July 25, p. 16.

Friedman, M. (1957). *A Theory of the Consumption Function*. Princeton Univ. Press, Princeton, New Jersey.

Friedman, M. (1968). "The Role of Monetary Policy," *American Economic Review* **58**, 1–17.

Friedman, M. (1980). "A Simple Tax Reform," *Newsweek*, August 18, p. 68.

Gordon, R. J. (1978). *Macroeconomics*. Little, Brown, Boston, Massachusetts.

Granger, C. W. J., and Newbold, P. (1974). "Spurious Regressions in Econometrics," *Journal of Econometrics* **2**, 111–120.

Hatanaka, M. (1975). "On the Global Identification of the Dynamic Simultaneous Equation Model with Stationary Disturbances," *International Economic Review* **16**, 545–554.

Laffer, A. B. (1980). "Tax Cuts Would More Than Pay for Themselves," *Los Angeles Times*, May 27, Part 4, pp. 2, 7.

Laffer, A. B., Ransom, R. D., and Weinburg, M. E. (1979). "The 'Prototype Wedge Model': A Tool for Supply-Side Economics," pp. 55–61. Wainwright Economics, Boston, Massachusetts.

Lucas, R. E., Jr. (1976). "Econometric Policy Evaluation: A Critique," *Carnegie-Rochester Conference Series* **1**, 19–46.

Nelson, C. R. (1979). "Recursive Structure in U.S. Income, Prices, and Output," *Journal of Political Economy* **87**, 1307–1327.

Plosser, C. I., and Schwert, G. W. (1978). "Money, Income, and Sunspots: Measuring Economic Relationships and the Effects of Differencing," *Journal of Monetary Economics* **4**, 637–660.

Sargent, T. J. (1981). "Interpreting Economic Time Series," *Journal of Political Economy* **89**, 213–248.

Sims, C. A. (1980). "Macroeconomics and Reality," *Econometrics* **48**, 1–48.

U.S. Department of Commerce, Bureau of Economic Analysis (1976). *The National Income and Product Accounts of the United States, 1929–74*. U.S. Government Printing Office, Washington, D.C.

U.S. Department of Commerce, Bureau of Economic Analysis (1977–1979). *Survey of Current Business*. U.S. Government Printing Office, Washington, D.C.

U.S. Treasury Department, Office of the Secretary (1947–1979). *Treasury Bulletin*. U.S. Government Printing Office, Washington, D.C.

Chapter 9

Persistent Growth Rate Differentials among States in a National Economy with Factor Mobility*

Victor A. Canto and Robert I. Webb

The relative performance of different state economies has been a matter of much interest to policymakers and the public in general. In a neoclassical world where factors are free to move across political boundaries, one would not expect to observe the existence of persistent product price or factor income differentials. Such differentials would disappear either through the trading of goods or factor migration.

This issue has engendered an extensive literature in economics of which a paper by Borts (1960) is representative of the early contributions.[1] Borts's

* A previous version of this paper was presented at the Center for the Study of Private Enterprise of the University of Southern California Conference on Taxation of Income from Capital held in Los Angeles on January 22, 1981, and the NBER Conference on State and Local Financing held in Cambridge, Massachusetts, on April 30, 1981.

[1] For an excellent summary of the earlier studies see Due (1961).

analysis suggests that although factor migration mitigates regional differences in income, persistent differences in factor returns nevertheless remain. The observation of seemingly persistent differences in *nominal* factor income across states ignores the possibility—pointed out by Coelho and Ghali (1971)—that such differences may merely reflect differences in price levels across states. Further, differences in tax rates across states may introduce perceived differences in after tax real income, independent of whether nominal income differs. Consequently, relevant persistent income differentials may be more apparent than real. More recent attempts to explain observed price and income differentials across political boundaries have emphasized differences in technologies [see Batra and Scully (1972)] or factor movement costs which may, in part, be influenced by state and federal fiscal policies [see Greenwood (1975) or McClure (1970)]. The effects of state fiscal policies on state relative economic performance, however, have not been adequately explored.[2] The intent of this paper is to develop and examine a neoclassical model which explicitly incorporates both state and federal fiscal policies in order to explain persistent differences in the relative performance of state economies.

In Section 1, a neoclassical model of an integrated economy is developed with two factors of production (one fixed and one mobile) which must decide between market and nonmarket activity across states. Within this framework, we show that trade in market goods and the migration of the mobile factor results in factor price equalization across states. Our model differs from Borts (1960) in that the assumption, in his model, of factor price equalization implies equality in per capita income across states, while our model permits both factor price equalization and persistent differences in factor incomes across states. This result may be traced to the assumption, in our model, that each factor has the choice of working in either the market or household sector. Consequently, although *full* incomes may be equated, *market* incomes need not be so. In our model, divergences in *market* incomes across states is attributable, in part, to the impact of state government fiscal policies on the supply of services of the immobile or fixed factor of production.

The influence of state fiscal policies on relative performance operates through any income or substitution effects which state spending and tax policies engender. To the extent that the state fiscal policies generate income effects or alter the after-tax incentives for market production to the fixed factor, the latitude of discretionary state fiscal policies is increased. The

---

[2] Earlier empirical studies [e.g., see Bloom (1960)] failed to find any association between state fiscal policies and relative economic performance. However, these studies failed to examine state expenditure and tax policies *relative* to those of other states. This model misspecification error may lead to biased results and explain the absence of relation between state fiscal policies and relative economic performance reported by these studies.

effects of state fiscal policy actions on the mobile factor differ since the mobile factor can migrate across state lines to arbitrage any differences in factor rewards. This clearly imposes some limitations on state economic policies.

As may be apparent, the issues examined in this paper lend themselves to a framework of analysis common to the trade literature. In this regard, individual states are analogous to small open economies (that is, where quantities adjust to assure factor price equalization), while, if the foreign sector is ignored, the U.S. economy is analogous to the closed world economy (that is, where prices change to equilibrate global or worldwide supply and demand).

In summary, we develop a neoclassical model of an integrated economy with gross-of-tax factor price equalization across state lines, which allows for differences in economic performance among states. In addition, the integrated economy approach suggests that relative prices are determined by the overall demand for and supply of goods and services in the U.S. economy. To the extent that state and federal fiscal policies affect the determination of relative prices, the influence of federal fiscal policy on relative prices will generate a proportionate common response in the state economies since the gross-of-tax prices are shared.

In Section 2, data on federal and (contiguous, or continental 48) state spending, transfer payments, and taxes covering the period 1957–1977 are employed to examine the influence of relative spending or tax rate policies on individual state economic performance as measured by personal income. Finally, the conclusions are summarized in Section 4.

1. THE MODEL

In order to capture as wide a spectrum of factor mobility as possible, factors of production are divided into those which are mobile (factor A) and those which are not (factor B).[3] The assumption that the total supply of each factor is exogenous at a point in time allows one to abstract from issues of capital accumulation or population growth. The absence of capital accumulation suggests that the two factors of production may be viewed as different types of labor. With respect to the mobile factor, it is assumed that all forms of barriers, both natural and man-made, among the different states are absent. The mobile factor, therefore, is presumed to incur no cost when moving across state boundaries. Neither factor faces any moving costs within a state. The immobile factor, on the other hand, faces a prohibitive cost if moving across

---

[3] For simplicity of exposition, factors are classified as either mobile or fixed. In principle, the analysis could also be extended to allow for differing degrees of factor mobility (i.e., adjustment costs). For a two-sector model with adjustment costs, see Mussa (1978).

state boundaries is contemplated. Immobile factors of production must therefore be employed within the state where they are located. Following Becker (1965), the services emanating from the two factors are assumed to have two alternative uses. One is in the production of market goods and the other is in the production of a household (nonmarket) commodity.[4] Non-market production in one state need not be physically similar to nonmarket production in another state. Household (nonmarket) goods produced by the immobile factor, however, must be purchased and consumed in the state where that factor is located.

In order to keep the full separation between market and nonmarket activity, market and nonmarket goods must be imperfect substitutes both in demand and supply. There must, therefore, be either a unique factor in the production of the nonmarket good or some other characteristic of the production relation to ensure imperfect substitutability.[5]

For the purpose of this paper, we assume that each state produces a single market good using similar technology. The market good production process is assumed to be linear, homogeneous, twice differentiable with both inputs indispensable, and is expressed as

$$Y_i = F(N_{Ai}S_{Ai}, N_{Bi}S_{Bi}) \tag{1}$$

where N_{Ai} and N_{Bi} denote units of factors of production within each state and S_{Ai} and S_{Bi} denote utilization rates for each factor within the state. The utilization rate is normalized so that it is always between zero and unity. And Y_i denotes state i's production of market goods.

In the absence of man-made or natural barriers to trade (e.g., tariffs and transportation costs, respectively), arbitrage will ensure that the price of market goods will be the same in each state. Similarly, the mobility of factor A ensures that the reward to that factor, R_{Ai}, will be the same in all states.

---

[4] The household commodity is assumed to be produced by the following linear homogenous, twice-differentiable production function:

$$Z = f(H, X)$$

where H denotes the amount of household time (i.e., leisure) and X the amount of market goods used in the production process. The cost of the household commodity for each factor in a given state i can be written as

$$\pi_{Ai} = \pi(R^*_{Ai}, 1)$$

$$\pi_{Bi} = \pi(R^*_{Bi}, 1)$$

where the price of the market good is the numeraire, and R^*_{Ai} and R^*_{Bi} denote the real after tax factor return (that is, the opportunity cost of leisure in terms of market goods).

[5] The assumption that the nonmarket commodity is produced and consumed in the household guarantees the imperfect substitutability conditions described.

Finally, given common technology across states, it follows that the rewards to fixed factors will also be equalized across states.[6]

The equalization of factor prices combined with the assumption of a similar linear, homogeneous technology implies that the proportion of factor services used in the production of market goods in any state will be the same as that of the rest of the economy; that is,

$$\frac{N_{Ai}S_{Ai}}{N_{Bi}S_{BI}} = \frac{N_{Aj}S_{Aj}}{N_{Bj}S_{Bj}} \qquad \forall i, j \ldots$$

---

[6] The general conditions under which trade is sufficient to equalize factor returns are well known in the literature [see Samuelson (1949)]. The effects of factor migration and factor price equalization are also well known [see Mundell (1957)].

In our model factor price equalization can be easily shown as follows: First, free trade assures that the price of the market good is equalized across states. Second, the price of the market good can be decomposed into the weighted sum of each factor's proportionate share of production costs times its respective *before tax* factor payments, or

$$P = \alpha R_{Ai} + (1 - \alpha)R_{Bi}$$

The above equation may be set equal to one since the market good is also the numeraire. Similarly, the average production cost for the mobile factor's household commodity can be written as

$$\pi_{Ai} = \theta R_{Ai}^* + (1 - \theta)$$

where θ denotes the share of leisure in the production of the household good. Third, if one assumes that state and local tax revenues are distributed only to the fixed factor, this guarantees that the mobile factor's full income is independent of its locality. Thus minimizing π_A will, in fact, be equivalent to maximizing the utility of the mobile factor since such actions will maximize household consumption (Z_A), which is the only argument in the factor of production utility function. Consequently, the mobile factor will migrate to the state with the lowest π_A. If mobile factors reside in all states this implies that

$$\pi_A = \pi_{Ai} \qquad \forall_i$$

Since the household good is not taxed (although the market goods input is), it follows that

$$R_{Ai}^* = R_{Aj}^*$$

which is the result that the mobile factor will be taxed at the same rate in every state.

The gross of tax relative factor cost in market production (R_{Ai}/R_{Bi}) and the tax rate on the mobile factor can be expressed in terms of the relative prices (R_A^*/P) and (R_A^*/π_A): Differentiating logarithmically the two relative prices and solving for (R_{Ai}/R_{Bi}) and t_{Ai} yields

$$E\left(\frac{R_{Ai}}{R_{Bi}}\right) = \frac{(1 - \theta)E(P/\pi_A) + \theta E(R_A^*/\pi_A)}{\theta}$$

$$t_{Ai} = -\frac{(1 - \alpha)\theta E(R_A^*/\pi_A) + (1 - (1 - \alpha)(1 - \theta))E(P/\pi_A)}{\theta}$$

where E denotes the d log operator.

Using this result and the market good equation yield $R_{Bi} = R_{Bj}$, even though $R_{Bi}^* \neq R_{Bj}^*$.

Thus, the ratio of output produced in a state to that of the U.S. economy will be equal to the ratio of the immobile factor services supplied in the state relative to that of the total services supplied by the factor in the U.S. economy; that is,

$$Y_i = \frac{N_{Bi} S_{Bi}}{N_{BUS} S_{BUS}} Y_{US} \tag{2}$$

The next sections of the paper discuss the determination of the equilibrium levels of the supply of factors to the market sector and the overall production of market goods.

1.1. The Supply of Factor Services to the Market Sector

In this model, factor services can be employed in the production of market goods or in the production of the household commodity (nonmarket activity). The market–nonmarket decision is based, in part, on the opportunity cost of the factor's services. The operational measure of opportunities in this paper is the full income measure developed by Becker (1965). In addition to the value of the total endowment of services, factors of production will also include in their full income measure the actions of the federal and local governments.[7] However, care must be exercised in the treatment of the effects of state and local government policies.

For simplicity and without loss of generality, it is assumed that there is at least one state that does not tax the mobile factor. Similarly, it is also assumed that if the factors of production do not pay any taxes, then they do not participate in the benefits provided by the revenues collected. Therefore, the state and local governments will not have any direct impact on the mobile factor, and any effect will be indirect insofar as the actions of the state governments collectively have an effect on overall U.S. prices.

The mobile factor cannot be taxed by any state at a rate higher than that of the state with the lowest tax rate. However, the actions of the state and local governments, in addition to the indirect effects described, will have a direct effect on the *immobile* factor insofar as the local government actions alter this factor's full income. All units of the immobile factor of production are assumed to be homogeneous. As a result, state and local government services and taxes are distributed equally among the immobile factors of production within any state.

---

[7] Since by assumption there is no unemployment of either factor of production (i.e., they are always engaged in either market or nonmarket activity), the market reward to each factor of production represents the appropriate measure to value the factor services—both market and nonmarket.

The analysis suggests that the utilization rate of the fixed factor will not necessarily be the same across states. Consequently, the states' output per unit of factor of production will differ insofar as the utilization rate of the fixed factor differs across state lines.[8]

Services provided by the federal government as well as taxes are assumed to be distributed among the two classes of factors of production according to their proportion in the economy.[9] Thus the actions of the federal government will have a direct impact on all factors of production in all states. In any state, the full income measure of the mobile factor can be expressed as

$$\Omega_{Ai} = \{N_{Ai}R_A + \alpha[\gamma G_f + \Psi TR_f - T_f]\} \tag{3}$$

where N_{Ai} denotes the state endowment of the mobile factor's services; α, the share of the federal government services and taxes accruing to a mobile factor; G_f, the federal government purchases of goods and services; γ, the value of the services provided by government services[10]; TR_f, the federal government transfer payments; Ψ, the value of the transfer payments (Ψ will be less than unity if there are tax collection or distribution costs); and T_f, federal tax revenues. Substituting the federal government budget constraint into the full income measure, the previous equation becomes

$$\Omega_{Ai} = \{N_{Ai}R_A + \alpha[(\gamma - 1)G_f + (\Psi - 1)TR_f]\} \tag{3'}$$

Similarly, the full income measure for the immobile factor of production can be expressed as

$$\Omega_{Bi} = \{N_{Bi}R_B + (\gamma - 1)G_{Si} + (\Psi - 1)TR_{Si} + (1 - \alpha)[(\gamma - 1)G_f + (\Psi - 1)TR_f]\} \tag{4}$$

where N_{Bi} denotes the state i endowment of the immobile factor; G_{Si}, state i government purchases of goods and services; and TR_{Si}, state i transfer payments.[11]

---

[8] It was previously argued that the gross-of-tax factor reward to the two factors of production would be equalized across states. Equalization of the gross-of-tax factor rewards, however, does not guarantee equalization of the after-tax factor rewards. In addition, the effects of state government spending policies will also alter the full income of each unit of the fixed factor. For these reasons the utilization rate may differ across states.

[9] It should be noted that, in this model, none of the factors of production can escape the taxation of the federal government.

[10] Conventional accounting techniques value government services at factor costs. However, there is no reason why the value of these services should equal their costs, as pointed out by Bailey (1971). Thus, in any analysis of fiscal policy, a provision should be made for this possibility.

[11] The above formulation implicitly assumes that the value of the government services provided by state or federal government services are the same.

The household demand for factors of production is postulated as depending on the factors' full income and the factor rewards as follows:

$$H_{Ai} = H_A[(\Omega_{Ai}/N_{Ai}), R_A(1 - t_A)] \tag{5}$$
$$(+) \qquad (-)$$

$$H_{Bi} = H_B[(\Omega_{Bi}/N_{Bi}), R_B(1 - t_{Bi})] \tag{6}$$
$$(+) \qquad (-)$$

where t_A and t_{Bi} denote the tax rates on the two factors of production and Ω_{Ai}/N_{Ai} and Ω_{Bi}/N_{Bi} denote the full income of a unit of a factor of production and the signs of the first derivatives are indicated in parentheses below the right-hand side of the equation. The factor market equilibrium can be expressed as

$$S_{Ai} = 1 - H_{Ai} \tag{7}$$
$$S_{Bi} = 1 - H_{Bi} \tag{8}$$

1.2. State-Specific Equilibrium

Substituting Eqs. (3)–(8) into Eq. (2) and differentiating totally yield[12]

$$EY_i = \frac{N_B}{\Omega_B} \eta_{B\Omega} \left[(\gamma - 1)d\left(\frac{G_{Si}}{N_{Bi}} - \frac{G_S}{N_{BUS}}\right) \right.$$
$$\left. + (\Psi - 1)d\left(\frac{TR_{Si}}{N_{Bi}} - \frac{TR_S}{N_{BUS}}\right) \right] - \eta_{BR}\left(\frac{dt_{Bi}}{(1 - t_B)} - \frac{dt_{BUS}}{(1 - t_{BUS})}\right)$$
$$+ EY_{US} \tag{9}$$

where E is the difference of the log operator and G_S and TR_S denote the sum of all state purchases of goods and services and transfer payments, respectively. N_B denotes the U.S. endowment of the immobile factor.[13]

A simple interpretation can be provided for Eq. (9). Within an integrated economy framework, two separate types of equilibria are of interest. The first is state-specific equilibrium, that is, that the equation of the demand and supply of goods and services and for factors of production within a given state. The second is overall equilibrium, that is, the equation of total demand and supply of goods and factors of production within the United States.

---

[12] See Appendix B for a formal derivation.

[13] It is important to note that since the states' (N_{Bi}) and the economy's (N_{BUS}) endowments of the immobile factor are given, the above equation can also be interpreted as the percentage change in output of the immobile factor.

The first type of equilibrium may be achieved through a redistribution of goods and the mobile factor of production among states.[14]

That is, if the demand for goods and/or factors of production does not initially equal the supply of goods or factors of production within the state, then the incipient excess demand or supply will generate a tendency for the relative prices in the state to change. However, the potential for arbitrage (through trade in goods or mobile factor migration) will dissipate any incipient change in relative prices. In the absence of international trade, such quantity redistributions will not necessarily achieve total equilibrium, since such flows only eliminate relative excess demand and supplies across states and, consequently, will not eliminate an economy-wide excess demand or excess supply. Aggregate excess demand may require an adjustment in the economy's relative prices in order to bring about overall equilibrium in all markets.

The important point is simply that since prices are equalized across states, a change in relative prices will tend to have the same proportionate effect in all states. Thus, part of the change in economic activity attributable to the relative price change will generate a component common to all states [i.e., the EY_{US} term in Eq. (9)], and, to a large extent, this component will be exogenous to the state government. However, to the extent that state and local governments can influence the full income and the net-of-tax factor reward of the fixed factor, the utilization rate, and then the total services supplied by the fixed factor, can be influenced by state spending and tax policies. As a result, output per unit factor of production may differ across states.

The change in state economic activity attributable to the state's economic policies will differ from that of the "average" performance in the other states to the extent that the state's spending and tax rate policies differ from those of the average of the other states. That this is the case is shown by the three terms in the brackets in Eq. (9). Finally, it is important to notice that, although the sign of the tax is unambiguously negative, the sign of the state's expenditures depends on the private sector's valuation of government services.

1.3. National Equilibrium

The demand for market goods within a single state is postulated as depending upon the state's total full income, the relative price of nonmarket

---

[14] If a state is assumed to be small relative to the United States, it will face given terms of trade (i.e., given gross-of-tax relative prices). Given the relative price and public spending and tax rates, the utilization rate for each factor of production will be determinate; thus, any change in supply of factor services must occur through a change in the state endowment. Similarly, the demand per unit of factor of production will be determinate; thus, any imbalance in the goods market must necessarily occur through a net "export" or "import" from other states.

activity, and state and federal tax and spending policies. That is,

$$AD_i = D_i(\Omega_{Ai} + \Omega_{Bi}, R_A, t_A, R_B, t_{Bi})$$
$$\qquad (+) \qquad (+)(-)(+)(-)$$
$$+ \phi G_{Si} + \phi G_f + \Theta T R_{Si} + \Theta T R_f \qquad (10)$$

where ϕ denotes the direct effect of state and federal government expenditures on aggregate demand, and θ, the effect of state and federal transfers on aggregate demand.[15] The distribution of income among the two factors of production is presumed not to affect the marginal propensity to spend. For ease of exposition, it is assumed that the private sector valuation per dollar of government expenditures is the same whether they are provided by the federal or any state government. In this case, the economy's aggregate demand for and supply of goods and services will be the sum across states and imposing goods market equilibrium yields:

$$AD_{US} = \sum AD_i = D_{US}(\Omega_{AUS} + \Omega_{BUS}, R_A, t_{AUS}, R_B, t_{BUS})$$
$$+ \phi(G_S + G_f) + \theta(T R_S + T R_f) = \sum i Y_i = Y_{US} \qquad (11)$$

Similarly, the overall economy factor market equilibrium can be expressed as

$$S_{AUS}(Y_{US}, R_A, R_B) + H_{AUS}(\Omega_{AUS}, R_A, t_{AUS}) = N_{AUS} \qquad (12)$$
$$\quad (+) \ (-)(+) \qquad\qquad (+) \ (-) \ (+)$$

$$S_{BUS}(Y_{US}, R_A, R_B) + H_{BUS}(\Omega_{BUS}, R_B, t_{BUS}) = N_{BUS} \qquad (13)$$
$$\quad (+) \ (-)(+) \qquad\qquad (+) \ (-) \ (+)$$

Equations (11)–(13) yield three equations with three unknowns (Y_{US}, R_A, R_B). Thus, one can solve for the equilibrium value of market output as a function of the expenditure and tax rate policies. The solution for the percentage change of the U.S. production of market goods can be shown to be of the following form:

$$EY_{US} = \beta_0 + \beta_1 d(G_S + G_f) + \beta_2 d(T R_S + T R_f) + \beta_3 dt \qquad (14)$$

where E is the first difference of the log operator, the β coefficients represent the reduced form solution to the structural model described in previous paragraphs, and t denotes the economy's average marginal tax rate whose coefficient can be shown to be negative. As before, the signs of the expenditure coefficients depend exclusively on the private sector valuation of public services and on whether these services are complements or substitutes for market goods.

---

[15] These coefficients critically depend on whether the government services are valued higher than the cost and also on whether the services provided are substitutes or complements for market goods.

The above equation suggests that in addition to federal government expenditures, state and local spending may also be important in the determination of the equilibrium level of market production. There is considerable literature on these issues [see, for example, Blinder and Solow (1974)]. The equation also indicates that the imposition of tax rates will generate a substitution effect away from market activity. Traditional macroeconomics usually assumes the disincentive effects of taxation to be small. However, in recent years this assumption has been criticized by many economists.[16]

To summarize the model, prices adjust in the U.S. market to ensure that at any point in time total U.S. demand equals total U.S. supply for both goods and factors. U.S. demand is, of course, simply the sum of the individual states' demand. Similarly, U.S. supply is the sum of the states' supply. By identifying supply and demand relation in each state, and summing across states, U.S. relative prices can be determined. Notice, however, that these prices are a necessary but not a sufficient condition for full equilibrium in the United States. While price changes equilibrate U.S. markets, there is nothing to ensure that they will equilibrate each individual state's market. The attainment of such full equilibrium also requires quantity adjustments among states.

The framework developed can be utilized to analyze the effects of federal and state spending and tax policies and their impact on economic activity. Some of the implications derived in this paper can be tested empirically. This is the subject of the next section.

2. SOME THEORETICAL AND EMPIRICAL CAVEATS

A stochastic version of Eq. (9) (which includes a constant term as a check for model misspecification) was estimated for each state where per capita personal income—deflated by the CPI—was used to measure state economic activity. Personal income was used due to constraints on the availability of data on other measures of state economic activity.[17] It should be noted that the theoretical model developed above requires that the same structure be imposed on all states without allowing for any regional differences.

One of the explanatory variables in our model is state expenditures. This variable was subdivided into state government purchases and state transfer payments for the purpose of estimation. Sample size and data aggregation considerations effectively preclude further subdivision of the state expendi-

[16] Recent contributions to this literature include the works of Boskin (1977, 1978), Burkhauser and Turner (1978), Canto (1980), Canto *et al.* (1979), Evans (1980), Feldstein (1974, 1978), Joines (1979), Schenone (1975), among others.

[17] The data employed in the tests below come from a variety of sources; a detailed explanation of the sources appears in Appendix A.

tures variable. The effects of government expenditures may be interpreted along the lines suggested by Bailey (1971). That is, $1.00 expended on state government services means $γ less expended on private sector services, where γ represents the private-sector valuation of state government services. If, on average, γ is positive and close to unity, then public expenditures will have no effect on the equilibrium level of output. It is important to note, however, that this does not necessarily imply that state government fiscal policies are unimportant. Imagine that γ is negative for some government services (i.e., government services are complements) and that for other government services γ is positive (i.e., government services are substitutes); then it is possible that cancellation may result, leaving an average γ close to zero. Given the small sample size and the level of aggregation of the data, it is not possible to distinguish between complements and substitutes. Therefore, we are constrained to estimate the average effect. This, however, does not allow one to infer whether the effects of individual government purchases will differ from the mean.

As for the expected coefficient for state transfer payments, one may again interpret these results along the lines of Bailey. In this regard, it is recognized that transfer payments merely represent a redistribution of wealth. Given the same marginal propensity to spend on market goods, there would be no aggregate income effect. As a consequence, one would expect a zero coefficient for aggregate transfer payments. However, in the presence of positive distribution costs, the coefficient might be positive. (If there is a requirement that there is an absence of work—for example, a means test—then the coefficient may be negative.)

Another explanatory variable used in our analysis is the differential tax rate among the various states. It should be noted that the data employed for the tax rate variable are highly aggregated and represent *effective average* tax rates and, as such, do not account for progressivity in the tax system.[18] Clearly, the use of effective average tax rates as a proxy for state marginal tax rates will result in less precise estimates. Further, given the level of aggregation, one cannot tell which types of taxes are important, merely that a disincentive effect appears to exist.

A natural question that arises in the empirical estimation of Eq. (9) concerns possible multicollinearity among the state explanatory variables. The state government budget constraint can be viewed as the total of purchases plus transfer payments, or, equivalently, taxes plus borrowing plus revenue

---

[18] Under a progressive tax system, an exogenous increase in a state growth rate will increase tax revenues more than proportionately. Therefore, the effective tax rates utilized in this study will unambiguously underestimate the true marginal tax rate. Thus, the degree of progression will induce a positive correlation between tax rates and economic growth thus biasing the estimated coefficient against the hypothesis that tax rates discourage market-sector production.

sharing. To the extent that borrowing and revenue sharing differ from zero, then this would tend to reduce the correlation between spending and the effective tax rates. In addition, it must be noted that the explanatory variables are expressed as changes in the deviation from the mean—which also tends to reduce any correlation between spending and tax revenues.[19]

The integrated economy approach suggests that the expected coefficient for the U.S. growth rate for each state is unity. There are two related possibilities as to why the growth rate coefficient may differ from unity where differentials persist. One possibility is that low-wage states are catching up with the rest of the states; that is, the process of adjustment is not instantaneous. In this case, the coefficients for this variable of those states may even exceed unity or the intercept term in Eq. (9) may be positive. A second possible reason for observing a coefficient different from unity is that state fiscal policy may alter the degree of openness of the economy.[20] That is, fiscal policy may make it more or less insulated. If the local policy is not desired, then the mobile factor leaves the economy and the remaining residents (the fixed factors) consume more of the locally produced goods. It is possible that the level of integration decreases and the local good becomes a nontraded good.[21] As a consequence, the local good then becomes less directly influenced by overall supply and demand shifts.

The theoretical analysis also yields an equation describing the national equilibrium in terms of government (local, state, and federal) expenditures and tax rate policies. There are, however, several difficulties involved with the estimation of Eq. (14). First, Eq. (14) was derived under the assumption that the U.S. equilibrium can be modeled as a closed economy. Since the United States is, in fact, an open economy in an integrated world economy, Eq. (14) ignores possible influences from the rest of the world. The omission of these potentially relevant variables from the regression may induce bias

---

[19] We estimated the correlation among the different explanatory variables and found that, in most cases, the correlation between state explanatory variables was less than 0.25. In some cases, however, the correlation was in excess of 0.5. There was high correlation between state tax and transfer payment variables for North Carolina, Rhode Island, Virginia, Louisiana, Colorado, and Delaware. There was also a high correlation between state government spending and taxes for Oregon, Missouri, California, and Colorado. Finally, there was a high correlation between state transfer payments and government expensitures for North Carolina, South Carolina, Tennessee, Utah, Virginia, Washington, Missouri, Colorado, and Nebraska. In most cases, the multicollinearity issue does not present a problem, however; the above variables may be collinear, and the equations for those states should be viewed with caution.

[20] One way to distinguish these two hypotheses would be to allow for some stock adjustment costs. We did not attempt to test for this in this paper, given our desire to impose the same structure on each state and the limited sample size of our data.

[21] Notice we already have nontraded goods—i.e., household goods. If more of the local goods become nontraded goods, then they will be less responsive to overall supply and demand shifts, and more responsive to local supply and demand shifts. As a consequence, there will be less consonance or harmony between local and overall economic activity.

in the estimated coefficients and inflate the estimate of the residual variance. Of course, in an open economy framework, estimation of the state, national, and overall equilibrium, would require that individual government fiscal policy variables be measured relative to the world economy. Second, in addition to the above problem, there is the potential for multicollinearity among the explanatory variables.[22] Third, the neglect of the highly progressive character of the federal income tax system could seriously bias the tax rate coefficient.[23] It is apparent, for these reasons, that estimation of the U.S. equilibrium equation is beyond the scope of this paper.[24]

3. EMPIRICAL EVIDENCE: THE STATES' PERFORMANCE

The first step in carrying out the empirical analysis is to estimate single equations for each of the states. In an effort to conserve space, the ordinary least square results will not be discussed in gretat detail.[25] However, there are some features of the analysis that deserve some attention: (1) The coefficient for the U.S. growth rate was positive and significant in the 46 equations for which the F-statistic was significant at the 95 percent level. (2) The coefficient for the states' government purchases variables was positive and significant only in seven equations and insignificant for all others. (3) The states' transfer payment variables was significant in four equations, in two of which the coefficient was negative. (4) The tax rate variable was found to be negative and significant in 34 of the equations.

The single-equation estimates suggest the possibility of homogeneity of coefficients across states, in which case the data could be pooled into a single time series–cross section regression.[26] Chow (1960) and Fisher (1970) have

---

[22] The correlation coefficient between the transfer payments and changes in the effective tax rates is -0.55.

[23] On this issue see footnote 16.

[24] Recently Canto (1980) has estimated a variant of Eq. (14) by utilizing transfer function analysis and measures of the economy's tax rates on income from labor and capital that account for the progressivity of the tax system.

[25] Seemingly unrelated regressions for the various regions are reported in Appendix C.

[26] The estimated coefficients of the pooled cross section–time series regression (with standard errors reported in parentheses) and summary statistics are

Constant	Δ in Y_{US}	$\Delta\left(\dfrac{G_i}{POP_i} - \dfrac{G_{US}}{POP_{US}}\right)$	$\Delta\left(\dfrac{TR_i}{POP_i} - \dfrac{TR_{US}}{POP_{US}}\right)$	$\Delta(t_i - t_{US})$
0.00013	1.010	0.000707	0.000693	-5.03
(0.00144)	(0.0138)	(0.0000541)	(0.000181)	(0.235)

R^2 (adjusted for degrees of freedom) $= 0.898$

$F(4, 1029) = 1954.27$

Durbin–Watson $= 2.22$

Sum of squared residuals $= 1.860$

suggested the following F-test for homogeneity of coefficients across equations using the sum of squared residuals:

$$F_{(K(M-1), M(N-K))} = \frac{(\text{ESS}_{\text{R}} - \text{ESS}_{\text{UR}})/K(M-1)}{(\text{ESS}_{\text{UR}})/M(N-K)}$$

where M denotes the number of states; N, the time period; K, the number of explanatory variables; ESS_{R}, the sum of squared residuals for the pooled regression; and ESS_{UR}, the sums of squared residuals of all the individual time-series regressions.

Since the estimated value of the F-statistic, 12.8, exceeds the critical $F(235,768)$ at the 1 % level, one can reject the null hypothesis of homogeneous coefficients across states. Therefore a separate equation for each of the states must be estimated.

The single-equation estimates are predicated upon the assumption that the explanatory variables are predetermined for each state. This may be a reasonable assumption for the U.S. growth rate variable if the state is small relative to the union. It may also be a reasonable assumption for the local government purchases of goods and services variable. However, it is clearly not a reasonable assumption for the state transfer payments and tax rate variables. This becomes apparent when one considers that the automatic stabilizer feature of modern fiscal policy ensures that part of the spending variable is related to the level of economic activity.[27] Thus, by construction the transfer payment and tax rate variables used in this study will be endogenously determined, and as a result the ordinary least squares estimates may suffer from simultaneous equation bias. In order to allow for this, Eq. (9) was reestimated using two-stage least squares with instrumental variables or the two-stage Cochrane–Orcutt technique where appropriate.

3.1. The States' Performance Relative to the National Economy: Simultaneous Equation Estimates

Table 1 reports the simultaneous equation estimates for each state using two-stage least squares with instrumental variables or the two-stage Cochrane–Orcutt technique where appropriate.[28] The equation for 12 of the states—Arkansas, Colorado, Delaware, Louisiana, Mississippi, Missouri,

---

[27] These government programs may be thought of as setting the criteria governing eligibility for transfer payments rather than total expenditures. In this sense, the eligibility criteria are analogous to a tax rate schedule and total transfer payment to tax revenues, in which case transfer payments per person as well as the effective marginal tax rates are endogenously determined.

[28] Values of all the variables lagged one period as well as the contemporaneous value of the U.S. per capita income, and the state purchase of goods and services are used as instruments.

Nebraska, Nevada, Rhode Island, Utah, West Virginia, and Wyoming—indicated an insignificant F-statistic at standard significance levels when this technique was applied.[29] As a consequence, these states are excluded from the discussion of the significance of the individual explanatory variable below.

Examination of the estimated equations indicates that the constant term is positive and significant for Kentucky and Texas. The intercept term is negative and significant for Michigan and Ohio.

The preceding theoretical analysis suggests that the value of the growth rate coefficient should be unity. The hypotheses cannot be rejected for 30 of the 36 states with significant F-statistics. For the remaining six, the coefficient is *insignificant* for 4 states—New Hampshire, North Dakota, Ohio, and South Dakota—significant and less than two standard errors below unity for New Jersey, and more than two standard errors above unity for Michigan.

Examination of the coefficients on the state purchases of goods and services variable indicate positive and significant coefficients for four states—New Hampshire, New Jersey, New Mexico, and Ohio. Similarly the transfer payment variable was found to be positive and significant in two states—Maine and Indiana. For none of the states was the coefficient of any of the states' spending variable found to be negative and significant. With respect to the states' tax rate variable, 19 states report negative and significant coefficients at the 95 % confidence level. It is well to note that some of the states for which the tax rate variable is insignificant are those for which we earlier suspected multicollinearity. In particular, the equation for California indicated a high degree of correlation between the spending and tax rate variables.

Rejection of the homogeneity of coefficients across equations precludes the possibility of pooling the data and reporting the empirical analysis in a more compact manner. An alternative way to present the joint significance of the coefficients of one of the fiscal variables across all 48 equations may be obtained by using the binomial distribution. This, of course, assumes that the coefficients are independent (which in the absence of any prior information to the contrary may be a reasonable assumption). The binomial distribution yields the probability density function for a given number of successful outcomes (i.e., significant coefficients) X or

$$\lambda = \frac{n!}{s!(n-s)!}(1-q)^{n-s}q^s$$

where n is the number of observations (48) and q the probability (5 %). The null hypothesis is that the fiscal variable has no effect on economic activity.

---

[29] In the text, we use the 10 % two-tailed (5 % one-tailed) test as the critical value for accepting or rejecting the significance level of a coefficient.

TABLE 1

Simultaneous Equation Estimates[a,b]

State i in $\Delta \ln Y_i$	Constant	Δ in Y_{US}	$\Delta\left(\dfrac{G_i}{POP_i} - \dfrac{G_{US}}{POP_{US}}\right)$	$\Delta\left(\dfrac{TR_i}{POP_i} - \dfrac{TR_{US}}{POP_{US}}\right)$	$\Delta(t_i - t_{US})$	R^2	F	DW	ρ	SE
Alabama	0.00992	0.822*	−0.0000638	−0.00151	−1.77	0.569	4.96	2.15	—	0.0175
	(0.00923)	(0.266)	(0.000487)	(0.00306)	(4.93)		(4.15)			
Arizona	0.000353	0.640*	0.00000675	−0.00361	−2.65	0.645	6.36	—	−0.346	0.0197
	(0.0109)	(0.212)	(0.000337)	(0.00325)	(2.10)		(4.14)			
Arkansas	−0.0108	1.24*	−0.000862	−0.00189	−11.24**	0.385	2.20**	—	0.136	0.0310
	(0.0195)	(0.405)	(0.000518)	(0.00437)	(4.97)		(4.14)			
California	0.00346	0.677*	0.000136	−0.0000214	0.854	0.692	7.84	—	−0.471	0.0124
	(0.00392)	(0.157)	(0.000210)	(0.000452)	(1.24)		(4.14)			
Colorado	0.0274	0.471	−0.000739	−0.00472	1.45	0.082	0.312**	—	−0.201	0.0245
	(0.0166)	(0.299)	(0.000637)	(0.00275)	(3.05)		(4.14)			
Connecticut	−0.00967	1.20*	−0.000321	−0.00114	−2.55	0.515	3.70	—	−0.142	0.0183
	(0.00705)	(0.260)	(0.000219)	(0.00275)	(1.46)		(4.14)			
Delaware	0.0161	−0.210	−0.000251	−0.00266	−1.90	0.444	2.80**	—	−0.565	0.0388
	(0.0128)	(0.470)	(0.000269)	(0.00379)	(2.27)		(4.14)			
Florida	−0.00728	1.03*	−0.000217	−0.00459	1.20	0.597	5.56	1.98	—	0.0237
	(0.0131)	(0.331)	(0.000471)	(0.00604)	(6.29)		(4.15)			
Georgia	−0.00185	1.15*	0.000581	−0.00155	−8.43*	0.820	17.09	2.21	—	0.0147
	(0.00617)	(0.172)	(0.00405)	(0.00129)	(2.88)		(4.15)			
Idaho	−0.0147	1.48*	0.000838	−0.000534	−3.97*	0.738	9.85	—	−0.270	0.0522
	(0.0146)	(0.405)	(0.000539)	(0.00374)	(1.25)		(4.14)			
Illinois	−0.00414	0.959*	−0.000269	−0.00147	−0.683	0.771	12.65	1.97	—	0.0144
	(0.00550)	(0.186)	(0.000262)	(0.00135)	(1.08)		(4.15)			
Indiana	−0.00184	1.39*	0.000424	0.00562*	−3.27*	0.878	25.16	—	−0.420	0.0139
	(0.00565)	(0.196)	(0.000354)	(0.00184)	(1.39)		(4.14)			

240

State										
Iowa	-0.00154 (0.00976)	0.923* (0.481)	-0.0000182 (0.000860)	-0.000167 (0.00243)	-6.19 (4.43)	0.769	12.50 (4.15)	2.11	—	0.0265
Kansas	0.00620 (0.0123)	0.784* (0.334)	-0.000223 (0.000618)	-0.000506 (0.00503)	-3.39* (1.95)	0.514	3.96 (4.15)	2.20	—	0.0285
Kentucky	0.00981* (0.00421)	0.973* (0.133)	-0.000155 (0.000183)	-0.000337 (0.00158)	-0.152 (1.04)	0.801	15.08 (4.15)	1.88	—	0.0121
Louisiana	-0.018 (0.0336)	0.994* (0.350)	-0.000729 (0.000566)	-0.00529 (0.000697)	-6.10 (7.57)	0.076	0.309** (4.15)	1.91	—	0.0291
Maine	-0.00867 (0.00726)	1.29* (0.258)	-0.000346 (0.000317)	0.000672* (0.00333)	-4.94* (2.57)	0.682	7.52 (4.14)	—	-0.964	0.0262
Maryland	0.00331 (0.00914)	0.904* (0.313)	-0.0000221 (0.000332)	-0.00268 (0.00488)	-0.335 (1.05)	0.488	3.57 (4.15)	1.97	—	0.0189
Massachusetts	-0.000556 (0.00654)	1.06* (0.232)	-0.000357 (0.000343)	-0.000684 (0.000578)	-6.09 (3.51)	0.613	5.93 (4.15)	2.02	—	0.0171
Michigan	-0.0207* (0.0112)	1.66* (0.329)	-0.000615 (0.000562)	0.00293 (0.00293)	-0.165 (2.25)	0.743	10.11 (4.14)	—	0.334	0.0233
Minnesota	-0.00706 (0.00742)	1.40* (0.238)	-0.000365 (0.000421)	-0.000377 (0.00150)	-3.20* (1.59)	0.740	9.98 (4.14)	—	-0.390	0.0205
Mississippi	0.00476 (0.0145)	0.912 (0.316)	0.000833 (0.000585)	-0.00244 (0.00266)	-6.50* (2.80)	0.356	2.07** (4.15)	1.85	—	0.0267
Missouri	-0.0155 (0.0201)	1.18 (0.718)	0.00223 (0.00216)	-0.00530 (0.00692)	-16.36 (17.4)	0	0** (4.15)	1.72	—	0.0411
Montana	-0.00669 (0.0136)	1.53* (0.602)	-0.000391 (0.000399)	0.00745 (0.00699)	-4.36* (1.58)	0.625	6.26 (4.15)	2.07	—	0.0394
Nebraska	0.0109 (0.0171)	1.44 (0.871)	-0.00119 (0.00146)	0.0118 (0.0133)	-4.69 (6.41)	0.138	0.601** (4.15)	1.93	—	0.0470
Nevada	-0.00538 (0.0123)	0.633* (0.374)	-0.000251 (0.000321)	-0.00309 (0.00251)	-6.19* (2.15)	0.371	2.07** (4.14)	—	-0.413	0.0353
New Hampshire	0.00740 (0.00972)	0.608 (0.399)	0.00153* (0.000606)	-0.00337 (0.00474)	-6.67* (2.85)	0.719	9.6 (4.15)	1.93	—	0.0222

(continued)

241

TABLE 1 (*continued*)

State i in $\Delta \ln Y_i$	Constant	$\Delta \ln Y_{US}$	$\Delta\left(\dfrac{G_i}{POP_i} - \dfrac{G_{US}}{POP_{US}}\right)$	$\Delta\left(\dfrac{TR_i}{POP_i} - \dfrac{TR_{US}}{POP_{US}}\right)$	$\Delta(t_i - t_{US})$	R^2	F	DW	ρ	SE
New Jersey	0.00615 (0.00580)	0.627* (0.175)	−0.000483* (0.000267)	−0.00113 (0.00138)	−1.83* (1.08)	0.664	7.4 (4,15)	2.08	—	0.0129
New Mexico	0.00717 (0.0107)	0.594* (0.297)	0.000598* (0.000307)	−0.00213 (0.00252)	−2.77 (2.59)	0.589	5.01 (4,14)	—	−0.462	0.0231
New York	−0.00681 (0.00734)	1.21* (0.270)	−0.000223 (0.000195)	−0.001001 (0.000970)	−2.29* (1.40)	0.648	6.45 (4,14)	—	0.279	0.0160
North Carolina	0.00572 (0.00773)	0.814* (0.252)	0.000802 (0.000875)	−0.00101 (0.00231)	−12.07* (6.31)	0.605	5.74 (4,15)	1.74	—	0.0182
North Dakota	0.0176 (0.0212)	0.114 (0.632)	−0.0000580 (0.000625)	−0.00224 (0.00618)	−9.62* (2.04)	0.935	50.30 (4,14)	—	−0.638	0.0435
Ohio	−0.0137* (0.00472)	1.32 (0.150)	0.000455* (0.000252)	0.000452 (0.00150)	−6.06* (2.35)	0.899	33.43 (4,15)	1.73	—	0.0120
Oklahoma	0.00922 (0.0104)	0.625* (0.253)	0.0000876 (0.000256)	0.0000692 (0.00133)	−3.03 (2.38)	0.489	3.35 (4,14)	—	−0.04	0.0178
Oregon	0.00887 (0.00907)	0.635* (0.285)	0.0000784 (0.000243)	−0.000853 (0.00138)	−0.703 (2.42)	0.549	4.55 (4,15)	2.01	—	0.0179
Pennsylvania	−0.00785 (0.0100)	1.09* (0.264)	0.0000415 (0.000372)	0.00189 (0.00243)	0.546 (1.85)	0.767	12.35 (4,15)	1.93	—	0.0127
Rhode Island	0.00171 (0.0124)	0.510 (0.456)	−0.000486 (0.000545)	0.00749 (0.00652)	−9.57* (4.33)	0.407	2.57** (4,15)	1.87	—	0.0313
South Carolina	0.0130 (0.00936)	0.990* (0.307)	0.000219 (0.000456)	−0.00117 (0.00215)	−0.206 (3.73)	0.573	4.70 (4,14)	—	−0.103	0.0215

South Dakota	−0.00195 (0.0213)	0.0262 (1.10)	0.00193 (0.00142)	−0.0146 (0.0164)	−5.91* (3.45)	0.791	13.25 (4,14)	—	−0.187	0.0568
Tennessee	−0.00666 (0.00931)	1.27* (0.217)	0.000247 (0.000397)	−0.00103 (0.00222)	−7.98* (3.47)	0.728	9.39 (4,14)	—	−0.347	0.0163
Texas	0.0103* (0.00546)	0.701* (0.173)	0.000215 (0.000459)	−0.000548 (0.00177)	−2.90* (1.29)	0.809	14.88 (4,14)	—	0.334	0.0109
Utah	0.0131 (0.00931)	0.617* (0.279)	−0.000442 (0.000564)	0.00120 (0.00469)	2.30 (2.95)	0.282	1.38** (4,14)	—	−0.083	0.0188
Vermont	0.00401 (0.0145)	0.888* (0.495)	0.000498 (0.000331)	0.00702 (0.00629)	−3.39 (2.25)	0.684	8.12 (4,15)	1.99	—	0.0377
Virginia	0.0122 (0.00793)	0.814* (0.295)	0.000182 (0.000428)	−0.00160 (0.00260)	−0.0832 (1.55)	0.577	5.12 (4,15)	1.95	—	0.0176
Washington	−0.00693 (0.00732)	0.982* (0.274)	0.0000837 (0.000543)	−0.00258 (0.00315)	−6.54* (3.28)	0.498	3.47 (4,14)	—	−0.501	0.0238
West Virginia	0.0103 (0.0120)	0.551 (0.366)	−0.000156 (0.000423)	−0.00224 (0.00290)	−6.72 (4.38)	0.206	0.098** (4,15)	2.27	—	0.0334
Wisconsin	0.00193 (0.00599)	1.01* (0.193)	−0.000127 (0.000276)	−0.00125 (0.000939)	−3.29* (1.44)	0.693	7.91 (4,14)	—	−0.414	0.0169
Wyoming	0.0306 (0.0245)	0.604 (0.994)	0.000377 (0.000301)	0.00679 (0.0151)	−7.78* (2.93)	0.248	1.23 (4,15)	1.50	—	0.0525

[a] Standard error in parentheses. An asterisk indicates significance at the 5% level; a double asterisk indicates insignificance at the 1% level.

[b] Instruments:

$$L\Delta \ln Y_i, \ L\Delta \ln Y_{US}, \ \Delta \ln Y_{US}, \ L\Delta(t_i - t_{US}), \ L\Delta\left(\frac{G_i}{POP_i} - \frac{G_{US}}{POP_{US}}\right), \ \Delta\left(\frac{G_i}{POP_i} - \frac{G_{US}}{POP_{US}}\right) \text{ and } L\Delta\left(\frac{TR_i}{POP_i} - \frac{TR_{US}}{POP_{US}}\right),$$

where L denotes the LAG(1) operator.

One would expect to find nq significant coefficients by chance. The mode or most likely outcome is 2.48 successes with a probability of 0.215.

Upon inspection of Table 1 it is apparent that the number of successful outcomes for the government purchases, transfer payments, and tax rate variables are 4, 2, and 22, respectively, with a corresponding probability of 0.127, 0.266, and 1.72×10^{-11}.

Although the assumption of independent outcomes may not be entirely correct, the probability for each outcome implied by the binomial distribution is highly suggestive. The probability of outcomes for the government purchases and transfer payments variables is of the same order of magnitude as that of the null hypothesis, while the probability of the tax rate outcome is 10 orders of magnitude smaller than that expected by the null hypothesis.

In summary, the information in the sample is consistent with the implications of our model. In particular, these results (1) strongly support the integrated economy approach, (2) suggest a negative relation between state tax rates and its economic performance, and (3) indicate that government spending variables are generally insignificant.

The latter point deserves some additional explanation. The insignificance of the government spending variable is in large part predictable for the following reason. At the margin, the empirical estimates suggest that average values of government services equal their cost (i.e., $\gamma = 1$) and as a result would have no impact. The fact that government expenditures do not appear to have an impact on economic activity does not imply that government expenditures are necessarily wasteful. On the contrary, these results are consistent with an "optimal" behavior on the part of the government. Abstract from the substitution effects that nonneutral taxation may generate and it is seen that a government policy that maximizes the economy's total wealth (inclusive of government services) is one that makes the value of government services equal to their costs (i.e., $\gamma = 1$). Thus, if anything, the evidence suggests that states' governments have pursued an optimal spending policy, as defined above. A note of caution is in order, however, since, as we mentioned, this optimum neglects the substitution effects generated by tax rates which may reduce the level of income. Once the distortionary effects of nonneutral tax rates on the economy are taken into account, it becomes apparent that an "optimal" government spending policy requires that the value of the services provided be sufficiently large to cover the factor costs of the sources provided as well as the costs generated by the nonneutral tax rates (i.e., $\gamma > 1$). In this case, the reduced form coefficient for the public spending variable will be unambiguously negative.

Similarly, given the structure of the theoretical model advanced above, one might expect correlation of the disturbances across equations. Zellner (1962) has suggested the use of seemingly unrelated regression analysis to

TABLE 2

Seemingly Unrelated Regressions: Regional Performance Relative to the Nation[a]

Region	Constant	$\Delta\left(\dfrac{G_R}{POP_R} - \dfrac{G_{US}}{POP_{US}}\right)$	$\Delta\left(\dfrac{TR_E}{POP_R} - \dfrac{TR_{US}}{POP_{US}}\right)$	$\Delta(t_R - t_{US})$
New England	−0.00240	0.000440*	−0.000740*	−2.278*
	(0.00264)	(0.000209)	(0.000298)	(1.03)
Middle Atlantic	−0.00286	0.000141	−0.0000330	−1.47*
	(0.00203)	(0.000130)	(0.000477)	(0.851)
Southeast	0.00355	0.000238	−0.00167	−3.72*
	(0.00396)	(0.000401)	(0.00125)	(2.20)
Midwest	−0.00232	−0.000218	0.000623	−2.91*
	(0.00180)	(0.000297)	(0.000608)	(0.724)
Great Plains	−0.000961	0.000114	−0.000969	−4.65*
	(0.00452)	(0.000493)	(0.00143)	(1.46)
Mountain	−0.00279	0.000318	−0.00145	−2.54*
	(0.00437)	(0.000238)	(0.00120)	(0.998)
Far West	−0.00264	0.000180	0.000111	−0.366
	(0.00235)	(0.000176)	(0.000441)	(0.740)

[a] An asterisk denotes significance at the 5% level.

obtain more efficient estimates in such cases. We estimated a variant of Eq. (9) using the seemingly unrelated regression technique to measure state economic performance relative to its region and economic performance relative to the national economy.

3.2. The Regional Performance: The Seemingly Unrelated Regression Results

Table 2 reports on the seemingly unrelated regressions on the regions' growth rate differential (relative to the U.S. growth rate). It is apparent that the results are quite consistent with the previously reported results. The coefficients for the constant term was not significant for any region. The government purchases and transfer payment variables are significant only for the New England states. In contrast, the coefficients in the tax rate variable are negative and significant for all regions except the Far West.

4. SUMMARY AND CONCLUSIONS

This paper attempts to explain the existence of apparent persistent income differentials among states in a national economy with factor mobility. A simple neoclassical model is advanced with a single market good and two factors of production—one fixed and one mobile—which must decide whether to engage in market or household production. The mobile factor is able largely or entirely to escape state (but not federal) taxes while the fixed factor is unable to escape either state or federal taxes. Although government services received are included in income by both factors of production, state fiscal policies are explicitly introduced into the model since it is recognized that such policies may alter the incentives to engage in market and household production. Consequently, if household and market goods are imperfect substitutes, *market* incomes may diverge across states (although *full* incomes need not) as individual state fiscal policies alter the relative incentives to engage in market and household production. This contrasts with previous studies which have emphasized differences in technologies or price levels across states or the presence of significant factor movement costs in order to explain observed persistent differentials in market income.

The essence of our model is contained in Eq. (9), which relates the percentage change in state income to differences in per capita state spending (which is divided between state purchases of goods and services and state transfer payments relative to average per capita state spending) and differences in effective state tax rates relative to average state tax rates. In order to allow for simultaneity among the dependent and the explanatory variables —specifically transfer payments and effective tax rates—Eq. (9) was estimated using two-stage least squares.

If the individual income effects induced by the state spending variables and the state financing of its spending (i.e., taxes) offset each other, as one aggregates over individuals to the state level and governments are neither more nor less efficient in providing services than the private sector, then one would expect zero coefficients for these two variables. Substitution effects, however, do not tend to cancel out as the aggregates over individuals. As a consequence, our model implies a significant negative relation for the tax rate variable.

Data on state population growth rates, per capita state spending, and tax rates were examined. A stochastic version of Eq. (9) which included a constant term was estimated. The empirical results indicate that the model is quite robust and the results are fairly consistent across the techniques employed. In particular, the constant term was rarely significant. This result is contrary to the implications of theories which explain income differentials as temporary phenomena which are eliminated as factor prices are equilibrated across regions. Similarly, the government purchases and transfer payments variables were significant in only a few instances. One explanation for this result is that states are pursuing optimal spending policies. That is, abstracting from substitution effects, the optimal state fiscal policy would be to make the private valuation of government services equal to the money expended on them (i.e., $\gamma = 1$), in which case the government spending variables should have no significant impact on relative state economic performance. However, where substitution effects are important and our analysis indicates that the differential tax rate variable appears to have a consistent negative and significant effect across states, a policy of equating γ to unity may indicate excessive spending. This suggests that γ should exceed unity in order to minimize any "excess burden" loss. Of course, our analysis does not take into account distributional effects which may result in different spending optima. In addition, these results suggest that to the extent that substitution effects are important, state relative performance can be influenced by state tax rate policy. The evidence from the single-equation estimates indicates that the coefficient for the U.S. growth rate is positive and in most cases not significantly different from unity. This suggests support for the integrated economy view.

Genetski and Chin (1978) use cross-sectional analysis to measure the effect of relative tax burden on economic activity. In sharp contrast with our results, they report a weak contemporaneous effect of the relative tax burden on economic activity. The use of cross-sectional analysis, however, implicitly assumes homogeneity of the tax rate coefficient across states. Our analysis, which encompasses the time period of the Genetski and Chin study, suggests that the pooling of data across states (and thus cross-sectional analysis) is inappropriate since one may reject the hypothesis of homogeneity of coefficients.

It should also be noted that the empirical analysis presented in this paper is capable of explaining the differences in economic performance among states without specific reference to such regional exogenous factors as climatic conditions or mineral wealth.

Examination of the seemingly unrelated regressions of states' performance relative to the region yields results consistent with the individual state equations. This result contrasts with past studies on factor migration which have tended to ignore the tax effects. This also has implications for the success of predatory tax policies. It should be emphasized that there is an effect on the U.S. economy resulting from the average state tax rate. Consequently, if all states engage in predatory or beggar-thy-neighbor tax policies, there may be no *relative* gain, but there may be an *absolute* gain due to the reduced average marginal tax rates. Although our results indicate support for the integrated economy approach, regional differences still exist. This is evidenced by the systematic differences in the magnitude of the tax rate coefficients across regions.

The empirical analysis of this paper suggests the conclusion that individual state fiscal policies can and do influence relative state economic performance. In contrast, federal fiscal policy mainly influences absolute or national economic performance. As a result, the empirical analysis suggests that both state and federal fiscal policies matter in the determination of the overall economic performance of a state or region.

APPENDIX A. DATA SOURCES

The data used in this study came from a variety of sources reporting on aggregate U.S. annual time series from 1957 to 1977. Data for federal government purchases of goods and services, federal transfer payments, federal tax revenues, and personal income at constant prices are taken directly from the *National Income Accounts.* Population figures were obtained from the *U.S. Department of Commerce Bureau of Census Current Population Reports.* Tax revenues and state expenditures and transfer payments were obtained from *U.S. Department of Commerce States' Government Finances.* Finally, the states' personal income figures were taken directly from *U.S. Department of Commerce Bureau of Economic Analysis.*

APPENDIX B. DERIVATION OF STATES' PERSONAL INCOME

By differentiating logarithmically, Eq. (1) yields

$$EY_i = ES_{Bi} - ES_{BUS} + EY_{US} \tag{A.1}$$

where $E = d$ log operator.

By differentiating logarithmically, the immobile factor demand for non-market services yields

$$
\begin{aligned}
EH_{Bi} = \frac{\eta_{B\Omega_i}}{\Omega_i} & [R_B N_{Bi} ER_B + (\gamma - 1) dG_{Si} + (\Psi - 1) dTR_{Si}] \\
& + (1 - \alpha)(\gamma - 1) dG_f + (1 - \alpha)(\Psi - 1) dTR_f \\
& - \eta_{BR} ER_B - \frac{dt_{Bi}}{(1 - t_{Bi})}
\end{aligned}
\tag{A.2}
$$

where $\eta_{B\Omega}$ denotes the income elasticity of demand for household services and η_{BR} the demand elasticity with respect to the factor reward.

Differentiating the factor market equilibrium condition yields

$$ES_{Bi} = - \frac{H_{Bi}}{(1 - H_{Bi})} EH_{Bi} \tag{A.3}$$

assuming symmetric behavior among the different states, that is,

$$\eta_{B\Omega_i} = \eta_{B\Omega_j}$$

and substituting Eqs. (A.3) and (A.2) into Eq. (A.1) yields

$$EY_i = \left[\frac{N_B}{\Omega_{B_i}} \eta_{B\Omega} (\gamma - 1) \left(\frac{dG_{OI}}{N_{B_i}} - \frac{dG_S}{N_{BUS}} \right) \right.$$

$$\left. + (\Psi - 1) \left(\frac{dTR_{Si}}{N_{B_i}} - \frac{dTR_S}{N_B} \right) \right] - \eta_{BR} \left(\frac{dt_{Bi}}{(1 - t_{B_i})} - \frac{dt_{BUS}}{(1 - t_{BUS})} \right)$$

$$+ EY_{US}$$

where

$$G_S = \sum G_{Si}, \qquad TR_S = \sum TR_{Si}, \qquad H_{BUS} = \sum N_{Bi} \qquad (A.4)$$

Also, since N_{Bi} is constant by assumption

$$\frac{dG_{Si}}{N_{Bi}} = d \left(\frac{G_{Si}}{N_{Bi}} \right), \qquad \frac{dG_S}{N_{BUS}} = d \left(\frac{G_S}{N_{BUS}} \right)$$

$$\frac{dTR_{Si}}{N_{Bi}} = d \left(\frac{TR_{Si}}{N_{Bi}} \right), \qquad \frac{dTR_S}{N_{BUS}} = d \left(\frac{TR_S}{N_{BUS}} \right)$$

APPENDIX C. THE STATES' PERFORMANCE RELATIVE TO THEIR REGION: THE SEEMINGLY UNRELATED REGRESSION ESTIMATES

Although the empirical estimates reported in the previous sections do not reject the hypotheses of an integrated economy (i.e., we could not reject the hypothesis that the U.S. growth rate coefficient was different than unity), states within a geographic region may be more similar to each other than states in other regions (e.g., due to similar climatic conditions). This suggests that one may obtain more precise estimates of the effects of the explanatory variables by estimating a variant of Eq. (9) in which the state's performance is measured relative to its region. Similarly, given the structure of the theoretical model developed, one might expect correlations of the disturbances across equations. This suggests the use of seemingly unrelated regression analysis.[30]

---

[30] The use of this technique should increase the efficiency of the estimates. In addition, the similarity of states within a region permits more precise measures of the effects of the variations in the explanatory variables.

TABLE 3

New England States' Seemingly Unrelated Regressions[a]

State	Constant	$\Delta\left(\dfrac{G_i}{POP_i} - \dfrac{G_R}{POP_R}\right)$	$\Delta\left(\dfrac{TR_i}{POP_i} - \dfrac{TR_R}{POP_R}\right)$	$\Delta(t_i - t_R)$
Maine	0.00407	−0.000368	0.000668	−5.96
	(0.00846)	(0.000384)	(0.000924)	(0.929)
New Hampshire	0.000649	0.000541*	0.0000192	−3.62*
	(0.00351)	(0.000224)	(0.000409)	(0.917)
Vermont	0.00499	0.000203	−0.0000722	−4.31*
	(0.00596)	(0.00021)	(0.000779	(0.544)
Massachusetts	0.000745	−0.000257*	−0.000218	−1.13*
	(0.00168)	(0.000117)	(0.000204)	(0.651)
Rhode Island	0.00391	0.000162	−0.000519	−1.95*
	(0.00559)	(0.000218)	(0.000643)	(1.00)
Connecticut	−0.00539*	−0.000112	−0.000867*	−0.565
	(0.00186)	(0.0000906)	(0.000271)	(0.509)

[a] An asterisk denotes significance at the 5% level.

TABLE 4

Middle Atlantic States' Seemingly Unrelated Regressions[a]

State	Constant	$\Delta\left(\dfrac{G_i}{POP_i} - \dfrac{G_R}{POP_R}\right)$	$\Delta\left(\dfrac{TR_i}{POP_i} - \dfrac{TR_R}{POP_R}\right)$	$\Delta(t_i - t_R)$
New York	−0.00231	−0.0000208	0.000470*	−2.04*
	(0.00209)	(0.0000905)	(0.000281)	(0.425)
New Jersey	0.000378	0.000318*	0.00103*	−1.96*
	(0.00232)	(0.000128)	(0.000420)	(0.435)
Pennsylvania	−0.00131	−0.000140	0.0000693	−1.95*
	(0.00242)	(0.000176)	(0.000479)	(0.573)
Delaware	−0.00685	0.000513	0.000610	−2.47
	(0.0128)	(0.00307)	(0.00329)	(1.82)
Maryland	0.00317	−0.000190	−0.000837	−0.453
	(0.00371)	(0.000166)	(0.000775)	(0.436)
Virginia	0.0115*	0.00000664	0.000824	−2.22*
	(0.00364)	(0.000152)	(0.000605)	(0.505)
West Virginia	0.00313	−0.000409*	0.000216	−2.28*
	(0.00621)	(0.000212)	(0.000979)	(0.886)

[a] An asterisk denotes significance at the 5% level.

A variant of Eq. (9) which involved moving the region's growth rate to the left-hand side to yield the differential growth was estimated for each region.[31] For estimating purposes, the U.S. economy was divided into the following seven regions: New England (NE), Middle Atlantic (MA), Southeast (SE), Midwest (MW), Great Plains (GP), Mountain (MT), and Far West (FW). The regressions for these regions are shown in Tables 3–9. It is recognized that this is an arbitrary but nevertheless commonly used method of regional classification. Other methods of dividing the nation into regions would be equally arbitrary.

TABLE 5

Southeast States' Seemingly Unrelated Regressions[a]

State	Constant	$\Delta\left(\dfrac{G_i}{POP_i} - \dfrac{G_R}{POP_R}\right)$	$\Delta\left(\dfrac{TR_i}{POP_i} - \dfrac{TR_R}{POP_R}\right)$	$\Delta(t_i - t_R)$
North Carolina	0.00244	0.0000798	0.000526	−2.09*
	(0.00228)	(0.000234)	(0.000800)	(1.20)
Kentucky	−0.00190	0.000194	0.000906	−0.981
	(0.00352)	(0.000179)	(0.00102)	(0.777)
South Carolina	0.00419	0.000114	0.000557	−1.56
	(0.00379)	(0.000201)	(0.000881)	(1.15)
Georgia	0.00128	0.000322*	−0.000495	−4.62*
	(0.00181)	(0.000147)	(0.000450)	(0.824)
Florida	−0.00823*	0.0000670	−0.00168	−2.37
	(0.00446)	(0.000273)	(0.00298)	(1.72)
Alabama	0.000841	0.000263	0.00151*	−5.92*
	(0.00280)	(0.000286)	(0.000824)	(1.41)
Mississippi	0.00589	0.000495*	−0.000200	−2.59*
	(0.00398)	(0.000215)	(0.000796)	(0.772)
Louisiana	−0.00805*	0.000246	−0.00183*	−1.72*
	(0.00440)	(0.000165)	(0.00111)	(0.735)
Arkansas	0.00421	0.000471*	0.00161	−6.26*
	(0.00501)	(0.000196)	(0.00117)	(1.16)
Tennessee	−0.00218	−0.000229	0.00292*	−3.48*
	(0.00183)	(0.000173)	(0.000892)	(0.700)

[a] An asterisk denotes significance at the 5% level.

[31] The rationale for this is that the importance of a state relative to its region is substantially larger than that of a state relative to the U.S. economy. Thus, the assumption that for a state the region growth rate is a predetermined variable is questionable. Moving the region growth rate to the left-hand side implicitly assumes that the variable coefficient is unity. In light of the evidence reported in Sections 3.1 and 3.2, it does not seem to be an unreasonable assumption to make.

TABLE 6

Midwest States' Seemingly Unrelated Regressions[a]

State	Constant	$\Delta\left(\dfrac{G_i}{POP_i} - \dfrac{G_R}{POP_R}\right)$	$\Delta\left(\dfrac{TR_i}{POP_i} - \dfrac{TR_R}{POP_R}\right)$	$\Delta(t_i - t_R)$
Ohio	−0.00377	−0.000167	−0.0000157	−1.33*
	(0.00332)	(0.000179)	(0.000906)	(0.785)
Indiana	0.00354	0.000639*	0.00107	−0.658
	(0.00284)	(0.000248)	(0.00114)	(0.441)
Illinois	−0.00138	−0.00000307	−0.000967*	−0.388
	(0.00249)	(0.000163)	(0.000675)	(0.553)
Michigan	−0.000655	0.000448	0.00141	−2.42*
	(0.00449	(0.000346)	(0.000967)	(0.877)
Wisconsin	0.00281	−0.0000971	0.000309	−1.18*
	(0.00258)	(0.000161)	(0.000473)	(0.519)
Minnesota	0.00905*	−0.0000901	−0.00229*	−3.86*
	(0.00495)	(0.000250)	(0.00118)	(0.706)
Iowa	0.00239	−0.000345	0.00261*	−6.61*
	(0.00527)	(0.000281)	(0.000892)	(1.53)
Missouri	−0.00207	0.000576*	−0.00131*	−4.41*
	(0.00471)	(0.000341)	(0.000913)	(0.913)

[a] An asterisk denotes significance at the 5% level.

TABLE 7

Great Plains States' Seemingly Unrelated Regressions

State	Constant	$\Delta\left(\dfrac{G_i}{POP_i} - \dfrac{G_R}{POP_R}\right)$	$\Delta\left(\dfrac{TR_i}{POP_i} - \dfrac{TR_R}{POP_R}\right)$	$\Delta(t_i - t_R)$
North Dakota	−0.00485	0.000485	−0.00201	−8.58
	(0.0102)	(0.000423)	(0.00196)	(5.86)
South Dakota	−0.00684	0.0010979*	−0.00224	−7.01
	(0.00694)	(0.000353)	(0.00184)	(5.16)
Nebraska	0.00254	0.000235	−0.00174	−5.09*
	(0.00488)	(0.000219)	(0.001129)	(0.802)
Kansas	0.000679	−0.000464	0.000782	−2.48*
	(0.00427)	(0.000281)	(0.000689)	(0.840)
Oklahoma	−0.000191	0.0000519	−0.000341	−3.22*
	(0.00363)	(0.000214)	(0.000752)	(1.34)
Texas	0.000492	−0.000252	0.00321*	−5.51
	(0.00204)	(0.000295)	(0.00115)	(0.701)

[a] An asterisk denotes significance at the 5% level.

TABLE 8

Mountain States' Seemingly Unrelated Regressions[a]

State	Constant	$\Delta\left(\dfrac{G_i}{POP_i} - \dfrac{G_R}{POP_R}\right)$	$\Delta\left(\dfrac{TR_i}{POP_i} - \dfrac{TR_R}{POP_R}\right)$	$\Delta(t_i - t_R)$
Montana	−0.00576	−0.0000466	−0.000442	−4.78*
	(0.00675)	(0.000202)	(0.00177)	(0.635)
Idaho	−0.00120	0.000109	0.00129	−5.80*
	(0.00592)	(0.000249)	(0.00176)	(0.751)
Wyoming	0.00908	0.000197	0.00445*	−4.73*
	(0.00808)	(0.000143)	(0.00184)	(1.02)
Colorado	0.00128	0.000108	0.00179	−5.17*
	(0.00329)	(0.000226)	(0.00114)	(0.723)
New Mexico	−0.0000396	0.000314	0.00123	−4.86*
	(0.00513)	(0.000265)	(0.00157)	(0.721)

[a] An asterisk denotes significance at the 5% level.

TABLE 9

Far West States' Seemingly Unrelated Regressions[a]

State	Constant	$\Delta\left(\dfrac{G_i}{POP_i} - \dfrac{G_R}{POP_R}\right)$	$\Delta\left(\dfrac{TR_i}{POP_i} - \dfrac{TR_R}{POP_R}\right)$	$\Delta(t_i - t_R)$
Washington	0.00278	−0.0000630	0.000658	−2.60*
	(0.00385)	(0.000125)	(0.000543)	(0.929)
Oregon	0.00350	−0.000128	−0.000207	0.00268
	(0.004448)	(0.000188)	(0.000562)	(0.0851)
California	−0.000993	0.000128	0.000104	−1.31*
	(0.000885)	(0.0000968)	(0.000305)	(0.605)
Nevada	−0.00546	−0.000402	−0.00161	−2.76*
	(0.00961)	(0.000369)	(0.00144)	(1.21)
Utah	0.00544	−0.000369	0.0000548	1.52
	(0.00404)	(0.000271)	(0.000610)	(0.982)
Arizona	0.000256	0.000331	−0.00122	−2.90*
	(0.00548)	(0.000239)	(0.000704)	(1.01)

[a] An asterisk denotes significance at the 5% level.

ACKNOWLEDGMENTS

We wish to express our sincere appreciation to the participants of the conferences and the following individuals: Fischer Black, Paul Evans, Douglas H. Joines, Arthur B. Laffer, Marc Miles, Janet K. Smith, John Shoven, and Arnold Zellner for their many valuable comments. Sin Poe Soh provided computational assistance.

REFERENCES

Bailey, M. J. (1971). *National Income and the Price Level*, 2nd ed. McGraw-Hill, New York.
Batra, R., and Scully, G. (1972). "Technical Progress, Economic Growth and the North–South Wage Differential," *Journal of Regional Science* **12**, 375–386.
Becker, G. (1965). "A Theory of the Allocation of Time," *Economic Journal* **75**, 493–517.
Blinder, A. and Solow, R. (1974). "Analytical Foundation of Fiscal Policies," in *The Economics of Public Finance* (A. Blinder *et al.*, eds.). The Brookings Institution, Washington, D.C.
Bloom, C. (1961). "State and Local Tax Differentials and the Location of Industry," *National Tax Journal*.
Borts, G. (1960). "The Equalization of Returns and Regional Economic Growth," *American Economic Review* **50**, 319–347.
Boskin, M. (1977). "Social Security Retirement Decisions," *Economic Inquiry* **15**, 1–25.
Boskin, M. (1978). "Taxation, Saving, and the Rate of Interest," *Journal of Political Economy* **86**, S3–S28.
Burkhauser, R., and Turner, J. (1978). "A Time-Series Analysis on Social Security and Its Effect on the Market Work of Men at Younger Ages," *Journal of Political Economy* **86**, 701–716.
Canto, V. (1980). "The Influence of Tax Rates on GNP and Potential Output," Univ. of Southern California, Los Angeles, California.
Canto, V., Joines, D., and Webb, R. (1980). "Revenue Effects of the Kennedy Tax Cuts," Univ. of Southern California, Los Angeles, California.
Chow, G. (1960). "Test of Equality between Sets of Coefficients in Two Linear Regressions," *Econometrica*, 591–605.
Coelho, P., and Ghali, M. (1971). "The End of the North–South Wage Differential," *American Economic Review*.
Due, J. (1961). "Studies of State–Local Tax Influences on Locations of Industry," *National Tax Journal* **14**, 163–173.
Evans, P. (1978). "The U.S. Labor Market—Some Empirical Estimates 1929–1976," Stanford Univ., Palo Alto, California.
Feldstein, M. (1974). "Social Security, Induced Retirement, and Aggregate Capital Accumulation," *Journal of Political Economy* **82**, 905–926.
Feldstein, M. (1978). "The Effect of Unemployment Insurance on Temporary Layoff Unemployment," *American Economic Review* **68**, 834–846.
Fisher, F. (1970). "Tests of Equality Between Sets of Coefficients in Two Linear Regressions: An Expository Note," *Econometrica* **38**, 361–366.
Genetski, R., and Chin, Y. (1978). "The Impact of State and Local Taxes on Economic Growth," Hanes Economic Research Office Service.
Greenwood, M. (1975). "Research on Internal Migration in the United States: A Survey," *Journal of Economic Literature* **13**, 397–433.
Joines, D. (1979). "Government Fiscal Policy and Private Capital Formation." Ph.D. Dissertation, Univ. of Chicago, Chicago, Illinois.

McClure, C. E. (1970). "Taxation, Substitution, and Industrial Location," *Journal of Political Economy* **78**, 112–132.

Mundell, R. (1957). "International Trade and Factor Mobility," *American Economic Review* **57**, 231–235.

Mussa, M. (1978). "Dynamic Adjustment in the Heckscher–Ohlin–Samuelson Model," *Journal of Political Economy* **86**, 775–792.

Samuelson, P. (1949). "International Factor-Price Equalization Once Again," *Economic Journal* **59**, 181–197.

Schenone, O. H. (1975). "A Dynamic Analysis of Taxation," *American Economic Review* **65**, 101–114.

Zellner, A. (1962). "An Efficient Method of Estimating Seemingly Unrelated Regression and Tests for Aggregation Bias," *Journal of the American Statistical Association* **55**, 348–368.

Chapter 10

The Missing Equation: The Wedge Model Alternative*

Victor A. Canto and Marc A. Miles

INTRODUCTION

The most commonly used framework of analysis for macroeconomic policy during the past several decades has been the IS–LM model. However, in recent years, various economists have become dissatisfied with the ability of the IS–LM model to analyze economic phenomena. One source of dissatisfaction with the IS–LM framework has been the well-known fact that the system of equations which characterizes the standard model is underdetermined. The system then becomes operational only by introducing an exogenous assumption. Traditionally, in order to close the system, either short-run price rigidity or full employment has been assumed. However, reliance on either of these assumptions requires neglecting the interaction between the product and factor markets in the determination of the equilibrium level of income (nominal or real).

* Originally published in the *Journal of Macroeconomics*, Spring 1981, Vol. 3, No. 2, pp. 247–269. © Wayne State University Press, 1981

This paper develops a third, alternative method for closing the IS–LM system of equations by systematically incorporating the economy's work–leisure decision. By including this additional decision constraint, the interactions between the product and factor markets can be explicitly considered. The result is a more general set of results regarding the effects of economic policy on the determination of output, employment, and the price level, of which the two traditional alternatives are only special cases. In particular, the model shows how the actions of government influence the size of "wedges" between the gross payments to factors and their net rewards. The adjustment in the size of the wedges in turn affects the supply and demand for factors, influencing the level of aggregate production and employment. It is then shown that the results of the more general model are consistent with recent empirical findings, and that the model developed in this paper is capable of analyzing and providing an interpretation of observed macroeconomic behavior in recent years.

The paper is organized as follows. Section 1 reviews the standard IS–LM framework and describes the indeterminancy of the system of equations. Section 2 develops the more general alternative way to close the system of equations. In Section 3 substitution effects traditionally neglected by the standard IS–LM representations are incorporated into the IS curve. Finally, in Sections 4–6 the new framework of marcroeconomic analysis is used to analyze the effects of government expenditures, nonneutral taxes, and deficit financings.

1. THE IS–LM FRAMEWORK

The closed economy IS–LM model can be summarized by the following two equations:

Income–expenditure sector:

$$AD \equiv C(Y) + I(r) = Y \tag{1}$$

Monetary sector:

$$M^d(i, PY) = M^S(i) \tag{2}$$

where Y is real income; r, the real rate of interest (the relative price of bonds in terms of goods); i, the nominal interest rate (the relative price of bonds in terms of money); C, real consumption expenditures[1]; I, real investment

---

[1] For simplicity, and without loss of generality, it is assumed that consumption depends on current income. The analysis can be easily modified to make consumption a function of wealth or permanent income without qualitatively altering the results obtained in this paper.

expenditures[2]; AD, aggregate expenditures on goods and services; M nominal money balances; and P, the price level (the relative price of goods in terms of money).

Given the absence of inflationary expectations, the model involves three unknowns (Y, r, P) in two equations. In order, then, to separate the equilibrium levels of nominal income into their price level and real income components, the model requires the so-called missing equation[3] to make the system determinate. The traditional assumptions used to close the system of equations usually take one of two forms:

1.1. Neo-Keynesian Approach

The existence of fixed contracts, excess capacity, and underemployment of factors of production are commonly invoked to justify the assumption of a constant price level in the short run. This assumption implies that a change in a nominal variable translates into an equal change in the corresponding real variable, clearly making the IS–LM system of equations determinate.

The constant price level assumption implies that the relative price of goods in terms of money is fixed. In this case, equilibrium in the money market requires that the asset price of money (the interest rate) change to eliminate any disturbance in that market. In addition, the constant price level implies that the relative price of bonds in terms of goods r and the relative price of bonds in terms of money i are always equal. Alternatively stated, real assets (equities) and nominal assets (government bonds) are perfect substitutes. The perfect substitutability assumption implies that, in general, monetary policy influences real economic activity both in the short and long runs (i.e., money is not neutral). As a result one cannot make use of the classical dichotomy.

1.2. Neoclassical Approach

The neoclassical model assumes price flexibility and that the economy tends toward its "natural" rate of employment. Thus factors in the economy are fully employed and production will be at its natural or full-employment level Y^*.

Equilibrium requires that relative prices change to eliminate any disturbance in the economy. Assuming no inflationary expectations, the nominal

---

[2] The formulation of investment in Eq. (3) implicitly assumes that the expected inflation rate is zero, in which case $i = r$. In the more general case, r and not i is the argument of the investment function.

[3] See Friedman (1974).

and real interest rates are equal. Since r is the only relative price entering the IS, stable equilibrium requires that r change to equilibrate the goods market and P change to equilibrate the money market.

Monetary policy has no permanent effect on the real variables (i.e., money is neutral in the long run). However, short-run effects may be generated by unexpected changes in monetary policy. If one assumes perfect foresight and certainty, as we shall for the remainder of the paper, then all changes in monetary policy are fully anticipated, and the price level changes instantaneously to offset any undesired change in monetary policy. In this case money is neutral both in the short and long runs (i.e., the classical dichotomy holds both in the short and long runs).

2. A MORE GENERAL MODEL

It is apparent from the discussions in the previous section that the assumption used to close the IS–LM system of equations is extremely important in any comparative static analysis. The assumptions made determine which variables change to eliminate any initial disturbance in the economy.

A third, alternative way to close the IS–LM system of equations is now considered. Let us follow Becker (1965) by explicitly assuming the existence of household or nonmarket activities. The household commodity is produced by combining market goods C with household time L. It is also assumed that these commodities are the only arguments in the economy's utility function.

The introduction of the household commodity implies that the demands for consumer goods and leisure time are derived demands, and depend, in part, on the relative price of the household production inputs (i.e., on the relative price of leisure time in terms of market goods w). Therefore, the position of the goods market equilibrium conditions (IS curve) now also depends on the real wage rate; that is,

$$C^d(Y_f, w) + I(r) = Y^S \tag{1'}$$

Consumption depends on Y_f, where Y_f represents the economy's full income, that is, real market income Y plus the value of leisure time wL.

The production function for market goods is assumed to be linear homogeneous, twice differentiable with both inputs indispensable;

$$Y^S = L_m f(K_m/L_m) \tag{3}$$

where L_m and K_m represent the amount of labor and capital services employed in the market sector. The market and household sectors employ the same factors of production. Hence total employment is subject to the economy's factor endowment constraint[4]:

$$K_m^d(Y^S, w/r) = \bar{K} \tag{4}$$
$$\quad (+) (+)$$

$$L^d(Y_f, \ w) + L_m^d(Y^S, w/r) = \bar{T} \tag{5}$$
$$\quad (+) (-) \qquad (+) (-)$$

where K_m^d and L_m^d represent the market sector derived demand for capital and labor services, L^d the derived demand for household (leisure) time, and the sign under a variable represents the sign of the partial derivative of the dependent variable with respect to the independent variable. The factor market employment equations introduce two additional equations to the IS–LM system of equations. However, only one new relative price (w/r) is introduced. If the equations are independent, the augmented system of equations are determinate.

As in the neoclassical model of the previous section, price flexibility, perfect foresight, and certainty are assumed. Thus all changes in monetary policy are fully anticipated and money is neutral both in the short and long runs. One can therefore dichotomize the economy into a real (product and factor market) sector, where real variables are determined, and a monetary sector, where nominal variables are determined.

From Eq. (3) it is apparent that, since capital is inelastically supplied to the market sector, labor employment and production goods in the market sector are uniquely determined by the equilibrium wage rental ratio. It is also apparent from Eq. (1) that investment is uniquely determined by the real interest rate and that, given market production Y, consumption is also uniquely determined. It is apparent then that r and w/r are sufficient, given technology and factor endowment, to characterize the real sectors of the economy. The next step in the analysis is to develop a graphical solution to the determination of the equilibrium real interest rate and wage–rental ratio.

The equilibrium division of labor between market and household employment is summarized in Eq. (5). Notice that this equation is a function of both w and r. Thus, there are a number of potential equilibrium values for r and w/r which together clear the labor market. These sets of values are shown in Fig. 1 as the $T^d = T^s$ curve. The curve has a negative slope. *Ceteris paribus,* an equiproportionate increase in the wage and rental rates does not change the

---

[4] The supply of capital services in the economy is simply the sum of all previous investment spending (assuming no depreciation). Hence, if investment spending is positive, the economy's capital endowment is increasing over time. However, at any point in time the supply of capital is a given quantity $\bar{K}$. The total supply of labor is also given at a point in time (24 hours per day per person), although population may be growing over time.

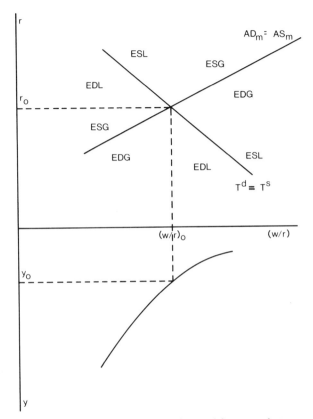

Figure 1. Equilibrium in the product and factor markets.

market demand for labor services. However, the increase in wage rate does tend to reduce the demand for leisure, generating an incipient excess supply of labor. In order to maintain the labor market equilibrium, the incipient excess supply must be eliminated. Given the wage rate, a reduction in the rental rate produces the desired result by increasing the demand for market time. The previous analysis implies that the area above the $T^d = T^s$ curve represents an excess supply of labor and the area below it an excess demand for labor.

The goods market clearing conditions [Eq. (1′)] is also an equation in two unknowns (w and w/r) and is represented graphically in Fig. 1. The $AD_m = AS_m$ curve is upward sloping. *Ceteris paribus*, an equiproportionate increase in w and r has no initial impact on aggregate production. However, the increase in w tends to increase consumption expenditures, while the increase in r tends to reduce investment expenditures. The net effect on aggregate demand for goods is ambiguous. If the investment effect dominates, as is assumed here,[5] there is an incipient excess supply of market goods. Given the wage rate, a reduction in the interest rate increases investment expenditure and reduces market production, thus generating an offsetting excess demand for market goods. Areas below the $AD_m = AS_m$ locus represent excess market good demand, while the area above represents an excess supply.

As shown in Fig. 1, the intersection of the market goods and labor market clearing loci yields a set of r and w/r which simultaneously clears both markets and automatically accounts for the interaction effects between the two markets generated by the substitution effects in household production. Furthermore, the curve in the lower half of Fig. 3 describes the relation between the wage–rental ratio and aggregate market output. As the wage–rental ratio falls, the desired capital–labor ratio falls, which, given the supply of capital, requires an increase in the market employment of labor. Since more factors of production are employed, market output rises. To put it more formally, since goods in this model are produced by a linear homogeneous production function, with capital fixed at a point in time, diminishing marginal product implies that output is negatively and uniquely related to the wage–rental ratio.

The determinacy of the real sector of the economy has been illustrated. In addition, the real interest rate and market income combined with inflationary expectations determine the demand for real balances. Given this demand, and given the money supply, the price level is also determinate. Clearly the assumptions which guarantee the short- and long-run neutrality of money are made only to simplify the graphical illustration of the determinacy of the system of equations. If the assumptions which guarantee neutrality are violated, then the system of equations has to be solved simultaneously and the graphical solution becomes more complicated.

In the next section the system of equations developed here is transformed graphically into the (r, Y) space to facilitate the comparison with the more familiar IS–IM analysis.

3. THE IS CURVE REVISITED

The representations of the goods and labor market clearing conditions in the more traditional (r, Y) space can be easily derived from the market clearing loci in the $(r, w/r)$ space. Consider point A in Fig. 2. The coordinates

---

[5] The justification for this assumption is that, as will be shown later, the upward sloping $AD_m = AS_m$ curve corresponds to the standard IS curve of the more traditional analysis.

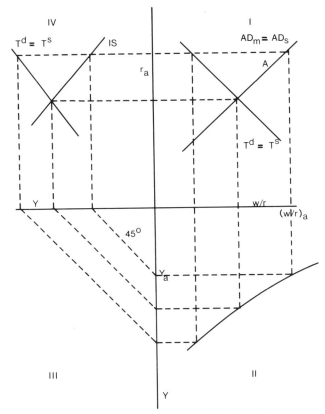

Figure 2. Representation of the model in the (r, Y) space.

of A indicate the equilibrium set of relative prices $[r_a, (w/r)_a]$ for which the goods market clears. As shown in the second quadrant, one can solve for the equilibrium level of output Y_a consistent with $(w/r)_a$. Through the use of a 45° line, Y_a can be translated onto the fourth quadrant horizontal axis. In that quadrant, (Y_a, r_a) represents the coordinates of a combination of interest rate and income for which the goods market clears. Therefore, the point must be on the IS curve. All other points on the IS^6 and $T^d = T^s$ curves in the fourth quadrant can be derived in a similar manner.

The IS curve derived in this section systematically incorporates the substitution effects between goods and time in the production of the household commodity as well as the substitution effects between capital and labor in

---

[6] As in the traditional IS–LM analysis, the slope of the IS curve is negative. However, it must be pointed out that the negative sloped IS depends on $AD_m = AS_m$ having a positive slope.

the production of market goods. Since, as relative prices change, factors choose more or less leisure, and producers choose more or less labor, the equilibrium level of market production cannot be determined independently of the factor market equilibrium condition.

Recent empirical evidence confirms the existence of goods–leisure substitution and capital–labor substitution effects in market sector production. In their study of Social Security, Burkhauser and Turner (1978) estimate that the Social Security retirement test has raised the work week (reduced leisure consumption) over two hours above what it would otherwise be for a prime-age male. Research by Boskin (1977), Quinn (1977), and Burkhauser (1976), however, indicates that constraints on market work, such as the Social Security retirement test, reduce the labor supply of older men. More recently, Feldstein (1978) has examined the effects of unemployment. He concludes that "[a]n increase in the UI (unemployment insurance) benefit replacement ratio from 0.4 to 0.6 raises the predicted temporary layoff unemployment rate by about 0.5 percentage points, or one-third of the current average temporary layoff unemployment rate of 1.6 percent." In a study which also takes a broader view of taxation to include reductions in transfer payments caused by increases in market income, Laffer (1978) finds that inner-city residents sometimes face marginal tax rates on market income in excess of 100 percent. Using U.S. data covering the period 1931–1977, Evans (1978) estimates the relations between changes in employment or hours of work and fiscal policy variables. He reports a strong negative effect of taxes on labor supply, the estimated elasticity being 0.48. He also reports an elasticity of substitution between capital and labor in the production of market goods in excess of unity.

While the effects reported by the several studies cited above may be individually small, they may not be small collectively. Furthermore, these studies have strong implications for the effects of tax rates and other variables on production. These effects are consistent with Friedman's (1968) and Lucas's (1978) arguments that the "natural" rate of employment and the economy's "potential" output may be influenced by real variables. As we shall show in the next two sections, this model is also useful for analyzing some often overlooked effects of the government sector.

4. THE EFFECTS OF GOVERNMENT EXPENDITURES

The government sector is viewed in this model as performing two simultaneous fiscal functions: providing goods to the private sector through government expenditure and obtaining the revenue to pay for the goods supplied. Both of these functions may have nonneutral effects on the economy. In this section we concentrate on the expenditure effects by considering the effect of an increase in government expenditure financed by neutral taxation. In the following section we reverse the neutrality assumption to consider the case of nonneutral taxes.

Conventional accounting techniques value government expenditures at factor cost. However, there is no *a priori* reason to assume that the private sector values the services provided by the government at their cost. This issue has been discussed by Bailey (1971). To the extent that the government expenditure has a positive value to the private sector (government- and private-sector goods are substitutes), it replaces or "crowds out" private-sector expenditure. The economy's aggregate expenditure function becomes

$$AD_m = C(Y_f, w) + I(r) + (1 - \gamma)G \tag{1''}$$

where γ is an index that measures the private-sector valuation of government services. If $\gamma = 1$, the private sector values the government services at their factor cost and complete "crowding out" occurs.

Incorporating the resulting effects on private-sector consumption through changes in full income, the total impact on the goods market resulting from an increase in government expenditures is therefore

$$dAD_m = \left(1 - \frac{\partial C^d}{\partial Y_f}\right)(1 - \gamma)\, dG \tag{6}$$

Whether an increase in government expenditure leads to an initial excess demand or supply of market goods depends on the private-sector valuation of government services.

To the extent that the private-sector valuation of public services differs from their costs, the economy's opportunities change and income effects are generated. The income effects in turn influence the economy's aggregate demand for labor services as follows:

$$dT^d = -(-\gamma)\frac{\partial L^d}{\partial Y_f}\, dG \tag{7}$$

Equations (6) and (7) illustrate that the government's ability to shift aggregate demand and to stimulate measured output and employment depends critically on the private sector's valuations of government services. If the value of these services is equal to their cost ($\gamma = 1$), private purchase reductions offset dollar for dollar the change in government expenditure. Only if the value of government services is less than their cost ($\gamma < 1$) does an increase in expenditure lead to an increase in aggregate demand and measured market output and employment. Thus a necessary condition for the balanced budget multiplier effect is that the value of government services be less than their cost.

The effects of a transitory increase in government expenditure when $\gamma < 1$ are shown graphically in Fig. 3. Equation (6) shows that when services are valued at less than cost, total aggregate demand rises, creating excess demand for market goods at the old equilibrium. The $AD_m = AS_m$ and the IS curves therefore shift to the left of the original curves to $AD'_m = AS'_m$ and IS', respectively. Similarly, Eq. (7) shows that the resulting reduction in aggregate full income reduces the demand for leisure time, creating an excess supply of labor. Therefore, the labor market equilibrium curve shifts to the left to $T^{d'} = T^{S'}$.

Since capital is supplied inelastically to the market and the total demand for labor falls, the wage–rental ratio unambiguously falls to $(w/r)_1$. The decrease in the wage–rental ratio in turn implies an increase in the market

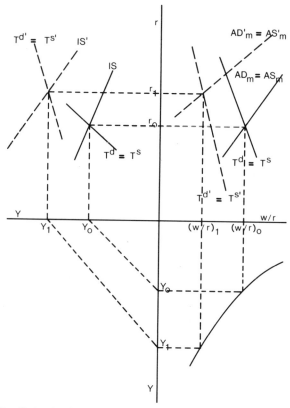

Figure 3. The effects of an increase in government expenditure for the case where the value of the public services provided are less than their factor costs ($\gamma < 1$), financed by neutral taxes.

employment of labor services, absorbing the labor released from leisure activities. The increase in factor employment unambiguously increases market output to Y_1.

Since the government is assumed in this example to be less efficient than the private sector ($\gamma < 1$), resources in the economy are being wasted. Part of the waste may occur at the expense of future consumption. As Fig. 3 shows, the higher level of measured income is associated with a higher real rate of interest r_1. The higher rate means fewer current investment projects are profitable. Part of the waste may also be occurring at the expense of leisure consumption, since less time and goods are now employed in that sector. These two effects together illustrate an interesting point: if the success of public policy is measured in terms of short-run increases in measured market output and the level of employment, this criterion may lead to a selection of policies which reduce the overall economy's well-being.

The analysis of the previous paragraphs unambiguously shows that investment tends to fall in the short run as a result of the increase in current government expenditure. The increase in public expenditure created by reducing wealth generates an excess supply of future goods and time, which *ceteris paribus* leads to a reduction of future relative prices. However, since in the long run the capital stock is endogenously determined, use cannot be made of the assumption that capital is inelastically supplied at a given time in order to determine the change in the rental rate. Therefore, in order to determine the long-run effects of transitory changes in expenditure, a more elaborate model which explicitly accounts for the long run is required. As it stands, the model developed in this paper is consistent with several long-run specifications, and long-run effects remain an open question.

5. THE EFFECTS OF NONNEUTRAL TAXES

Consider now the effects of the other fiscal function of the government sector, obtaining the revenue for the government expenditure. In order to concentrate solely on the effects of taxes on output and employment, it is assumed in this section that the private sector values the services provided by the government at precisely their factor cost ($\gamma = 1$). In this case there is no change in aggregate wealth as the level of aggregate government expenditure changes, and hence no shift in the aggregate demand for goods and factors from this effect. However, changes in the tax rates do induce relative price changes which affect the goods and factor markets.

Different forms of taxation generating the same level of revenues may produce different types of substitution effects. Thus, in order to illustrate the effects of taxes, a specific form of taxation must be assumed *a priori*. In this section the government is assumed to finance all expenditures through a sales tax of t percent.

An increase in government expenditure requires an increase in the sales tax rate t. The sales tax does not distort the input choices between capital and labor in the production of market goods. However, the sales tax does create a wedge between the gross receipts of market labor and the net goods purchased, thus reducing the real net of tax market wage rate and the rate of return on capital, or, alternatively, raising the price of market consumption relative to leisure consumption now and in the future. Thus, the sales tax distorts the work–leisure choice and induces a substitution away from market goods and into leisure consumption. Finally the sales tax also distorts the investment decision and will induce a reduction in investment.

In terms of the algebraic model, the effects of the sales tax can be incorporated into two additional equations and amplifications of three other equations. The additional equations reflect the wedge between the gross and net market wage and rental rates:

$$\bar{w} = (1 - t)w \tag{8}$$

$$\bar{r} = (1 - t)r \tag{9}$$

where w is the gross wage rate in market activities, $\bar{w}$ is the net of tax wage in market activities, and t is the sales tax rate. Similarly, $\bar{r}$ and r represent, respectively, the net and gross of tax rental rate of capital. Equation (8) implies that a sales tax distorts the value to an individual of a unit of time in leisure production compared with in-market production. The returns from market production must first be converted into market goods, which are taxed, before they are consumed. The tax rate introduces a wedge between the gross and net of tax wage rates, generating substitution effects away from market activity.

The effects of the wedge between gross and net market returns are then incorporated into the model through Eqs. (8) and (9) by substituting the net of tax market wage rate $\bar{w}$ for the gross wage w:

$$L^d(Y_f, \bar{w}) + L^d_m (y, w/r) = \bar{T} \tag{5'}$$
$$(+)(-) \quad (+)(-)$$

$$C^d = C^d(Y_f, \bar{w}) \tag{10}$$
$$(+)(+)$$

$$I^d = I^d(r) \tag{11}$$
$$(-)$$

The positives and negatives below the variables again indicate the signs of the partial derivatives.

The net effect of the increased expenditure ($\gamma = 1$) financed by sales taxes on the goods and labor markets is therefore as follows:

$$dAD_m = \underset{(+)(-)}{\frac{\partial C}{\partial w}\frac{\partial \bar{w}}{\partial t}} + \underset{(-)(+)}{\frac{\partial I}{\partial r}}\underset{(+)}{\frac{\partial r}{\partial t}} \quad dt \quad < 0 \tag{12}$$

$$dT^d = \underset{(-)(-)(+)}{\frac{\partial L^d}{\partial w}\frac{\partial \bar{w}}{\partial t}} dt \quad > 0 \tag{13}$$

The increased sales tax creates an excess supply of goods and an excess demand for labor at the initial equilibrium prices. In terms of Fig. 4, Eqs. (12) and (13) show that the $AD_m = AS_m$ and $T^d = T^s$ and IS curves shift to the right. The new intersection of the curves is clearly at a higher wage—rental ratio, implying a smaller market employment of labor and less market output. The gross of tax return to capital r unambiguously increases. Sales taxes then tend to reduce market output, employment, and investment in the short

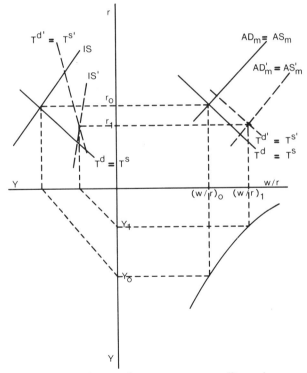

Figure 4. The effects of an increase in government expenditure where $\gamma = 1$, financed by a nonneutral sales tax.

run. As previously discussed, in order to determine long-run effects a more elaborate model is required.

An important proposition stemming from this analysis is that the substitution effects generated by the tax rate make it less likely that the balanced budget multiplier is positive. In addition to the requirement from the last section that the value of government services be less than the cost to the government ($\gamma < 1$), a positive balanced budget multiplier requires the expansionary effects of increased government expenditure to be sufficiently large to dominate the negative substitution effects that the tax rate generates.

These substitution effects tend to be neglected in simple income–expenditure macromodels. The neglect can be traced to the failure to incorporate explicitly the role of capital, and the subsequent reliance on the "missing equation" assumptions. Under one assumption, the economy is underemployed and below its potential capacity utilization. Therefore, for all practical purposes, in the relevant range factor supplies are perfectly elastic. Relative prices do not change, and no substitution effects are generated. Thus, government intervention is required to stimulate aggregate demand and to achieve "full" employment and "potential" output. The other common assumption is that the market sector is fully employed, so that the economy's aggregate supply of market goods and factors is completely inelastic. In this case an increase in aggregate demand resulting from increased government expenditures only leads to an increase in relative prices with no change in aggregate supply. Under this assumption, the private market is simply "crowded out" of the market.

However, our more general model of output shows that output is jointly determined by shifts in the economy's aggregate demand and supply functions (income or expenditure effects), as well as the substitution effects due to relative price changes. Models that neglect any of these effects can therefore result in misleading policy conclusions. This conclusion is reinforced by the mounting evidence of the importance of the substitution effects. The importance of substitution effects resulting from tax rates on the equilibrium level of employment has been pointed out by Evans (1978) and Feldstein (1978). The importance of hours of work and the retirement decision has been shown by Burkhouser and Turner (1978) and Boskin (1977). Feldstein (1974a, b) and Joines (1978) have stressed the effects of taxes on capital formation, and Boskin (1978) the effects of taxes on savings. Macromodels should therefore incorporate the substitution effects without neglecting the importance of shifts in the economy's aggregate demand for, and supply of, goods and factors of production. The model described in this paper is one attempt to develop such a general equilibrium model. From it we learn that more than just one relative price is required to determine the equilibrium level of output and employment of an economy.

6. DEFICIT FINANCING: THE MONEY AND BOND MARKETS

Until this point the discussion has assumed that the government's budget is always balanced. However, the analysis is now extended to consider a government which is subject to a budget constraint:

$$G = Tx + \dot{M} + \dot{B}$$

where Tx is the level of tax revenues, and $\dot{M}$ and $\dot{B}$ the increases in the money supply and government bonds. The government is therefore capable now of running a budget deficit in a given year, financed by issuing money or bonds. Given the government's new abilities, how is the preceding model affected? More specifically, does the real sector of the economy remain completely independent of the monetary and bond sectors? The answer, it turns out, depends on whether the private sector anticipates its future tax liabilities, and whether tax rates are fixed in nominal or real terms.

6.1. Bond Financing

Financing government expenditure with money or bonds can affect the real sector of the economy in two possible ways. First, if the future tax liabilities associated with these forms of government debt are not observed or properly discounted by the private sector, private sector assets are perceived to exceed private sector liabilities, increasing perceived private wealth. Second, even if these wealth effects do not exist, the imposition of future taxes may alter, say, current relative to future consumption patterns, producing real effects.

The issue of whether government bonds are net wealth has received considerable attention. Barro (1974) has shown the theoretical conditions under which bonds will not represent net wealth. The existence of a net wealth effect has been investigated by, among others, Barro (1978), Feldstein (1976), and Kormendi (1978).

Conflicting results are reported by the different writers. The structure of the model developed in this paper is easily adaptable to either alternative, and it is not the object of this paper to deal with the issue. The point we want to emphasize is that, even accounting for wealth effects, the various substitution effects generated by different potential tax rates associated with a given level-of debt remain to be accounted for.

In order to determine the substitution effects of debt financing, the precise nature of the taxes imposed to finance the bond or money redemption must be known. While there are a large number of possibilities, only two are considered to illustrate the issue. First, consider a person who does not have to pay any taxes this year, but next year will have to pay what he would have paid this year plus the accrued interest. This example illustrates the simple case of bond financing of current tax liabilities. Obviously, if the individual understands his choices (and discounts consumption at the market rate of interest), it makes little difference to him when he pays the taxes. While there are no wealth effects, bond financing produces the same substitution effects as current taxation.

Second, consider the case where tax rates (say, income tax rates) are computed to yield a desired amount of revenue over the life cycle. During some years revenues will exceed expenditures, and the government will retire some of the debt incurred in years in which revenues fell short of expenditures. Clearly, in this case bond financing required in the years in which expenditures exceed tax revenues does not generate additional substitution effects over and above the ones implied already by the tax rates.

6.2. Money Financing

Whether money is net wealth and how alternative rates of inflation may affect real variables are matters that have been extensively discussed in the economics literature. An excellent exposition of the existing theories can be found in Dornbusch and Frenkel (1973).

If, for example, fiat money does not represent net wealth, the only effect of continued money deficit in a closed economy is inflation. If expectations are rational, given that in this model there is perfect foresight and certainty, all price changes are instantaneous. However, it is interesting to point out that even if money is not net wealth, progressive taxation of nominal income implies that changes in the price level will alter the economy's marginal tax rate. This marginal tax change in turn generates substitution effects away from market activity into nonmarket activity. Thus monetary policy in this case has a real and permanent effect on the economy.

7. CONCLUDING REMARKS

This paper, by systematically incorporating work–leisure substitution effects and explicitly accounting for the factor market equilibrium condition, develops an alternative way to overcome one source of growing dissatisfaction with the IS–LM framework.

Our model provides an explanation of how economic policy can influence the economy's "natural" rate of employment and potential "market" output. It is also shown that the model developed is sufficiently general to incorporate as special cases the models we have described—the neoclassical and the neo-Keynesian versions. Although in order to simplify the graphical exposition only the case of neutral money is considered, the model is sufficiently general to be easily modified to allow for the nonneutrality of money.

The importance of the substitution effects can be highlighted by contrasting some standard results of the traditional income expenditure models with those of the models presented in the paper. An increase in transfer payments financed by an increase in the economy's tax rate does not alter the economy's disposable income and, according to the standard formulation, has no effect on output and employment. Although no income effects are generated, the substitution effects generated by the tax transfer policy remain to be analyzed. The increased tax rates tend to discourage market activity, and the equilibrium level of market production tends to fall as a result of the substitution effect. Given the money stocks, the proportion of goods to money falls and the price of goods in terms of money rises.

Another standard result is the value of the balanced budget multiplier (BBM). Bailey (1971) has shown that a necessary condition for the BBM to be positive is for the value of the services provided by the government sector be less than their cost ($\gamma < 1$). However, to the extent that the change in marginal tax rates generates a substitution effect away from market activity, Bailey's condition is no longer sufficient to guarantee the BBM result. The sufficient condition is that the value of the services provided must be sufficiently lower than their cost to ensure that the expenditure effects dominate the substitution effects.

We cannot claim that our attempt to account for the supply side of the economy is unique. Models such as Hall (1978) which explicitly account for the supply side are becoming more and more frequent in the economics literature. Yet certain fundamental differences remain between these models and ours. First of all, some of these models are underdetermined and must still rely on a "missing equation" in order to close the system. Hall, for example, arbitrarily fixes the initial price level. In contrast, by including an explicit employment equation for labor and capital services, our model is not underdetermined, and the real returns to both capital and labor and the price level are endogenous to the model. Second, the emphasis on different types of substitution effects produces different dynamic analyses. For example, in our model the effect of a tax cut is to lower gross-of-tax (market) relative prices, not raise them. Our model suggests that tax reductions increase the supply of goods, lowering the price level, not raising it.

Our analysis suggests that any attempt to redistribute income through transfer payments financed by increases in tax rates reduces the association between effort and reward, and, as a result, the incentives to produce market goods falls. The production of market goods decreases, and the price level tends to increase. Another interesting implication of our analysis is that to the extent that substitution effects are important, a tax rate reduction will lead to an expansion in market production and the taxable base. To the extent that the tax base expands, the loss of revenue from the tax rate reduction is partially offset. Empirical evidence on the effects of tax rate changes on tax revenues is limited. An analysis by Canto *et al.* (1979) of the effects of the 1962 and 1964 Kennedy tax cuts suggests that some expansion of economic activity and no significant loss of revenue occurred as a result of the Kennedy tax cuts.

The model also produces different implications for bond and money financing: even if bonds and money are not net wealth, substitution effects may be generated by deficit financing which alter the equilibrium level of output. In the case of money financing, real effects may result if there is progressive taxation of nominal income. In the case of bond financing, one must specify the nature of the taxes to be imposed to finance the debt in order to establish the substitution effects and then determine the effect on output.

REFERENCES

Bailey, M. J. (1971). *National Income and the Price Level*, 2nd ed. McGraw-Hill, New York.
Barro, R. J. (1974). "Are Government Bonds Net Wealth?" *Journal of Political Economy* **82**, 1095–1117.
Barro, R. J. (1976). "Reply to Feldstein and Buchanan," *Journal of Political Economy* **84**, 343–349.
Barro, R. J. (1978). "Social Security, Saving and Capital Accumulation: A Brief Review," Univ. of Rochester.
Becker, G. S. (1965). "A Theory of the Allocation of Time," *Economic Journal* **75**, 493–517.
Boskin, M. (1977). "Social Security Retirement Decisions," *Economic Inquiry* **15**, 1–25.
Boskin, M. (1978). "Taxation, Saving, and the Rate of Interest," *Journal of Political Economy* **86**, S3–S28.
Burkhauser, R. (1976). "The Early Pension Decision and Its Effect on Exit from the Labor Market," Ph.D. dissertation, Univ. of Chicago.
Burkhauser, R., and Turner, J. (1978). "A Time-Series Analysis on Social Security and Its Effect on the Market Work of Men at Younger Ages," *Journal of Political Economy* **86**, 701–716.
Canto, V., Joines, D., and Webb, R. (1979). "Empirical Evidence on the Effects of Tax Rates on Economic Activity," *Proceedings of the Business and Economic Statistics Section*, American Statistical Association.
Dornbusch, R., and Frenkel, J. (1973). "Inflation and Growth Alternative Approaches," *Journal of Money Credit and Banking* **5** (1), Part 1, 141–156.
Evans, P. (1978). "The U.S. Labor Market: Some Empirical Estimates 1929–1976," Stanford Univ., Palo Alto, California.
Feldstein, M. (1974a). "Incidence of a Capital Income Tax in a Growing Economy with Variable Saving Rates," *Review of Economic Studies* **41**, 503–513.
Feldstein, M. (1974b). "Tax Incidence in a Growing Economy with Variable Factor Supply," *Quarterly Journal of Economics* **88**, 551–573.
Feldstein, M. (1976). "Perceived Wealth in Bonds and Social Security: A Comment," *Journal of Political Economy* **84**, 331–336.

Feldstein, M. (1978). "The Effect of Unemployment Insurance on Temporary Layoff Unemployment," *American Economic Review* **68**, 834–846.

Friedman, M. (1968). "The Role of Monetary Policy," *American Economic Review* **58**, 1–17.

Friedman, M. (1974). "A Theoretical Framework for Monetary Analysis," in *Milton Friedman's Monetary Framework* (R. J. Gordon, ed.). University of Chicago Press, Chicago, Illinois.

Hall, R. E. (1978). "The Macroeconomic Impact of Change in Income Taxes in the Short and Medium Runs," *Journal of Political Economy* **88**, S71–S86.

Joines, D. (1979). "Government Fiscal Policy and Private Capital Formation," Ph.D. Dissertation, Univ. of Chicago, Chicago, Illinois.

Kormendi, R. C. (1978). "Government Debt, Government Spending and Private Sector Behavior," Univ. of Chicago, Chicago, Illinois.

Laffer, A. (1978). "Prohibitive Tax Rates and the Inner City: A Rational Explanation of the Poverty Trap," in *Economic Study*. Wainwright Economics, Boston, Massachusetts.

Lucas, R. E. (1978). "Unemployment Policy," *American Economic Review* **68**, 353–357.

Quinn, J. (1977). "The Microeconomic Determinants of Early Retirement: A Cross Section View of White Married Men," *Journal of Human Resources* **12**, 329–346.

Index